THE ELOQUENT "I"

Style and Self in
Seventeenth-Century
Prose

THE ELOQUENT "I"

Style and Self in

Seventeenth-Century Prose

JOAN WEBBER

The University of Wisconsin Press

Madison, Milwaukee, London

1968

Published by
The University of Wisconsin Press
Box 1379
Madison, Wisconsin 53701
The University of Wisconsin Press, Ltd.
27–29 Whitfield Street, London, W.1
Copyright © 1968
by the Regents of the University
of Wisconsin
All rights reserved
Printed in the
United States of America
by Vail-Ballou Press, Inc., Binghamton
New York
Library of Congress Catalog
Card Number
68–19573

FOR JULIAN

I have heard Rabbi Hirsch,
the disciple of our Rabbi, say:
"A teacher like Rabbi Melech has not been known since
the days of the *Tannaim* and *Amoraim*.
But our Rabbi has better eyes."
I have come to learn since that time that,
though eyes are important,
they are not the most important things about a man.
The important thing is what the eyes seek
to see when they exercise their power of vision.
And that is not determined by the eyes.

Rabbi David of Lelov,
in Martin Buber's *For the Sake
of Heaven*

PREFACE

IN THIS STUDY OF LITERARY SELF-CONSCIOUSNESS, IT HAS NOT BEEN A part of my intention to explain why such a phenomenon occurred in seventeenth-century England, and therefore it may be well at least to comment briefly on the problems which such an explanation would involve. The art of the period has already been overexplained, in works which find "the seventeenth-century mind" created out of all sorts of revolutionary occurrences that make the seventeenth century a watershed between the Middle Ages and the modern world. This dramatic viewpoint is best modified by the recognition that every age is one of crisis and transition; this one, as Douglas Bush suggests, is more transitional than most because disruptive and creative forces have combined to "speed up the normal process of change" (*English Literature in the Earlier Seventeenth Century*, Oxford, 1962, p. 1). And instead of talking about cause and effect, between historical occurrences and literary styles, it is probably better to speak of significant parallels. This aspect of the problem, as well as the question of how to determine when parallels are significant, is at least clearly introduced in *Seventeenth Century Science and the Arts*, edited by Stephen Toulmin (Princeton, 1961). The most relevant essays are Stephen Toulmin's "Seventeenth Century Science and the Arts," and Douglas Bush's "Science and Literature." Toulmin distinguishes between the Sceptics, who refuse to see relationships anywhere, and the Enthusiasts, who find them everywhere. Somewhere between these two extremes a path has to be found, but Toulmin believes that our knowledge and our methods are not yet sufficiently advanced to insure success.

Of course, as Douglas Bush notes, there was no such thing as "the seventeenth-century mind," any more than there is such a thing as a twentieth-century mind. There were many different minds reacting to many different stimuli, and, by their reactions, creating other stimuli for other people. That is to say, any one man helps to create his age as much as he is created by it. And one can never be sure how many totally personal elements enter into a work apparently influenced by *zeitgeist*. When Donne wrote that the new philosophy called all in doubt, he gave twentieth-century critics a touchstone for the claim that the new science made seventeenth-century literature pessimistic, but, as Douglas Bush points out, Donne "was writing after years of heavy personal trials" (Toulmin, p. 50). So many possible things could have influenced the writing of that complex, mocking line, from Donne's Roman Catholic birth to the fact that he had been commissioned to write a memorial poem for Elizabeth Drury and wished to mourn her hyperbolically.

The most that I want to do here, then, is to offer a few seventeenth-century phenomena as possible stimuli to the development of self-consciousness. Science was changing man's position in space; he was beginning to think differently about time. He had increasing mobility in social rank. Opening up to him were more and more choices (or recognition of the desirability of choices) of vocation, dwelling place, religion, politics, and prose styles. Foreign travel was more available, and so were foreigners. Some brands of Protestantism encouraged introspection. All these things were happening during the reign of Elizabeth, of course, and the earliest of these writers were born in the sixteenth century. Thereafter, expanding opportunities to make choices led to increased choosing, increasing repressiveness by governors, and increasing necessity to choose whether or not to accept the status quo. The partly cyclical nature of this progression is apparent, and each part of the sequence contains possibilities for an accompanying intensification of self-consciousness. Donne, isolated in childhood by his Catholicism, was as a young man fired from his job on account of his marriage, and subsequently forced by James I to choose the priesthood or nothing. Milton was "church-outed by the prelates." Lilburne thought himself unable to exercise a trade because of court-granted monopolies. Parallels for such misfortunes can, of course, be found in any age. The most that I can conclude here is that men of particular temperaments encountered particular circumstances that may have increased a self-awareness already present or potential. And they lived, as Burton says, in a scribbling age.

And so do we. This book about their books is one which I have wanted to write for fifteen years, although in its first conception its features were indistinct, and although during most of that time my intention was to write it at about the age of sixty. That it makes its appearance thus prematurely is, I hope, at least partially atoned for by the fact that many learned and good friends and colleagues have been at hand to prevent some of the follies with which it would otherwise be marred. The following are only the debts of which I am most conscious.

Although he will not know it until he reads these words, this book was inspired by William Haller. Helen C. White and Julian Markels helped me to define its scope. At midpoint, when I was too deep in close detail, Madeleine Doran helped me to rethink my whole design. Early chapter-drafts were read and criticized, and encouragement warmly given, by Malcolm Griffith, Robert C. Jones, Thomas Kranidas, Julian Markels, Louis L. Martz, John T. Shawcross, and Stanley Stewart. I am particularly indebted to Walter Davis, whose suggestions were influential in my analyses of Donne and Burton.

At various stages of thinking and writing, I have benefited from conversations or correspondence with Dennis Donovan, Robert M. Estrich, John Hollander, Donald R. Howard, Ruth Hughey, David Kettler, William Krueger, Clayton Roberts, and Victor Rowley. A faculty seminar directed by Arnold Hauser gave me the opportunity to try out the Lilburne chapter.

My work on Traherne was in part made possible by the generosity of James M. Osborn and Carol Marks. Mr. Osborn unhesitatingly allowed me to read and to reproduce passages from the manuscript of Traherne's "Select Meditations," which will be published under his editorship as a companion to the two-volume Oxford edition by H. M. Margoliouth. Miss Marks furnished me with typescripts and proofsheets, before they were in print, of her essays on Traherne and the general introduction to the now-published edition, by Carol Marks and George Guffey, of Traherne's *Christian Ethicks* (Ithaca, 1967). A briefer version of my chapter on Traherne was first printed in *Papers on Language and Literature*, II (Summer, 1966), 258–64. This material is here reproduced by permission of the editors.

I am indebted to the graduate student members of two seminars in seventeenth-century prose, at the Ohio State University and at the

University of Washington, for allowing me to use them as a sounding-board for my theories and for contributing their own ideas to my project. Among these students, I owe special thanks to John Fleischauer, who checked my notes, proofread the manuscript, and, with Janet Fleischauer, compiled the index.

For the facilitation of my work at various stages, I am indebted to Albert J. Kuhn, chairman of my department; Joseph Mullin, who was my teaching assistant in the spring of 1967; Miss Harriet C. Jameson, Head of the Rare Book Library at the University of Michigan; Mr. Richard Ploch, Curator of Rare Books at the Ohio State University Library; and Mr. Ploch's assistant, Mrs. Serena Bradshaw. The Ohio State University has been generous with funds for typing, travel, and research assistance.

If this book was written with any particular readers in mind, certainly among the foremost are Rosalie L. Colie and Richard D. Altick, who read the whole manuscript as soon as it was presentable. I should like also to mention here the expert readers for the Press, Arthur Barker and A. B. Chambers. I am grateful to all these severe and sympathetic critics for their extensive, relevant, and helpful comments upon my work. The errors that now remain represent my invincible ignorance in the face of their admonishments.

For a woman scholar, in particular, non-intellectual debts may be crucially important. These are among the most vivid of mine. My daughter Rachel, who is a few months younger than the first-written chapter of this book, has shown remarkably little jealousy of typewriters, and has kept her parents cheerful through the most desperate authorial crises. A grant from the Guggenheim Foundation enabled me to take a year off from teaching without losing the indispensable services of Mrs. Helen Pearson, who runs my household with such unparalleled and loving wisdom that my husband, my daughter, and I have fared the better, rather than the worse, for my absorption in the seventeenth century.

To my parents, to Helen Pearson, to William Haller, and (always above all) to my husband Julian Markels—each in different, unmeasurable ways—this book and I owe the most. I hope that it may be worthy of them, and of their witnesses to human values.

J. W.

Columbus, Ohio
Christmas, 1967

NOTE ON
DOCUMENTATION

The editions of works cited in the text, and abbreviations used in citing, are given below. I have followed the spelling, punctuation, and capitalization of the editions being used, except that in the case of quoted prefatory material italic and roman passages have been reversed.

John Donne. *Devotions Upon Emergent Occasions* (London, 1624). References are to section (that is, Meditation, Expostulation, or Prayer), Station, and page.

John Bunyan. *Grace Abounding to the Chief of Sinners*, ed. Roger Sharrock (Oxford, 1962). Citation is by page.

John Lilburne. The tracts are cited in the notes. Original editions have been used unless otherwise noted.

Robert Burton. *The Anatomy of Melancholy*, ed. Holbrook Jackson, 3 vols. (London, 1932). References give part, section, member, and subsection as applicable, except that references to the preface give page number in Part I. References to the section "Religious Melancholy" are to an as yet unpublished edition of this section by Dennis Donovan and are identified by the letter "D." See the Bibliographical Appendix for a discussion of this edition.

Richard Baxter. *Reliquiae Baxterianae*, ed. Matthew Sylvester (London, 1696). References give part, section, and page.

Sir Thomas Browne. *Religio Medici* in *The Works of Sir Thomas*

Browne, ed. Geoffrey Keynes, 4 vols. (Chicago, 1964), Vol. I. References are to part and section.

John Milton. *Complete Prose Works of John Milton*, ed. Don M. Wolfe and others, 4 vols. to date (New Haven, 1953–). References are to volume and page.

Thomas Traherne. *Centuries, Poems, and Thanksgivings*, ed. H. M. Margoliouth, 2 vols. (Oxford, 1958), Vol. I. References are to century and meditation.

CONTENTS

THE ELOQUENT "I"

Style and Self in
Seventeenth-Century
Prose

CHAPTER I

STYLE AND SELF IN SEVENTEENTH-CENTURY PROSE

MY INTENTION IN WRITING THIS BOOK HAS BEEN TO OFFER AN AP-
proach to the study of seventeenth-century prose which might supplement the method made available to us by the distinguished and
still invaluable scholarship of Morris Croll. Seventeenth-century literature contains a number of works of prose nonfiction in which the
self-conscious first person singular is so important that it can be employed by the critic as a central means to a definition of the nature
of the style. This method is here demonstrated upon eight works by
eight different writers, each, in his different way, of major importance in his age. The terms "conservative Anglican" and "radical
Puritan" are defined and employed as broad literary categories to
suggest that each of these writers represents a significant variation
upon one or the other of two styles of self-expression.

The literary self-consciousness so noteworthy in Donne and a few
of his contemporaries is a peculiarly seventeenth-century phenomenon. The eight men to be considered here are very different from
earlier writers, who, with few exceptions, did not explicitly consider
or question the nature of selfhood. They are also different from
writers of the Romantic age, who flaunt their lonely individuality,
and from those after the mid-nineteenth century, whose thought is
increasingly served by a highly technical vocabulary of self-analysis.
In these seventeenth-century writers, individuality is real but limited,
self-consciousness extreme, but untrained in modern techniques of
introspection. These eight men had an unprecedented choice of traditions within which to find themselves—and the choice itself bred
self-consciousness—but they could not eschew traditions altogether.
Those which they accepted involved group meanings and identities,
and their truths were thought to be objective and absolute.

3

My study is limited to some prose works written approximately between 1620 and 1680, and bound together by their authors' common need to express, defend, or define themselves in a literary way, within the context of a turbulent, creative age. The English Revolution, occurring at the center of this period, sets a mark of violent change and conflict upon it. The only post-1660 writers included here are still preoccupied with Revolutionary or pre-Revolutionary styles and issues, and do not belong to the literary period of the Restoration.

My definition of literary self-consciousness, for the purposes of this study, is very carefully limited to works which partake of the nature of confession, and display in varying degrees a specific set of literary characteristics. Thus, while cutting across a number of genres in my selection of works to be discussed, I am hypothesizing another genre whose rules explain why I can include Donne but not Andrewes, Burton but not Hobbes.

By seventeenth-century literary self-consciousness, I mean the writer's crucial and unremitting awareness that he is the subject of his own prose, whether or not he is literally writing autobiography. Each of these men is vastly and precisely interested in himself either as a sensitive human being placed in time for some important purpose, or as a literary artifact (his own) designed to reflect eternity. It is not a seventeenth-century phenomenon, but a necessary fact of life that he and his world create one another: in showing himself, he shows his time. More typically seventeenth-century is his habit of generalizing his "I" into a representative of all Englishmen, or a cosmic personality symbolic of all men.

As a writer, he is explicitly interested in his prose and often comments extensively upon it, becoming his own first critic. And although he may be full of pretended indifference toward the reader, he is constantly reacting to the reader—striking poses, asking for sympathy, even asking the reader's cooperation in the writing of the book. Literary self-consciousness, then, includes consciousness of self as subject, in all the richness of the self as product and maker of his age; consciousness of self as style and thereby as a way of linking subject with object; consciousness of self in the eyes of the reader, or object, which may mean either opposition to or union with that reader.

I have chosen works whose nature or strategy most clearly forces the writer to identify himself with his words, and writers who are most aware of becoming so identified. Prose nonfiction, which significantly flourishes in this period, is the obvious mode. It lacks the protective devices both of fiction and of poetry: one inevitably assumes that in this medium a writer is who he says he is. Introduce here the first person singular, and life and art become more explicitly interwoven than they do anywhere else: Montaigne, whose essays influenced more than one of these Englishmen, tells us that he has made his book no more than the book has made him.[1] The self-consciousness that caused him to choose the essay form to begin with is increased as he continues to expose himself in that form, inevitably affecting the style of every page.

Once this "genre" is established, its most interesting representatives seem to divide up into two clearly distinct literary categories, to which I have given the names "conservative Anglican" and "radical Puritan."[2] The terminology is not lightly chosen. My whole argument will make clear the literary justification for my choice of these words, and that is my primary concern. But of course Anglican prose has to have been written by someone who was an Anglican, and there *is* a significant correlation between the prose and the world-view. The correlation is less likely to exist in unself-conscious prose or in poetry, which is practically incapable of being self-conscious in the way of prose because it is so well protected by its obvious stylistic conventions and thresholds.

The term "conservative Anglican" is unexceptionable, I think. Modern historians disagree sharply about the meaning of the word "Puritan."[3] More accurate historical words for my authors, at least before 1640 and after 1660, might be "separatist," or "nonconformist," not to mention individually applicable sectarian labels. But it was necessary to find a word more suggestive of broad ideological and stylistic patterns, and sufficiently affirmative and resonant to offer a positive alternative to "Anglican." Although even today "Puritan" can be used as a term of disapproval, at least in itself it implies something valuable, and its stylistic connotations are suitable to my analysis. Distinctions made in the past, by such literary historians as Edward Dowden, have helped to remove for us the historical drawbacks of the word, and contributed to it some of the evocativeness that "Anglican" already had. As an essential qualification, I include the adjective "radical" (making a union that would have been historically contradictory before 1640), to define more closely the period and nature of the Puritanism to be considered here.

Within these two categories, then, of conservative Anglican and radical Puritan, the Anglican works in which the appearance of the "I" can most easily be studied are Donne's *Devotions Upon Emergent Occasions*, a kind of spiritual autobiography written during convalescence from a serious illness; Browne's *Religio Medici*, a long essay explaining and defending his faith; Burton's *Anatomy of Melancholy*, a layman's analysis of that pervasive Renaissance ailment, preceded by a lengthy preface to the reader; and Traherne's *Centuries of Meditations*, religious meditations probably written with a particular friend-in-the-faith in mind. These four pieces of literature, while they are very different one from another, possess in common most of a set of characteristics definable as the Anglican "I."

On the radical Puritan side are Bunyan, whose *Grace Abounding* provides the very best example of the Puritan spiritual autobiography; "Free-born John" Lilburne, the purest literary example of the self-conscious radical, whose story we must trace through a number of political tracts; and Milton, from whose prose I have selected as most relevant five antiprelatical tracts written at a crucial time in his own career and in English history. These Puritans are all more different from one another than the Anglicans are, since Puritanism is not one ideology, but many different ones—and left-wing Puritanism, in particular, splits into faction after faction. Hence we have here Bunyan, a Baptist; Milton, an Independent; and Lilburne, a Leveller who turned Quaker in his middle age. Nevertheless, the fact that all of them can be called Puritans, the reason why, and the effect upon the literary "I" make a clear enough bond among them for analysis to be possible.

It seems unlikely that self-consciousness is to be found in writing that cannot be identified as either conservative or radical. Whatever may have been written by men who were neither significantly sustained by the traditions of Anglican conservatism nor willing to commit themselves to radical changes in the world, their viewpoints, or non-viewpoints, are not ordinarily expressed in highly memorable, strongly egocentric prose. The one important exception to be considered here is the Puritan Church-of-Englander Richard Baxter, whose painfully honorable, self-chosen, and self-assertive mid-road position is described in an almost artlessly epic life-and-times autobiography, *Reliquiae Baxterianae*, published posthumously. While he finally belongs with the Puritans rather than the Anglicans, he provides a dividing line and a rule-proving exception.

Given these eight writers, we have a very considerable range of prose—devotions, meditations, extended essay, spiritual autobiography, history of a life and times, medical-psychiatric encyclopedia, and political tract. Thus it is possible to study the appearance of the self-conscious "I" in a wide range of settings, and to recognize that in this century, while it does foster and is fostered by the formal autobiography, it can turn up almost anywhere—that in Anglican writing, in fact, autobiography is its least probable form. It is significant that the political tracts are written by Puritans and the meditations by Anglicans, and it cannot therefore be argued that the "I"'s present themselves differently only because of the accident of genre. Of course some Anglicans wrote political tracts, and some Puritans wrote meditations.[4] But we have to do with the best writers, in their most obviously self-conscious works. The fact is that the self-conscious Puritan "I" expressed himself most readily in action, and the Anglican in meditation. The chosen forms, then, are a result more than they are a cause.

The terms "conservative Anglican" and "radical Puritan," once they are carefully defined as literary categories, broadly summarize the major contrasts in styles of selfhood between the two groups of writers considered in this book. In the following description of these contrasts, it is of course assumed that, as in any definition of style, no one writer can be expected to exhibit every characteristic: in fact, one reason for setting these generalizations at the beginning rather than the end of the book is to insure the recognition that every work here represented is a variation upon one of the paradigms.

The conservative "I" is meditative, anti-historical, obscure and ambiguous, symbolic. He lives upon the inheritance of the Anglican past, sustaining and sustained by it. Time for him is an aspect of eternity;[5] there is nothing new under the sun; every man is like Adam, who contained all. The typically Anglican metaphor of man as a little world is predominant in the conservative's self-analysis. Overcoming space and time, this symbol can unify the shared experience of the race. Thus is generated the "cosmic personality."

Yet, in his self-consciousness the Anglican writer cannot simply make himself a symbol and be done with it. That he recognizes in

7

himself conflicting moods, thoughts, and sensations is part of his acceptance of himself as a little world, but he has to learn to deal with
his conflicts as an individual, seeing that he is not a simple, all-of-a-
piece mechanism. His "I" is obscure, ambiguous, many-sided, because that is how he looks to himself. The complexity of his style
imitates the complexity of his sense of himself, both in his use of
such metaphysical figures as optical illusion, paradox, and word play,
and in stylistic shifts from one point to another in his prose. He is
aware that "he" need not even be the same person from moment to
moment.

His prose is apt to be tinged with melancholy. He is a conservative
partly because he knows that so long as death exists there is no
Utopia, progress is limited, and life is tragic. Yet this recognition,
linking life and death in his consciousness, makes his prose responsive
to the constant rhythms of life. And despite his melancholy it is the
conservative rather than the radical who has the sense of humor. He
is better able to laugh at life, better able to accept his insignificance,
to be amused even by his own fascination with himself. More likely
than the radical to be blessed with security, education, and status,
and much less likely to be wholly preoccupied with temporal issues,
he has more time for play as well as for introspection: for all these
reasons, he is much more likely to engage in the play of art.

At the opposite extreme from the conservative, the radical "I" is
active, timebound, as simple and visible as possible, desirous of being
taken literally and seriously as a man living in a hostile world. Instead of beginning with Man, he begins with himself; instead of beginning with generalizations, he begins with concrete details. Where
the conservative prefers poetry, he prefers history, and in current
events he finds his place in life. His spiritual self-exploration is always temporal: How have I progressed (or regressed) from day to
day? rather than, What am I like as a human being? Politically, his
destiny is to be one of God's Englishmen, to prophesy the millen-
nium, or to assist in the fulfillment of God's purpose for England in
the bringing about of an earthly Utopia in time. Both because he
begins with the literal facts and because his role is to a large extent
defined for him by his conception of history, he has less occasion
than the Anglican to see himself very complexly or very subjec-
tively. Possessed of a simple literal strength, his prose is less volatile
and less resonant than that of the Anglican.

The experience of conversion is not as important to Anglicans as to Puritans, and the more Calvinist the doctrine, the more stress seems to be laid on the incompatibility of election with despair.[6] Thus, the saved Puritan, despite the frequent discomfort of his daily life, may feel it incumbent upon him to suppress all tendencies toward melancholy in order to convince himself of his salvation. If he is political, he believes that direct action in this world can have some permanent value, that man is capable of progress, that therefore he can take part in the bringing about, at the least, of man's substantial betterment, at the most, of Utopia. In this respect, his view of the world is the opposite of tragic, and death, for which he claims always to be prepared, is actually of minor importance in his consciousness.

Yet, while he always insists that he is cheerful, he inevitably encounters disillusion. He looks for progress and fails to find it; the climactic moments of his life are scenes of public trial or punishment which should lead men to change of heart, but do not. His absorption in immediate causes and his relative indifference to the constant rhythms of life may give his prose a topicality and a lack of resonance, which contrast sharply with the Anglican mode. What he writes is distinguished by its gravity, though he may be self-consciously capable, as Milton is, of "grim laughter," [7] and he has a genius for making his enemies look ridiculous. But to the extent that art is play, he finds it hard to accept, and he often sees the conservative as someone who plays with words, because he cannot believe that such play may be serious.[8]

The self-conscious Anglican, viewing himself both with mirth and with dismay, may achieve a more balanced self-knowledge in his sense of man's ambiguity, discontinuity, and relative unimportance, and in the greater extent to which he is aware of and free to use psychology. Yet the very depth of his knowledge causes him to adopt disguises and run from his own perceptions, at least in public. The Puritan may achieve a steadier and graver vision, less bounded by a fragmented and playful self-consciousness, but hindered by less habitual subjectivity, less range of viewpoint (and less sense of proportion), less capacity for free psychological probing.

It is thus, first of all, that the "I" defines himself to us as an "I," in terms of the whole context from which he speaks. Secondly, he defines himself to us as an "I" in terms of his relationship with his art,

9

or with the paper on which he writes. As this is a self-conscious age, it is an age tremendously conscious of language: the individual writer, in every paragraph he sets down, reveals his anxiety to understand the character of words, in themselves, and in relation to him in manuscript or in print. This is true of both Anglicans and Puritans, although their conclusions differ.

To begin with a standard cliché set in a new context, what has "holding up the mirror to nature" to do with writing about oneself? Does the writer believe that his "I" *mirrors* his eye? *We* know, at any rate, that the image we see in the mirror cannot correspond exactly with what others see: it is what we choose or are conditioned to behold there. The problem becomes much more complicated when the person creating the mirror image by looking into the mirror is aware of other people looking on as that mirror image is formed, people who cannot see *him*, but can see the image of himself that he has chosen to present. That is our position as readers of his work.

Let us ignore for the moment the effect of the audience, which is to be our third consideration, and confine ourselves to the connection between the writer's eye, and the "I" that he creates. Essentially, the differences between the relationship that the Anglican has with the paper on which he writes and that which the Puritan has are these. The Anglican turns himself into art, while the Puritan turns art toward life, using art for the benefit of life. For the Anglican, the mirror image is primary; the Puritan's emphasis is on what the image reflects, and how it can be used. For the Anglican, the world is already artificial because it constitutes the art of God. The phrase "the Book of the Creatures" is not a metaphor; everything in the world is symbolic; and word and world are only two different ways of bodying forth divine truth.[9] To turn oneself into art is only to become more fully realized.

For the time being, then, for the Anglican, art and life are much closer to one another than usual; it is much easier than usual for the person looking in the mirror to say to himself, Which is which? Just as nature's artificiality makes it more meaningful as the art of God, so the more *literary* the "I," the more he takes precedence over the creating eye, and can enter into a relationship with the eye that is reciprocal, creating as he has been created. Robert Burton, for example, writing of melancholy to avoid melancholy, puts on the persona of Democritus, Jr., son of the laughing philosopher. The laughing "I" may teach the eye to smile.

The Anglican is not disposed, when he sets himself before the mirror, to imagine that the eye that is mirrored there has any kind of simple existence. One reason why he engages in this activity is to find out who he is. Discovering that he changes from moment to moment, he allows his style to do the same thing. Unlike him, the style can continue to reflect these changes—the book can *be* simultaneously three different faces of John Donne, as in the *Devotions*,[10] while he can be and feel himself to be only one at a time. In this sense, too, the book can be more himself than he is.

Moreover, the more literary the "I," the more "I" and eye together achieve a symbolic existence that transcends personality and begins to claim infinite vision. It is partly because the boundary between art and life is so blurred that the work of art acquires the advantages of both. And it is partly because in his literariness the "I" evokes all his rich literary past as present in him. Thus, we see confirmed in the Anglican's negotiation with his art the impulse toward symbolic characterization and cosmic vision that typifies the way in which he represents his context.

The radical writer in this age cannot help sharing in a sense of the liveliness of words and language: Milton, like Donne, speaks of books as the progeny of their writers.[11] But because the Puritan is turned so much more toward the reality of current events than the Anglican is, he tends to see the function of books wholly in terms of life. So it happens that while in Anglican prose the life-art boundary is forever being blurred by life's incorporation into art, in Puritan prose it is blurred by the effort to make art into life. One has the sense less of a reciprocal creation ending in the predominance of the literary "I" than of an attempt to reproduce the literal eye, to make the mirror give way to reality.

Instead of saying, Who am I? to the mirror image, the Puritan says to himself, or to it, Here is who I am, or intend to be. His statement involves considerable display of concrete details, "proof of identity." To some extent, a reciprocal relation still operates. The Puritan diarist lays out these details as a way of self-examination, so as to be able to improve himself. The propagandist lays them out as a means of self-defense, or as a way of projecting himself into society. In the conscious or unconscious ways in which these details are selected (for they are selected, no matter how literal or unbiased he tries to be), the "I" of the manuscript becomes a different person from the narrator, and may act upon the narrator, helping him to create himself in that image.

As the Anglican's view of himself is affected by his concept of the world as art, the Puritan's is shaped by his sense of himself as an instrument of God's will.[12] In varying degrees, the emergent "I" has to be subdued to his role in life, and the personal made impersonal. And as God uses him, so the Puritan uses the paper on which he writes, and in this way, it becomes an instrument rather than a reflecting mirror. Then the relationship between him and the paper is one-way rather than reciprocal. The results affect the relationship between the self-conscious narrator and his audience, to which we can now turn.

A literary "public," like the modern use of the word, comes into being for the first time in the sixteenth century with the proliferation of printing houses.[13] The audience of a printed work can no longer be limited; the author has to consider the possibility that his book may be read by almost anyone. The emerging self-consciousness of these authors must inevitably be complicated by the fact that, if they are to be authors, their self-awareness must be publicly learned.

Though the Anglican meditates upon himself in private, he is constantly aware that he may be overheard. He is aware that he is using a pen or pencil, and he knows that words committed to paper have a way of being read by others. Given his degree of self-consciousness, he is always aware of the possibility that he is only holding the pen because he wants his words to be read, of the possibility that they will be read whether he so desires or not, of the possibility that they ought to be read (from which, or before which, arises the question of whether they are good enough to be read, or whether he ought to be engaging in this kind of activity at all). On the one hand, he claims to have no desire to publish, pretends to be completely unaware of an audience; on the other hand, he prepares the manuscript for its readers as carefully as he can.

The reliable old criterion—Is it for the glory of God?—no longer comes so readily or so simply to the writer's mind. The stimulation of the admiring audience is too present. At best, the writer must have a double focus: he offers himself, as Donne does in his *Devotions*, simultaneously to God and the world.[14] Seeing, and seeing that he sees—and is seen; writing, and conscious of the complex relationship between the "I" he thinks of as himself and the "I" which emerges on paper; conscious too that this relationship—and his attitude toward the literary "I"—will differ from the reader's, he may produce an "I" that plays games with the audience, teasing them about his identity in a way that had very seldom been tried in earlier literature. Between providing enough biographical details to identify himself clearly, and masking as Democritus, Jr., Robert Burton, for example, asks us to believe that his book was written by the man-in-the-moon, or by no one, *nemo*. We see, then, reasons from still another point of view, for the fragmentation, obscurity, and ambiguity of the Anglican "I."

And yet, after all, the audience is there, and despite all his hesitations the man is writing to that audience. We observe that the Anglican does not write autobiography directly; rather, he invites the reader to share with him in the investigation of some "subject," like a doctor's religion, or the anatomy of melancholy. The investigation can seem shared because the style is meditative. The writer allows the reader to follow the course of his mind as he contemplates his subject: thus, in a sense, the reader has to write the book himself—and in the process, he and the author become one, yet not one. The investigation can seem shared, too, because it is never finished. Not only does the meditative style itself suggest work-in-progress,[15] but the whole form of the book is left open: Donne's meditations are cyclic; Traherne invites his reader to add to what he has written. Thus, while on one level the reader seems to have been ignored or rejected, on another the most significant kind of participation and communion is required. On this profounder level, the phrase "to the glory of God" may again become operative, since for the Anglican the brotherhood of men is communion in Christ.

The Puritan autobiographer is still explicitly justified by that old criterion because his autobiography is likely to be exclusively focused on those aspects of his life which he takes to be directly revelatory of God's mercies, because the form of the work, usually centering on conversion, is accepted and standardized,[16] and because he is less likely to be subject to as much literary self-awareness as the Anglican is—he tends to be, and to choose to be, less sophisticated. Usually, too, he thinks of his autobiography in terms of no audience at all, or of a very well-defined audience—his own family or parish. Hence, he is less likely to feel so self-conscious about the idea of publishing.

When his work is more explicitly political, publishing actually becomes his whole purpose. His prose is active and public; his intention is to change the world. To the extent that public self-exploration is involved, it is generally less subjective and at the same time less symbolic than in conservative prose. He may be presenting himself as prophet. He may write for the purpose of bearing witness in his own person to the injustices of the opposition. Even if he is not the ostensible subject, he may feel required to become so momentarily in order to defend himself against the calumnies and slanders that men in public life are heir to. In any case, he has some specific audience in mind—and a specific temporal reason for writing to this audience. He tries to mask himself only when he might otherwise be prosecuted for treasonable utterances. Ordinarily he wants to be known.

Before he thinks of a relationship with the pen and paper, he thinks of that audience. He does not want to meditate with his hearers; he wants to impress his message upon them. His prose may be very repetitious, either because he is trying to persuade or because he means simply to attack, in which case he may think of words as weapons. Then the page becomes an object, to be thrown in fury at his opponents.

His publishing worries are directly opposite to those of the conservative. It is hard for him to find a willing and competent printer, hard to read proof (he may be in jail, or simply too busy), hard to be sure of adequate distribution (he may be censored or suppressed). His writing, under temporal pressure, may be hastier and less finished, more authentically spontaneous and colloquial, but less artistic than that of the conservative. Certainly it is likely to be more plain and rude, more direct, more popular, less mannered.

It is in these ways that the eyes of conservative and radical meet those of their readers, then and now. If they could have understood each other better, their art would not be so distinctive or so sure. Richard Baxter demonstrates, in fact, how perilous and self-denying a task it can be for an artist to attempt to intermediate, to interpret, to stand between two different ideologies or styles. Yet I assume this to be the proper work of the critic, since it requires objectivity and disinterested appreciation, and since, whether or not he is able to live up to its demands, it provides the critic with a vocation worthy of the name.

CHAPTER II

DONNE AND BUNYAN:
THE STYLES
OF TWO FAITHS

IN LATE NOVEMBER OR EARLY DECEMBER, 1623, JOHN DONNE, THE famous Dean of Paul's, and a favorite preacher at the court of James I, fell ill of the relapsing fever,[1] and, in anticipation of his own demise, hastened the marriage of his daughter Constance to the retired actor Edward Alleyn. Edward LeComte's nomination of Alleyn as a father figure for Constance [2] sets off fascinating reverberations, since Donne himself was such a player of parts. At this time, he not only provided Constance with a dramatic replacement for himself; he provided the world with one, too, in his *Devotions Upon Emergent Occasions.* Then, somewhat anticlimactically, he recovered, and, outliving Edward Alleyn, saw his *Devotions* through three editions before his death.

Some thirty-seven years later, in 1660, John Bunyan, a Baptist preacher and former tinker, was arrested and charged with holding a conventicle. He was one of the first to suffer the repressive effects on dissenters of the Restoration settlement, but the results of his imprisonment were surely not what its Anglican administrators had in mind. His twelve-year confinement, while it worked immeasurable hardships upon his family,[3] was humane and at times even perfunctory. It gave him leisure to conceive and write books which, for many generations of readers, were to take second-place only to the Bible. Here *Pilgrim's Progress* may well have been begun. Here he wrote his spiritual autobiography, *Grace Abounding.*

Ideologically, personally, culturally, these two men are a world removed from one another. Their different uses of the "I" are very clearly distinguishable. And yet they do unexpectedly have much in common besides their Christian names. Their likenesses, especially as evidenced in the two works to be discussed here, make a comparison of their "I"s more possible, more relevant, and more exciting. Both books were written by preachers at a time when they were unable to preach, Donne because he languished in sickbed, and Bunyan because he languished in prison. These books, then, might be considered "second-choice"; they are not what their authors most wanted to be doing. Though both men were prolific writers, their principal business was the spoken word. Since both admired and imitated Saint Paul, considering themselves, like him, reformed sinners, they believed it proper to preach about themselves, as he did. In a period of crisis and isolation, deprived of books and auditors, they looked within, and wrote of what they saw.

The subjective pattern detailed by both men presents an alternation between joy and grief, hope and despair, which, as Henri Talon says of Bunyan, "constitutes the rhythm of our author's life and perhaps, in varying intensity, of every human life." [4] Both Donne and Bunyan, at least during the periods of their lives with which they are here concerned, were highly emotional, highly prone to extremes of feeling. Both were preoccupied with their souls' health. Both books end on a note of uncertainty; while Bunyan has resolved to stand fast and Donne's illness has abated, still Bunyan allows for the possibility of further pain, and in Donne's last meditation, the physicians warn of the possibility of a relapse.

The religious needs of the two men were somewhat similar. Both spend a good deal of time in their narratives voicing intellectual doubts, and both resolve their doubts in emotion rather than reason. Donne begs for God's thunder, and gets it in the organ voice of the prayers of the Anglican church. Bunyan, in a fine climactic passage, cries out, "I will leap off the Ladder even blindfold into Eternitie, sink or swim, come heaven, come hell; Lord Jesus, if thou wilt catch me, do; if not, I will venture for thy Name" (*G.A.*, p. 101). Bunyan was early attracted by Anglican ritual; Donne was by nature a passionate, rebellious man. Had circumstances been different, their roles might have been reversed.

Finally, directed by the fact that the sincerity of both men has been questioned,[5] we can find parallels in the effect of their self-consciousness upon their art. Mirrors and rulebooks guide the emergent self-awareness of the age, in the mannered confusion of life and art on the one hand, and the proliferation of how-to-do-it books (the art of living, loving, dying) on the other.[6] A seventeenth-century man who checks his progress in the mirror (like Donne), or is converted by the book (like Bunyan), may be different from his predecessors, but is probably no less sincere. And the art that he produces may exemplify a particularly valuable kind of originality just because one is constantly aware of the artist's awareness of his situation and his craft.

The question of sincerity confronts us head-on in the dedications of these two books, in the different arguments and styles in which the two men explain their reasons for publishing such personal writing. Donne's book is dedicated in a highly mannered and witty style to Prince Charles, soon to be Charles I:

MOST EXCELLENT PRINCE,

I Have had three *Births;* One, *Naturall,* when I came into the *World;* One *Supernatural,* when I entred into the *Ministery;* and now, a *preter-naturall* Birth, in returning to *Life,* from this *Sickness.* In my *second Birth,* your *Highnesse Royall Father* vouchsafed mee his Hand, not onely to sustaine mee *in it,* but to lead mee *to it.* In this *last Birth,* I my selfe am borne a *Father:* This *Child* of mine, this *Booke,* comes into the world, *from* mee, and *with* mee. And therefore, I presume (as I did the *Father* to the *Father*) to present the *Sonne* to the *Sonne;* This *Image* of my *Humiliation,* to the lively *Image* of his *Maiesty,* your *Highnesse.* It might bee enough, that *God* hath seene my *Devotions:* But *Examples* of *Good Kings* are *Commandements;* and *Ezechiah* writt the *Meditations* of his *Sicknesse,* after his *Sicknesse.* Besides, as I have liv'd to see, (not as a *Witnesse* onely, but as a *Partaker*) the happinesses of a part of your *Royal Fathers time,* so shall I live, (*in my way*) to see the happinesses of the times of your *Highnesse* too, if this *Child* of mine, inanimated by your gracious Acceptation, may so long preserve alive the *Memory* of

> *Your Highnesse*
> *Humblest and*
> *Devotedst*
> JOHN DONNE

For Donne, the king or prince is the significant audience, since all meaning is vested in him. The prince's power of patronage is just one aspect of this: whether Donne lives or dies, the dedication of the book to Charles guarantees the extension of *Donne* into Charles' reign. The book is born of his sickness, and so is he. It becomes both his child and his twin, and is also an "I" to live after him. He is not content to have it merely *an* other self; it is somehow a whole family of other selves.

The most interesting sentence in the dedication is this: "It might bee enough, that *God* hath seene my *Devotions:* But *Examples* of *Good Kings* are *Commandements;* And *Ezechiah* writt the *Meditations* of his *Sicknesse,* after his *Sicknesse.*" It is not clear whether he means that, since God saw him at prayer, it might be thought that he had no reason to write anything down at all, or that, since God read the manuscript, there might be no reason to publish it. Since the devotions are supposed to be taking place during his illness, and since he speaks of Hezekiah as writing his meditations after his illness, the more probable meaning is the former; the unwritten devotions might be thought sufficient. But there is ambiguity, and it is relevant, since the actual and written devotions, Donne praying and the written page, are being so closely identified with one another. Perhaps the devotion is the act of writing.

But why must there be an audience? If the sentence permits a backward reference, then one argument might be that since examples of good kings are commandments, and since King James presented his spiritual son John Donne to God, then Donne should present *his* spiritual child (the book) to the prince, soon to become God's representative. As Donne was brought to life by James, so the book will be "inanimated" by the prince. The immediate reference is more obvious, although also complicated. King Hezekiah, mortally ill, prayed to have his life extended, and God granted his wish. He then repeated a psalm reflecting upon his illness, praising God for his deliverance, and asserting that he would tell his children of God's goodness.[7] Thus, in reading of Donne's deliverance, we see Donne reading of Hezekiah's deliverance and citing what must have seemed to him a prototype of his own situation in order to prove his right to make his devotions public. If Hezekiah was simply repeating a psalm suited to the occasion, and written by someone else,[8] still another mirror image is added to the succession.

The sentence preceding this one, of course, has already provoked the life-art, reality-image confusion, when Donne says that as he presented himself (the book's father) to James (Charles' father), he will present the son to the son, "This *Image* of my *Humiliation* to the lively *Image* of his *Maiesty.*" The first presumption is made to justify its re-enactment; the original will justify the copy. But meanwhile, art and life are equated in the comparison of Donne's book to Prince Charles, as the image is presented to the image, the son to the son.

This type of dedication is standard. But the kinds of ambiguity involved and the mirrors-within-mirrors images of conscious devotion are very Donnean. He had never published anything personal before. That he did it at this time, still confined to what everyone had feared was his deathbed, argues a unique strength and complexity of motivation that only partly emerges in this cryptic and mannered prose. Such motivation we find, I think, in the whole character of the book, but first of all in the unusually close connection between the life —and near death—of the author, and the book's creation.

R. C. Bald, in a brilliant final act of scholarship, left us this information about the *Devotions:*

Constance Donne was married to Edward Alleyn on 3 December 1623, and we have Alleyn's word for it that the marriage occurred while Donne was ill: "Thus past it on till the beginning off your sickness and then you desire[d] our maryag showld bee performed with as much sped as might bee." If Donne had not passed, or had only just passed the crisis of his fever by 3 December, he must have fallen ill during the last few days of November. The *Devotions* were entered in the Stationers Register on 9 January, presumably after having been scanned by the licenser and, if Donne's correspondence is to be believed, after having been seen by more than one of his friends . . . On 1 February Donne was able to send a presentation copy to the Queen of Bohemia enclosed in a dated letter to one of her ladies, who was to hand it to her. The book turned out to be larger than Donne anticipated, as it consists of 27 sheets, and thus would have taken about a month to pass through the press. If we assume that the book was in the printer's hands for the whole of January, we must then assume that the book was written during December. Yet this forces us to believe that the book was written in only a few weeks by a man who had very nearly died, whose body was weak and exhausted by his illness, and who was in the early stages of a long and slow convalescence. Even when the book was in the press, he was barely able to sit up in a chair in his bedroom, but had been unable as yet to leave it. For the circumstances of its composition Donne's *Devotions* can have few, if any, parallels in the annals of literature.[9]

I have quoted Mr. Bald at length both to do justice to his account and to emphasize its importance for us. A few years later, Donne was to pose in his graveclothes for a picture that, according to Walton, "became his hourly object" [10] as he lay dying. In 1624, he was still able to be his own artist, and, in the face of death, to strive for publication.

Besides the dedication, one literary device in particular, placed at the entrance of the work, informs us of its extraordinary artfulness. Disguised as a table of contents, a Latin poem in dactylic hexameters describes the various stages of Donne's illness. The poem is called "*Stationes*, sive *Periodi* in *Morbo*," and the opening lines, halved by the tiny pages of the 1624 edition, will serve to illustrate the verse, which would be entirely unremarkable if it were not so entirely unexpected:

> 1. *Insultus* Morbi primus;
> 2. *Post, Actio Laesa;*
> 3. *Decubitus* sequitur tandem;
> 4. *Medicusq;* vocatur;
> 5. *Solus* adest; 6 *Metuit;*
> 7. *Socios* sibi iungier instat.

Broken up according to their numbers, the pieces of the poem then serve one by one, throughout the book, to introduce the twenty-three "*stationes*" into which it is divided. Thus, the Latin poem is not just mirrored by the devotions. It is explicated, and seen in this light, the *Devotions* are an *explication de texte*. Donne is artist, art, and critic, all three. And this is his sermon upon his own text, to and upon his own soul.

From the midst of a consuming illness, in which one would imagine his whole impulse would have been to devote himself to God, he made sure that in the posture of devotion he should be self-consciously immortalized as art. I believe it consistent with his dedication and table of contents, as well as with all his religious writings, to suggest that for him the perfect achievement of the art was essential to the perfect act of devotion, because for Donne to live was at least as much a literary as a physical endeavor. Mr. Bald's description of his convalescence bears dramatic witness to that.

The publication of the *Devotions* was partly a manifestation of real gratitude to King James, who gave Donne spiritual life (in the ministry) and physical health (in sending the royal physician to nurse him through his illness). Still, Donne's eyes question the public reaction: "But let me stop, *my God*, and consider; will not this look like a piece of art, & cunning, to convey into the world an opinion, that I were more particularly in his care, then other men? And that heerein, in a shew of *humilitie*, and *thankfulnesse*, I magnifie my selfe more then there is cause?" (*Dev.*, Expos. 8, pp. 186–87). Gratitude to James and to God do mingle with vanity and desire for immortality: that is already clear in the dedication. But publication may also have been partly occasioned by the unusual isolation that his sickness forced upon him. He had expressed his desire to die in the pulpit.[11] In the *Devotions*, his complaints about his solitude repeatedly suggest that he does not feel whole when he is alone: "But *Lord*, thou art *Lord of Hosts*, & lovest *Action*; Why callest thou me from my calling? *In the grave no man shall praise thee*; In the doore of the grave, this sicke bed, no Man shal heare mee praise thee: Thou hast not opned my lips, that my mouth might shew *thee* thy praise, but that my mouth might shew *foorth* thy praise" (*Dev.*, Expos. 3, pp. 53–54). If he can exercise his meditations only in private, then in some way he must manage to have them overheard. Yet, despite the necessary qualifications to Anglican individuality suggested in Chapter I, and exemplified by the fact that in the foregoing passage he speaks in Scriptural language, the devotions are personal; it is himself he exposes to view. The dilemma implied in the dedication is everywhere apparent in the body of the *Devotions*.

Bunyan in *Grace Abounding* avoids this dilemma from the outset. Thinking as common man toward common men, he dedicates his book to his congregation, his "children," in whom he finds life: "Your hungerings and thirstings also after further acquaintance with the Father, in his Son; your tenderness of Heart, your trembling at sin, your sober and holy deportment also, before both God and men, is great refreshment to me: *For you are my glory and joy*, (I Thes. 2.20)" (*G.A.*, p. 1). Instead of the heavy and repeated stress on the "I," the emphasis is all on "you," or "your." If Donne is to find life in the "I" of his book, that is where his attention has to be centered. Bunyan is *using* his book as a way of continuing to find life in his "children." Hence, the book and the "I" of the book become instruments, means to an end.

Never in Donne's dedication or in the *Devotions* themselves is it suggested that his offering himself to the world as he does is simply to testify to God's goodness, or to provide inspiration to others. It would almost seem that the complexity of pose is a direct result of his refusal to stress this possibility: he could so easily have provided a supporting interpretation of Hezekiah's story. Bunyan does find it necessary to justify what he is doing, but for him the justification is easy:

Moses (*Numb.* 33. 1, 2) writ of the Journeyings of the children of *Israel*, from *Egypt* to the Land of *Canaan*; and commanded also, that they did remember their forty years travel in the wilderness. *Thou shalt remember all the way which the Lord thy God led thee these forty years in the wilderness, to humble thee, and to prove thee, to know what was in thine heart, whether thou wouldst keep his commandments, or no,* Deut. 8. 2, 3. Wherefore this I have endeavored to do; and not onely so, but to publish it also; that, if God will, others may be put in remembrance of what he hath done for their Souls, by reading his work upon me (*G.A.*, p. 2).

In this passage the double intention of *Grace Abounding* becomes clear. It is, first of all, a personal exercise in remembrance; and then, secondly, when published, a tool to be used by others in their own memory exercises. How are they to use it? "By reading his work upon me." The phrase is very striking, first in its obvious subordination of Bunyan to God, and then in its use of the word "work." Although the word can slide back and forth between "book," and "action" or "effect," here it points toward the latter meanings, and focuses Bunyan's whole biography away from art, toward life. The contrast is total with the mirror-within-mirror literary self-consciousness that informs Donne's prose.

Bunyan says at the end of his preface that he could have written his book in a much higher style if he had thought it right to do so. He did allow himself this liberty in his dense employment of Biblical quotations and citations in the preface itself. This standard practice places his autobiography in the traditional context that gives it significance: "I now once again, as before from the top of *Shenir* and *Hermon,* so now from *the Lions Dens, and from the Mountains of the Leopards* (Song 4. 8), do look yet after you all, greatly longing to see your safe arrival into THE desired haven" (*G.A.*, p. 1). On the one hand, evidence of salvation is to be found in plain, everyday experiences; reference must always be first to the individual daily life of the common man. On the other hand, reference to the Bible can explain and generalize that life, and make it more dramatic. In his preface, Bunyan goes very far toward making allegory of himself and his congregation. Then, consciously bringing himself down to earth, he makes allegory and realism touch briefly, before rejecting the former method for the present: "Have you never a Hill *Mizar* to remember? Have you forgot the Close, the Milk-house, the Stable, the Barn, and the like, where GOD did visit your Soul?" (*G.A.*, p. 3). And immediately after this he makes his comments about style. This book is to be confined to barn and milk-house, to the specific places and events which must be acknowledged before allegory can become meaningful. Like Donne's, Bunyan's is a chosen style. But its purpose is to reflect a consciousness less literary and more utilitarian, less inwardly than outwardly directed.

Bunyan's twelve years in prison gave him time to recall to himself the most significant episodes in his spiritual life. Remembering for him involved reliving; that is a difference between his autobiography and those of less memorable Puritans. Yet it is still a past, recollected and analyzed, and more or less summed up at the end of the volume: There I was; here I am now. This kind of perspective is conducive to successful story-telling, as the reception of the book makes clear. Unlicensed and poorly printed, Bunyan's book was used up like a commodity. Despite the very large printings, only three copies of the first edition remain: it was literally read to pieces.[12]

Already, then, in these few pages, distinct differences between Donne and Bunyan, and between the Anglican and Puritan sensibilities, have begun to emerge. Donne's prose is mannered, witty, and cryptic; his art, which for him is a higher form of life, centers itself on the showing forth of his symbolic "I." Bunyan uses his book to send a message or sermon to his "children," who constitute his life. He too lives in his work, but as a remembrance of God's work upon him, as example (or exemplum) more than as symbol.[13] Both God and the congregation so far have received more stress than he has. Bunyan chooses to keep his style relatively concrete and literal. From the type of prose so far visible, and the different presentations of the "I"s, we may expect Donne's to tend toward an associative, poetic style, and Bunyan's toward chronological narrative.

The differences suggested by the dedications make themselves felt on every page of the two works, beginning, of course, with the use of the first person. Particularly significant contrasts may be drawn between Donne's and Bunyan's presentation of the "I" with relation to the implied narrator and to spectators implied or present; the "I" as timeless (Donne) or temporal (Bunyan); the "I" as historical character (Bunyan) or generalized symbol (Donne); the "I" as cosmic (Donne) or localized (Bunyan). These patterns do overlap one another, being different aspects of the same subject rather than different subjects. In considering all of them, it may be useful to keep in mind as touchstones (never as causes) one pair of contrasting figures that can to some extent summarize the differences between the Anglican and Puritan ways of relating the self to the world. These figures are the microcosm and the wayfaring pilgrim.[14]

Dependent upon the old theory of correspondences, the idea of man as little world at once gives the Anglican an opportunity to see himself reflecting and reflected by a larger mirror-image, and in the process of such reflection to depart from absolute realism. In his symbolic identity with all things in time and space, he is familiar with the mysterious and remote. He can also fragment, or anatomize himself, into component symbols, each with its separate significance, arteries being rivers and so on. The Puritan figure of the pilgrim, on the other hand, implies men moving through history, achieving self-consciousness partly by intercourse with other men, achieving their meaning by finding vocations within the historical flow of time. The Bible explains where they have come from, where they are, where they are going, in terms quite specifically applicable to current events. The immediate and down-to-earth matters much more than the mysterious and remote: the theory of correspondences is simply irrelevant or untrue. The Anglican's favorite Old Testament character is Adam, who includes all men, while the Puritan prefers Biblical characters wholly immersed in history.

Donne's choice of subject is self-conscious in the mirror-gazing sense. Physical illness makes it necessary for him to be especially aware of himself—looking in the mirror for symptoms: "So that now, we doe not onely die, but die upon the Rack, die by the torment of sicknesse; nor that onely, but are preafflicted, super-afflicted with these jelousies and suspitions, and apprehensions of *Sicknes*, before we can cal it a sicknes; we are not sure we are ill; one hand askes the other by the pulse, and our eye askes our own urine, how we do" (*Dev.*, Med. 1, p. 4). He has chosen a particularly private subject. Physically, he is confined to bed and denied visitors. His solitude heightens his self-awareness and makes him more than usually inclined to anatomize himself. He is quick to descant upon reality; perhaps his proneness to hypochondria causes him to anticipate and magnify his symptoms.

Later, when first one doctor and then several become involved in the case, he watches them watching him:

I observe the *Phisician*, with the same diligence, as hee the *disease*; I see hee *feares*, and I feare with him: I overtake him, I overrun him in his feare, and I go the faster, because he makes his pace slow; I feare the more, because he disguises his fear, and I see it with the more sharpnesse, because hee would not have me see it. He knowes that his *feare* shall not disorder the practise, and exercise of his *Art,* but he knows that my *fear* may disorder the effect, and working of his practise (*Dev.,* Med. 6, pp. 115–16).

This building of an audience into the work itself is characteristic of Donne. He often looks past himself in the mirror to see who is look- ing on, and then recognizes that his own poise is accordingly affected. But here, in this deathly illness, the price of self-conscious- ness is high. The tight, clipped rhythm of the prose reflects the fe- vered sense of time's quickening as Donne nearly condemns himself to death before his time.

Just as in the first passage Donne in a sense invented the disease, here he has invented the doctor, who does not speak, but is inter- preted from the point of view of an "I" whose objectivity we have no reason to trust. This kind of eye-witness is usual in Donne. Recall "The Exstasie," where he hypothesizes first a Platonic lover, and later "some lover such as wee," to behold a private scene. He con- stantly imagines himself under observation, imagines a complexity of reaction on the part of the observer. And because Donne is never justified by "evidence," the chief reaction of the reader is to become more aware of the extreme self-consciousness of the "I." The lookers- on whom he invents are there to mirror for him some feeling of his own.

Bunyan, too, has chosen a subject that requires constant self- examination, but even though he deals directly with his spiritual con- dition—which one would assume to be more private than physical illness, his manner is considerably less private and subjective, less no- ticeably self-conscious. For one thing, instead of pretending that the reader does not exist, he talks to him, rather than (except as he quotes himself to the reader) to himself or to God:

But one day (amongst all the Sermons our Parson made) his subject was, to treat of the Sabbath day, and of the evil of breaking that, either with labour, sports, or otherwise: (now I was, notwithstanding my Religion, one that took much delight in all manner of vice, and especially that was the Day that I did solace my self therewith.) Wherefore I fell in my conscience under his Ser- mon, thinking and believing that he made that Sermon on purpose to shew me my evil-doing; and at that time I felt what guilt was, though never before, that I can remember . . . (*G.A.,* pp. 9–10).

Perhaps the most obvious characteristic of this prose in contrast with Donne's is that it lacks the atmosphere of solitude. We are never told that the "I" of this narrative is in prison. Bunyan does not provide himself with that very available excuse and setting for self-analysis, and thus he completely avoids that opportunity for examining himself in private. On the contrary, the "I" of his narrative is in constant contact with everyday, outdoor activity. Not only is he not in prison; he is also never at home. He is always to be found in public places, as, here, at a sermon, and his sense of what is happening within him must always compete with and/or be tested by what seems to be a reasonably objective version of reality.

Bunyan's inner thoughts never seem out of proportion with that reality. In the passage above, we are told that Bunyan was a Sabbath-breaker, that the preacher spoke against Sabbath-breaking, and that therefore Bunyan thought the sermon was aimed at him. It could be true, if the preacher knew his congregation. But Bunyan further saves himself from Donne's self-centering of reality by the use of three words, "*thinking and believing* that he made that Sermon on purpose." Here interpreter-Bunyan distances himself from his earlier "I," for the very purpose of correcting the earlier self's vision.[15]

Like Donne, Bunyan often has onlookers, to whom he is extremely responsive:

But one day, as I was standing at a Neighbors Shop-window, and there cursing and swearing, and playing the Mad-man, after my wonted manner, there sate within the woman of the house, and heard me; who, though she was a very loose and ungodly Wretch, yet protested that I swore and cursed at that most fearful rate, that she was made to tremble to hear me; And told me further, *That I was the ungodliest Fellow for swearing that ever she heard in all her life; and that I,* by thus doing, was able to spoile all the Youth in a whole *Town, if they came but in my company.*

At this reproof I was silenced, and put to secret shame; and that too, as I thought, before the God of Heaven . . . (*G.A.,* pp. 11–12).

Bunyan's observers are almost always located in time and space, and given their own parts to play in the action of the story. They are never there only to observe, and their objective importance is as clear to the reader as to Bunyan himself. The whole of the drama, then, is much more externalized. There is a great deal of speech in Bunyan's narrative, and, even when he phrases it as indirect discourse, it seems public and literal.

One particular kind of observer, constant in Puritan prose, makes an interesting exception to this pattern. We may call him the Slanderer. Although he sometimes has a local habitation and a name, often he has neither. His purpose is to undermine a man's public position by accusing him of a questionable private life, and especially of indiscretions with women. In this self-conscious age, slander had become a criminal offense, but was still only partially controllable; and of course different standards of tolerance were applied to pro- and anti-government slanderers.[16] Every Puritan has a standard Biblical response to such charges: "Now these slanders . . . I glory in, because but slanders, foolish, or knavish lies, and falsehoods cast upon me by the Devil and his Seed; and should I not be dealt with thus wickedly by the World, I should want one sign of a Saint, and Child of God. *Blessed are ye* (said the Lord Jesus) *when men shall revile you, and persecute you . . .*" (G.A., p. 93). Yet neither Bunyan nor any other Puritan is able to bear meekly charges which cast doubt on the validity both of his conversion and of his calling, and strike, in him, at the faith he holds. In the effort to justify himself against the Slanderer's distortion of truth, Bunyan is moved to hyperbolical response:

My Foes have mist their mark in this their shooting at me. I am not the man, I wish that they themselves be guiltless, if all the Fornicators and Adulterers in *England* were hang'd by the Neck till they be dead, *John Bunyan*, the object of their Envie, would still be alive and well. I know not whether there be such a thing as a woman breathing under the Copes of the whole Heaven but by their apparel, their children, or by common Fame, except my Wife (G.A., p. 94).

Donne's self-consciousness leads him to imagine the thoughts of his doctors. Bunyan is made self-conscious partly at least by the accusations of his slanderers. One's sense of Bunyan's isolation is heightened by this portrayal of himself as the only just man in an unjust society. He moves *in* society in a way that Donne does not, but he is set off from it, because he is always being measured or measuring himself against its demands. With the Slanderer his rage is great, because he is so limited in his ability to strike back. The Slanderer is the under-voice of conservatism, blindly but powerfully attacking the unknown. We will hear of him again.

Where Donne actively invents the casts of his inner dramas, Bunyan suggests that he is continually being invented by other people. There is, of course, the conversion pattern that he must follow, and he is reminded of its importance by voices that come (or seem to come) from without. One's sense of his being acted upon is much increased by his habitually making himself the object of the sentence, or speaking of himself in the passive voice, another characteristic way in which the called Puritan describes the continuing experience of vocation:

It would be too long for me here to stay, to tell you in particular how God did set me down in all the things of Christ, and how he did, that he might so do, lead me into his words, yea and also how he did open them unto me, make them shine before me, and cause them to dwell with me and comfort me over and over . . . (*G.A.*, p. 39).

And now was that word fulfilled on me, and I was also refreshed by it . . . Thus was my Soul at this time, (and as I did then think for ever) set at liberty from being again afflicted with my former guilt and amazement (*G.A.*, p. 61).

The passive expresses vocation as well as the related sense of being predestined and thereby unable simply to choose one's own path. God acts upon him.

The "I" is created or creates himself by means of (Puritan) or in spite of (Anglican) human time. The chief obvious difference between *Grace Abounding* and the *Devotions* is that one is literally autobiographical and the other is not. Autobiography in its literal, chronological sense, and as practiced by really self-conscious men, not just by diarists recounting external events, is a Puritan, not an Anglican habit. The self-conscious Puritan hopes to be able to move in time, in some sort of meaningful progression of events, from bad to good, from heathen to Christian (or from unsaved to saved), from tyranny to Utopia, from the City of Destruction to the New Jerusalem. The Anglican, committed to an older view, has no belief in progress: his whole posture is likely to be contemplative rather than active. In meditation, he seeks to learn the significance of what is. Thus we see in Bunyan a chronological account of years that are finished, of a struggle that exists in the past and in the memory; in Donne, a picture of a mind presently in travail, which can know, almost simultaneously, states of pain and states of rest. The illness is ended, and yet it still is wholly present.

Donne writes in the present tense, eclipsing time; he makes the experience happen to him on the printed page:

In the same instant that I feele the first attempt of the disease, I feele the victory; In the twinckling of an eye, I can scarse see, instantly the tast is insipid, and fatuous; instantly the appetite is dull and desirelesse: instantly the knees are sinking and strengthlesse; and in an instant, sleepe, which is the picture, the copy of death, is taken away, that the *Originall, Death* it selfe may succeed, and that so I might have death to the life (*Dev.*, Med. 2, pp. 25–26).

There can be no transitions from one state of mind to another because there is no room in Donne's technique for commentary on the experience; that is one reason for the separation of the *Devotions* into independently titled paragraphs, each concerning a separate mood or stage. Donne-the-author is absent; there is only Donne-the-work. Past and future cease to have meaning, and there is only an ever-changing present captured and created in art.

Bunyan recounts experiences that have happened to him in the past, and the page, the written narrative, is a seldom-adequate medium for describing these experiences:

I cannot now express with what longings and breakings in my Soul, I cryed to Christ to call me. Thus I continued for a time all on a flame to be converted to Jesus Christ, and did also see at that day such glory in a converted state, that I could not be contented without a share therein. Gold! could it have been gotten for Gold, what could I have given for it! had I had a whole world, it had all gone ten thousand times over, for this, that my Soul might have been in a converted state (*G.A.*, p. 24).

He presents himself as *a* mortal man *in* time, the passage laced with changing tenses that call attention to the fact of time's movement, whereas Donne's identification of himself with the printed page seems to absolve him of mortality and time. It is entirely typical that Bunyan insists on his inability to recreate the experience (thus opposing art and life) while Donne's passage ends with the author's witty metamorphosis into art.

In *Grace Abounding*, we are shown Bunyan the "I"-in-process, and his feelings are clearly rendered through the interpreter-Bunyan of many years later. Thus we are immediately made aware of the passage of time in a completely different way from that in which we experience it in the *Devotions*. We watch Bunyan changing from year to year, and we also know that time exists and that Bunyan has changed, because interpreter-Bunyan is clearly an older man by whom these earlier experiences are being relived or recreated.

Stylistically we are informed of the difference between the two Bunyans in numerous ways. Interpreter-Bunyan signals his presence almost sentence-by-sentence, with such interjections as "I say," "you must know," "thought I," and "I thank God." As we have seen, he tells us sometimes that he cannot or will not report certain earlier feelings or events. Sometimes he explains an event that he could not understand at the time: "But so foolish was I, and ignorant, that I knew not the reason for this sound . . ." (*G.A.*, p. 30). Such passages as these are particularly apt ways of marking the difference between the experience and the recording of it, since they show clearly that the two Bunyans are different, existing in different periods of time.

Bunyan constantly mentions the time at which something happened, or the length of time during which he continued in a given state of mind or way of life. Even if these times are approximate and undated, they provide a sense of temporal significance: "But about ten or eleven a Clock one day, as I was walking under a Hedge, full of sorrow and guilt God knows, and bemoaning myself for this hard hap . . . suddenly this sentence bolted in upon me" (*G.A.*, p. 44); "That Scripture would lie all day long, all the week long; yea, all the year long in my mind, and hold me down" (*G.A.*, p. 44). One qualification of Bunyan's method needs to be made. The fact that in a very real sense he has brought his whole struggle to the present, making it palpable and vivid in his mind, is most obviously represented by his frequent use of the word "now," in a context charged with immediacy: "And *now* was I both a burthen and a terror to myself, nor did I ever so know, as *now*, what it was to be weary of my life, and yet afraid to die. Oh, how gladly now would I have been anybody but myself!" (*G.A.*, p. 45). He relives the experience with a vividness which gives his book much of its power and distinguishes it from more pedestrian and more typical Puritan autobiography. Still *was* vies with *now* in this passage, *then* with *now* in his vocabulary. It is always obvious that the time of the experience much precedes the time of writing; the narrator remains in the present while the actor visits the past. The chronological notation of time is definitive, and therefore even in the midst of pain, bad times can be endured:

So soon as this fresh assault had fastened on my Soul, that Scripture came into my heart, *This is for many days*, Dan. 10. 14. and indeed I found it was so: for I could not be delivered nor brought to peace again until well-nigh two years and an half were compleatly finished. Wherefore these words, though in themselves they tended to discouragement, yet to me, who feared this condition would be eternal, they were at some times as an help and refreshment to me.

For, thought I, *many days* are not for ever . . . (*G.A.*, p. 62).

Donne too proceeds through a spiritual-physical crisis, but he indicates periods of time nowhere, and any forward movement is highly qualified by several structural devices implied by his word "*stationes*," or "stations," which describes his alternative to chronological time. I have already pointed out that this word first appears in the title to his introductory Latin poem, which is then broken up into headings for the twenty-three stations, or sections, of the book. Thus before we begin to read the story of Donne's illness, we have already read it immortalized in timeless Latin. And yet both the poem and the story through which it weaves are in the present tense, here used perhaps like God's Hebrew, which (says Donne) has only one tense because all times are one to Him.[17]

In the body of the book, each station is in turn divided into three sections—Meditation, Expostulation, and Prayer—illustrating despair, doubt, and peace, so that any forward movement is again qualified by a constant recognition of a permanently self-divided state. Two significant passages in the meditations illuminate his employment of the word "stations":

All things are done in *time* too; but if we consider *Tyme* to be but the *Measure of Motion*, and howsoever it may seeme to have three *stations, past, present*, and *future*, yet the *first* and *last* of these *are* not (one is not, now, & the other is not yet) and that which you call *present*, is not *now* the same that it was, when you began to call it so in this Line . . . (*Dev.*, Med. 14, pp. 333–34).[18]

Though thou remove them [specific days, time, months] from being of the *Essence* of our *Salvation*, thou leavest them for *assistances*, and for the *Exaltation* of our *Devotion*, to fix our selves, at certaine *periodicall*, & *stationary times*, upon the consideration of those things, which thou hast done for us . . . (*Dev.*, Expos. 14, pp. 342–43).

What these passages seem to mean in relation to the *Devotions* is this. On the one hand, time is meaningless: past, present, and future alike are scarcely tangible. On the other hand, for the sake of devotions, we can fix ourselves upon certain symbolical times (or, to refer to my earlier discussion of the table of contents, for the sake of better understanding, we can explicate a poem which cannot be paraphrased). Thus, the three sections of each station in the *Devo-*

tions represent a psychological rendition of the constant flow of time in their portrait of a mind that is now dejected (in the meditations), now turbulent (in the expostulations), now exalted (in the prayers).[19] At the same time, the gathering together of the three as a station, each station representing a highly symbolized stage of Donne's illness, suggests that time can be redeemed and stilled through the creation of a symbolic pattern that gives the temporal phenomenon of the illness a permanent spiritual meaning.

Finally, the word "station," in another sense which Donne could hardly have escaped, refers to the Catholic service of the Stations of the Cross, in which a series of prayers is uttered before each of fourteen representations of Christ in his progress toward Calvary. At Donne's fourteenth station, in fact, the physicians recognize that he is at the critical stage of his illness. In the service of the Stations, the faithful follow in the path of Christ, imitating his progress, standing before the pictured or sculptured representations to make a tableau facing a tableau. Donne's use of the word "stations" thus underlines the public context in which he hoped to justify and immortalize his private experience.

Let me now briefly illustrate this theory in practice. At the twelfth station, the physicians apply pigeons to the soles of the feet in order "to draw the vapors from the Head."[20] Here Donne completes the three-part sequence in the prayer:

And as thou hast caried this thy *creature* the *Dove*, through all thy wayes, through *Nature*, and made it naturally proper to conduce medicinally to our *bodily health,* Through the *law*, and made it a *sacrifice* for *sinne* there, and through the *Gospel,* and made it, & thy spirit in it, a witnes of thy *sonnes baptisme* there, so carry it, and the qualities of it home to my *soule*, and imprint there that *simplicity*, that *mildnesse*, that *harmelesnesse*, which thou hast imprinted by *Nature* in this *Creature.* That so all *vapours* of all disobedience to thee, being subdued under my feete, I may in the power, and triumphe of thy *sonne,* treade victoriously upon my *grave*, and trample upon the *Lyon,* and *Dragon,* that lye under it, to devoure me (*Dev.,* Prayer 12, pp. 308–9).

Donne need not wait until the end of some period of days or years to be delivered, since this kind of salvation is available at any point in the sequence. The rendering of the experience into symbolism enables the "I" to tread upon his own grave, in other words, to conquer time. The "I" becomes art, making himself an emblem of his own spiritual struggle.

The chronological and utopian aspects of Puritan thought explain other characteristics of the stylistic difference between Bunyan and Donne. Because Bunyan moves from one point to another in time and meaning, the more effectively his prose can move the narrative forward, the better it can sustain his meaning. Hence, he is more likely than Donne to discover the techniques of narrative, and to prefer pace to decoration. His description of the several stages of his decision to give up bell ringing as sinful takes 260 words, where Donne needs 5,000 words to ring all the possible changes upon the passing-bell as symbol of man's unity. Having nowhere to go, he can move around and around his symbolic subject, in meditative and associative, rather than chronological, prose.

One of the commonest words in Bunyan's book, especially in the earlier parts, is the verb "to walk." He had to walk, of course, in his work, and in the course of his walking some of his most meaningful experiences occurred. Walking brought him closer to heaven. Words describing travel are, in fact, often used in contexts that blur the distinction between literal and metaphorical:

Thus therefore for several dayes I was greatly assaulted and perplexed, and was often, when I have been walking, ready to sink where I went with faintness in my mind . . . (*G.A.*, p. 21).

Now I remember that one day as I was walking into the Country, I was much in the thoughts of this, But how if the day of grace be past? and to aggravatate my trouble, the Tempter presented to my mind those good people of *Bedford*, and suggested thus unto me, That these being converted already, they were all that God would save in those parts, and that I came too late, for these had got the blessing before I came (*G.A.*, p. 22).

In the light and encouragement of this word, I went a pretty while . . . (*G.A.*, p. 23).

In the second of these three quotations, the word "conversion" appears. To the Puritan, conversion or change is the painful day-to-day experience of learning to conform to the will of a mysterious God, and then attempting to find out whether grace has been granted. Whether or not it happens all at once, or over a long period of time, it does happen *in* time, although from that point forward the Puritan may sense himself as living on more than one level, as partaking somehow in allegory. Journey, walking, conversion bring the Christian to the New Jerusalem.

The words in the *Devotions* that correspond to Bunyan's travel words are "change," "translate," "transform," and "transmute."

Man's changefulness is a condition of mortal life. Moreover, Donne is well acquainted with the paradoxes of Christianity, particularly those characterizing the main events of Christ's life and the Church's sacraments, as examples of double meaning that allow for transmutation. Considered symbolically, the bread and wine of the Eucharist are the flesh and blood of Christ. No forward movement is necessary; one must simply use the goods of this world as doorways to eternity. Change is instantaneous, and, again, chronological progress is without meaning. The symbolic character of the Anglican way of thought is here reinforced. For Donne, in the *Devotions*, all the external manifestations and trappings of his illness—physicians, fever spots, pigeons, bells, and so forth—have this sacramental nature. So another difference between Donne and Bunyan (and Anglican and Puritan) is the difference between a sacramental and a non-sacramental view of reality.

The way in which Donne uses, or ignores, time demonstrates that by gathering timeless human meanings into himself, he makes his individual "I" a symbol representing all men. Bunyan, on the other hand, in dissociating himself from the society of the Slanderer, and in submitting himself to the severing power of time, becomes more isolated as Donne becomes less so. This point becomes still clearer in the persona's third type of self-expression—as historical character (Bunyan) or generalized symbol (Donne). Where Bunyan confines himself to his own experience, Donne generalizes his predicament to—or from—that of all men. The Anglican's habits of thought are more closely allied to the deductive reasoning of old philosophies, while the Puritan gravitates toward the inductive reasoning of the new. No Anglican or Puritan is necessarily conscious of an issue; each naturally uses what is appropriate to the sustenance of his values and interests. To put it another way, it is the difference between symbol and exemplum. Donne is all men; Bunyan is an example of what a man can be. It is also beginning to be the difference between poetic and scientific (or evidential) truth.

Bunyan takes personally everything that happens to him; specific events of his life seem to him the best of all possible evidence of God's grace. In his opening sentence he tells his readers that he wants to begin by giving "a hint of my pedegree, and manner of bringing up; that thereby the goodness and bounty of God towards me, may be the more advanced and magnified before the sons of

34

men" (*G.A.*, p. 5). Specific occurrences surrounding and comprising his conversion are clear and vivid. Physical events and dates are mingled in such a way that it would be impossible to mistake this autobiography for anyone else's: God saved him from drowning once in "a crick of the Sea," and again in Bedford River (*G.A.*, p. 7); he and his wife came together "without so much houshold-stuff as a Dish or Spoon," but she had with her *The Plain mans Pathway to Heaven*, and *The Practice of Piety*, which her father had left her (*G.A.*, p. 8); he ministered in Bedford; on the road between Elstow and Bedford he was tempted to try to work a miracle, making the dry places puddles, and the puddles dry (*G.A.*, pp. 18–19); he loved and worried about his blind child more than any of the others (*G.A.*, p. 98). He spares us the most mechanical phraseology of the standard autobiographies, and the vivid concreteness of particular temptations is no one's but his own.

In Donne's *Devotions* we are provided with almost none of this homely, immediate information. His book describes the course of an illness which afflicted him at the time of writing, and his illness is equated with spiritual disease. We know enough about his physical condition to diagnose it in modern terms. But we are told very little else about his circumstances, nothing of his family, dwelling place, position, or age, and almost nothing of his life preceding the illness. The opening lines of the *Devotions* cry out, "Variable, and therefore miserable condition of Man; this minute I was well, and am ill, this minute. I am surpriz'd with a sodaine change, & alteration to worse, and can impute it to no cause, nor call it by any name. We study *Health*, and we deliberate . . ." (*Dev.*, Med. 1, pp. 1–2). The alternation observable between the general and the particular, man and Donne, "we" and "I," does in itself definitively distinguish Donne's "I" from Bunyan's. Donne begins with a generalization about man's estate, in sickness and health assuming his lot to be that of fallen humanity. Significantly, he shares this very illness with many others, as one victim of an epidemic. While he may rebel against having to share man's common fate, he is not forced to quiver with uncertainty about the meaning of specific details of his life.

He can see very well that there is a difference between the general and the particular, between the tradition to which he belongs and his own individuality, but the existence of the distinction is strange to him—it both irritates and excites him, and he intensifies the problem by putting emphasis upon it. Hence, the alternation between "I" and "we"; the cosmic "I"; the generalizing parenthesis in an especially self-conscious figure: "Miserable and, (though common to all) inhuman *posture*, where I must practise my lying in the *grave*, by lying still, and not practise my *Resurrection*, by rising any more" (*Dev.*, Med. 3, pp. 46–47). Between general and particular, a new tension exists. Donne cannot simply say "I" or "we."

While Donne's consciousness is coextensive with man's (he and mankind being involved and contained in one another), Bunyan questions whether he has any place among men at all. While he published his autobiography as a way of helping and consoling others who might be encountering similar experiences, and while he was certainly aware that his conversion followed a pattern, his moment-to-moment account of his successes or failures shows us a man standing alone:

But the same day, as I was in the midst of a game at Cat, and having struck it one blow from the hole; just as I was about to strike it the second time, a voice did suddenly dart from Heaven into my Soul, which said, *Wilt thou leave thy sins, and go to Heaven? or have thy sins, and go to Hell?* At this I was put to an exceeding maze; wherefore, leaving my Cat upon the ground, I looked up to Heaven, and was as if I had with the eyes of my understanding, seen the Lord Jesus looking down upon me, as being very hotly displeased with me, and as if he did severely threaten me with some grievous punishment for these, and other my ungodly practices (*G.A.*, p. 10).

In an instant, Bunyan is cut off from all humanity. Other players in the game vanish. Only he, of all those playing at cat at such and such a place and such and such a time, was aware of a voice that unexpectedly required a choice between heaven and hell. No generalization protected him against its force or allowed him to consider the "thou" as plural. Having worked through to a belief in his own salvation, Bunyan could offer his own experience as an example for others, but he could not, as Donne could, symbolize his plight as it occurred. Nor, I think, could most Puritan writers. The preacher, finally, conversant with many particular cases, including his own, could build the moral allegory of *Pilgrims Progress*, which transmutes all particular men into General Man; but to do this, he had to put aside the self-conscious voice entirely, and, so to speak, objectify his findings.

We have seen some slight evidence of this beginning to happen in

the preface to *Grace Abounding*. It also happens during the course
of the narrative that the preacher comes momentarily to the fore in
the person of interpreter-Bunyan, and then we get passages like this,
where Bunyan is obviously generalizing:

(And I am very confident, that this temptation of the Devil is more than
usual amongst poor creatures then many are aware of, even to over-run their
spirits with a scurvie and seared frame of heart, and benumming of conscience: which frame, he stilly and slyly supplyeth with such despair, that
though not much guilt attendeth the Soul, yet they continually have a secret
conclusion within them, that there is no hopes for them; *for they have loved
sins, therefor after them they will go,* Jer. 2. 25 & 18. 12.) (*G.A.,* p. 11).

This sudden and extreme distancing of the subject, from "I" to
"poor creatures" and "them," is dramatic. And Bunyan's inclusion of
the paragraph within parentheses is interesting. He recognized that
he was changing his style.

Disapproving or even unaware of much of Donne's whole system
of correspondences, Bunyan separates general from particular completely, concentrating first on the particular, in autobiography, then
on the general, in allegory. While diary and autobiography certainly
have strong obvious tendencies toward allegory, still the two forms
for the time being remain separate. Bunyan is not yet ready to talk
about Common Man, because he is so preoccupied with the common
man that he himself is. Like most Puritans, he spends his time compiling evidence. There has to be more diary than allegory, more item-
ization of detail than literary production.

By his use of external personal detail, and by his objective location
of himself in time and space, Bunyan persuades us to accept and trust
him as a person. Insofar as Bunyan-the-interpreter succeeds as narrator, we read the story from his point of view. With him, we fall into
sympathy with the life story of the younger Bunyan, accepting him as
a person "like ourselves." Still, interpreter-Bunyan, of whom we are
often unaware, is a person of enough sophistication to see all around
the younger Bunyan, and to guide our responses to him—a fact
which should be remembered when we judge the "I" of this work.

In Donne's book, there is only the one "I," with a widening vision,
unlocated in time and space. Superficially ignoring the reader, he
catches us up in other ways—by his inclusive symbolism, by his
shifting between "I" and "we," and by the rhythms of his rhetoric.
By his use of these rhythms, he makes us take each moment of the

sickness as he takes it, accepting the cyclic psychological movement from despair to hope to confidence, and the cyclic esthetic movement from flat realism to febrile questioning to symbolic art. To the extent that we can share his rhythms and his language, we are brought with him to the tense union of particular with general, "I" with "we," one man with all men.

Elsewhere I have traced the particular sentence patterns which comprise these rhythms,[21] and I do not want to reproduce the entire argument here. The point is that the movement of this prose is meditative in a particularly purposive way—that the flat Senecan periods of the meditations imitate the feeling of negation and despair that the imagery and word choice encourage; that the turbulent periods of the expostulations break up that sense of deadness, and replace it with a feverish life; and that finally both give way to the stately Anglican cadence of the Book of Common Prayer, where man is wholly reconciled to God. Donne's italics, as well as many other stylistic devices, help to point up these rhythms and enable the reader to hear his voice.

There are other rhythms as well. From the significant repetition of single words, to the choral refrain effect of a sentence given at the beginning of a paragraph and then varied at the end (Meditation 1, for example), repetitions account for much. Worth mentioning here, again, is the broken-up poem whose Latin cadences so greatly affect the tone of the whole work.

The rhythms of Bunyan's prose are those of common speech, the colloquial rhythms of a man speaking to men. His genius lies in his ability to reproduce and to heighten these rhythms, depending upon the occasion being described. For example, when he recounts his most crucial experiences, the language is intensified by means of repetition, italicization, direct quotation, and exclamation:

So as I was a going home, these words came again into my thoughts, and I well remember as they came in, I said thus in my heart, What shall I get by thinking on these two words? this thought had no sooner passed thorow my heart, but the words began thus to kindle in my Spirit, *Thou art my Love, thou art my Love*, twenty times together; and still as they ran thus in my minde, they waxed stronger and warmer, and began to make me look up; but being as yet between hope and fear, I still replied in my heart, *But is it true too? but is it true?* at which, that sentence fell in upon me, *He wist not that it was true which was done unto him of the angel*, Act 12. 9 (*G.A.*, p. 29).

Both men in different ways catch us up in an immediate sharing of experience through the compelling rhythms of their prose. Both also allow us different kinds of esthetic distance from personal experience, corresponding to the sacramental and homiletic approaches. Hoping to teach by example, Bunyan presents his story reportorially, in narrative form, making a distinction between the preacher and the story, Bunyan-now and Bunyan-then. Donne leads the reader, through shared experience, to see himself as a type of mankind. Rather than separating himself from his experience in any way, Donne makes it formal, public, and symbolic.

Finally, the two "I"'s differ with regard to space. Where Bunyan limits his existence in space by use of concrete detail, Donne expands his in order to create a cosmic personality. Their common interest in bells will usefully illustrate the contrast. Discovering that bell-ringing was sinful, Bunyan learned to give it up a little at a time:

I thought that such a practice was but vain, and therefore forced my self to leave it, yet my mind hanckered, wherefore I should go to the Steeple house, and look on: though I durst not ring. But I thought this did not become Religion neither, yet I forced my self and would look on still; but quickly after, I began to think, How, if one of the Bells should fall: then I chose to stand under a main Beam that lay over thwart the Steeple from side to side, thinking there I might stand sure: But then I should think again, Should the Bell fall with a swing, it might first hit the Wall, and then rebounding upon me, might kill me for all this Beam; this made me stand in the Steeple door, and now thought I, I am safe enough, for if a Bell should then fall, I can slip out behind these thick Walls, and so be preserved notwithstanding.

So after this, I would yet go to see them ring, but would not go further than the Steeple door; but then it came into my head, how if the Steeple it self should fall, and this thought, (it may fall for ought I know) would when I stood and looked on, continually so shake my mind, that I durst not stand at the Steeple door any longer, but was forced to fly, for fear it should fall upon my head (*G.A.*, pp. 13–14).

Bunyan's imagination in this sequence operates tenaciously and personally, binding him closer and closer to the objects of his guilt and forcing him to take immediate literal action in regard to them. Realism is foremost both in the concreteness of details given—main beam, thick walls, the way the bell swings, and so forth, and in the concreteness of each of Bunyan's responsive actions. The story has to be told chronologically, with each movement in the sequence included. Committed to a literal rehearsal of the facts as he (at least) wishes us to suppose that he remembers them, Bunyan-narrator can allow Bunyan-actor to occupy no other part of space and time than those very limited places and times in which the event could actually have occurred.

As Donne lies ill in bed, he thinks about the passing bell in a personal way: it tolls for him. But already the facts are distorted, since it is not literally his funeral bell. In raising the bell to a symbol and himself to mankind's representative, he begins by reminding himself of other bells, and of writings about bells which enrich the meaning of this one at the same time that they cause its personal relevance to fade: "We have a *Convenient Author*, who writ a *Discourse of Bells* when hee was prisoner in *Turky*. How would hee have enlarged himselfe, if he had beene my *fellow Prisoner* in this *sicke bed*, so neere to that *steeple*, which never ceases, no more than the *harmony of the spheres*, but is more heard" (*Dev.*, Med. 16, pp. 388–89). Like most of Donne's puns, the play on the word "enlarged" is very fruitful. The meditator gains freedom from personal bondage, and increased freedom of language in the inspiration afforded by the bells; by these means, he may himself become a larger person. Perhaps he is also to be enlarged by becoming Donne's bedfellow. At any rate, Donne's next step is to begin to suggest for himself the possibility of that kind of human extension. He associates himself with another man by saying that his death is as likely, his sinfulness as certain as those of the man for whom this bell now tolls. At this point, then, he is already in his imagination both himself and the dead man. Elevation to universality follows, in the famous passage: "No man is an *Iland*, intire of it selfe; every man is a peece of the *Continent*, a part of the *maine*; if a *Clod* bee washed away by the *Sea*, *Europe* is the lesse, as well as if a *Promontorie* were, as well as if a *Mannor* of thy *friends* or of *thine owne* were; Any Mans *death* diminishes *me*, because I am involved in *Mankinde*; And therefore never send to know for whom the *bell* tolls; It tolls for *thee*" (*Dev.*, Med. 17, pp. 415–16).

The more detail Bunyan supplies in the presentation of his story, the clearer its boundaries become: it happens in a limited time and space. The farther Donne elaborates his meditation, the more extensive he becomes. His limits are those of human consciousness, ultimately definable only in terms of the earth or the cosmos. Specifically, here we notice first of all that as soon as he thinks, "they . . .

may have caused it to toll for me," he also thinks, "for *thee*." It is a variation on his characteristic shifting between "I" and "we." Just as typical is the microcosm-macrocosm imagery which identifies mankind with the earth. Donne's daring with his figures reflects his literary, controlled use of his experience, whereas Bunyan's experience is presented as if it were only accidentally literary, because he happened to record it.

The contrast between the "artificial" and the "natural" record becomes even clearer if we compare passages where both writers involve themselves at once in something other than literal reality. In the following passage, Bunyan describes what he calls "a kind of Vision," in which he saw the people of Bedford on the sunny side of a mountain, and himself on the cold side, with a wall between:

About this wall I thought myself to goe again and again, still prying as I went, to see if I could find some way or passage, by which I might enter therein, but none could I find for some time: at the last I saw as it were, a narrow gap, like a little door-way in the wall, thorow which I attempted to pass: but the passage being very straight, and narrow, I made many offers to get in, but all in vain, even untill I was well nigh quite beat out by striving to get in: at last, with great striving, me thought I at first did get in my head, and after that, by a side-ling striving, my shoulders, and my whole body; then I was exceeding glad, and went and sat down in the midst of them, and so was comforted with the light and heat of their Sun.

Now, this Mountain and Wall, &c., was thus made out to me; the Mountain signified the Church of the living God; the Sun that shone thereon, the comfortable shining of his mercifull face on them that were therein: the wall I thought was the Word that did make separation between the Christians and the world: and the gap which was in this wall, I thought was Jesus Christ, who is the way to God the Father, *Job.* 14.6. *Mat.* 7.14. But for as much as the passage was wonderful narrow, even so narrow, that I could not but with great difficulty, enter in thereat; it shewed me, that none could enter into life but those that were in down-right earnest, and unless they left this wicked world behind them; for here was only roome for Body and Soul, but not for Body and Soul, and Sin (*G.A.*, pp. 19–20).

The sense of spatial constriction strikes one very forcibly here. It is, of course, part of the character of this vision that such constriction has to exist, but it is also in the character of *Grace Abounding*. One has the same sense of spatial oppression in the episode with the bell tower, and in many other passages where Bunyan seems pinned to specific time and place, or forced from moment to moment to move from one limited space to another.

Bunyan is dealing with a dream or vision whose symbolism is in-trinsic to it; all he can do is try to find the "right" interpretation. And notice here the wording of the sentence that introduces the in-terpretation, "this Mountain and wall, &c. was thus made out to me," suggesting that Bunyan himself had nothing to do with it.[22] Just as in his reporting of events, he ascribes control of his experience and his understanding to an agent other than himself, here he suggests that both dream and its meaning were simply given him as scribe. The Biblical echoes, meanwhile, reveal the source of the vision.

Donne does not have visions, and the traditional character of his symbolism is obscured by its immense sophistication. At the thir-teenth station of Donne's *Devotions*, "*the Sicknes declares the infec-tion and malignity thereof by spots*" (*G.A.*, p. 312), and the sym-bolic meaning he ascribes to the spots is spelled out, if anything, too plainly:

My *God, my God,* thou hast made this sick bed thine *Altar,* and I have no other *Sacrifice* to offer, but my self; and wilt thou accept *no spotted sacrifice?* Doeth thy *Son* dwel bodily in this flesh, that thou shouldst looke for an un-spottednes here? Or is the *Holy Ghost,* the *soule* of this *body,* as he is of thy *Spouse,* who is therfore *all faire, and no spot in her?* or hath thy *Son* himself no *spots,* who hath al our stains, & deformities in him? Or hath thy *Spouse,* thy *Church,* no *spots,* when every particular limbe of that faire, & spotles body, every particular *soule* in that *Church* is full of staines and spots? Thou bidst us *hate the garment, that is spotted with the flesh.* The *flesh* it selfe is the *garment,* and it spotteth it selfe, with it self (*Dev.*, Expos. 13, pp. 320–21).

Very clear here is the way in which Donne becomes both subject and object of his meditations. He offers himself as sacrifice; the flesh sullies itself with itself. He is his own creation, an artificial and sym-bolic character, whereas Bunyan presents himself always as a human being made by God, upon whom God works his will. While Donne's fever spots presumably appeared unexpectedly, like Bun-yan's vision, Donne is instantly prepared to employ them as the sym-bolic subject of a many-levelled exegesis. Eventually, they become his equivalent of Bunyan's narrow passageway to grace:

Even my *spotts* belong to thy *Sonnes* body, and are part of that, which he came downe to this earth, to fetch, and challenge, and assume to himselfe. When I open my *spotts,* I doe but present him with that which is *His,* and till I do so, I detaine, & withhold *his right.* When therfore thou seest them upon me, as *His,* and seest them by this way of *Confession,* they shall not appear to me, as the *pinches of death,* to decline my feare to *Hell;* (for *thou hast not left thy holy one in Hell,* thy *Sonne* is not there) but these *spotts* upon my *Breast,* and upon my *Soule,* shal appeare to mee as the *Constellations* of the *Firmament,* to direct my contemplation to that place, where thy *Son* is, thy *right hand* (*Dev.,* Expos. 13, pp. 326–27).

Concentrating wholly upon himself, again he finds himself merging with the universe. He is both contained and container, both the soul seeking heaven, and the constellations that light the way. Bunyan in his vision moves from one place to another. Donne simply expands, becomes fragmented, eventually occupies the whole universe. The very cause of his confinement, the spots of the fever, becomes the instrument of his "enlargement."

There is certainly a playfulness, too, about his extension of fever spots into so complex a symbol. This playfulness is intrinsic to metaphysical wit, in its penchant for making farfetched analogies, in its capacity to view the same object in several different lights, and in its fascination with transformation. Donne uses all these devices here. The exegetical character of this exercise gives the reader an opportunity to share the play. In a sense, he is led to believe that the whole process is very logical, especially if he remembers, as Donne would have, the connection between the words "spots" and "spotless" and the Latinate "immaculate," with its religious connotations. It is amazing to see the least esthetic aspect of his illness become the starry firmament above his head, but our amazement is made respectful by the knowledge that he has earned the right to work the transformation.

Like most Puritans, Bunyan is interested only in thought directly translatable into action, especially a certain kind of action. Bunyan hoped that he could find a place to stand where the bell would not fall on him, and he hoped to be able to get to the sunny side of the mountain. While the bell episode is meant partly to illustrate Bunyan's ignorance of God at the time, it is nevertheless a typically Puritan hope, whether expressed in such limited terms as these or in those that filled the minds of men who wanted to build Utopia. The Puritans believed it possible to move physically, in space and time, from a place that was not safe and perfect to one that was, and their whole lives were given to this quest. It is united, of course, with their desire for spiritual progress, but the fact that this too is commonly described as physical movement is significant. Donne, in contrast, believes that the bell summons all men to die, whoever and wherever they are, that man's estate is miserable, and that the only hope is not in any kind of movement or progress, but in making time and space themselves open into eternity, just as the temporal fever spots, so limiting and limited in their "real" character, are made to become a vehicle of Donne's enlargement from the confines of time and space. Both Bunyan and Donne, in their different handlings of different material, bring the "I" to a point where he represents all men. But Donne's "I" has also become symbolic and non-representational, where Bunyan's functions as a representative human being in an allegorical situation.

A consideration of Donne's and Bunyan's conscious choices of language and of their comments on language can help us to understand the different theories of style according to which they proceed. I have already touched upon their contrasting types of imagery. Bunyan never uses the microcosm-macrocosm analogy that is Donne's stock-in-trade. For Donne, man is not only a little world, but, as I have already suggested, he frequently becomes the world, both in analogies (his veins are rivers, and so forth) and in importance. Metaphor unites and transforms. But for the Puritan the world is a more hostile place, more definitely allied with flesh and devil, and the individual is a pilgrim wayfarer or soldier passing through it.

In minor figures of speech, Bunyan makes constant and almost exclusive use of simile: "my heart . . . was as a clog on the leg of a Bird" (*G.A.*, pp. 25–26); "they had as good have told me that I must reach the Sun with my finger" (*G.A.*, p. 26); "I have found my unbelief to set as it were the shoulder to the door" (*G.A.*, p. 26); "I found myself as on a miry bog" (*G.A.*, p. 27). Donne is much more prone to use metaphors or symbols, eliminating "like" or "as" from the figure.

Yet the distinction which Bunyan consistently makes has nothing to do with a failure of the imagination or with the prissiness that we commonly call Puritanical. Donne is accustomed to dealing in ritual and symbol; for him, these unite world and spirit. For Bunyan, the particular symbols and rituals of Anglicanism are divisive, needlessly arbitrating for him between man and God. Therefore he wishes to dispense with the very tools upon which Donne relies for an orderly, coherent world. At the same time, Bunyan is less well-equipped than Donne, for a variety of reasons, to cope with a world that has not been ordered for him. He has less education and less familiarity with the printed word. He rejects various kinds of authority which Donne takes for granted and uses as boundaries or points of stability. His imagination thus is both unschooled and unbounded. He has to trust it, for through it comes his prized direct communication with the Almighty; but he cannot trust it, because it is itself unruled. These two factors—his need to accept the imagination and his unpreparedness to understand it—put him much more at the mercy of language and of the world than Donne is.

Simile is a simple way of controlling the imagination, and it is analogous here to the habit of breaking apart generalization and concrete detail, of substituting allegory and personal narrative for symbolism. If you say that one thing is like another, you can keep the two distinct and unconfused in your mind more easily than if you fuse them in metaphor.

The one place where Bunyan does not typically use simile is where he describes the power that thoughts and words are able to exert upon his mind—"this thought would when I stood and looked on, continually so shake my mind"; "these words broke in upon my mind." For here he speaks not in metaphor but in literal truth, insofar as such experiences can be literally described. And it is just when Bunyan begins to express himself in this way that Donne pulls back or finds himself at a loss. Donne wants to be ravished by God, struck by God's thunder, but he is too sophisticated and self-centered, too fully in control of his world to be able to open himself to such raw, direct experience. His religious experience, like Bunyan's, is formulated in language, but it is the ordered, disciplined language of Anglican ritual.

Unless he is careful to keep it in its place, Bunyan does not use language; it uses him. Donne modulates Scripture into his own imagination, and makes it speak in his voice. An apt example is this passage from his meditations on the tolling bell:

The *voice*, thy *hand* is in this *sound*, and in this *one sound*, I heare this *whole Consort*. I heare thy *Jaacob* call unto his *sonnes*, and say; *Gather your selves together, that I may tell you what shall befall you in the last daies:* He saies, *That which I am now, you must bee then*. I heare thy *Moses* telling mee, and all within the *compasse* of this *sound, This is the blessing wherewith I blesse you before my death;* This, that before your death, you would consider your owne in mine. I heare thy *Prophet* saying to *Ezechias, Set thy house in order, for thou shalt die, and not live;* Hee makes us of his *familie*, and calls this a setting of *his* house in order, to compose *us* to the *meditation of death*. I heare thy *Apostle* saying, *I thinke it meet to put you in remembrance, knowing that shortly I must goe out of this Tabernacle*. This is the *publishing* of his *will*, & this *bell* is our *legacie*, the applying of *his present condition* to our use. I heare that which makes al sounds *musique*, and all *musique* perfit; I heare thy *Sonne* himselfe saying, *Let not your hearts be troubled* . . . (*Dev.*, Expos. 17, pp. 421–23).

The perfect control of Scripture and of art which enables Donne to "hear" these voices speaking in a concert that leads to a controlled and beautiful climax in the words of Christ is typical of Donne's imagination, as it is of Anglican ritual, which was thought to exemplify the beauty of holiness. Here also is manifest the "I" as cosmic personality, in Donne's ability both to participate in time and to surpass it. He hears the speakers, in their own times; he makes himself one with them ("he makes us of his familie"), and at the same time he compresses all these speakers and their occasions into a single moment when a bell tolls in London for all mankind.

Now compare these typical encounters between Bunyan and Scripture:

Lord, thought I, if both these Scriptures would meet in my heart at once, I wonder which of them would get the better of me. So me thought I had a longing mind that they might come both together upon me; yea, I desired of God they might.

Well, about two or three days after, so they did indeed; they boulted both upon me at a time, and did work and struggle strangly in me for a while; at last, that about *Esaus* birthright began to wax weak, and withdraw, and vanish; and this about the sufficiency of Grace prevailed, with peace and joy (*G.A.*, pp. 66–67).

When I had with much deliberation considered of this matter, and could not but conclude that the Lord had comforted me, and that too after this my wicked sin; then methought I durst venture to come nigh unto those most fearful and terrible Scriptures, with which all this while I had been so greatly affrighted, and on which indeed before I durst scarce cast mine eye, (yea, had much ado an hundred times to forbear wishing of them out of the Bible, for I thought they would destroy me) but now, I say, I began to take some measure of incouragement, to come close to them, to read them, and consider them, and to weigh their scope and tendence.

The which when I began to do, I found their visage changed; for they looked not so grimly on me as before I thought they did: And first, I came to the sixth of the *Hebrews*, yet trembling for fear it should strike me . . . (*G.A.*, pp. 69–70).

Where Donne assimilates Scripture into himself—makes it speak Donne—Bunyan encounters it, or fragments of it, as if it were another person. We know that Donne is in control of his concert, because all the members of it speak in turn at his bidding. Bunyan describes his younger self as having no control over his conflicts, except to the extent that he has a part, which is sometimes active and sometimes passive, in the proceedings. Sometimes he becomes the arena in which the Scripture battle rages; sometimes he himself can take one part against another. He is never "enlarged" by the presence of these passages within him, though he may be liberated as a result of struggle with them.

Donne's whole experience of life is literary, and indissolubly connected with the experiences of scholars and other writers whose works he knew. All creation is God's book, and he applies this cliché even more widely than was common in the age.[23] To him, things are words, and life has reality only when it becomes verbal; it is only then, too, that it acquires order and discipline, for, as he says in colloquy with the Trinity, "If your consultation determine in writing, if you refer me to that which is written, you intend my recovery; for all the way, *O my God*, (ever constant to thine owne wayes) thou hast proceeded *openly, intelligibly, manifestly by the book*" (*Dev.*, Expos. 9, p. 217).

God's works are to be *read*, all of them. They may also be translated: "Let me think no degree of this thy correction, *casuall*, or without *signification;* but yet when I have read it in that language, as it is a *correction*, let me translate it into another, and read it as a *mercy;* and which of these is the *Originall*, and which is the *Translation;* whether thy *Mercy*, or thy *Correction*, were thy primary and original intention in this sicknes, I cannot conclude, though death conclude me . . ." (*Dev.*, Prayer 7, pp. 173–74). The fever spots, in their final metamorphosis, become God's writing: "These *spots* are but the *letters*, in which thou hast written thine owne *Name*, and conveyed thy selfe to mee . . ." (*Dev.*, Prayer 13, pp. 329–30). Donne, in fact, is an example of God's writing, just as everything else is, and his creation of himself in language in this book is a sort of imitation of God's creation of him.

Always, for Donne, experience and its literary rendition are inseparable. Bunyan, in the midst of a moving episode, may long for a recording pen, but that wish passes as does the experience itself, because for him there *is* a vast difference between a ploughed field and a printed page:

Yea, I was now so taken with the love and mercy of God, that I remember I could not tell how to contain till I got home; I thought I could have spoken of his Love, and of his mercy to me, even to the very Crows that sat upon the plow'd lands before me, had they been capable to have understood me, wherefore I said in my Soul with much gladness, Well, I would I had a pen and ink here, I would write this down before I go any further, for surely I will not forget *this* forty years hence; but alas! within less then forty days I began to question all again (*G.A.*, p. 30).

Desire to write down the experience, or to talk about it, *follows* the experience but is not a necessary part of it.

To say that to Donne things are words and to Bunyan words are things is stretching the truth just slightly. While Donne puts the whole world into language, Bunyan finds language acting a part in the world; words strike him with objective force. To him at times Scripture seems more a blank physical power than a printed book: "Then did that Scripture seize upon my soul" (*G.A.*, p. 56); "Then would the former sentence, as the conclusion of all, fall like a hot thunder-bolt again upon my Conscience" (*G.A.*, p. 50).

Again, Donne's greater ability and desire to create order is apparent. Bunyan, in relation to words, is subject to dreams, visions, and voices, which he takes seriously, putting himself at their mercy. Donne hears and sees nothing except what he wants to, and what he does hear is consciously ordered. Bunyan talks of reading the Bible less often than of hearing at crucial moments verses whose source he does not know. His world is more magical and arbitrary than Donne's, partly because it is a peasant world, partly because he has to allow it to be in order to free himself of certain constricting traditions of the establishment.

Their different views of language are closely related to another primary difference in sensibility between them—Donne's persistent wit and Bunyan's sobriety. Donne, thinking himself on his deathbed, puns as if his life depended on it: his puns have been so immense nowhere else except in the "Hymne to God the Father," also written in sickness. Bunyan, in much less desperate circumstances, rejects any opportunity to smile at his younger self, and explicitly refuses to indulge in any play with style:

I could have enlarged much in this my discourse of my temptations and troubles for sin, as also of the merciful kindness and working of *God* with my

Soul: I could also have stepped into a stile much higher then this in which I have here discoursed, and could have adorned all things more then here I have seemed to do: but I dare not: *God* did not play in convincing of me; the *Devil* did not play in tempting of me; neither did I play when I sunk as into a bottomless pit, when *the pangs of hell caught hold upon me:* wherefore I may not play in my relating of them, but be plain and simple, and lay down the thing as it was . . . (*G.A.*, pp. 3–4).

Naturally, Bunyan cannot "lay down the thing as it was"; the phrase suggests a complete bypassing of language, as does the phrase quoted earlier where he invites his people to "read God's work upon me." The *thing* cannot be laid down except by being put into words, and in order to do that, interpreter-Bunyan must make constant choices—between one episode and another, and between one word or phrase and another. Nevertheless, the aim—to submit language to reality—is important.

Whether presented in the form of words that "bolt in upon him" (words as things), or of more conventional experience, Bunyan's reality is recognizable partly by its seriousness. One way to get rid of sin and error is to give up games—cat, bell-ringing, dancing, all had to be forsaken. Conversion is an abandonment of the enticements of the world in favor of a sterner existence. One may suggest that in the Puritan's world there is no time for play because all energies are consumed in action. Analogously, there is no time for the play of art, but only for careful reporting of events.

Bunyan's God has no sense of humor, in his work or in his language. The messages Bunyan receives from him are brief, and sometimes cryptic, often seeming less like language than like physical blows. Donne's God, on the other hand, delights in play of words, as Donne points out here in justifying his own style:

My *God*, my *God*, Thou art a *direct God*, may I not say, a *literall God*, a *God* that wouldest bee understood *literally*, and according to the *plaine sense* of all that thou saiest? But thou art also (*Lord* I intend it to thy *glory*, and let no *prophane misinterpreter* abuse it to thy *diminution*) thou art a *figurative*, a *metaphoricall God* too: A *God* in whose words there is such a height of *figures*, such *voyages*, such *peregrinations* to fetch remote and precious *metaphors*, such *extensions*, such *spreadings*, such *Curtaines* of *Allegories*, such *third Heavens* of *Hyperboles*, so *harmonious eloquutions*, so *retired* and so *reserved expressions*, so *commanding perswasions*, so *perswading commandements*, such *sinewes* even in thy *milke*, and such *things* in thy *words*, as all *prophane Authors*, seeme of the seed of the *Serpent*, that *creepes*, thou art the *dove*, that flies (*Dev.*, Expos. 19, pp. 479–81).

This hath occasioned thine ancient *servants,* whose delight it was to write after thy *Copie,* to proceede the same way in their *expositions* of the *Scriptures,* and in their composing both of *publike liturgies,* and of *private prayers* to thee, to make their accesses to thee in such a kind of *language,* as thou wast pleased to speake to them, in a *figurative,* in a *Metaphoricall language;* in which manner I am bold to call the comfort which I receive now in this sicknesse, in the *indication* of the *concoction* and *maturity* thereof, in certaine *clouds,* and *recidences,* which the *Physitians* observe, a discovering of *land* from *Sea,* after a long and tempestuous *voyage* (*Dev.,* Expos. 19, pp. 486–87).

These passages are almost infinitely suggestive. Samuel Johnson might here find himself anticipated, in Donne's elegant comment on "remote and precious metaphors," and daringly refuted in the series of words that equate more literal writers, profane writers, and the devil. Opposed to the creeping serpent of literalism is the flying dove, conveyor of facility in tongues; and a high-flown style thus becomes a vehicle, even a sign of grace.

The opportunity for play of wit arises because Donne conceives of the purpose of Scripture differently than Bunyan does. For Bunyan, cryptic passages must be solved; there must be literal interpretations, literal solutions to the whole text of the Bible because the Bible is an instrument of edification, intended to be useful to men. And as God did not play in writing the Bible, Bunyan will not play in writing his own book.

For Donne, edification is of course the Bible's principal use. But Donne's God constantly runs the risk of being misunderstood through abundance of metaphor.[24] Obscurely magnificent passages, featuring, perhaps, "*extentions, . . . spreadings, . . . Curtaines of Allegories,*" are intended for admiration as well as for instruction. God here, as he is the Word of the Bible, makes himself an object of contemplation. He presents Himself in the Bible, and in the three faces of the Trinity, as a Being, mysterious, unknowable, delighting in "*third Heavens of Hyperboles.*" And Donne, made in God's image (who is made in whose image?), reflects back his own three faces in the triple stations of the *Devotions,* and his own "height of figures" in their metaphors and puns.

Bunyan's Bible plays a role in his life. It, and fragments of it, strike him like weapons, call upon him to do this or that, force him to respond, to move forward. Donne's Bible is something which one can enter "for our *satisfaction,* and for our *Inquisition,* for our *Instruction,* and for our *Admiration* too." Centuries of many-levelled exegesis had taught men, in a sense, how to write the Bible as they read it, to enter into an "inventive" (in the Renaissance sense) relationship with this text similar to that which Donne ideally establishes with his reader in the *Devotions*. It is a literary relationship.

The whole subject of the use of the Bible by Puritans and Anglicans is, of course, a book in itself. My intention here has been merely to suggest very briefly that Donne and Bunyan, in their different attitudes toward the Bible, and in their different concepts of its Author, naturally enough reveal the same attitudes that they have toward life, and to some extent the same concepts that they have of themselves.

These can now be briefly summarized. Donne's prose is analytical, psychological, subjective, meditative, private, self-centered, and literary. The "I" tends to make himself the center of things, the object of contemplation. He both insists upon and denies an audience. He rejects the opportunity to justify his writing in utilitarian terms. He is ambiguous, elusive, highly self-conscious, and creates his own reality. Constantly turning himself and experience into art, he absolves himself from time and reaches toward the limits of space, thus achieving a cosmic personality which sees itself as one with all men. The self-centeredness of the prose is qualified by the fact that "I" and "we" are so interchangeable, by the fact that the "I" symbolizes all men.

Bunyan's prose is reportorial, straightforward, apparently objective, taking place in public, and inviting the reader to see him as an instrument of use rather than an object of contemplation. He tries to describe himself as simply as possible, with a distant narrator correcting the earlier Bunyan's errors in vision. His only obvious distortions come as an attempt to answer the distortions of the Slanderer, who speaks for the conservative underworld. His prose is directly addressed to his congregation, and thereby to the reader, who consequently never feels like an eavesdropper. Writing autobiography, Bunyan submits himself to the demands of time and space, and so speaks as an isolated human being. His material is particularized and he rarely makes generalizations about Man. He chooses to submit language to life, showing himself at the mercy of experiences which are then described as accurately as possible.

Donne's prose encourages a reciprocal relationship with language. The writer creates and is created by his prose. The reader, experiencing meditation, is invited by Donne to become part of the "I" and so of all men, since time and space are obliterated. To some extent, Bunyan too is created by his book. But it is also clearly meant to be used as a guide, and in it Bunyan is an exemplum.

If we are sometimes annoyed with Donne's excessive artificiality, his excessive control, we may become bored with Bunyan's refusal to control his own destiny, with the extent to which he puts himself at the mercy of experience. Their strengths are one with their weaknesses, and alert us once more to the different emphases of their interests. Donne turns life into art, and thereby immeasurably enriches man's potential range of sensibility, duration, self-expression, communion with others. There can be no forward movement, but there can be the fullest possible use of what *is*. The Anglican "I" is obviously conducive to meditative literature, to poetry, and to the kind of symbolic (not allegorical) fiction that plays with space and time. As Donne employs it, its weakness is its unwillingness to take a fresh view of life. Its elaborate metaphors can obscure as well as illuminate reality. His personality can be cosmic because he is his world.

In reaction to this kind of artificiality, splendid as it is, there is bound to be a turning away from art toward life. Necessarily he who does this, like Bunyan, will be at the mercy of experience. His concentration is outward, and his role is subject to the limitations of a time-bound world. Less independent and disciplined than Donne's, his imagination lacks control and humor. But the freshness and vigor of his experience lend urgency and immediacy to a prose in which the techniques of "realistic" fiction are already being exercised.[25] In fact, the likeness of accurate reporting to documentary fiction provided England's strongest impulse to the rise of the novel, as is evident in the familiar progress of English fiction from Bunyan to Defoe and onward.

CHAPTER III

JOHN LILBURNE:
THE EYE OF A POLITICAL
RADICAL

IN THE POSSESSION OF THE METROPOLITAN MUSEUM OF ART IN NEW York City is a seventeenth-century portrait in oil on canvas said to have been painted by Robert Streater and once identified as a picture of John Lilburne or possibly of John Milton.[1] It is a strange final meeting for these two radical Englishmen, the one so remarkably famous in his own day and now almost unknown, the other much less widely valued in life, but now firmly established as England's greatest nondramatic poet. Perhaps some expression about the eyes caused the uncertainty in identification. Both were said to have fine eyes, although both suffered from blindness.[2] Both assigned themselves a central place in the drama of England's civil wars, and William Haller justly calls Milton Lilburne's "spiritual next of kin."[3] Their brands of self-consciousness are very similar, and very different from the typical Anglican mode.

Many of the differences between Lilburne and Milton can be foreseen in the conditions of their early lives. Milton was brought up in London, in respectable middle-class circumstances, by his father, a self-made businessman, who was able to send his son to St. Paul's school. And the father was a man of culture as well, a serious musician, who provided his son from his youngest years with the capacity both for a fiercely Puritan individualism and for an indestructible admiration of the classics, for art that endures when wars are over and the men who fought them, dead.

Though Lilburne's parents had served the royal family at Greenwich, where he was born in 1615, his real roots were in Northumberland, Percy country, on the Scottish border, where he did most of his growing up. He was not, he says, "one of the dronessest Schoole Boyes there,"[4] but clearly formal education played a minor role in his life. In his early twenties he became a London apprentice who improved his time by reading Foxe's *Book of Martyrs*, the Bible, and assorted Puritan and separatist tracts. Restless and pugnacious as he was, he inevitably encountered the political radicals of his day. From being a disciple of Burton and Prynne, he rapidly emerged as a leader in his own right of the Levellers, who stood in practice for the principles of freedom and democracy that they believed the Revolution had been fought to achieve. More bitterly opposed to the Long Parliament than he had ever been to the House of Lords, he became more rather than less radical as he grew older: he died a Quaker and was given a Quaker funeral.

His milieu was that "troubl'd sea of noises and hoars disputes" [5] into which Milton was so reluctant to descend. Far from distracting him and diverting him from his usual interests, the wars gave him meaning and purpose. Milton's orderly and extensive preparation for writing the great poem was interrupted by the outbreak of civil war. Nothing in Lilburne's early life suggests that his future was to be at all remarkable before he found and accepted the role of revolutionary. He came of a cantankerous, stubborn family with a flair for histrionics; his father was the last man in England to claim the right to trial by combat. Given his disposition, his role was, more than that of most men, created by his times. In recognizing his unique fitness for this role of revolutionary, in devising his movements and his lines from scene to scene, Lilburne expressed his particular brand of self-consciousness. Unlike Milton, he did not soar sublime above the earth. He walked upon it, and his prose can be described with the same adjective that modern scholars use to describe him—popular. He was, they say, the most popular man in England.[6]

The word, used in our modern sense, is new in the seventeenth century, and it is difficult to imagine it applied more fitly to anyone else than to Lilburne. It was said of him in his own time that the New Model Army was "one Lilburne throughout,"[7] and that the common people adored him "as the onely *Oracle of Truth*." [8] Consistently, throughout his whole life, he made himself a symbol of the people, of the "any one" who might as well be everyone. As he says in *The Just Defence of John Lilburne*:

. . . for what is done to any one, may be done to every one: besides, being all members of one body, that is, of the English Commonwealth, one man should not suffer wrongfully, but all should be sensible and endeavor his preservation; otherwise they give way to an inlet of the sea of will and power, upon all their laws and liberties, which are the boundaries to keep out tyranny and oppression; and who assists not in such cases, betrayes his own rights, and is over-run, and of a free man made a slave when he thinks not of it, or regards it not, and so shunning the censure of turbulency, incurs the guilt of treachery to the present and future generations.[9]

In this tract he claims that he never chose his unpeaceful existence, but that always willful infringement of his rights as an Englishman forced him to defend in his own name "the right, freedome, safety, and well-being of every particular man, woman, and child in England."[10] It was this vocation of his which made him so popular, and so relevantly central a figure in his own tracts. Whether his title is *The Legall Fundamentall Liberties of the People of England* or *The Just Defence of John Lilburne*, his material is almost always autobiographical in an intentionally symbolic way.

Professor Haller made the passage I have quoted the epigraph of his edition of Leveller tracts, and it is certainly the most eloquent expression of a belief which is present in all of these writings. One is reminded immediately of the comparable "No man is an island" passage in the *Devotions* of Donne, who meditated upon life and death, being and non-being, in the symbolic mutilation of the body of mankind. Lilburne thinks of himself, first of all, as a member not of mankind or even of Christendom, but of the modern English Commonwealth, whose just laws he should uphold against the sea of chaos, for the good of all. He stands at a crucial point in history, with an action to perform at peril of being thought a traitor by present and future generations. Everything that he ever does or writes is undertaken as an act committed in time, and dependent upon a temporal context for its clarity. Unlike Donne, who pretends to ignore the reader, Lilburne has in mind men who will support and men who will bodily attack him. He is continually fighting for his life, and for the well-being of the nation; if his words were not going to be directly effective upon men's minds and actions, there would be no point in his writing at all.

From this very brief contrast of Lilburne with Donne, an underlying question may arise: Can Lilburne's tracts be called literature, so scattered and hasty as they are, so topical, so deeply submerged in time? Critics have repeatedly belittled the effectiveness of both his life and his work,[11] and it is to some extent my intention to argue from a different point of view. Practically speaking, the archetypal character Lilburne's tracts achieve, simply because he is so central and symbolic a figure in them and in his time, makes them highly useful in a contrast of conservative with radical prose. But beyond this practical fact, the strength of Lilburne's personality and the single-mindedness of his devotion to the ideal of freedom help to raise these tracts, both in style and in content, above the ephemeral propaganda from which he nevertheless learned many of his attitudes and techniques.

The strongest possible argument against treating these tracts as art is that they reverse what we usually understand to be the artistic process. Their intended function is not to take the stuff of life and transform it into art, but somehow to mythologize life itself, as life. Instead of using himself as material for his own autobiography, Lilburne is interested in using his writing as one way of improving his position in the world, and, of course, of improving the world too. The art is a by-product. Thus it is never possible to consider his tracts as their own excuse for being, and it is sometimes difficult for the critic to decide whether he is writing biography or literary criticism.

The reader will observe in the character of this problem an antithesis to the optical illusion so common in Anglican prose, intentionally created by the artist to give the audience a sense of confusion about whether what it sees is real or artificial. The Anglican is always turning life into art; the Puritan tries to turn art back toward life. Both blur the life-art borderline, but for different reasons. Lilburne's stand, if he had one, would be that there is no point to art unless it can serve life in some practical way. The critic of his style must often feel himself explicating backwards, so to speak, against the movement of the prose. Yet even from this rather negative viewpoint there is clearly much to be gained from opposing Lilburne's "I" to those of others.

That he makes himself a symbol points up at the outset the peculiar character of his Puritanism. He presents himself both as a fascinating, even romantic, individual and as God's symbolic Englishman, on the one hand providing more intimate individual detail about himself than an Anglican would, and on the other hand giving himself a more universal significance than a typical Puritan would. The idea of the calling, the doctrine of predestination, and Foxe's *Book of Mar-*

tyrs combine to give the political radical something like a figural (in Auerbach's terms) justification of his role in history.[12] He is there to fulfill what has been foretold, and to do it in limited historical terms, losing none of his human realism. A more immediate explanation, quite compatible with the other, is the particular Leveller impulse toward awakening of group consciousness and mass political activity.[13] One dramatic and successful means toward this end was to cause the people to identify themselves with Lilburne.

His first step is to be entirely visible. Far from swathing his rhetoric in levels of meaning as an Anglican would, or creating an "I" that either teases us or fragments itself, he refuses even to admit the existence of a persona, or the possibility that anywhere at any time, in print or out of it, he is other than the one John Lilburne, "*semper idem*," "John Lilburne as ever I was in my life," "having never forsaken nor changed my principles from better to worse the space of one hour." [14] At every point he takes the reader into his confidence in regard to the details of his private life. Even his marriage is a matter of public record, from the letter of courtship he wrote from prison in 1637 [15] to the letters he and his wife exchanged during his exile in 1653.[16] These he treated like any other documents to be appended to his tracts. Indeed, if one subtracts from his autobiographies the time spent in the army, in jail, on trial, and in exile, there is not much time left for a private life. The typical domestic scene between the Lilburnes, as recorded in the tracts, is staged between two windows, the one in his prison cell, the other in a house opposite, but forty yards distant, which is as near as she was permitted to come.[17] From these two windows they conversed. (Both, needless to say, were accustomed to public speaking.) In prison he courted her, from the appropriate London prison he named his son Tower, and while out on bail he died (the only event he could not describe in his tracts). His portrait is reproduced in Richard Overton's *Remonstrance of Many Thousand Citizens*, with bars across the face, under the legend, "The Liberty of the Freeborne Englishman, Conferred on him by the house of lords." A typical revolutionary, he lived his life in public (and publicized it in print), available to the judgment and the love of all.

Naturally, one has to assume throughout this rendition some selection of detail and considerable slanting in presentation. If anything in Lilburne's life is inconsistent with the portrait of a romantic protagonist who suffers constantly and unjustly in the cause of freedom, it is not included. The idea is to provide so much detail that absolute frankness is taken for granted, especially by supporters eager to live vicariously in the person of their unchanging hero. Surface visibility also allows him some room for below-surface maneuvers; because (unlike many others) he almost always signs his tracts, he can sometimes take advantage of anonymity to praise or agree with himself, thus giving his claims added weight: "God will provide, above hope: out of the thicket shall come a Ransome for this his beloved Isaac . . . God cannot suffer so abominable wickednesse: He can turne the hearts of a whole *Presbyterian Jury*, (if it should come to that,) in an instant, and make them to see their owne *Liberties* burning at the stake in him: that his Sufferings are but a *Preface* to their *Tragoedy*. . . ." [18] The fact remains that, in general, his intention is to be one person, to play one role, in print or out, in public, in private, in life and art, to make thoughts, feelings, writings and actions match. This one person is to be both an ordinary man and a symbol of all men. The insistence that his peril and his rights are those of all runs through his tracts like a refrain.

As he presents himself to us, he is singularly free of melancholy, that most characteristic of seventeenth-century ills, and there is relatively little introspection too. An inward glance in one of his last tracts, *The Resurrection of John Lilburne*, is therefore the more significant. Here he expresses his only self-criticism, that he coveted to be esteemed among the sons of men something more than Divine Wisdom would have it.[19] Indeed, he has been almost universally accused of vanity by his modern critics, but so have most seventeenth-century writers; it is certainly, in part at least, that their self-consciousness is something new, and in their inexperience they allow themselves to look vain. A modern writer with any sophistication would not speak of himself as a pearl in a dunghill; neither would he, like Sir Thomas Browne, congratulate himself upon his freedom from the sin of pride.

In other respects, the problem is our failure to read accurately. More than anything else, Lilburne's self-consciousness is that of a man convinced that he is to play a central role in history, and that he is entirely capable of playing it. Some minor techniques he borrows—for example, religious cant, the almost automatic use of certain well-worn Biblical phrases: ". . . if the Lord so order it that I may have Liberty to speake, I doubt not but by the might and power of my God, in whom I rest and trust, valiantly to display the weapons of a good Souldier of *Iesus Christ;* Come life, come death . . . ." [20] In this same line, his frequent comparisons of himself with Christ are surprising to us, where they would not have been to his contemporaries. Here he merely uses their clichés to express the confidence that as convert and social prophet he was expected to possess. Perhaps the least egotistical aspects of his rhetoric, they are also the least original and the least accurate for his purposes, and he uses them less and less as time goes on. More political than spiritual, he is much more cognizant of the material issues at stake than most men of his time; religion is inevitably a means of expression and action, but it does not cause him until late in life to question his worthiness. He is too busy and too symbolic. To question himself would be to question God's Englishmen, for whom he stands.

Lilburne's egotism is really a rocklike faith in the God-givenness of his vocation, an ability to turn everything he does, and everything that is done to him, to good purpose. The following three passages are all taken from the same tract, *Innocency and Truth Justified,* where typically he includes his standard generalizations, the latest episodes in his autobiography, and his latest plans for social action. One cannot help being impressed by the confidence with which he moves from one kind of material to another, equally sure both of his principles and of the value of a particularly demeaning event in his life. First, his characteristic stand on equality:

I professe, I am to learne (to conceive,) that any man in *England:* that professes himselfe to be a man, (and not a god) hath justly by any pretended prerogative or priviledge whatsoever . . . exemption from the lash and rigor of the Law more than my selfe, or the meanest free man in *England,* and I doe seriously protest, my judgement is, that what single person soever he bee, whether King, Lord, or Member of the House of Commons that treads under foot the Law made by common consent, and Acts as if he were subject to none, is an absolute Tyrant, and no Ordinance of God, and so not by any to be obeyed.

Second, a description of the psychological effect of unfair and undemocratic treatment. Typically using himself as an example or central character, he describes his reward for the successful capture of a castle:

His Lordship fell a calling of me Rogue, Rascall, and base fellow, and asked me whether he or I was Generall, and told me, the Armie was to much troubled with such busie Rogues as I was, and he would send me farre enough from it, and also told me, I deserved to be hanged, and would not suffer me to speake one word in my owne defence, but turned away from me in a greater fury then ever I see him in, in my dayes; his carriage being a cleere Demonstration to me, that he in a manner scorned to accept of the Castle, because I had taken it. Which carriage, did so vex and perplex my very soule, as I was never more I thinke, in my dayes, and so cooled my courage in fighting, that I could never from that day to this present houre, draw my sword, nor ingage my life in the way of a Souldier, with that freenesse, alacrity, and cheerfullnesse, as formerlie I had done.

Third, a challenge to William Prynne, a former Puritan martyr now become a member of the establishment and hence one of Lilburne's villains:

This I say to him, I both dare and am able, (for all his vapours which I esteeme no more then God did *Adams* fig leaves, with which he would have covered his nakednesse) to meet him, and a whole Squadron of such heady and light men, face to face, upon equall tearms, upon any ground in England, to justifie and maintaine my present cause against him, whether it be Religion, or the publique liberty of the free people of England, the equall tearmes I desire, is no more but this, that I may have as free libertie to speake, write and print as himselfe, and I will set my hand to what ever I doe, and seale it with my blood.[21]

Lilburne's essential style is a very bare one. He uses few metaphors, rarely lets us know what anything looks like, and avoids frequent recourse to devices of rhetoric. Ordinarily, he will not even build to a climax, except in courtroom speeches, unless the climax simply happens, chronologically. Thus the sentences, unimpeded by strong punctuation or direction, flow freely, taking their movement and their drama from Lilburne's emotions and actions as they are expressed from moment to moment.

This ever-present sense of time, evoked first of all by the fact that he writes as things happen, so that in a given tract there is always a past, a present, and a future, is part of what maintains our interest; coordinating conjunctions and other weak links between sentences keep the prose unhurried and relaxed, at the same time holding our attention in the flow of time; and the automatic coupling of Lilburne's own affairs with his general principles or with major affairs of state provides the human drama that makes the principles interesting, as he is well aware. Yet the language is typically unpretentious and colloquial, and he presents himself, in the second passage, in a somewhat unflattering context—or so it would appear. Actually, he is willing to present himself in any kind of context.

What he implies in the total fabric of this style is this: I am a man like you, living a life in time like you, and my life, just as it is, has great value. That is to say, the artlessness of the presentation is intentional.[22] Lilburne believed in extemporaneous writing and speaking, partly because he thought Scripture supported it, partly because he recognized its effectiveness for him. He saw it to be a way of drawing in the common man. Practised as he was in his artless art, he knew that one can make use of any passing thought. The psychological frankness of the second passage is a way of arousing his readers to remember that they, too, have been in such situations, a way of stimulating them to self-consciousness and thence to social awareness. And it is a way of setting the reader up for his challenge to the establishment in the third passage, and of making that challenge more exciting and dramatic.

His critics say that Lilburne had no sense of humor; that is part of the reason why they find his vanity excessive.[23] Certainly, if humor is to be defined as a friendly and reconciling power, which endows its possessor with a sense of proportion and draws the sting from pain, Lilburne does not have one. In this sense, perhaps humor is inevitably part of the rhetoric of moderation that is so congenial to the Anglican *via media*, and antipathetic to the Puritan zealot.

Yet Lilburne's tracts are often funny. When he was being tried for treason, the courtroom was packed with his admirers. And according to one spectator, when the prosecution read out passages from Lilburne's works, as illustrations of his guilt, it "pleased the People as well as if they had acted before them one of Ben Jonson's plays." [24] Even when some allowance is made for the possible histrionics of the prosecution, the comment is immensely illuminating in suggesting the kind of response which Lilburne's style must have called forth. The man was on trial for his life, yet the people, who were solidly on his side, were able to be diverted as if they were watching a satirical comedy. One aspect of his humor, obviously, is his ability to lampoon authority, taunting its inability to keep Lilburne quiet and at the same time consistently reminding it of its failure to be what it promised, as shown in this title page:

AS YOU WERE OR The Lord General Cromwel and the *Grand Officers* of the *Armie* their REMEMBRANCER. Wherein, as in a glass they may see the *faces of their Soules* spotted with *Apostacy, Ambitious breach of promise,* and hocus-pocus-*juggleing* with the honest *Soldiers,* and the rest of the *Free-people of England.* to the end that, haveing seene their deformed and *fearfull visage,* they may by returning to doe their first *pretended* workes, wipe of their spots, mend their *deformities* & regaine their *lost Credit* . . . .

The satire is meant to be corrective, just as in Ben Jonson. Much of its comicality must have derived from combined shock and relief at the release provided from false decorum, false respect for authority. Lilburne's approach is based on a new kind of *decorum personae,* first announced by Martin Marprelate,[25] in which rhetoric is to suit the character of the persons at whom the tract is aimed. Lilburne "unmasks" his enemies by describing their outward appearance in terms of their inward illness, or by equating them directly with anything generally thought indecent: "I judg the two *forementioned lying base Apostates,* to be so abominably vile, that I judg not my excrements mean enough upon equal terms to ballance against them . . . ."[26]

Thomas Kranidas has eloquently opposed to Anglican insistence on outer decency Milton's insistence on harmony and wholeness.[27] And I have already shown that Lilburne's first intention, like Milton's, was to present himself as a whole person, matching inside and outside. Vituperative or indecorous language may fitly expose the indecency of false pretentions, especially on the part of men who caused the revolution in the name of freedom and now deny freedom to those who fought for it. Significantly, the one direct connection between Milton and Lilburne is Lilburne's appreciation of Milton's insistence that the English people must practice inner freedom, rather than relying on others to take care of things from without.[28] His rage, like Milton's, is against the hypocrisy or indifference that makes many men unsound and subject to decay. And the definition of humor with which I began is simply irrelevant to the Puritan cause. Gentle humor can only be satisfactory to a society generally content with itself, where proportion and harmony are the rule. Lilburne's aim, like Milton's, is to raise England by harsher methods to a state in which that kind of humor can be appropriate.

More uniquely important to Lilburne's thought, and humor, is his instinct for levelling people, insisting on the equality of all men under the law. The complete identification which the common people had made with Lilburne was based largely on his willingness to represent them at all times, and their amusement at his encounters with authority was a vicarious pleasure. His refusal to take off his hat in Star Chamber, his infuriating offers to debate with anyone at all, his insistence upon being addressed as Lieutenant Colonel, are not evidence of personal vanity but of his complete acceptance of his responsibility to uphold the dignity of the common man.[29]

In his defense of his rights, in fact, he often risks personal absurdity without a second thought. Situations occur which must have amused his own supporters, and which provide the greatest pleasure to the modern reader, contributing everywhere to our enjoyment of his personality, and undercutting the vanity. It is very funny when, in the midst of the solemn proceedings of the treason trial, surrounded by pompous judges who have effectively blocked all his other efforts to gain time to prepare a brief for himself, he calls for a chamber pot to be brought to him in the court room, uses the waiting time to study his books, and then uses the chamber pot.[30] He is frequently comical in his insistence on his rights in what would seem unimportant or at best unexpected situations—his rights, for example, in the Tower of London, a sort of boardinghouse of a prison:

But thirdly, what ground have you, upon any pretence whatever framed by your selfe, to lock me up in my chamber, as soon as candles are lighted, seeing I am in a moated and double walled Prison, where you have not only a Train-band, but also great store of your owne Warders to secure me?

And therefore, I tell you plainly, I shall never condiscend to be locked up sooner then that convenient houre of 8.a clock, the accustomed hour of the place, which is much sooner then they are in other prisons, that I have been in.[31]

Whether or not he was aware of the humor in all these situations, he is certainly not concerned with any traditional decorum; he will defend his principles and his rights to the last hundredth of an inch under any conditions and with any weapons. He is willing to be absurd in order to say what must be said if he is to keep faith with all those whose miserable lives he is attempting to uplift; and social status cannot be decorously revolutionized. Humor of incongruity is perhaps an inevitable by-product when commoner strives against aristocrat.

It is also a by-product of Lilburne's total commitment to his cause, his inability to calculate effects or select issues. With his whole being devoted to one great issue, he becomes like Bergson's mechanical man, reacting predictably to every situation, accepting every challenge from moment to moment in time, without trying to assess the relative importance of each or to protect the dignity of his image. For one who cannot compromise with reality enough to accept the heroism of Oliver Cromwell, the only kind of heroism possible is that of the absurd. But in the age and in the man there is still a saving idealism. A. L. Morton compliments him very deftly: "Yet, whether he is writing badly or well, it is always an unmistakable man who writes. Lilburne's style has always, like his character, something of the grandeur as well as a little of the absurdity of a national monument."[32]

The attention that we have had to pay to action suggests one final way in which Lilburne directly creates the "I" of his prose. Because he was so physically active and so magnificently capable of dramatic gesture, one is constantly aware, in and around and after the language, of symbolic uses of his body, both by himself and by others. One remembers Lilburne whipped through the London streets at a cart's tail, tossing banned books into the crowd as he stands in the pillory doing penance for the crime of distributing banned books, pleading the case of the common man in trial after trial (a Hollar engraving shows him standing at the bar with his copy of Coke in hand), returning from exile to face death. Such public, dramatic gestures, in themselves enough to ensure popular devotion, help to explain why Lilburne's style can be so bare and yet so interesting; they are one means by which he turns the prose toward life without wholly assimilating life into it. One might even suppose that here words are superfluous, but such a supposition misses the point.

It has already been made clear that life-art boundaries in Lilburne's prose are practically impossible to maintain because he wants and provides almost no distinction between the "I" of the prose and the "I" of the author. The fact that the "I" of the prose makes constant reference to himself as author also blurs the boundaries, although this is a technique common to the age. Both Puritans and Anglicans build their literary theories into their literature, discussing their art as it is in process of becoming art. Extreme significance always is attached to the relationship between the man and the word, and Lilburne's practice is distinct only in the peculiarly Puritan and Lilburnian character of its existence.

He is an extremely prolific writer, the constant flow of publication being made possible partly because, like many radical Puritans, and in direct opposition to Anglican principle, he insists upon spontaneous utterance. Just as he feels compelled to fight the battle of every freeborn Englishman, he trusts in God to speak through his Englishmen, and cites Matthew 10:19–20 for justification: "But when they deliver you up, take no thought how or what ye shall speak: for it shall be given you in that same hour what ye shall speak. For it is not ye that speak, but the Spirit of your Father which speaketh in you." [33] Measuring the degree of his inspiration by the number of manuscript pages he thinks himself able to fill, he writes that "my God hath filled my soule so full of Heavenly matter, that had I but a current vent, I could *ex tempore* write an hundred Sheetes of paper to you, filled full of Heavenly expressions of the Lords goodnesse, faithfulnesse, loving kindnesse and Truth." [34] Thus, prolific spontaneity becomes a sign of God's favor.

I shall often have occasion to mention the characteristic insistence in this age upon writing, as if writing were a way to keep alive. For Lilburne, writing in itself, though it can temporarily measure his inspiration, is not enough; active and famous as he is, he must publish, to assert his rights and to maintain a sense of his own integrity. Near the end of his life, banished from his country on pain of death and burdened with a staggeringly unfair fine, he searches for a place "where Safely to abide and print without offence." [35] His wife, knowing this to be a main source of his difficulties, begs him to be still, but he argues that there are "undeniable reasons WHY I AM COMPELLED TO PRINT." [36] Pen and sword throughout his life he has offered to the service of his country, but the more thoroughly he sees himself rejected, the more fully he turns to printing as the only kind of action available.

The need to print has far from simple causes. If it is true that it has to do with Lilburne's sense of integrity, it is also true that it springs from very practical impulses. At one point, after he had been committed to the Tower, the newssheet *Mercurius Pragmaticus* prophesied: "Now the next time that John comes abroad it will be in Print, I warrant you, to wire-draw the whole Story of the businesse, with all the secrets of the designe." [37] Printing was a way to transcend imprisonment, to maintain his freedom and popularity even from jail,[38] and that was important because he was in jail so much of the time. Printing was also a means to personal safety, as he reminds us in *As You Were*. Rumors had him on the one hand a regicide, on the other a secret correspondent of Charles II; in Holland both Cavaliers and Roundheads were out to get him. To publish a double-column account of the facts, in Dutch and English, was to provide himself with some necessary life insurance. Finally, in the *Just Defence*, he says that silence in the face of false accusations is tantamount to an admission of guilt. There is no fear of that from Lilburne!

From the very beginning to the very end, both his cause and his means of attack have to do with language. He first attracted the notice of the crumbling government of Charles I when he became an agent to bring into England so-called seditious and scandalous books printed in Holland. He says he was the first man ever to refuse to take the oath *ex officio* in the Star Chamber. For years he was imprisoned in the Tower of London, which was among other things a library, and here he studied the records and charters that gave him much of the knowledge of laws, customs, and legal history that he was to use in defending himself at the bar and in print.[39] Although his complaints about both monarchy and commonwealth are numerous, the main source of his difficulty is the censorship laws, which deny him the right to print his views. And he has to go on printing them because censoring his books is the same thing as censoring him.

The tract is a weapon. To deprive Lilburne of pen and ink is to disarm him and render him helpless; in tract after tract, this is listed among the most grievous woes of prison life: "I have been almost two yeares in Prison: First, in Newgate; and then secondly in the Tower *devorsed from my wife, debarred of my friends, deprived of pen, Inck and paper*."[40] Like many of his colleagues, Lilburne believed that writing is combat, a way of duelling with one's enemies. When the Army was organizing in opposition to Parliament, one of their first aims was to "keepe a partie of able penn men at Oxford and the Army."[41] It is beautifully symbolic that one of the two chief Leveller meeting places, jestingly named the two new houses of Parliament, was a tavern called the Mouth.[42]

As words and soldiers together issue from the Mouth, the concept of the word as something which communicates is almost overshad-

THE PURITAN IN HISTORY

John Lilburne at the bar: the frontispiece of
The Triall of Lieut.-Collonell John Lilburne

(1649)

owed by the concept of word as weapon. For Lilburne, the tract is something to break the fangs of his adversaries ("this bone to pick"); [43] it is like Sampson's foxes with firebrands at their tails.[44] Hence the skill with which he uses vituperative adjectives, one of his very few rhetorical tricks, as in the following examples: "all the rest of his bloody-minded, pretended reformed fellow-clergy Presbyters"; "that lying, deceitful, forsworn, and bloodye Sect"; [45] "your decaying, tottering, spirituall, Babilonian, Anti-Christian Kingdome"; [46] "*O brave, unerring, unsinning, and everlasting, nonesuch Parliament.*" [47]

The Puritan radical is not averse to real exchanges of views. One need only recall the Army debates at Putney to be assured of that. Lilburne offered to debate with almost anyone from the very first time he came in conflict with society; but the offer of a twenty-two-year-old apprentice to debate publicly with the Archbishop of Canterbury could scarcely have been expected, by anyone except Lilburne, to result in a real encounter:

I pray you, take notice of his great learned Arguments, which he used to confute me, and defend himselfe, which were these:

Let him be lockt up close prisoner, in the basest place in the *Wards of the Fleete;* for so runne the words of the Order; and let none come at him, least he should infect any of the people with his errours . . .

Oh! Scholasticall Arguments indeed; Alas! poore man, are your eyes so sore, that they cannot endure to looke upon the Sunne . . . ?

But before them I made this challenge, and desired them to tell it to the Bishops, that I would dispute with them all before my Dread Soveraigne . . . And their Arguments and replication to this my challeng, was: Lay him fast in Iron chaines, Armes, and Leggs, coupled together . . . . [48]

Lilburne's handling of these episodes employs the kind of irony that Milton called "grim laughter," suitable to the "serious uncasing of a grand imposture." [49] It is understandable that after some experience of this kind of treatment Lilburne should also develop methods of speaking not primarily concerned with allowing equal time to the other side.

Thus language becomes on the one hand a club, on the other a means of exposure. Confident in the power of words to bring about eventual justice, Lilburne sees no need for diplomacy; if his enemies will not give him what he wants simply because it is right, then there is no hope for them. Consider, for example, the opening sentence in "A Coppy of a Letter Written by John Lilburne, Close Prisoner in the Wards of the *Fleet*, which he sent to *James Ingram* and *Henry Hopkins*, Wardens of the Said *Fleet*. Wherein is fully discovered their great Cruelty exercised upon his Body":

Sirs, You are both so rooted in oppression and so malicious in thirsting after innocent blood, that the actions of the one, may be attributed and judged, to be the actions of you both; there is such a harmony betwixt you in *wickednesse*, so that I will now put you both in the singuler number, and write unto you, as if you were but one; Desireing to let you understand, that in *December* was 2. yeares, the Devil Your old Father, *John* 8, 44. (for my *innocencie*) *cast me into Prison*, and *William Laud* his obedient Sonne, got me committed to your custodie to be *tormented*, in which Art you are very exquisite, and expert; and your plots to murther me, and to take away my *innocent blood* from me, have not been a few, which have been, and still are so palpable, that they cannot be hid from the world; unto the view of which I have already in part, in my Printed Books, layd them open in a brief way: but much more then I have in publique said, have I yet behind truly to declare.

In this letter he expresses enormous confidence in the power of print to undo villainy. He is surprised, in fact, that what he has already published has not yet taken effect, but he warns his jailors that if they should murder him he has left them a legacy of language in his will, "a biting whippe to lash and scourge your fat and knavish sides," which his executor has orders to publish with marginal notes.

In all this there begins to emerge an implicit theory of language that can be joined with my earlier comments on language as action supplementary to the literal activity of its author and directed toward the creation of Utopia. Language is also a specialized commodity, serving to give reality to such abstractions as "the rights of Englishmen." The repetitiveness of Lilburne's tracts, far from involving any waste motion, seems to endow these abstractions with force and substance, making more and more obvious their proper application to the specific situations in which Lilburne becomes involved. This is perhaps a particularly modern, Renaissance use of language. Much more primitive, and appropriate to Lilburne's character as folk hero, is the concept of language as weapon, possessed of magical power to strike down the adversary.[50]

Structurally, Lilburne's tracts may be considered either as dramatic performances, or as imitations of the saint's life in Foxe's *Book of Martyrs*. In view of the Puritans' sense of drama and their use of Foxe in writing their own "plays," these two ways of analyzing the tracts are entirely compatible. Foxe himself was dramatic enough, and they envisaged themselves as writing the next and perhaps the most glorious act of the great Christian drama that he had recorded.[51]

It was a commonplace in Anglican pamphlet literature of the civil wars that the Puritans closed the theaters in order to cut off competition for their own comedies (the proceedings of Parliament) and tragedies (the trial of the king).[52] But long before this, they were constantly living out dramas of life and death. Mr. Haller makes these perceptive comments on the public torture of Lilburne's mentors, Prynne, Bastwick, and Burton:

> The London mob had probably never beheld upon the boards of the Globe or the Swan a more moving drama than that which Prynne, Bastwick and Burton enacted in the Star Chamber and the old palace yard, enacted with full measure of that gift for histrionic gesture and utterance which was the common possession of the English populace. These men were the rivals as well as the enemies of the players, and of the playwrights too. As soon as time would allow, after Prynne and his fellows had been dragged off to prison, there appeared another illicit pamphlet in the streets of London.[53]

As for Lilburne, he "was ready in the wings the moment his elders left the boards." [54]

The Puritan rejects art for life, studiedness for spontaneity, drama for reality. Yet his reading of history fills his life, just as it is, with symbolic and eternal meaning. A memorable and favorite phrase of Lilburne's—"for all my short eternity in this world" [55]—suggests all this, in its apparently paradoxical view of time. The tract as dramatic performance reproduces dramatic situations featuring Lilburne as protagonist. The antagonists, of course, are the enemies against whom Lilburne's words are shot as weapons. The audience for the drama is made up of Lilburne's admiring friends, who play a more or less passive role.

In Anglican prose, the self-conscious narrator talks to himself, argues with himself, plays in one person different parts. He is in control to the extent that he does not have to be governed by a response from another person, as does Lilburne, who is and is not the author of the drama in which he stars. It was said of pugnacious Lilburne, and he repeated the remark himself, that if only John Lilburne were left alive, John would quarrel with Lilburne. But naturally things never came to such a pass; John always had plenty of enemies, and never needed, like Donne, to fight with himself.

Perhaps the most vivid example of Lilburne's drama is a tract whose literary validity may seem questionable because it is simply a transcript of what was said and done at a trial—Lilburne's trial for treason; and because, although he certified its validity, Lilburne did not make the transcript himself. The fact is, though, that this is only an extreme example of the realistic framework that Lilburne's writings always have, that both the movement of the trial and most of the speaking in it are Lilburne's, and that the trial represents the climax of all his writing and of his career. No single piece of his work has less claim to be called his art, yet this trial must be considered the keystone of his life and art partly because it is here that the two become absolutely one and the same.

The scene is provided for us, and so is a degree of tension natural to the circumstances. The picture of seventeenth-century justice which emerges bears striking resemblance to that portrayed in the court scene of *The White Devil*. Like Vittoria Corombona, Lilburne is given both more and less than his due. He is consistently allowed to dominate the scene, consistently permitted more freedom of speech than we would allow a defendant, and yet at the same time is deprived of rights that we would consider elementary. The result is that he stands forth in very bold relief, both because he takes the center of the stage and because he commands our sympathy as he does it.

On the first page of *The Triall of Lieut. Collonell John Lilburne*, the names of the participants are printed, as in a playbill. From the opening page, Lilburne, who has a tremendously well-developed sense of melodrama, consistently upstages and outtalks his judges, provoking them into such feeble rejoinders as these:

L. *Col. Lilb.* I desire nothing but Councell, and a little time to consult with them, and to produce my Witnesses, and a Copy of my Indictment; if not, I am willing to die as the object of your Indignation and malice, do your will and pleasure.
L. Keble. *We are willing to die too.*

Lieut. Col. Lilb. . . . Sir, I have within me I blesse God, that will be a portion of comfort to me, to carry me through all your mallice and injustice.
L. Keble. *Never talk of that which is with you; God is in us as well as in you: never make a flourish of what is in you; for the feare of God is before our eyes as well as yours* . . . .[56]

The judges are clearly intimidated by the highly partisan audience. They stand firm on a limited number of issues, as that in cases of treason no defense lawyer is permitted, but they allow Lilburne almost unlimited talking time, which he uses as he sees fit, both to argue the particular procedural issues, and to orate upon himself. The judges' feeble efforts to match Lilburne's claims obviously win them no sympathy: after all, they are not on trial. And they have tried to stack the cards in advance, just because they know the filibustering power of Lilburne's monologues:

Lord Keeble. Mr. Lilburne, *I shall add this more to it, that you at this time, have here such a Court, which never any of your condition ever had in* England, *so many Grave Judges of the Law.*
L. Col. Lilb. *Truly I had rather have had an ordinary one Sir, I mean a legall and ordinary Assises or Sessions.*
L. Keeble. *But this you have, & this is to take off or prevent, that which you would do now, if there had been one Judge & no more, and if you had not had this great presence of the Court, you would have been malepart, and have out talked them, but you cannot do so here.*[57]

It was habitual with Lilburne to act as his own attorney: earlier in his life, he had insisted upon it, saying that he could trust no lawyer to speak for him.[58] At the same time, here he manages to play both sides of the fence by claiming to be at a disadvantage because he has not been allowed counsel. In all his protestations of his inability to defend himself, he is role-playing to some extent. He knew at least some Latin and Greek, and he had by this time spent years studying the law. He pretends ignorance and naiveté because he speaks as the people's representative, in defense of the rights of any freeborn Englishman. Thus, for purposes of the trial, he is ignorant of other languages than English, and of the complexities of laws in whatever language they are written. We must recognize, despite his protests to the contrary, that here at least there is a difference between the man and the persona.

The results of Lilburne's arguments bear melodramatic witness to the physical power that all his words seemed to possess. It is no wonder that the Law required company:

L. Col. Lilb. Well then, if it must be so, that you will have my bloud right or wrong, and if I shall not have on [*sic*] houres time to refresh me, after my strength is spent, and to consider of that which hath been alledged against me, then I appeale, (which he uttered with a mighty voice) to the righteous God of heaven and earth against you, where I am sure, I shall be heard and find access, and the Lord God Omnipotent, and a mighty Judge betwixt you and me, requier and requite my bloud upon the heads of you and your posterity, to the third and fourth generation; immediatly after the uttering of which the Scaffold fell down, which was on the left hand, which occasioned a great noise and some confusion by reason of the peoples tumbling . . . .[59]

In the following passage, he concludes his final statement to the jury:

And therefore, I desire you to know your power, and consider your duty, both to God, to Me, to your own Selves, and to your Country; and the gracious assisting Spirit, and presence of the Lord God omnipotent, the Governour of Heaven and Earth, and all things therein contained, go along with you, give counsell, and direct you, to do that which is just and for his glory. [*The People with a loud voyce, cryed* Amen Amen, *and gave an extraordinary great hum, which made the Judges look something untowardly about them, and caused Major Generall* Skippon *to send for three more fresh Companies of Foot Souldiers.*][60]

The calling up of fresh companies of foot soldiers in response to Lilburne's speech is a confirmation of this whole aspect of the theory of language and rhetoric which he represents. His words are, and are opposed by, active physical force.

Like the passages from Lilburne's books, the trial itself is as exciting as a play by Ben Jonson, and has what some would consider the additional advantage of being true. In this nonfiction seventeenth-century drama, the author simultaneously wrote, acted, and directed the script. To the surprise of his judges, he was acquitted, as he would have been by any jury of his peers. It was the high point of his career. Nothing quite so important ever happened to him again, and moreover it became clear to him that even such an acquittal as this would not bring down the government and sweep his Levellers into power. Rather, as is foreshadowed here, it caused the government to increase the repressive measures exercised against him. If he could not be killed, he could be imprisoned for the rest of his life. At least in this respect, the pen, powerful as it was, could not resist the sword.

The picture of Lilburne as martyr brings us to consideration of the structural influence upon his work of the great Renaissance martyrology. While much of the material of *The Triall* could be employed in an extension of Foxe's *Book of Martyrs*, the more narrative and specifically functional tracts are more obviously indebted to that Elizabethan source. In Foxe's book, the stories of saints and martyrs, many of them sixteenth-century Englishmen, are given in documentary fashion, with all possible objective records included, such as verbatim accounts of interrogations and trials, letters, warrants, and so forth. The intention is to provide a history of Christianity in the stories of its saints, and particularly to explicate the history of the English as God's chosen people. Lilburne, like Milton, takes this view of things for granted in his tracts, as well as his own central role in the manifestation of England's destiny. An important complication, however, is that Lilburne, as his own biographer, has not only to collect the documents; he has first to create them. And the primary purpose of their creation is presumably not that they may become autobiography, but that they may have their natural function as letters, petitions, polemics, and so forth. Even the longest autobiographical tracts, such as *The Legall Fundamentall Liberties of the People of England,* were, as this title suggests, intended to serve more than an autobiographical function; they were to be weaponry and propaganda. As with Foxe, any given tract may include four or five or more different exhibits. A private letter written in 1638 is included in a tract dated 1645. Petitions seeking a compromise settlement instead of a trial are appended to the account of the trial itself. Warrants, petitions, letters, pleas, speeches are imbedded in the tracts wherever relevant. Therefore, the function, intended audience, and point of view of these publications are curiously manysided.

The tracts are filled from the very beginning with vivid concrete autobiographical detail. We are told when, where, in whose companionship, against what odds each adventure occurs. The detail is active, dramatic, very exciting and romantic. Here is the opening sentence of his very first tract, *The Christian Mans Triall,* describing his first arrest by the Royalists:

Upon Tuesday last the 11, or 12. of *December,* 1637 I was treacherously and Judasly betraied (by one that I supposed to be my friend) into the hands of the Pursevant, with foure of his assistants, as I was walking into a narrow lane, called *Soperlane,* being walking with one *John Chilliburne,* servant to old Mr. *John Wharton,* in *Bow-lane* a Hotpresser Which *John* had laid the plot before for my apprehension, as I am able for to prove and make good, that he shall not be able with truth to deny it. And at my taking the Pursevants were very violent [with] me, and having by force got me into a shop, they threw me over a Sugar-chest, to take my Sword from me, and cried out for helpe, and said he had taken one of the most notoriousest dispersers of scandalous bookes that was in the Kingdome, for (saith he) he hath dispersed them from one end of the Land to the other.

To the average Londoner, who had never read a novel, such an opening page must have been practically irresistible. It involved him immediately in intrigue and adventure, not by carrying him to some far-off part of the world, but by dramatizing events taking place in his own city, on familiar streets, among his neighbors. Foxe had done the same thing, but this was even more up-to-date. Its style, like Foxe's, is that of the popular theater.

Constantly, the reader is made to be a present audience. In *A Worke of the Beast,* he includes in full his speech from the pillory: "Now here againe I speake it in the presence of God, & all you that heare mee." [61] Typically, he intersperses the printed speech with vivid stage directions: "And here a bout I put my hand in my pocket, and puld out Three of worthie *D. Bastwicks Bookes* and threw them among the people and said, There is part of the bookes for which I suffer, take them among you, and read them, and see if you finde any thing in them, against the Law of God, the Law of the Land, the glory of God, the honour of the King or state." [62] Often, such interruptions are caused by others, in which case they habitually seem as eerily timed as the collapse of the scaffold in response to Lilburne's calling upon God's justice. His speech from the pillory was twice interrupted by Royalist commands that he hold his peace. The second time the request punctuated the following sentence: "Alas if men should hold their peace in such times as these, the Lord would cause the verie Stones to speake to convince man of his cowardlie baseness." [63] This, his first public appearance, was, interestingly enough, the moment chosen by the Lord for Lilburne's conversion and calling. In the midst of this experience, uniquely occurring in public, Lilburne calculated its effects.[64] Later, ostensibly for lack of ink, but surely to make his torture palpable to the reader, he sets his name, John Lilburne, to what he says is "written with part of my owne bloud." [65]

Because he is so conscious of being a man in history, one thing that is always clear, given the inevitable problems caused by his use of both Old Style and New Style dating, is the time and place of writing. In the earliest years, the tracts are datelined with such hopeful tags as these: "Printed in the yeare the Beast was Wounded 1638"; "Printed in the yeare of hope, of ENGLANDS purgation, & the Prelates dissolution. ANNO 1639." [66] Later, as it begins to seem possible to Lilburne that the wounders of the Beast are not going to bring about Utopia, these tags become less frequent, and more gloomy,[67] but the dating becomes much more specific, including month and day as well as year. The Puritan writer is far more committed to history than any previous writers had been: his tracts both create history and are imbedded in it. Hence, the unlikelihood that any one of them can seem whole in itself, though Lilburne's tracts taken all together do constitute a kind of autobiography. In this respect, one might notice his constant cross-advertising of his books. References and allusions are allowed at every point to lead the reader out of one work and into others:

> But after I had sufficiently baited both you and your unjust house; you sent me to *Newgate a hundred pound in mony, I thinke to get me to hold my peace,* and the 14 of October 1645, most honorably Voted me out of Prison, and so your self being my acuser, prosecutor and Judge, Justified me in this contest, the relation of which you may at large read in that notable book called *Englands Birth-right* [this was printed anonymously], and in my *Epistle of two sheets of paper* in print *dated* 25. July 1645. but especially in my Large Book forementioned, and called *Innocency and Truth Justified* . . . .[68]

Only in the trials, where references to other works are cited as evidence by the prosecution, and so are given at sufficient length to be self-explanatory, does this technique contribute to the integrity of the immediate situation. With each successive addition to his autobiography, past chapters are thus implied, making a strange blend of that active, immediate, oral style with historical footnotes. But the method of Puritan biography is always to record chronology, progress through time.

The Freemans Freedome Vindicated may conveniently be used as an example of Lilburne's documentary technique, since it is a relatively brief affair of some twelve pages. Published on June 19, 1646, it bears the following subtitle:

> *A true Relation of the cause and manner of* Lieut. Col. Iohn Lilburns *present* imprisonment *in* Newgate, *being thereunto* arbitrarily *and* Illegally *committed, by the* House of Peeres, *June* 11. 1646. *for his delivering in,* at their open Barre, *under his* Hand *and* Seal, *his* PROTESTATION, *against their* incroaching *upon the* Common Liberties *of all the* Commons *of* England, *in endeavouring to try him,* a Commoner *of* England, *in a criminall cause, contrary to the expresse tennour and forme of the* 29. Chap. *of the great* Charter *of* England, *and for making his legall and just appeal, to his competent, propper and legal* Tryers *and* Judges, *the* Commons *of* England, *in* PARLIAMENT *assembled.*

This tract is typically addressed to "True bred *Englishmen,* that have a life to lay down, for the defence of your just Liberties and

Freedomes." Its purpose is to tell them how his liberties have been abused, and thereby presumably to stimulate them to action. That is, he wishes both to educate and to arouse. He first summarizes his troubles of the moment. Then he introduces his strategy. First, he wrote a letter to his attorney instructing him to draw up a plea. The letter follows. On June 10, he was summoned to answer questions in regard to a tract published on June 6. There follows "The PRO-TESTATION, PLEA and DEFENCE OF Lieutenant Colonell JOHN LILBURNE. *Given to the Lords at their Barre*, thursday June 11. 1646." The theme is that the Lords are not qualified by law to try a commoner. Thereupon, he goes on to relate, he was sent to Newgate, and he includes the charge, "*for exhibiting to this house* a scandalous and contemptuous Paper." Next, a letter, claiming that he has been badly treated, is addressed "*To the Gentleman Usher of this House, or his Deputy, to be delivered to the Keeper of New-gate.*" There follows a petition to the House of Commons, begging them to use their proper jurisdiction to save him. He then adds to the tract a postscript, containing a "generall Proposition" to the effect that all men are equal, and government should be by free consent of the governed. This proposition ends one third of the way down page twelve. Lilburne can never bring himself to leave a page unfilled: "Courteous countrymen to fill up this vacant place I shall desire thee to read the words of the Declaration of the House of Commons, published 27. *Ianu.* 1641." The declaration has no immediate relevance to this tract; it argues that the king is guilty of treason.[69]

This tract is briefer than most, less coherent than many because there is less narrative surrounding the documents. But it is a good illustration of the sort of multiple viewpoint that typifies his work. The original purpose on June 19, 1646, was to enlighten sympathetic readers, and stir them to action. Their long-range function is dual. First, it is to bear a continuing witness to the work of John Lilburne in the world and thus to outlive, "and be (I hope) as good as winding sheets unto"[70] those who opposed him. Second, it is to provide realism and believability for the future readers (that is, ourselves) of the autobiography of John Lilburne. It seems inevitable that in some way he must have been aware of this second purpose, just because he knew how popular and durable was Foxe's *Book of Martyrs*.

Much of the appeal of Lilburne's pamphlets springs from their intention to involve the reader actively. We have already seen numerous techniques by which he achieves this end, from the active character of the prose itself to its documentation of contemporary history. There are even accidental factors that work in his favor. The effort to get hold of a pamphlet could in itself be strenuous and dangerous. The circulation of a pamphlet among ten people already makes those ten people allies, part of a movement.[71] The type with which the pamphlets were printed was inevitably worn and faulty, the printers scrambled type size and multiplied errors with what sometimes seems like the gayest abandon, and Lilburne was rarely able to proofread: hence, such appeals to his readers as this made them practically editors:

Courteous Reader, by reason I am prohibited to have Pen, Ink, and Paper; I am forced now to write a peece, and then a peece, and scarce have time and opportunity seriously to peruse and correct what I write; and in regard I cannot be at the Presse, either to correct, or revise my own lines (which besides is attended with many difficulties and hazards) I must intreat thee, as thou readest, to amend with thy Pen, what in sence or quotations may be wanting, or false; & I shal rest thy true and faithfull Country-man, ready to spend my bloud for the fundamental Lawes and Liberties of *England*, against any power what-ever that would destroy them.[72]

Here, as so often, Puritan technique corresponds, on its different plane, with one that the Anglican is likely to use. By chosen literary means—for example, the meditative style, the Anglican invites the reader to participate with him in the making of the book or the fulfillment of its making and meaning. The Anglican technique is contrived; the Puritan one is enforced by circumstance. But it is interesting that in both cases the reader becomes something more than a mere spectator.

Lilburne had to go farther, for his intention was not literary involvement so much as it was direct action in the world. The most obvious device is the petition, which the Levellers employed to some extent as an educational instrument. Whether circulated by itself, or later attached to a tract, it was the best possible evidence that the active cooperation of the reader was required. In the tracts, the people are constantly exhorted, both implicitly and explicitly, to mass protest: ". . . therefore up, and as one man, to the Parliament with a Petition, to displace all those *Monopolizers*, and to put honest *Englishmen* into their places . . . ."[73] The tract called *Rash Oaths Unwarrantable* includes five interrelated petitions with accounts of their fate. The first was ignored; a certificate to it resulted in its bearer being imprisoned. The second was ignored. The third was judged seditious and burnt with the others "by the hands of the common hang-man." At this point Lilburne advises the petitioners that they have nothing left to petition for, except to inquire what a petitioner's privileges are. They reject his advice, and petition, also unsuccessfully, for an investigation of Parliament. The tract concludes with an Army petition, asking what the Army continually and unsuccessfully demanded—arrears, discharge from foreign service, allowances to war widows, and so forth. The circulation of such petitions in the first place gave the people a voice; their presentation with historical commentary showed the people that their voice was not respected. And these two factors together created a party. Meanwhile, Lilburne, in his petitions, in his tracts, and in his own person is constantly providing activity, amusement, and inspiration.

Though Lilburne's most explicit and conscious reasons for writing were immediate and topical,[74] he did also want and intend to continue to live in print. At any rate, that is where he does live now. The prolific self-consciousness of his prose, and its preoccupation with language and print, show how deep a part of him authorship was. Though he chose not to present himself as a literary man, because such a person is not a common Englishman, one comes finally to realize that a literary man is preeminently what he was. It is impossible to conceive of him otherwise; he does not even exist for us otherwise; and the skill with which he has concealed this fact from us and perhaps from himself, too, is his most impressive feat.

The sense we have of the urgent connection between his writing and the life surrounding it, the sense of the writing being turned toward and serving life, is also created by the prose and is part of its quality. When this characteristic manifests itself in specific local demands, we cannot honor them; we cannot sign Lilburne's petitions. But even for Lilburne, the petitions had a wider function; they were educational. For us, if they are a justifiable part of the whole design, they provide a local illustration of the large demand for commitment to human equality and justice that this prose makes of all its readers. That I think is a legitimate demand.

At the age of forty-one, in his final imprisonment in Dover Castle, John Lilburne became a Quaker. In his tract called *The Resurrection of John Lilburne*, he and his wife speak of the work that God is doing upon them, such work "as shall make us study our selves more than we have done." Now he distinguishes between his outer name "JOHN LILBURNE," and the "new, or inward spiritual name," which "no man knowes but he that hath it." [75] But if this conversion led to more profound self-analysis than he had engaged in previously, he left no record of it. The Lilburne that remains to us is the political John Lilburne, who, like John Milton and George Foxe, never publicly doubted his salvation.

But this same John Lilburne was a lifelong creator and student of himself. This Lilburne whom we know, his author's chosen image mirrored in the prose, is the symbolic common Englishman that Lilburne chose to be, and he repeatedly affirms and insists upon this identity in every successive overlapping section of his autobiography. Documenting vividly and fully the life of a political martyr, these sectional tracts are climaxed by the full-scale drama of the treason trial, and then descend gradually into stillness in the record of the subsequent years. The story that they tell is as compelling and at least as well-presented as anything in Foxe's *Book of Martyrs*. Although Lilburne cannot claim credit for the technique, its application is novel, and the result is art.

CHAPTER IV

ROBERT BURTON:
THE ANATOMY
OF DEMOCRITUS, JR.

WE HAVE SEEN IN DONNE THE ANGLICAN'S PERSISTENT EFFORT TO TURN life into art and to find in art among other things a means to anticipate one's own death and look back upon his life. The same dizzying confusion of one mode of being with another occurs in the life and work of Robert Burton, onetime fellow of Christ Church, Oxford, and author of that huge 842-page folio volume, *The Anatomy of Melancholy*.[1] The epitaph which he composed for himself, and which is inscribed upon his bust in Christ Church Chapel, reads as follows: "Paucis notus, paucioribus ignotus, hic jacet Democritus Junior, cui vitam dedit et mortem Melancholia."[2]

If Democritus Junior is a made-up character, the persona in whose name Burton wrote the *Anatomy of Melancholy*, then this epitaph is nonsense. A fictitious character does not die just because his author does. But if Burton *is* Democritus Junior, then he is both a "real" person and a persona, hence both mortal and immortal. Known to few as Burton, unknown to fewer as Democritus, he was given life and death by Melancholy. Here the possible meanings are numerous. The malady of melancholy was Burton's life. Writing the *Anatomy of Melancholy* was Burton's life. The *Anatomy* gave life to Democritus Junior. But Melancholy, man's portion in life, finally brought Burton to his death, and in some sense (for example, the sense in which Democritus lived through successive editions or stages of growth of the book) Democritus Junior died with him.

From all the available evidence, it would seem that the *Anatomy* was Burton's life. It might even be said that the book is a prototype for the transformation of man into art, and Burton was, I think, as conscious of what he was doing as a seventeenth-century writer could be. At present, at least, it would be impossible to write a conventional biography of him: Douglas Bush put almost all the facts we have into a footnote in his *English Literature in the Earlier Seventeenth Century*.[3] With the help of a few more details, some consideration of Burton's literary methods, and some responsible speculation, M. Jean Simon was able to write a biographical chapter; but Simon calls Burton's life "le désespoir du biographe." [4] Burton was born in Leicestershire in 1577, entered Brasenose College, Oxford, in 1593, was elected a Student of Christ Church in 1599, and lived at Christ Church for the rest of his life. He was granted the B.A. in 1602, the M.A. in 1605, and the B.D. in 1614. In 1616 he became Vicar of St. Thomas's in Oxford. The force and passion, subtlety and wit of his nature are more fully realized in his book than they seem ever to have been in his daily life.

Burton's age was Janus-faced, among other reasons, because of the way it stood between the oral past and the printed future.[5] A man could "live" in print, and in several ways. For the first time he could really have access to a world of books of all kinds: he could read both Aristotle and the latest news out of Brazil, and thus control the world and time without leaving his study.[6] Certainly the opening up of such a world amidst the great intellectual excitement of the period made possible what might seem to us an extravagant affection for reading, not as the good substitute for experience that earlier writers had found it, but as experience itself, both dangerous and compelling. Donne's "Hydroptique immoderate desire of humane learning and languages" [7] comes at once to mind. And if reading is experience, writing is life, and the life of the book indistinguishable from the life of the man. Pepys thought himself half-dead when he could no longer see to make his own journal entries,[8] and Burton tells us that the seventeenth century is such a "scribbling age" because men write to prove themselves alive (Pt. I, pp. 22–23).

In his own effort to live in prose, Burton adopts the pseudonym of Democritus Junior, but he does not maintain that pseudonym consistently. The shifting back and forth among his various selves and the commentary upon these selves constitute the most important and complex stylistic technique in the *Anatomy*. The "I" is not always the same "I," nor is it possible always to be sure who is supposed to be speaking at any particular time.

Burton's most limited "I" is Robert Burton the historical being, who provides simple autobiographical details: I was born in Warwickshire; my patroness is Lady Frances, Dowager Countess of

Exeter (Pt. II.2.3); I drink no wine (Pt. II.5.1.5); at Oxford we use smoke of juniper to sweeten our chambers (Pt. II.2.3); I have no wife or children (Pt. I, p. 18). These comments are introduced in scattered places throughout the book, and have been found sufficient by more than one critic for a full-scale psychological portrait of Burton the man.[9] At the same time, Burton in his second edition and thereafter deletes his name from the title page (although from the third edition on he included his picture), and asks us to believe that his book has no author at all, that it was written by the man-in-the-moon, or by no one (Pt. I, p. 15). In the course of *this* shift, he actually moves from no one to no one, from the *nobody* that is Robert Burton, M.A., to the book so comprehensive in scope that it can have been written by no one, because everyone is included in it.

This shift from anonymity to anonymity is effected partly by the creation of Democritus Junior. He is the supposed author of the book, as is explained in the very long preface, "Democritus Junior to the Reader," in which Burton discusses his style, his persona, his reasons for writing his book, and his attitudes toward the reader. Burton says he adopted this pseudonym for the obvious reason that it gives him more "liberty and freedom of speech"—that is, it stretches the private man into a public and ageless creature, the son of an ancient Greek, who can laugh at folly without fear of reprisal. He intends also to continue the work of Democritus the anatomist, who dissected animals in order to find out more about the nature of man.

Knowing something about Democritus the atomist as well as about Burton's method of procedure, we can add at least one other reason for the pseudonym. The atoms of Democritus fell ceaselessly through space, combining and recombining by chance—and thus the world of men came into being. Burton, too, combines atoms—fragments from the books of other men that came to him by chance as well as choice—and thus the world of the *Anatomy* is created, haphazardly, though also, of course, at Burton's whimsical pleasure. Lucretius, Democritus' apostle, stressed the liberating power of the atomic theory to free men's minds from superstitious fears, and Burton's book is partly inspired by the same intent. Both the malevolent will of Satan and the old humoural system are shown in this anatomy to be often less significant than they had been thought in determining a man's destiny—and a proper knowledge of physic and psychology, meanwhile, can help a man to rule himself.[10]

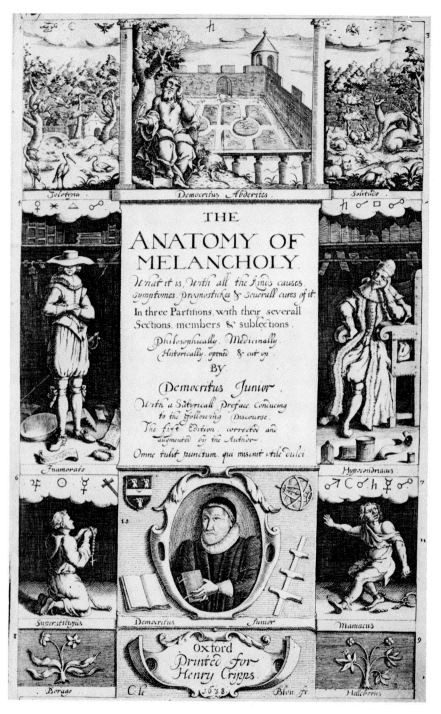

THE ANGLICAN IN ART
Robert Burton in the engraved frontispiece of
The Anatomy of Melancholy (5th edition)

Certainly, the explicit and implicit rationale of this persona is impressive, but Burton's intentions are too complex to allow him to give the persona full independence. The very fact that he has to explain his choice of the name undercuts Democritus' plausibility, and makes us conscious of Burton the author. Again, the technique mingles life with art. Melancholy is Burton's subject. But melancholy is equated with nothing less than the whole mind of man, which is represented in this book by Burton's mind. Since Burton's mind, or life, is both the book and the writing of the book, then the book and its writing must become the subject matter of the book and its writing. As usual with Anglican writers, one is forced to resort to the analogy of mirrors within mirrors.

The creation of the book life is the means by which Burton says he can overcome the melancholy of his worldly life: "I write of melancholy by being busy to avoid melancholy." "This playing labour," he calls the business of writing, and explicates his pun by describing authorship as a kind of parallel to the labor of childbirth (or of excretion): "I had *gravidum cor, foedum caput*, a kind of imposthume in my head, which I was very desirous to be unladen of, and could imagine no fitter evacuation than this" (Pt. I, pp. 20–21). In the highly important pages on his own style in the preface, he tells us that the book would have been written in Latin if he could have found a publisher willing to undertake the task. And he also pretends to apologize for its disheveled condition—like that of an unlicked bear cub; he says there was no time for the polishing he would like to have done.[11] But six editions and twenty years later, when the book is 60 per cent *longer* than it was and many changes have been made, the dishevelment is as much as ever a part of its character.[12] Now he says that he could not revise because it would just have been too difficult: he would rather start over with another book than attempt to correct this one.[13] All these comments, of course, encourage us to think of the book itself as a living person—by accident of birth English rather than Roman, full of faults that multiply as he grows older, able to increase his knowledge more easily than he can improve his character. In growing as it does over this extended period of time, the book literally imitates the growth of a living being. And since it is, in effect, Burton's collected works, it must have taken up a good deal of his actual life span.

The question of how to name this book-personality cannot be simply answered, and not just because Democritus is rarely mentioned beyond the preface. There is in the book a sense of universality that is almost more than can be defined by the term "cosmic personality" if that term is only to describe the mind of Burton or Democritus. It *is*, of course, literally the mind of Burton that is expressed here. But it is the mind of Burton, not at any one point in history, but at six different points all combined. And when we add up these six different views, we are including in them the omnivorous reading of a lifetime. This quantitative and spatial presentation of what could not have simultaneous literal existence is perhaps the main reason why one constantly has the sense of a third person, besides Burton and Democritus, a person who is represented by them but is larger than the sum of his parts. The cosmic personality is given its nature and scope primarily by quotations, by the use of resonant oral material, and by the specific cultivation of cosmic language and imagery. Each of these techniques reflects this odd blurring of focus between Burton in one or another of his roles and the larger totality into which he seems to be absorbed.

The book grows, most notably, by absorbing quotations. Burton accuses himself of plagiarism, though he defends his right to "this my Macaronicon" on the grounds that he has made sufficient acknowledgment of his borrowings (by and large he has), and that "the matter is theirs most part, and yet mine, *apparet unde sumptum sit* (which Seneca approves), *aliud tamen quam unde sumptum sit apparet;* which nature doth with the aliment of our bodies incorporate, digest, assimilate, I do *concoquere quod hausi*, dispose of what I take" (Pt. I, p. 25). The suggestion of organic growth is purposeful; the "I" digests and assimilates other writings into himself. Dom Jean Leclercq has reminded us of the similarity between eating and talking in an oral culture.[14] Here Burton takes advantage of a typographical age to dramatize an oral-age phenomenon.

The use of quotation extends the personality in another dimension. If the book's basic character is necessarily English, it is nevertheless a macaronic English; the character becomes a world citizen through quoting Greek, Latin, and Italian, and referring to sources representing many other countries and times as well.[15] There are places where it is difficult to tell where Burton's "I" leaves off and the source begins, or vice versa, partly because the assimilation is effective, partly because he sometimes has parallel sentences alternating within a single period, partly because he often provides free translations of passages that have already been partly quoted in the original, so that the progression may be from the original, to the original paraphrased, to Burton, or some more complex version of that sequence. Quotations are often misquoted, to produce a further blurring. Some of his more endearing uses of quotation occur in passages that would seem to be very immediate or very personal, as in the passage given above where he defends his style, or when he says of himself, "I have no wife nor children good or bad to provide for" (Pt. I, p. 18). Such employment of quotation warns us that even in Burton on his lowest or most specifically autobiographical level, we are dealing with a person whose life is books. "The mind is all" (Pt. II.3.3), he says; and his mind is this storehouse and assimilator of learning.

The assimilation of the quotations could not be complete unless Burton were really willing to plagiarize. Since he is not, he acknowledges his sources by calling attention to them in an unequalled stream of varied synonyms for "as so and so says": "approves," "declares," "hath commented," "gives an instance," "relates," "observes," "holds," "repeats," "supposed," "confirms," "condemns," "cries out on," "prescribes," "rings," "explodes," "laughs to scorn," "cracks," "scoffs," "witnesseth," "denounced," "subscribes," "mutters." The endless list represents a kind of mastication, Burton or the book chewing on the approval or muttering of others, reminding us that assimilation is in process. Very often Burton neglects to say in the text *whose* crying out or ringing he has cited, identifying the author only as "he"—"as he says." One can find the reference in a note, but the text suggests such familiarity with the source that again one experiences it as being more than half assimilated.

There are inevitably a number of unacknowledged quotations, many of them representative of the furnishing of a seventeenth-century mind: "If he be in sorrow, need, sickness, or any other adversity" (Pt. I.1.1.); "the remembrance of it is most grievous unto us" (Pt. II.3.5); "death is but a perpetual sleep" (Pt. II.3.5); "*O quam te memorem*" (Pt. II.2.4). Some phrases recur again and again, in changing contexts. "*Spretaeque injuria formae*," [16] for example, is to Burton an enormously evocative line because it recalls an archetypal example of action and psychological reaction. These phrases, recurrent and reminding, help to establish the impression that the book is a living mind, containing familiar echoes. In our own time, stream-of-consciousness writers have made more disciplined and structural use of such material.

Burton's constant and massive use of authorities, directly and indirectly quoted, has frequently evoked the critical comment that he is so busy giving all the arguments on all sides of a subject that he has no time to be on any side himself, or that his own position is weakened or buried.[17] There are several answers to this objection, at least one of which directly bears on the suggestion that the book-personality encompasses its personae.

Burton himself, and perhaps Burton when represented as Democritus, is antagonistic toward useless or theologically impertinent questions: "I will end the controversy in Austin's words, 'Better doubt of things concealed, than to contend about uncertainties, where Abraham's bosom is, and hell-fire'" (Pt. II.2.3); "But why should the sun and moon be angry, or take exceptions at mathematicians and philosophers, whenas the like measure is offered unto God Himself, by a company of theologasters?" (Pt. II.2.3). He will mention such issues both as illustrative of the means to certain kinds of melancholy, and as enjoyable subjects for speculation when one is in the right mood. But, like Sir Thomas Browne, he is more interested in the speculation than in the conclusion.

When there are practical problems—controversies over the efficacy of medicines, for example—he also often hesitates to give unequivocal answers, and here his position is a kind of relativism. While he believes in authority, he has no belief that one authority can know everything, or that one medicine can heal all men. He is most skeptical about absolute, generalizing statements on any subject. And he will try to find the relationship between the absolute statements and specific cases: for example, some say carp are good to eat; some say they are bad; the solution may be that it depends on where they have grown and fed. Some say one medicine is good for melancholy; some say another: the solution may be that every melancholy man is a special case, and must find his own cure. He will find the cure *in books*. But Burton's amassing of authorities is done not just for the sake of thoroughness, but because he sees that not all authorities are relevant to the needs of all. Repeatedly, he suggests that one of the merits of his book is its gathering into one place the varied views that might otherwise be difficult for a reader to come by (D., p. 297; Pt.

III.4.2.6). Thus, here is another Janus-point: this all-inclusive, ency-clopedic, Renaissance mind of a book is an advertisement for the age of specialization. Doctors, says Burton, who claim the ability to cure all kinds of ills are quacks.

Burton, nevertheless, as Burton, does express his opinion con-stantly on all sorts of subjects. The reason his opinions are not more evident is that he is only one among innumerable characters and points of view represented in the book. The defense for his inclu-siveness on the most comprehensive level is that the book-mind is a universal one, including all sorts and conditions of men and argu-ments, and taking sides with none. It becomes no one by being ev-eryone. On both its most important levels, when we consider the *Anatomy* as a medical book and when we consider it as a universal mind, the answer to the objection that Burton weakens his own posi-tion is that he does not *have* a position in the same sense in which the authors whom he quotes do. His whole purpose is to include as many different positions and possibilities as he can.

Words from a thousand books are assimilated by the speaker, as if he were eating and growing fat on them. The oral past is joined with the written present, the encyclopedic present with the specialist fu-ture. A second important way in which the book achieves life and cosmic extension involves another Janus-use of oral and print cul-tures. The "life of the mind" is the opposite of sterile or quiescent because the "I" is so colloquial and gossipy in manner, and because many of the sources upon which this lively mind loves to feed are resonantly oral.

These are not entirely separable points. The "I" controls the tone of the book, and, as we shall see, his tone, even when he is reporting on the contents of quite sober and scholarly books, is robustly anec-dotal, rather than analytical. He proceeds by telling stories.[18] Thus, even sources which one could never think of as oral in themselves become so in Burton's handling of them. And yet it is clear that he is gossiping about *books*. Typically, he justifies his lowbrow gossiping with a Latin quotation: "I say farther with him yet, I have inserted (*levicula quaedam et ridicula ascribere non sum gravatus, circum-foranea quaedam e theatris, a plateis, etiam e popinis*) . . ." (Pt. III.1.1.1). That he sees no contradiction in his choice of a Latin quo-tation to defend his description of *current* levities is explained by the fact that for him current levities may be fetched from Homer as well as from modern medical books, but very rarely direct from life. The book-personality, feeding on this material, spans the centuries and also enjoys the freedoms and the peculiar resonances both of sound and print.

Burton supplies sound effects to illustrate his stories: "Sound trumpets, fife and drums" (Pt. I.2.2.2); "he will ride a gallop, a gallop, etc." (Pt. II.3.3); "let drums beat on, trumpets sound taratantarra" (Pt. II.3.7). And sometimes, as I shall show at length later on, he constructs scenes made up of dialogue direct and partly direct. In other words, he uses the printed page to evoke sound. That he thinks both in speech and print is evident from the way he habitually couples the two in speaking of his own work: "These following lines, when they shall be recited or hereafter read" (Pt. I, p. 38); "*facite haec charta loquatur anus*" (Pt. III.1.1.1); "I am not willing to publish it [a last remedy for jealousy]; if you be very desirous to know it, when I meet you next I will peradventure tell you what it is in your ear" (Pt. III.3.4.2). We, of course, use words like "speak" and "write" interchangeably, but more as dead metaphors than with conscious intent. Burton's language is clearly designed to call attention to itself, and has the effect of presenting him as a gossip, chattering like an old woman, or whispering in his listener's ear.

Although he sometimes sneers at contemporary literature like "English chronicles, playbooks, news sheets" (Pt. I.1.1.4), his own library was full of such reading matter, and his book contains innumerable references to plays both classical and contemporary. Role-playing is important for him, and for the cure of the melancholy patient, and, of course, he reiterates the familiar metaphor of life as a play: "We must so be gone sooner or later all, and as Calliopius in the comedy took his leave of his spectators and auditors, *Vos valete et plaudite, Calliopius recensui*, must we bid the world farewell (*exit* Calliopius), and having now played our parts, for ever be gone" (Pt. II.3.5). Typically, he stuffs the quotation into his own sentence, without wholly assimilating it. It is engulfed, trapped, his property, yet it retains its own life and dramatic worth—and typically he includes a stage direction, so that the dialogue is supplemented by action.

I shall have considerably more to say about Burton's various dramatic poses in my discussion of his relationship with his readers. In this consideration of his enlivening of written sources, the relevant

role is that of gossip. Some of the best illustrations of Burton's colloquial manner are in the section on love-melancholy, a section which
was very dear to him and upon which he lavished particular attention in the successive editions of the *Anatomy*, so that its growth in
volume is greater than that of other parts: [19]

I could tell you such another story of a spindle that was fired by a fair lady's
looks, or fingers, some say, I know not well whether, but fired it was by report, and of a cold bath that suddenly smoked and was very hot when naked
Caelia came into it: *Miramur quis sit tantus et unde vapor*, etc. But of all the
tales in this kind, that is the most memorable of Death himself, when he
should have stroken a sweet young virgin with his dart, he fell in love with
the object. Many such could I relate which are to be believed with a
poetical faith (Pt. III.2.2.2).

It is not unusual for Burton to treat a source thus casually, with a
"some say" or "by report," or even to pretend or to admit that he is
ignorant of or has forgotten his source. These devices and his willingness to mingle fact with fiction combine with the liveliness and intrinsic interest of his stories to produce in the reader just that blend
of belief and disbelief with which one so often listens to gossip. His
intimate address to the reader, "I could tell you," is typical, and increases one's sense of listening to confidences. The nature of the material itself in this section heightens an effect which Burton achieves
everywhere in the *Anatomy*.

His own faith in the printed page sometimes seems absolute. In one
of his personal comments, he tells us that his mother had a talent for
healing the sick. One of her remedies involved a spider and an amulet,
comprising a cure which Burton thought "most absurd," "till at
length, rambling amongst authors," he "found this very medicine in
Dioscorides, approved by Matthiolus, repeated by Aldrovandus,"
whereupon he "began to have a better opinion of it" (Pt. II.5.1.5).
Having listed a number of writers who speak of palm trees falling in
love, he evidently still feels some doubt himself, and hastens to add
these comments:

If any man think this which I say to be a tale, let him read that story of two
palm-trees in Italy, the male growing at Brundusium, the female at Otranto
(related by Jovianus Pontanus in an excellent poem, sometime tutor to Al-
phonsus Junior, King of Naples, his secretary of state, and a great philosopher), "which were barren, and so continued a long time," till they came to
see one another growing up higher, though many stadiums asunder. Pierius, in
his Hieroglyphics, and Melchior Guilandinus, *mem. 3, tract. de papyro*, cites

this story of Pontanus for a truth. See more in Salmuth, *Comment, in Pancirol. de nova repert. tit. 1, de novo orbe*, Mizaldus, *Arcanorum lib. 2*, Sandys' Voyages, *lib. 2, fol.* 103, etc. (Pt. III.2.1.1.).[20]

Philosophy supported by poetry, and poetry by travel books! In another place, he interrupts a listing of successful love baits to say, "Who cannot parallel these stories out of his experience?" (Pt. III, 2.2.4). But what follows this question is an anecdote about a gallant named Speucippus, taken from "that Greek Aristaenetus," and Burton never does get around to telling us about his own experience (except that by this time the reader expects Burton's experience to be of this or that Greek writer, rather than of daily life).

What does he mean when he says, "Many more such could I relate which are to be believed with a poetical faith?" For one thing, he means to qualify his faith in books in at least one important way. He is not trying to prove anything by the scientific method. Rather, he wants to set down those tales which best illustrate the human condition, by means of the universal human method of gossip. Source and accuracy of information are less important than vividness, and illumination of what the gossiper would have us believe. Even the palm trees serve in this respect as illustrations both of the human desire for marvels and of the fierceness of human love, for "if such fury be in vegetals, what shall we think of sensible creatures? how much more violent and apparent shall it be in them!" (Pt. III.2.1.1). This theory of Burton's is precisely spelled out many times in such comments as these: "These are tales, you will say, but they have most significant morals, and do well express those ordinary proceedings of doting lovers" (Pt. III.2.2.4); "Whether this be a true story, or a tale, I will not much contend; it serves to illustrate this which I have said" (Pt. III.2.2.4).

Burton's most habitual, characteristic, and interesting kinds of sources are proverbs, myths, fables, and superstitions. He gathers in this material avidly and aptly, to such an extent that sometimes his whole style seems directly shaped by that of the proverb:

If thou be in woe, sorrow, want, distress, in pain, or sickness, think of that of our apostle, "God chastiseth them whom he loveth." "They that sow in tears, shall reap in joy" (Ps. cxxvi, 6). "As the furnace proveth the potter's vessel, so doth temptation try men's thoughts" (Ecclus. xxvii, 5); 'tis for thy good, *periisses nisi periisses:* hadst thou not been so visited, thou hadst been utterly undone; "as gold in the fire," so men are tried in adversity (Pt. II.3.1.1).

And so on. Again, it is clear that his book is not intended to prove in a "scientific" way; what Burton intends is to be true to human experience, and proverbs as the reflection of what has most frequently been thought and said would seem to him the quintessence of human experience.

His tales, like some of the phrases discussed earlier, often seem archetypal; they are familiar to most men as dream, nightmare, fear, or wish, e.g., the story of a man lost in a strange city who asks for lodging and is directed to a whorehouse (Pt. III.2.2.5); the man who jumped into the river when his sweetheart asked him for this proof of love, and then drowned because he could not swim (Pt. III.2.3); the poor drunk who was persuaded for a day, as a joke, that he was a great lord (Pt. II.2.4); the man who burned his birthplace (Pt. II.3.2). Of course there are madder tales as well (though still standard types), as he moves into the realm of the psychotic: the man who would not urinate for fear he would drown the city (Pt. I.3.1.3); the man who thought he was butter and would be melted by the sun (Pt. I.3.1.3). He is trying to delineate the range of human experience in melancholy by providing the illustrations that seem most evocative, that in fact achieve an almost mythic status by their very nature as well as by their occurrence in literature before and after Burton.

And while these tales have the quality of oral literature, they also share the distinction of having been written down. At the end of his longest listing of proverbs, Burton says, "Look for more in Isocrates, Seneca, Plutarch, Epictetus, etc., and for defect, consult with cheese-trenchers and painted cloths" (Pt. II.3.8). That is to say, if you are still not satisfied, look for popular proverbs written on wooden bowls and samplers. Burton's literary mind is a very inclusive one, and a kind of parallel to Jung's collective unconscious. All his tales are at least relatively sophisticated: the collective conscious has its life in print.

While he rejects superstitions with the zeal of a Lucretius, he frequently employs the myths that we might include under superstition: in illustrating one human vagary or another, he indiscriminately mingles tales of classical gods with those of men, their lives and loves being made to seem as relevant as ours. At the other end of the scale, his use of the fables of Aesop and others compares men to animals. He tests the range of humanity. Man, though a poor creature comparable to dog and pig, is also a fabulous and mythic creature, sharing even his faults with those of gods. And the book-mind is a cosmic personality, which itself includes and suffers the range of human possibility, time, and experience.

Burton's indifferent use of fact and fiction absolves him from the controversy as to whether history or poetry is a higher form. To him, all is equal so long as it is true to experience, in a way that is representative or symbolic, as is the case with the man who burned his birthplace. The oral-literary gossip technique mediates between fact and fiction, by its very rhetoric promising only that the speaker is intensely interested in human affairs. This technique gives Burton more freedom of range of experience and tone than would ordinarily be possible in a single work of art.

A related point which need not be exhaustively considered is that Burton's world is not only oral and literary: he makes constant reference in very specific ways to painting, sculpture, hieroglyphics, emblems, and music. Sometimes such references simply announce that no artist could describe the symptoms of melancholy, and thereby intensify our sense of the difficulty of his work. But even when this intention is present it may be combined with his desire to add another dimension to a description, as here:

> What therefore *Timanthes* did in his picture of *Iphigenia*, now ready to be sacrificed; when he had painted *Calchas* mourning, *Vlysses* sad, but most sorrowful *Menelaus*, and shewed all his Art in expressing variety of affections, hee couered the maides father, *Agamemnons* head with a vaile, and left it to euery spectator to conceiue what he would himselfe, for that true passion & sorrow *in summo gradu*, such as his was, could not by any art be deciphred. What he did in his picture, J will doe in describing the Symptomes of Despaire, imagine what thou canst, feare, sorrow, furies, griefe, paine terror angor, dismall, gastly, tedious, irksome, &c. it is not sufficient, it comes farre short, no tongue can tell, no heart conceiue it (D., p. 279; Pt. III.4.2.4).

Both here and in the following passage, the painting provides a kind of emblem for Burton's commentary: ". . . Albertus Durer paints Melancholy, like a sad woman leaning on her arm with fixed looks, neglected habit, etc.; held therefore by some proud, soft, sottish, or half-mad, as the Abderites esteemed of Democritus, and yet of a deep reach, excellent apprehension, judicious, wise and witty . . ." (Pt. I.3.1.2). Probably his most frequent references are to emblems, both because they combine words and pictures, and because the emblem books would have been much more available to a non-traveller than any other kind of art.

For just as the oral character of Burton's work is largely Burton's invention, so, with most of the other art works mentioned, his source is literary. The emblems are easy for him to see for himself. Otherwise, he must generally rely on the descriptions of others. Hence, his references to the other arts are often embedded in anecdotes of some sort, sometimes having to do with the artist's life, or with the particular reaction to the work of some melancholy viewer. Of all the seventeenth-century writers whose universe is made of words, Burton may have had the most limited personal life and the largest reading life; of all these writers, he may have known the greatest variety of ways to experience and extend the world in language.

When we turn to Burton's own comments upon his task and its requirements, it becomes clear that while Democritus is allowed to be superior to time and space, this superiority is finally not enough; and since one Democritus is not adequate to his task, the cosmic personality must be mankind. We are often asked to follow in the footsteps of Democritus, who gives his credentials thus, in a passage which typically blurs Democritus with Burton:

I ward all with Democritus' buckler, his medicine shall salve it; strike where thou wilt, and when: *Democritus dixit*, Democritus will answer it. It was written by an idle fellow, at idle times, about our Saturnalian or Dionysian feasts, when, as he said, *nullum libertati periculum est*, servants in old Rome had liberty to say and do what them list. When our countrymen sacrificed to their goddess Vacuna, and sat tippling by their Vacunal fires, I writ this and published this (Pt. I, p. 122).

Democritus of old could not know all. Burton speculates about what might happen "if every man had a window in his breast . . . or . . . that he could *cubiculorum obductas foras recludere et secreta cordium penetrare*, which Cyprian desired, open doors and locks, shoot bolts, as Lucian's Gallus did with a feather of his tail: or Gyges' invisible ring, or some rare perspective glass, or otacousticon, which would so multiply *species* that a man might hear and see all at once . . ." (Pt. I, pp. 68–69). This is really what Burton-Democritus is trying to do, and he sees his task as infinite.

He tries to visualize what it means to see all men and all times, not just by strolling through pleasant landscapes or gathering anecdotes from a hundred different countries, but also by compiling statistics.

To learn how men suffer in war, for example, one may try to add up the number of men who have died in wars, or fought, or received wounds or decorations. How *many* men are all men? Consider in this typical passage the apparently intimate knowledge and concern, the fingertip information combined with occasional uncertainty:

The siege of Troy lasted ten years, eight months; there died 870,000 Grecians, 670,000 Trojans at the taking of the city, and after were slain 276,000 men, women, and children of all sorts. Caesar killed a million, Mahomet the second Turk 300,000 persons; Sicinius Dentatus fought in an hundred battles, eight times in single combat he overcame, had forty wounds before, was rewarded with 140 crowns, triumphed nine times for his good service. M. Sergius had 32 wounds; Scaeva, the centurion, I know not how many; every nation had their Hectors, Scipios, Caesars, and Alexanders. Our Edward the Fourth was in 26 battles afoot: and as they do all, he glories in it, 'tis related to his honour. At the siege of Hierusalem, 1,100,000 died with sword and famine. At the battle of Cannae, 70,000 men were slain, as Polybius records, and as many at Battle Abbey with us; and 'tis no news to fight from sun to sun, as they did, as Constantine and Licinius, etc. (Pt. I, pp. 56–57).

In this passage, too, he goes back and forth between general statistics concerning dead and wounded in single battles, and individual statistics about how many wounds one man received in his career. The disparate character of the figures makes its own contribution to the cosmic range. The method of narration is saga-like, with its nearly omniscient and all-present "I," but it is clear that this narrator's omnipresence is, as always, in his books, even though he has absorbed them as experience. Although he piles up numerous accounts, tabulating the deaths of millions of men, he cannot reach an end, and the sentence stops, as Burton's typically do, with an "etc." Although he has worn himself out, he accepts the fact that the subject is not exhausted: he cannot hold in his mind at once or set down on a page at once all the vicissitudes of man. The next best thing is to admit it by using the "etc.," letting the openness of the sentence suggest the infinity that the page cannot contain.

This sense of openness is not confined to a single technique. At the end of paragraph or section, we are constantly confronted by lines like "Read more in Poggius Florentinus, Valdanus, Plutarch, etc." His massive footnotes interlarding every page and almost every sentence perform a like function in supplying further details and references. And so we see that while so much literature, so much of time and space is being constantly assimilated into the book, the reader is also invited to move in the other direction and for both reasons to sense that the book is lacking in conventional boundaries. This openness of form is essential just because statistics cannot enclose infinity.

Not only is there an infinity of men: the psychological complications common to men are also infinite, even if one limits oneself only to the consideration of melancholy. After all, "if thou shalt either conceive, or climb to see, thou shalt soon perceive that all the world is mad, that it is melancholy, dotes" (Pt. I, p. 39). Almost any Puritan would have objected to Burton's assumption that melancholy is intrinsic to mankind: "You may . . . as soon find the motion of a bird in the air as the heart of man, a melancholy man" (Pt. I.3.1.4). Nevertheless, this is how Burton sees it, and therefore believes his task to be so labyrinthine and Herculean that one might as well reckon up the motes of the sun or the sands of the sea:

> To anatomize this humour aright, through all the members of this our *microcosmos*, is as great a task as to reconcile those chronological errors in the Assyrian monarchy, find out the quadrature of a circle, the creeks and sounds of the north-east or north-west passages, and all out as good a discovery as that hungry Spaniard's of *Terra Australis Incognita*, as great a trouble as to perfect the motion of Mars and Mercury, which so crucifies our astronomers, or to rectify the Gregorian calendar (Pt. I, p. 38).

Repeatedly, he compares the anatomy of melancholy to the most difficult problems that have been or could be devised, particularly problems having to do with the character of the world itself. It is as hard to figure out man as to map the world, because in the familiar microcosm-macrocosm analogy which he uses here, man *is* a world.

When Burton speaks of the "world" specifically, it is almost always in such a context as to suggest that the world is at man's mercy. Man creates or disposes of it as he will: "Alexander was sorry because there were no more worlds for him to conquer" (Pt. I, p. 60); man's sins "crucify the world" (Pt. I, p. 97); men "will so long blow the coals of contention till all the world be consumed with fire" (Pt. I, p. 56); men "blear the world's eyes by flattery" (Pt. III.1.3). Clearly what he is saying is that man destroys man by his vanity, for man himself is the only world there is. *Men* are killed, a million here, five thousand there: by these means, man or the world, and hence Burton as the book, is crucified. Therefore, " 'tis not one Democritus will serve turn to laugh in these days; we have now need of a 'Democritus to laugh at Democritus'; one jester to flout at another, one fool to fleer at another: a great stentorian Democritus, as big as that Rhodian Colossus" (Pt. I, p. 52).

Burton briefly makes the effort to construct his own Utopia, where he can be that Rhodian Colossus, and freely domineer. But although his interest in this project was sustained, as the changes through various editions show,[21] he could not commit himself to it as the solution to the world's problems. Though his suggestions are practical, he is only able to control his Utopia because it is entirely his own. And the more fruitful effort to be the stentorian Democritus is in his recognition that as men destroy each other, they may also laugh at and pity one another in themselves. Man is his own worst enemy, but men are all members of one body, the world, which is represented by the Rhodian Colossus that is the *Anatomy of Melancholy*.

The reasons for the fragmentation of Burton's persona become more apparent. He both identifies himself with this concept of man, and rejects it. He can sit apart, a little anatomist in a college garden—a nobody in his own book; or he can be Democritus the cynic, coolly analyzing man's frailties; or he can become the book, and, symbolically, all men.

In turning from Burton's "I" to the relationship between the "I" and the audience, one of the first things a reader is likely to notice is the shiftiness of the pose. Burton is constantly aware of the discrepancy between his own human limitations, and the wider capacities of Democritus and of the book personality. But he capitalizes upon this discrepancy by emphasizing his weakness. For example, after a lengthy exposition of the miseries of single women, he breaks off thus: "But where am I? Into what subject have I rushed? What have I to do with nuns, maids, virgins, widows? I am a bachelor myself, and lead a monastic life in a college . . ." (Pt. I.3.2.4). This kind of comment is always a sign that Burton is about to become his wiliest, most Chaucerian self. He closes these remarks by saying, "though my subject necessarily require it, I will say no more." And the paragraph ends. The reader, forced to conclude that Burton is putting his modesty before the demands of his subject, must also realize, even if partly unconsciously, that a bachelor who leads a monastic life may very well have experienced miseries something like those that trouble nuns, maids, virgins, and widows. Burton is using his personal life at this point to give his book-self additional interest and authority, even while he seems to be doing just the opposite. The apology implicitly makes the bridge between the externally restricted life of the unimaginative man, and the wide and rich experience of the imaginative author. Thus, when he continues in the next paragraph, "And yet I must and will say something more," the reader is relieved and impressed.

One particularly significant example of this technique shows clearly his awareness of the problem of limited versus cosmic personality. Discussing the nature of the universe, in his "Digression of Air," he has involved himself in a lengthy and satiric discussion of various theologies that attempt to explain the world or God. He then breaks off thus:

> But hoo! I am now gone quite out of sight, I am almost giddy with roving about: I could have ranged farther yet, but I am an infant, and not able to dive into these profundities or sound these depths, not able to understand, much less to discuss. I leave the contemplation of these things to stronger wits, that have better ability and happier leisure to wade into such philosophical mysteries; for put case I were as able as willing, yet what can one man do? I will conclude with Scaliger, *Nequaquam nos homines sumus, sed partes hominis; ex omnibus aliquid fieri potest, idque non magnum; ex singulis fere nihil* (Pt. II.2.3).

At the beginning, of course, he is still speaking satirically; and by stressing his weakness really emphasizes his own wisdom as against the follies of those who pry into and make pronouncements upon matters about which they know little or nothing. No one man or group of men can possibly set up to know all, but "*ex omnibus aliquid fieri potest*"—which is clearly just what Burton has done by setting up his book-personality, made up of his own varied personae together with the minds of men of all times. "*Ex omnibus aliquid . . . idque non magnum*"—hence the use of "etc." Only by including all that he can, and then leaving the book as open as he can, is it possible for him to suggest cosmic Man.

Burton's attitude toward his audience is clarified by his enumeration of the purposes for which he is writing—to avoid melancholy; to make clear, by "showing himself," that he knows something about melancholy; to make an antidote out of the prime cause of his disease; to help others out of fellow feeling; to make men know themselves; and to bring them to moderation. The first and third reasons imply that he can afford to be indifferent to the popular success his book may achieve. And he often tells us that if he does no one else good, he does good to himself, or that if no one else is interested in a given aspect of his subject, he is (Pt. II.3.1.1). His second reason for writing, though, commits him to appearing in public. "Peradventure [I write] as others do, for fame, to show myself (*Scire tuum nihil est, nisi te scire hoc sciat alter*). I might be of Thucydides' opinion, 'To know a thing and not to express it, is all one as if he knew it not' " (Pt. I, p. 21). Between "peradventure" and "might be," the reader cannot help sensing a kind of ambivalence in Burton about the propriety of this reason. The self must be confirmed by the testimony of others. An audience is necessary. But the suggestion of vanity involved in "showing oneself" keeps Burton's tone irresolute.

On the other hand, this ambiguity may be only another Burtonian trick. For if the presence of an audience confirms the book-personality, the book can create the kind of audience it wants, by building into itself a dialogue with that audience, or by employing the kind of manipulative rhetoric that I have already illustrated. Burton anticipates objections to his title, his subject, and his style, and answers them by giving reasons and precedents. He repeatedly and at length apologizes for his incompetence, only by some quick twist to cut the reader's ground from under him:

And for those other faults of barbarism, Doric dialect, extemporanean style, tautologies, apish imitation, a rhapsody of rags gathered together from several dung-hills, excrements of authors, toys and fopperies confusedly tumbled out, without art, invention, judgment, wit, learning, harsh, raw, rude, phantastical, absurd, insolent, indiscreet, ill-composed, indigested, vain, scurrile, idle, dull, and dry; I confess all ('tis partly affected), thou canst not think worse of me than I do of myself. 'Tis not worth the reading, I yield it, I desire thee not to lose time in perusing so vain a subject, I should be peradventure loath myself to read him or thee so writing; 'tis not *operae pretium*. All I say is this, that I have precedents for it, which Isocrates calls *perfugium iis qui peccant*, others as absurd, vain, idle, illiterate, etc. *Nonnulli alii idem fecerunt*, others have done as much, it may be more, and perhaps thou thyself, *Novimus et qui te, etc.* We have all our faults; *scimus, et hanc veniam, etc.*, thou censurest me, so have I done others, and may do thee (Pt. I, p. 26).

His artful listing of his faults is followed by the news that this faulty style is partly affected, which at once partly disarms the critic. Then after encouraging the critic again by his own self-criticism, he says that he has precedents for his style—and then undercuts himself by explaining that his precedents are as worthless as he is. Immediately, however, the bridge is made between worthless precedents and the reader, who may be guilty of similar displays: "thou censurest me, so have I done others, and may do thee." We will see this final technique used repeatedly in various ways in Burton's relationship with the reader. For if the audience is part of the book-personality, part of "Burton," then it makes sense for Burton repeatedly to force the audience to change places with him. The reversing of roles connects them, makes everyone see everything from all possible viewpoints, frees Burton from the spotlight, and again forces the question, Which is life and which is art? To put the effect of the technique in another way, since it is clear that Burton's folly reflects the world's (and the reader's), the reader has to accept his reflection or play the hypocrite.

Thus, not only is the making of the book-personality a main theme of the book; the reader's reaction is, too. And the readers, or all men, are part of the book in this way just as they are represented in its corporate personality, and in its infinitude of listings of symptoms, diseases, situations. "How shall I hope to express myself to each man's humour and conceit, or to give satisfaction to all?" he asks, and the question has a double effect. For, in a sense, he means that he wants to do just that: his aim is to include or imply everything. But, of course, he is also open-ending this problem as he does everything else. His book even implies readers who will not read *him;* no one can please all: "If you like not this, get you to another inn . . . go read something else" (Pt. I, p. 28).

Once the willing reader permits himself to be drawn into the book, another of its functions becomes clear. When Burton says he wants to make an antidote out of the prime cause of his disease, he means that he will avoid melancholy by writing about it; the construction of the book-self is psychotherapy. The reader is also to avoid melancholy by reading about it. Despite its grandiose typographical outlines, the book's practical purpose is not to make authoritative conclusions about this vast subject, but to act as medicine upon its readers. It is for this reason, obviously, that from edition to edition the creative and anecdotal sections of the book increase at such a disproportionate rate in comparison to the more scientific ones. It is true that Burton includes prescriptions in one or two instances, but he is anxious not to encourage that kind of do-it-yourself medicine. Hence, he is apt to put such passages in Latin, omit part of the technical directions, or refer the reader to another source. The book is to be, not to teach, medicine. That is one reason for such lengthy presentation of opposite viewpoints on various subjects, and another reason why he does not always move directly toward a reasoned and tested conclusion. The opposite viewpoints are interesting in themselves, as an aspect of humanity; and a reader who is able to become interested in humanity may be cured of melancholy.

A remedy for melancholy, according to Burton, is to be kept in the company of your friends, not to be left alone (Pt. II.2.6.4). Burton is not always friendly, but he never leaves the reader alone. Almost all his stylistic techniques force us to take an active part in responding to the prose—the apologies that take the drowsy reader unaware, the constant confrontations between Burton and his audience, the necessity of choosing this conclusion or that. Burton often directly challenges the imagination. Let the lover separate his mistress from her gorgeous attire, and then see if he still loves her: "Suppose thou saw her in a base beggar's weed, or else dressed in some old hirsute attires out of fashion, foul linen, coarse raiment, besmeared with soot . . . wouldst thou affect her as thou dost?" (Pt. III.2.5.3). Let the reader explicate or apply the text: "A mouse (saith an apologer) was brought up in a chest, there fed with fragments of bread and cheese, thought there could be no better meat, till coming forth at last, and feeding liberally of other variety of viands, loathed his former life: moralize this fable by thyself" (Pt. III.2.5.2). Burton consistently speaks to the reader, often in the imperative, either satirically or seriously ordering him to make personal application of the text: "Now go and brag of thy gentility" (Pt. II.3.2); "Be thou such a one; let thy misery be what it will, what it can, with patience endure it; thou mayst be restored as he was" (Pt. II.3.3). These directives are reminiscent of the part of the sermon called the "application," [22] in which the minister applies to his auditory the text that he has previously explained. They are a bit sharper in tone than the application generally is, but they share the oral immediacy that makes the listener sit up and take notice. Like earlier techniques, too, this helps to make of the reader what the book wants—to exercise a control as direct and personal as that of speech over the unseen audience.

Another very central way in which Burton involves the reader in his prose is the apparently informal sentence structure so common in his age.[23] The writer refuses to detach himself from his prose, but insists upon making the sentences appear to mirror his mind, not as that mind presents an ordered argument from which its own confusions and doubts have been abstracted, but rather as the mind struggles with these confusions and doubts from moment to moment.

This may be, in fact, like other techniques that I have mentioned, a means of compensating for the detachment of print. As the writer chooses to seem undisciplined, or to be constructing his order as he goes, he invites the reader to endure with him the pains and gratifications of self-discovery rather than easily reading the conclusions abstracted from the experiment. In a sense, reading the book under these conditions becomes the same task that writing it was; Burton's prose is singularly exhausting to read:

Some are afraid that they shall have every fearful disease they see others have, hear of, or read, and dare not therefore hear or read of any such subject, no, not of melancholy itself, lest by applying to themselves that which they hear or read, they should aggravate and increase it. If they see one possessed, bewitched, an epileptic paroxysm, a man shaking with the palsy, or giddyheaded, reeling or standing in a dangerous place, etc., for many days after it runs in their minds, they are afraid they shall be so too, they are in like danger, as Perkins, *cap.* 12, *sect.* 2, well observes in his Cases of Conscience, and many times by violence of imagination they produce it. They cannot endure to see any terrible object, as a monster, a man executed, a carcass, hear the devil named, or any tragical relation seen, but they quake for fear, *Hecatas somniare sibi videntur* (Lucian), they dream of hobgoblins, and may not get it out of their minds a long time after: they apply (as I have said) all they hear, see, read, to themselves; as Felix Plater notes of some young physicians, that studying to cure diseases, catch them themselves, will be sick, and appropriate all symptoms they find related of others to their own persons (Pt. I. 3.1.2).

Typically Burtonian, this period does not seem to contain all the information a speaker wants to present, in its best psychological form, from a given point of view. Rather, it tries to include unlimited possibilities, and the point of view threatens once or twice to shift from speaker to subject. There is no rigid attempt to maintain grammatical consistency, either, since that might require too much limitation of subject or viewpoint: hence, for example, his characteristic listing of parallel examples, including some not in parallel form, e.g., "if they see one possessed, bewitched, an epileptic paroxysm." The sentence is like a multiple-choice examination: "check one, or if none is applicable, explain under 'other' (etc.)." This kind of variety makes the sentence as inclusive as possible, offering the reader every opportunity to find in it his own experience, and to broaden his own experience by taking all this into himself, just as Burton has done. Both the references to other writers and the use of the "etc." permit an openness of meaning that does not limit the subject to what can be fitted onto the page.

Multiplication of parallel illustrations is, of course, characteristic of Burton's style; and although each writer has his distinctive way of handling this technique, it is also characteristic of the age. Leonard Goldstein has termed its use in Burton an unconscious operation of the quantifying tendency of Galilean science,[24] and I am sure that is at least a partial explanation. Wherever the impulse has its roots, it not only contributes in Burton to our sense of cosmic personality, but also becomes a robust literary tendency to try to seem an unpremeditating pioneer in this world of infinite variety—do not take time to choose between this word and that; use them both—the habit speeds up the tempo of the prose, increases its exuberance and plenitude, creating an effect of excited speech at the same time that it actually slows the thought to a conversational pace: "I know there be many base, impudent, brazen-faced rogues, that will *nulla pallescere culpa*, be moved with nothing, take no infamy or disgrace to heart, laugh at all; let them be proved perjured, stigmatized, convict rogues, thieves, traitors, lose their ears, be whipped, branded, carted, pointed at, hissed, reviled, and derided with Ballio the bawd in Plautus, they rejoice at it: *Cantores probos! babae!* and *bombax!* what care they?" (Pt. I.2.3.7). There is sequential, rhetorical, or psychological order in some of these listings, however haphazard they may be in general. To the extent that such order does exist, the staccato progression of the sentence becomes more evident: here Burton describes first the characters of the rogues, then the manner of their conviction, and then their punishment; and within these groupings there are lesser movements. Burton interrupts his sentences, or sharpens the tempo, not only by his staccato listings, but also by the use of imperatives, and by insertion of short clauses, exclamations, and Latin phrases, as notably illustrated in the sentence given above. Of course the usual shifts in point of view occur here too. The reader is not allowed to settle down emotionally; the tension of this kind of sentence structure prevents it, and keeps him in close contact with the book-personality, whose typographical and sentence-structural techniques have the emotional force of pronunciation and gesticulation.

More than most writers, Burton has caused his sentence structure to imitate the content of his sentences.[25] His style changes subtly as well as vastly, not just from one general subject to another, but from one mood or passing point to another: "So that as a river runs sometimes precipitate and swift, then dull and slow; now direct, then *per ambages;* now deep, then shallow; now muddy, then clear; now broad, then narrow; doth my style flow; now serious, then light; now comical, then satirical; now more elaborate, then remiss, as the present subject required, or as at that time I was affected" (Pt. I, p. 32). The river metaphor suggests again both variety and openness of theme. The range of style is, of course, another way of pleasing and including all sorts of men: "He respects matter, thou art wholly for words; he loves a loose and free style, thou art all for neat composition, strong lines, hyperboles, allegories; he desires a fine frontispiece, enticing pictures . . . that which one admires, another explodes as most absurd and ridiculous" (Pt. I, p. 27). All these, including the fine frontispiece with enticing pictures,[26] are represented in the *Anatomy*. But the primary intent is not to make a display of versatility, impressive as that versatility is, but to let the sentences really be the body of the book, or of mankind, in all man's infinite variety. Let me illustrate with two sentences chosen at random. In the first, the idea requires that the sentence provide a long cumulative build-up punctured rather quickly at the end, to imitate worldly success:

A knight would be a baronet, and then a lord, and then a viscount, and then an earl, etc., a doctor, a dean, and then a bishop; from tribune to praetor, from bailiff to mayor; first this office, and then that; as Pyrrhus in Plutarch, they will first have Greece, then Africa, and then Asia, and swell with Aesop's frog so long, till in the end they burst, or come down with Sejanus *ad Gemonias scalas* and break their own necks; or as Evangelus, the piper in Lucian, that blew his pipe so long, till he fell down dead (Pt. I.1.3.11).

In contrast to the straightforward movement toward a puncturing climax in the above sentence, the one that follows presents a labyrinthine involvement of clauses wound one around the other, to imitate the self-entrapment of increasingly more neurotic men:

So delightsome these toys are at first, they could spend whole days and nights without sleep, even whole years alone in such contemplations and phantastical meditations, which are like unto dreams, and they will hardly be drawn from them, or willingly interrupt; so pleasant their vain conceits are, that they hinder their ordinary tasks and necessary business, they cannot address themselves to them, or almost to any study or employment, these phantastical and bewitching thoughts so covertly, so feelingly, so urgently, so continually set upon, creep in, insinuate, possess, overcome, distract, and detain them, they cannot, I say, go about their more necessary business, stave off or extricate themselves, but are ever musing, melancholizing, and carried along; as he (they say) that is led round about a heath with a Puck in the night, they run earnestly on in this labyrinth of anxious and solicitous melancholy meditations, and cannot well or willingly refrain, or easily leave off, winding and unwinding themselves as so many clocks, and still pleasing their humours, until at last the scene is turned upon a sudden by some bad object, and they, being now habituated to such vain meditations and solitary places, can endure no company, can ruminate of nothing but harsh and distasteful subjects (Pt. I.2.2.6).

In some ways analogous, though flashier, is Burton's use of drama. Life turns out to be a play in Burton, as in so much of the art of this period, but Burton takes the metaphor much more seriously than most writers do, using theater figures on almost every page, making both himself and his readers actors in his tragi-comedy. Burton frequently asserts that he is on stage: "Be it therefore as it is, well or ill, I have assayed, put myself upon the stage" (Pt. I, pp. 26–27); "I am resolved . . . boldly to show myself in this common stage, and in this tragi-comedy of love to act several parts, some satirically, some comically, some in a mixed tone, as the subject I have in hand gives occasion, and present scene shall require or offer itself" (Pt. III.1.1.2). That he means to act several parts should alert us to the fact that in his dramatic scenes point of view shifts repeatedly, as both Burton and the reader move from one role to another. Burton's dramatic versatility is another way of creating the cosmic personality, and of involving the reader in the work.

When Burton simply *shows* himself upon the stage, his technique is monologue, with an audience obviously implied, as in the opening pages of the section on religious melancholy:

Giue me but a little leaue, and I will set before your eyes, in briefe a stupend, vast, infinite ocean of incredible madnesse and folly: a Sea full of shelues and rockes, Sands, gulfes, Euripes and contrary tides, full of fearefull monsters, uncouth shapes, roring waues, tempests, and Siren calmes, Halcyonian Seas; unspeakeable miserie, such Comedies and Tragidies, such absurd and ridiculous, ferall and lamentable fitts, that I know not whether they are more to be pittied or derided, or may be belieued, but that we daily see the same still practised in our dayes, fresh examples, *nova novitia*, fresh obiects, of misery and madness in this kind that are still represented vnto vs, abroad, at home, in the midst of vs, in our bosomes (D., p. 5; Pt. III.4.1.1).

As an introductory soliloquy, this is especially revealing, for while he speaks as an actor to an audience, promising spectacles, comedies, and tragedies, and speaking in macrocosmic terms, eventually he locates the drama in man's bosom. Within the confines of this book, then, which represents Burton, or Burton magnified to cosmic personality, Burton and his readers will be acting out the tragedies and comedies that are played within themselves: again there are mirrors within mirrors. What Burton means to set before the reader is the reader playing himself: "Thou thyself art the subject of my discourse" (Pt. I, p. 16).

The role-playing from one direction evolves out of the techniques Burton uses to manipulate and involve the reader. From another direction, it evolves out of simple quotations, and since I have earlier discussed Burton's use of quotations at some length, I need not go into much detail here. When he uses quotations to support a point that he is making, they do allow another voice to be heard, and his recognition of one value of this technique is apparent: "*Divitiae saeculi sunt laquei diaboli:* so writes Bernard; worldly wealth is the devil's bait: and as the moon when she is fuller of light is still farthest from the sun, the more wealth they have, the farther they are commonly from God. (If I had said this of myself, rich men would have pulled me a-pieces; but hear who saith, and who seconds it, an Apostle.)" (Pt. II.3.3) It is interesting to see him play his fool role against Bernard in such a way that the rich men, as is usual for the auditors of this Burton, end up the losers, men who attend to names but not to wisdom. But the use of the quotation in itself is not really important dramatically.

Much more interesting dramatic passages are those in which Burton allows himself and his reader to take an active part in the drama, and engages in the role-shifting of which we have seen some evidence already. In the following passages, he has been speaking in his priest-role, trying to comfort a victim of despair. He then moves into the other person's consciousness by paraphrase of his thoughts, rather than by direct quotation: "All this is true thou replyest, but yet it concernes not thee, 'tis verified in ordinary offenders, in common sinnes, but thine are of an higher straine, euen against the Holy Ghost himselfe . . . ." Halfway through this, he pulls back, speaks briefly of the sinner in the third person, and then almost immediately slides completely into the sinner's point of view:

In steed of Faith, Feare, and loue of God, repentance, &c. blasphemous thoughts that haue bin euer harboured in his mind, euen against God himselfe, the blessed Trinity: the Scripture false, rude, harsh unmethodicall: Heauen, hell, resurrection, meere toyes and fables; incredible, impossible, absurde, vaine, ill contriued; Religion, policy, an humane invention, to keep men in obedience, or for profit, invented by Priests and Lawgiuers to that purpose. If there be any such supreme Power, he takes no notice of our doings . . . (D., pp. 316–18; Pt. III.4.2.6).

The seemingly almost unconscious movement from one mind to another demonstrates extraordinary mental flexibility resulting, partly at least, from Burton's cultivated effort to understand a variety of viewpoints.

Two principal techniques used in his longer and more dramatic passages should be illustrated. In one, he plays third person commentator on a scene in which he also acts:

For look into the world, and you shall see men most part esteemed according to their means, and happy as they are rich . . . Every man seeks his acquaintance, his kindred, to match with him, though he be an oaf, a ninny, a monster, a goosecap, *uxorem ducat Danaen*, when and whom he will, *hunc optant generum rex et regina*, he is an excellent match for my son, my daughter, my niece, etc. *Quicquid calcaverit hic, rosa fiet*, let him go whither he will, trumpets sound, bells ring, etc., all happiness attends him, every man is willing to entertain him, he sups in Apollo wheresoever he comes; what preparation is made for his entertainment! fish and fowl, spices and perfumes, all that sea and land affords. What cookery, masking, mirth to exhilarate his person! . . . What dish will your good worship eat of? . . . What sport will your honour have? hawking, hunting, fishing, fowling, bulls, bears, cards, dice, cocks, players, tumblers, fiddlers, jesters, etc., they are at your good worship's command . . . Though he be a silly soft fellow, and scarce have common sense, yet if he be born to fortunes (as I have said) *jure haereditario sapere jubetur*, he must have honour and office in his course: *Nemo nisi dives honore dignus* (Ambros. *Offic.* 21) none so worthy as himself: he shall have it, *atque esto quicquid Servius aut Labeo*. Get money enough and command kingdoms, provinces, armies, hearts, hands, and affections; thou shalt have popes, patriarchs to be thy chaplains and parasites . . . (Pt. I.2.4.6).

Burton successively plays the detached observer, the amused observer, the would-be in-laws, and the sycophant. The reader is first invited to play the rich man when Burton begins to play the sycophant, speaking to a *you.* That role is briefly made unavailable when Burton steps back into his observer role, and then restored, more ironically than ever, when he again turns to the reader with the imperative, "Get money enough."

Burton's second major theatrical method dispenses with the detached observer, and constructs a kind of dialogue. There may be any number of speakers for a given viewpoint, and Burton shifts roles, or bequeaths roles to the reader at will. Part II, Section 3, Member 3 is wholly constructed in this way. Entitled "Against Poverty and Want, with such other Adversities," it begins with a fairly long speech on the blessings of poverty, spoken by Burton in his parish-priest role. Frequently signalling a change of speaker in this passage are the words "Yea but," first voiced thus: "Yea, but he hath the world at will that is rich, the good things of the earth: *suave est de magno tollere acervo,* he is a happy man, adored like a god, a prince, every man seeks to him, applauds, honours, admires him" (Pt. II.3.3). The argument then moves back and forth, between these two views, with various speakers voicing their discontent with poverty, or, less frequently, their contentment with it. During the course of the debate, Burton, in addition to his parish-priest role plays the part of servant to a lord; a malcontent poor man; an envious man; and a slave. He also addresses various *thou's*—a lord, a drudge, and a discontented wretch. Here the reader has many opportunities to accept one role or another, and is sometimes really forced to do so by the sharpness of Burton's tone: "That which St. Austin said of himself here in this place, I may truly say to thee, thou discontented wretch, thou covetous niggard, thou churl, thou ambitious and swelling toad, 'tis not want but peevishness which is the cause of thy woes; settle thine affection, thou hast enough" (Pt. II.3.3).

In speaking of love-melancholy, Burton says that "when a country fellow discommended once that exquisite picture of Helen, made by Zeuxis, for he saw no such beauty in it, Nichomachus, a lovesick spectator, replied, *Sume tibi meos oculos et deam existimabis,* take mine eyes, and thou wilt think she is a goddess, dote on her forthwith . . ." (Pt. III.2.3). One of Burton's principal efforts in his book has been to enable men to see through one another's eyes, and to recognize themselves in others. If his method has been successful, the conclusion to the first part of his book will have terrific impact. It voices a theme that we have heard expressed several times already, most notably in Donne's meditations on the bells, but Burton has brought us to it in a way that is all his own. He has been speaking of self-murder, which one would ordinarily think the loneliest and most alienating of acts, a purposeful severing of self from self, man from mankind. Even here, Burton insists that the survivor may conceive himself the victim: *"Quod cuiquam contigit cuivis potest.* Who knows how he may be tempted? It is his case, it may be thine: *Quae sua sors hodie est, cras fore vestra potest.* We ought not to be so rash and rigorous in our censures as some are; charity will judge and hope the best; God be merciful unto us all!" (Pt. I.4.1).

Finally, the "I" makes himself known through some characteristically Anglican and conservative themes: appearance and reality; discontinuity; time and eternity. Inevitably we have already seen something of them in sidelong glances. But since this is a book of many faces, it would be possible to concentrate on these themes alone as both subject and style of the "I" of Burton's book.

It is impressive evidence of the pervasiveness in the age of the theme of appearance and reality that a scholar like Burton, in many ways so much removed from seventeenth-century life, so thoroughly absorbed this theme into the character of his book. One major vehicle of its expression is Burton's wit: among its many other virtues, the *Anatomy* is a very funny book,[27] and its wit is based almost entirely on appearance-reality jokes. To suggest the range of wit that this theme can encompass, let me simply list a few examples. A rare pun: "bull bellowing pope" (is he bull or pope? what are the bulls that he bellows?). Mistranslation of Latin: *Veritas odium parit,* "verjuice and oatmeal is good for a parrot." (The Latin looks like one meaning, but has another.) Bawdy story: when the convent caught fire one night, the nun, in her haste to dress, put the monk's breeches on her head instead of her wimple (as the breeches appeared to her to be her wimple, so she appeared to others to be virtuous). False modesty: Burton claimed that his first edition was signed only at the publisher's insistence, and in subsequent editions removed his name, but put his picture on the title page, and left identifying autobiographical details scattered through the volume.

Burton has his own symbol for his Janus-faced age and for the elusive complexity of his book: "I will determine of them all, they are like these double or turning pictures; stand before which, you see a fair maid, on the one side an ape, on the other an owl; look upon them at the first sight, all is well; but further examine, you shall find them wise on the one side and fools on the other . . ." (Pt. I, p. 115).[28] The double picture has a third face. It is by thus capitalizing upon ambiguity that he solves his own dilemma of how to respond to man's follies: "*Fleat Heraclitus an rideat Democritus*, in attempting to speake of these Symptomes, shall I laugh with *Democritus*, or weepe with *Heraclitus*, they are so ridiculous and absurd on the one side, so lamentable and tragicall on the other, a mixt Sceane offers itselfe . . ." (D., p. 106; Pt. III.4.1.3). Here again Burton suggests a third face to the coin—the mixed scene, to which he can respond with a mixed passion. The theme of appearance and reality is ideally suited to such an aim, because in its ambiguity of character or tone, it is intrinsically witty, and in its implicit representation of this fallen world of appearances, it is intrinsically grave. A figure based upon this theme, then, always partakes of both elements, and can do so in many varying proportions depending upon whether the author wants to emphasize the comic or the tragic aspects of his subject.

The nun who thought the monk's breeches were her wimple, for example, becomes the subject of a funny story. Behind the bawdy humor, more serious kinds of deception are involved. By day, she appears to be a godly woman; at night, she gives rein to her true (lack of) character. Possibly she is self-deceived about her vocation. In larger terms, the anecdote criticizes the proclaimed purity, the actual corruption both of religious orders and of the Roman church.

Like any seventeenth-century preacher, Burton suggests that passion, imagination, and the devil are responsible for man's inability to distinguish between appearance and reality. "Love and hate are like the two ends of a perspective glass, the one multiplies, the other makes less" (Pt. I, p. 66, n. 4). Among his many tales illustrating the blindness of love to the reality of its object is this one: "Petrarch hath such another tale of a young gallant, that loved a wench with one eye, and for that cause by his parents was sent to travel into far countries; 'after some years he returned, and meeting the maid for whose sake he was sent abroad, asked her how and by what chance she lost her eye? No, said she, I have lost none, but you have found yours . . .'" (Pt. III.2.5.2). Imagination, which in Burton blends into madness, explains delusions: ". . . if it be extreme, they think they hear hideous noises, see and talk with black men, and converse familiarly with devils, and such strange chimeras and visions . . ." (Pt. I.3.1.3). But such delusions may also be caused by the devil, who is of course the father of lies. To these other causes, Burton, in his physician role, adds physical ailments. A man bitten by a mad dog sees dogs everywhere, especially in water (Pt. I.1.1.4). For these ailments, Burton has cures. His book is a serious effort to "repair the ruins of our first parents," [29] to free men of the ills that distort and blind their vision.

In his treatment of himself and his book, Burton often seems to be using the theme of appearance and reality merely to play games with the reader. His false apologies fall into this category, as does all his obfuscation of his own identity. Because of his habit of extensive quotation, he can say whatever he likes, and then, if anyone takes umbrage, disclaim responsibility: " 'tis all mine and none mine." The whole book becomes an optical illusion: looked at in one way, it is an encyclopedia; in another, an original treatise; in another, a living organism. All these devices are surely witty and exciting. And they also very clearly express the problem of emerging individuality that is so crucial in the seventeenth century. He appears to court the reader, yet in a way he is not even willing to admit that he wants to be read. He has a sense of separateness and individuality, yet he feels most whole when he is most at one with his learning and his traditions. The question here is not so much one of appearance and reality as of fragmented reality. The three sides of the coin are not simultaneously visible to mortal sight, but they must be made so.

The same kinds of comments may be made upon Burton's multiplicity of roles, his reversals of roles, his involvement of the reader, and his intentional confusion of art with life. Though in one sense he can be himself only, in another he is all the parts he plays, because his book-personality becomes cosmic. In the same way, in the book, he and the reader are one, both being the subject of Burton's discourse. And, as we have already seen, the book is Burton's life, and there is uncertainty about whether "life" and "art" are two different things. From his book, Burton surveys the scene of the world as if he were in a theater. Yet the theater is the book.

The most persistent type of appearance-reality motif, the figure of transformation, is a theme in its own right.[30] Some of Burton's uses of it could certainly be illustrated from what I have said of appearance and reality. Furthermore, his fascination with myths, legends, and religions that involve transformation—lycanthropia and metempsychosis, for example—is typical of this general preoccupation. But Burton's most frequent expression of it springs from Chrysostom's comparisons of sinful men to animals.[31] The causes of transformation for the worse are love, deceit, unbridled passion, poverty, superstition, and the devil. The causes of transformation for the better are love and repentance. Typical descriptions of transformation are these:

"Man in honour that understandeth not, is like unto beasts that perish," so David esteems him: a monster by stupend metamorphoses, a fox, a dog, a hog, what not? (Pt. I.1.1.1)

The major part of lovers are carried headlong like so many brute beasts; reason counsels one way, thy friends, fortunes, shame, disgrace, danger, and an ocean of cares that will certainly follow . . . yet they will do it, and become at last *insensati*, void of sense; degenerate into dogs, hogs, asses, brutes; as Jupiter into a bull, Apuleius an ass, Lycaon a wolf, Tereus a lapwing, Callisto a bear, Elpenor and Gryllus into swine by Circe (Pt. III.2.3).

To see a man turn himself into all shapes like a chameleon, or as Proteus, *omnia transformans sese in miracula rerum*, to act twenty parts and persons at once for his advantage, to temporize and vary like Mercury the planet, good with good, bad with bad; having a several face, garb, and character for every one he meets; of all religions, humours, inclinations; to fawn like a spaniel, *mentitis et mimicis obsequiis*, rage like a lion, bark like a cur, fight like a dragon, sting like a serpent, as meek as a lamb, and yet again grin like a tiger, weep like a crocodile, insult over some, and yet others domineer over him, here command, there crouch, tyrannize in one place, be baffled in another, a wise man at home, a fool abroad to make others merry (Pt. I, pp. 65–66).

Donne, speaking of his sermon auditory, has very similar things to say of man's character (he too picks up and varies Chrysostom's metaphor): man is a salamander in the fire of his lusts and ambitions, and a serpent in his seditions and indevotions. "How," asks Donne, "shall we raise this Salamander and this Serpent, when this Serpent and this Salamander is all one person, and must have contrary musique to charme him, contrary physick to cure him?"[32] Burton asks, "How shall I hope to express myself to each man's humour and conceit, or to give satisfaction to all?" (Pt. I, p. 28). The answer for both Donne and Burton was to make a contrary music of their prose, holding up to man his mirrored instability.

Appearance-reality, transformation, metamorphosis, fragmentation of reality decisively affect Burton's style, and, as Burton tells us, the style is the man (Pt. I, p. 27). He is what he would seek to cure. By putting on display his own weaknesses and paradoxes, both those that are actual in him and those potential ones that are realized only in the quotations and anecdotes that he assimilates into himself, he gives man the opportunity to strive, at least, for self-knowledge and self-control.

Very close to appearance-reality and sometimes overlapping with it is discontinuity, the expression of a feeling discernible in the seventeenth century that man is not the same person from moment to moment. As Montaigne says, "My selfe now, and my selfe anon, are indeede two." [33] This is one reason why Proteus and Mercury are such popular figures; it is another reason why the theme of transformation is so popular in the age. Among other reasons, man finds himself confronted by the problem of identity just because his personality is no longer stable and taken for granted, but, rather, needs to be continuously redefined. The sudden shifts in tone and point of view, the leaps from character to character in Burton's book all illustrate this tendency of the age. The restlessness of the style is partly accounted for by Burton's habit of suddenly breaking off one discourse and turning to another, usually with the explanation that he does not know what he is talking about. The additive organization of the book confirms our sense of a personality that remakes itself from one moment to another.

All seems to change, yet nothing changes. Like Sir Thomas Browne, Burton notes that "men are lived over againe." [34] "What Fagos, Epicures, Apiciuses, Heliogables, our times afford! Lucullus' ghost walks still, and every man desires to sup in Apollo . . ." (Pt. I.2.2.2). Again and again he repeats that below the constant shifting of appearances, all things remain the same:

'Tis not to be denied, the world alters every day; *Ruunt urbes, regna transferuntur,* etc. *variantur habitus, leges innovantur,* as Petrarch observes, we change language, habits, laws, customs, manners, but not vices, not diseases, not the symptoms of folly and madness, they are still the same. And as a river, we see, keeps the like name and place, but not water, and yet ever runs, *Labitur et labetur in omne volubilis aevum;* our times and persons alter, vices are the same, and ever will be; look how nightingales sang of old, cocks crowed, kine lowed, sheep bleated, sparrows chirped, dogs barked, so they do still; we keep our madness still, play the fools still, *nec dum finitus Orestes;* we are of the same humours and inclinations as our predecessors were; you shall find us all alike, much at one, we and our sons, *Et nati natorum, et qui nascuntur ab illis,* and so shall our posterity continue to the last (Pt. I, pp. 53–54).

Now I think it must be obvious that this description of life is also a description of Burton's book. The central figure is the river metaphor, which, of course, he also used to describe his style. It is ever different, yet ever the same, in constant movement and yet keeps the same name and place. It is never finished, and yet always complete, infinitely open and yet bounded.

The book imitates life under the aspect of melancholy. That is why it begins with the Fall, and that is why one thing that Burton almost never mentions or tries to describe is the eternal life. As many times as Burton describes himself as in a theater beholding the world, or mounted on a high hill, or otherwise possessed of a timeless vantage point, it is always to behold *this* world and its follies. He is the author and god of the world of this book. It is he, with his mixed passion, who resolves (as well as creates) its ambiguities and discontinuities. But his cosmic vision and his world are finally less than those of God, who began the world with the Creation, not the Fall, and sees it under the aspect of eternity. The only means by which man can attain to God is to reject this world and its follies, as Burton says in a rare passage describing quite a different kind of cosmic vision than that upon which the *Anatomy* depends:

He cannot (*Austin* admonisheth) be Gods friend, that is delighted with the pleasures of the world, *make cleane thine heart, purifie thine heart, if thou wilt see this beauty, prepare thy selfe for it. It is the eye of contemplation by which wee must behold it, the winge of meditation which lifts vs vp, and reares our soules, with the motion of our hearts, and sweetness of contemplation* . . . *he that loues God will soare aloft and take him wings, and leaving the earth flie vp to heauen, wander with Sunne and Moone, Starres and that heauenly troupe, God himselfe being his guide.* If wee desire to see him, we must lay aside all vaine obiects, which detaine vs and dazell our eyes, and as *Ficinus* aduiseth vs, get vs solar *eyes, spectacles as they that looke on the sunne* . . . In *Ficinus* words I exhort and beseech you, *that you would embrace and follow this diuine loue with all your hearts and abilities, by all offices and endeauors make this louing God propitious vnto you.* For whom alone, saith *Plotinus,* we *must forsake the kingdomes and Empires of the whole earth, Sea, Land, and Ayre, if we desire to be engrafted into him, leaue all and follow him* (D., pp. 17–19; Pt. III.4.1.1).

Of one thing we may be sure: this is not the voice of Democritus Junior. For his vision is limited to this world, and, like Dante's

Virgil, he cannot provide a guided tour of Paradise. From this we learn yet another perspective on one of the ambiguities with which we began. It is very tempting to believe that in the Renaissance, as E. M. Forster put it, "the printing press . . . had been mistaken for an engine of immortality." [35] But men of the sixteenth and seventeenth centuries had much less need than we to seize upon such a thought, because their immortality was already assured. Burton scoffs at people who think they can find immortality in print, and clearly understands that books, like their authors, die and are forgotten; human fame does not endure (Pt. I, pp. 23–27). It is partly because the book finally has that mortal character that it can be confused with life at all.

"Here lies Democritus Junior, to whom melancholy gave life and death." Democritus-Burton can no longer preside over his book-world, or see that the river of its growth continues to flow through time. If the book-world did not wholly die with Burton, certainly it began to die of its own mortality, that is to say, of melancholy. And the Democritus Junior part of Burton is also described in this epitaph, the part that wept and laughed over humanity. If he had a soul that by his death, freed of flesh and freed of print, was enabled to forsake the kingdoms of the earth, that is not mentioned in this memorial to his earthly self. Here, as always, the reader is left to draw his own conclusions about Burton, the *Anatomy*, and the meaning of art and life.

CHAPTER V

RICHARD BAXTER:
THE EYE OF
THE HURRICANE

RICHARD BAXTER'S LIFE AND WRITINGS ARE REPRESENTED HERE BY THE posthumously published history of his life and times, the *Reliquiae Baxterianae*. Baxter's is the eye of the hurricane,[1] representing his stormy age, utterly at its mercy, yet aware of it in its entirety in all his being. There is extreme tension. His "I" is maintained at the center, not by a calm indifference, but by the terrific opposing pulls of his own nature and his own world. He is a strong personality attempting self-effacement, a man seeking unity where there is only division.

A Puritan Anglican, he believed that adherence to sect, faction, party, or style was a selfish act, contrary to the interests of Christianity, Catholicism, and charity. For party to fight with party was for the body to dismember itself. And by this he means not Donne's conveniently symbolic body of mankind, but the body of the English church and nation in mid-seventeenth-century England. Identifying himself with this body, he tried as a Puritan Anglican to unite all Christians by his example, his actions, and his writings. His refusal to choose sides endows his writing with a doubleness of focus which, on the one hand, increases his inclusiveness, range, and power, and, on the other, diffuses through every aspect of his thought and every level of his style eclecticism, discontinuousness, and ambiguity. His style portrays the agony of dividedness in expressing the condition of an utterly self-divided man striving even against his own nature for unity and wholeness in a world which he knows can never be whole.

The effort to be at the center, giving up sect or party, is one kind of self-effacement. Another, more typically Puritan, comes from the concept of self as instrument. We have seen the effect of this belief upon Bunyan's prose, and in Milton are manifest the ways in which the "I" can be fully realized in spite of or even by means of identification of instrumentality with vocation. For Baxter, instrumentality implies self-abnegation, which he attempts to achieve. In this sense, it is at least to some extent incompatible with the writing of autobiography,[2] and it creates another ambiguity in his prose.

Being at the center, he chose not to choose or cultivate either a conservative or a radical style. He wanted to achieve a literary objectivity and transparency which would allow him as an instrument ("a pen in God's hands")[3] to set forth without distortion the ideas and conflicts of his age. Page by page, he did achieve a kind of stylelessness. Any given paragraph of his history may well show no significant uses of adjectives, metaphors, or sentence structure: here his centrality resists our stylistics. But we can analyze the work in large ways, speaking of its structure and purpose; of Baxter's own views of style; and of his "I." Here are clearly reflected the passions and conflicts of his age, the divisions of his mind.

One of the printed attacks upon Baxter is reminiscent of what was said about Lilburne's quarrelsomeness: *The Casuist uncased in a Dialogue between Richard and Baxter, with a Moderator between them for quietness sake.*[4] Baxter's condition is altogether different from Lilburne's, infinitely more complex. But it is true that he himself was a living dialogue. At the same time, just because he embodied these warring factions, he also embodied their irreconcilability. Loving though he was, he could not transcend human nature, and it is not insignificant that this great peacemaker of his age was noted for the hastiness of his temper. To recognize the complexity that could overtake a moderate Puritan is to discover a valuable contrast with the much more familiar and obvious complexities in Anglican writing, as well as with the relative straightforwardness of the radical Puritan style. Donne's contrary impulses are resolved in literary paradox that in turn may help us to make sense out of life. Baxter's oppositions and ambiguities are likely to be half-underground, not immediately perceptible in their entirety, and probably much less conscious. His style is less interesting as art than as the portrayal of an interesting, impressive man.

Richard Baxter was born in 1615, the year of John Lilburne's birth. His father, a much reformed gambler, had a modest country estate in

Shropshire, and the son grew up close to village people, and yet removed from them because they scorned the Baxters as Puritans. Measuring his father's godliness against the frivolity of the villagers, Baxter was from childhood inclined toward Puritanism, but always as a movement within the Church of England. His education was haphazard, but the piety stressed in his home was intensified in him by severe ill-health that began early and continued all his life. Expecting death from one week to another, he consciously obeyed the maxim, "Live each day as if it were to be your last," and as a result was ordained in the Church of England before he had actually tested his beliefs. When he did, he concluded that both conformists and nonconformists had merits, and all his life he remained a Puritan Anglican, in that age an impossible anomaly understood by neither side. Cromwell, whom he felt obliged to oppose as a usurper, gave him freedom to preach; Charles II, to whom he had remained loyal, deprived him of his ministry (as Baxter had expected he would) because he was unable to sign the unqualified oaths of obedience required.

He was then and still is acknowledged as a great man. Bishop Wilkins, his contemporary, said of him that if he had lived in primitive times he would have been one of the Fathers of the Church.[5] Others called him the "Bishop of Nonconformity." [6] Cromwell invited him to be preacher to his own regiment, and Charles II, at the time of the Restoration, named him one of his chaplains. Usually the representative of the nonconformists in meetings with king and prelates, he was twice offered a bishopric by Charles. Both sides courted him for his prestige, and damned him for his unwillingness to support either side wholeheartedly. From a perverse, ungodly people at Kidderminster, he made a great and devoted congregation, built up by methods which could have been, and before the Restoration had begun to be, a model for the whole church to follow. As a theologian, he had international fame, and was read in many languages, and consulted from Europe and America, as well as in England. Intellectuals regardless of party were his friends; among them were the scientist Robert Boyle; Charles II's Lord Chief Justice, Matthew Hale; the Cambridge Platonist Henry More; and Archbishop Tillotson. These facts need to be remembered, because, while he does mention most of them, he does so with characteristic self-effacement. Keenly aware of the dangers of fame and the need for humility, he minimizes his own importance, and other matters, in which he saw less need for caution, come through more clearly. The facts of his greatness, and of his great involvement in his age, help to assure us that his picture of his life and times will be a rewarding one. Taking a central position in religion and politics, he was also, as much as any nonconformist could be, at the center of religious and political affairs.

What Baxter's story is about from page to page is his lifelong effort to make peace among men. This subject is not in itself susceptible to stylistic analysis. Counterpointed against that large story are the very descriptions of the opposing forces, and of Baxter's own inner oppositions and ambiguities. These conflicting ideas, attitudes, and emotions are the texture of the work. Thus, even though the subject of the work is peace, almost everything in the work that is available to any kind of stylistic analysis militates against the idea of peace. The first "literary" effect of Baxter's vocation of peacemaker is so to wrest apart content and style that the work itself bears witness that failure was part of the vocation.

Baxter's own self-division is crucial. In some instances, he chooses to make separations, for example between body and soul. His discontinuous sense of time has various causes—the sense of time in the age itself, his illness, his growing belief that man himself cannot be trusted to remain the same from one moment to another (he had to trust his manuscripts to his close friend Matthew Sylvester when he died, but he was not even sure that he ought to do that).[7] His self-division, more nobly, springs from the very impulse that leads him to seek peace; his recognition that there is good on both sides leaves him suspended between conformity and nonconformity, unable to give himself wholeheartedly to either side, but able to see both more objectively, perhaps, than anyone else of his time. When he had been suspended from the ministry and had to apply for a license to preach as a sectarian, he refused to identify himself with any sect, but listed himself as a "mere nonconformist," meaning, as little of a nonconformist as possible.

The consistency of his position is both the matter and the style of his *Reliquiae.* Everywhere, his own self-division and the fragmentation of his world force him to reach out in opposite directions. He could not make a choice between prelacy and separatism, Arminianism and Calvinism, or justification by faith and by works. Even in the quest for peace itself, he was for freedom of worship, but could not agree to extend that freedom to Socinians or Papists. By instinct a controversialist, he set his heart on peace; a monastic, he eventually chose to marry; a great writer of books, he worried that men defeat their own ends by excessive publishing. Aligned with the humble and ignorant in his work, he made his closest friends among aristocrats and intellectuals. Independent and scornful of patronage, he nevertheless refused to allow himself the pride that rejection of patronage might foster. Contemptuous of pretentious learning, he regretted that he had never had time for some of learning's refinements.

It is everywhere apparent in Baxter that imperfection, and dividedness as the chief manifestation of imperfection, is the signal characteristic of mortal man. Whether one remains poised between two opposites, or chooses the more desirable of the two, reluctantly giving up the other, or endeavors to reach the best of both, the result is never satisfactory. The *Reliquiae Baxterianae* is both thesis and evidence.

The book is written in three parts, of which the first, written "for the most part" in 1664, was clearly intended to stand by itself. Baxter had expected to die soon enough so that this would be his whole autobiography. Concentrated on his life beginning with his birth, this section shifts back and forth between his story, and that of his times. It builds to the Restoration of Charles II, and to a concluding self-analysis, in which he considers the ways in which he has changed from youth to age.

Part II, written in 1665, is almost completely impersonal, and completely different in method. Covering a shorter period of time than Part I, and focused more upon debate and dialogue than upon action, it has correspondingly less chronological organization. Its central purpose is to describe and illustrate Baxter's continuous and monumental effort, under both Cromwell and Charles, toward the establishment of a truly catholic and united English church. It begins with an account of the different Protestant sects, and includes extensive consideration of doctrine and church practices relevant to negotiations among different sects and parties. It is heavily documented with specific evidence—letters, proposals, declarations, suggested revisions for the Book of Common Prayer, and so forth. Here also are related the bad times after the Restoration—the silencing of the ministers, the offer to Baxter of a bishopric in exchange for an unqualified oath of belief in and acceptance of the Royalist creed and party, the subsequent denial to him even of the curacy of his old parish at Kidderminster. This part ends with a brief and moving description of the plague, which he regards as God's judgment.

The third part opens with the words "Novem. 16. 1670. I began to add the Memorials following." From here on the work is again more personal, but it is less shaped than either of the preceding sections. Transitions again move us back and forth between the "I" and his society, but there is almost no shaping of the whole section, which has the appearance of a record kept from day to day, and comes to no climax or conclusion. With the final pages, labelled "*Additions of the Years* 1674, 1676, 1677, 1678, &c.," the work becomes truly fragmentary, no autobiography in fact, but simply a diary.

In considering the structure of the *Reliquiae*, I think one must first deal with an obvious objection that in its dishevelment it is simply not typical of Baxter's best work. But it is atypical because it is autobiographical. Compared to his other books, it *is* defective—unfinished, disconnected, less developed stylistically, full of the opposite pulls of which I have spoken. In his other works, he is chiefly concerned with specific audiences, and says relatively little of himself. And as they are polemical, they do endeavor to present a calm and unified persuading argument. But the *Reliquiae* enfolds the arguments of all these books, just as it actually describes the books as part of his life. Where some books are directed to papists, some to radical Puritans, and some to prelates, the *Reliquiae* tries to show why Baxter in these different writings appeared to so many people to be contradicting himself. It shows Baxter whole, being concentrated on him, rather than on some one of his specific interests. An autobiography *must* be unfinished. And Baxter's autobiography is discontinuous and divided just because he was and his life was. Given all the evidence, one is tempted to say that he could not have written his autobiography successfully by literary standards, and still have represented himself so well.

Confronted with the posthumously published 1696 edition of the *Reliquiae*, after having been introduced to Baxter through the more available but drastically abridged Everyman edition, one is astounded by its size. It may be smaller than Burton's life's work, but this is not by any means a life's work and it is not that much smaller. A large folio volume, it comes to over six hundred pages, not counting various appendices. And there is no question that the length, in itself, is a completely unavoidable aspect of Baxter's style. The editors of the 1707 edition of the *Practical Works* (which totals nearly four thousand folio pages) speak advisedly when they advertise their selection as a "standing Monument." Over the course of forty years of constant devotion to the ministry, of persecution, of illness, in a time of immense civil and religious turmoil, he wrote about one hundred and forty books.[8] The total includes works like *The Saints Everlasting Rest,* an 856-page quarto edition, written in a four-month period which he remembers as being unusually free because he was too ill to minister to his congregation. Baxter elsewhere apologizes for his prolixity, saying that it is necessitated by the thick-wittedness of his audiences, and that his natural tendency is to writing so obscure as to be cryptic,[9] but one hardly knows what to make of such a remark. He is never brief, unless expressly requested to be so. And certainly a brief autobiography could not have adequately represented him in all his great variety of being and immensity of energy, especially since this is a history of his life and times.

One can make out a reasonably good case for the structure of the *Reliquiae,* after the fact. There is esthetic balance, the documentary portion centered between the two more personal sections. The inclusion of documents, as I have shown in my chapter on Lilburne, is typical of post-*Book of Martyrs* histories. Since documents supposedly cannot lie, their use would seem to be the simplest way of assuring oneself and one's readers that the literal truth has been recorded. And Baxter depended desperately on history to set the record straight, since he was unable to protect himself in his own time from the floods of abuse set loose upon him from both Puritan left and Anglican right. Very often, he says of a disputed matter, "I leave it here on Record to the Notice of Posterity, that to the best of my knowledge" (Pt. II. 113, p. 278) this or that was so. The center of the *Reliquiae,* which is most fully concentrated on his own doctrinal quest for reconciliation of doctrinal differences and the achievement of a unified church, is the most vulnerable, from his point of view, and therefore the most in need of an entirely objective, factual presentation.

Further, it can obviously be argued that the whole biography has the shape of Baxter's life, the neatness of the first part giving way under pressure of age and external affairs to the necessity of a wider and wider openness of form. The opposition of the fairly clear and well-shaped opening to the fragmented conclusion reflects the opposition between the peace and relative coherence of Baxter's earlier years and the utterly chaotic and rootless existence that he was forced to lead after the Restoration. He had been seriously anticipating his own death for twenty years; his physical suffering was constant; and, in addition, he had experienced very harsh political and religious persecution. The emotionalism that he had in the past tried scrupulously to avoid is much more evident here, and contributes to the pervasive atmosphere of tension and upheaval. Thus, the literary biography imitates the real one, and so far there is little that seems remarkable.

But it must also be recognized that the structure of the *Reliquiae*, like that of some of his other works, is very much affected by the peculiar character of Baxter's sense of time. Had he not been so ravaged by illness, he might perhaps have thought about history more simply in chronological terms, as most Puritans did. As things were, he was forced to think of each moment as a separate gift of God. The fact that he had to write the *Reliquiae* at odd moments increases its fragmentariness. The tendency is most apparent, of course, in the last pages of the book, where every sentence is written under the expectation of death, and the inscriptions are brief and poignant.

Yet if he is the victim of time in one respect, in another he almost ignores it. The grace of additional years permitting him to add Parts II and III to his book, he was enabled to include material from the earlier years that he had skipped over before. Parts I and II thus overlap one another. Occasionally, material is repeated simply because he wants to dwell upon it, or to discuss it from a different viewpoint: in a marginal note, he writes, "Pardon the tediousness of three or four Sections, which repeat some of that which was mentioned before, because it is here put in as part of my Pacificatory Endeavors only" (Pt. II. 40, p. 179). Here there is the suggestion of a compartmentalization of experience. Another marginal note reads, "Though the Conjunction of the matter caused me to speak together of these things, yet the matter of this Section and the following was for time about two or three Years after that which followeth" (Pt. II. 43, p. 180). After giving brief histories of five different sects, he makes a transition, thus: "Having gone on thus far with the general Hints of the History of those times, because I would not obscure them by the Interpositions of my own Affairs, I now return to these, and shall set them also together, that they may be the better understood" (Pt. I. 128, p. 79).

These transitions almost always seem mechanical and awkward, because Baxter is so consciously turning from one kind of subject to another. He does not think of experience as all of a piece, as the Anglican would. Not only does he turn back and forth between himself and public affairs, but he subdivides these categories too, as in his separation of histories of the sects from other aspects of current events. When he talks about himself, he separates the history of his physical ailments from the history of his spiritual development, and both from the story of his ministry at Kidderminster. The result is another kind of discontinuity, which also interferes with a smooth chronological account.

For though he is trying to write history, he is simply not committed to an historical way of thought. He is fascinated by order and method; he is influenced not only by medieval logic, but also by the contemporary Puritan and scientific tendencies to compartmentalize and divide. Odd distortions of vision and perspective are created. While it separates moment from sequential moment, this viewpoint foreshortens history, pulling together into a moment's apprehension events that must have taken place over a considerable period of time. Powicke points this out in discussing a passage concerning Baxter's ministry, where Baxter unintentionally gives the false impression that he successfully initiated half a dozen spiritual projects all at once:

I preached before the War twice each Lord's Day; but after the War but once, and once every *Thursday*, besides occasional Sermons. Every *Thursday* Evening my Neighbors that were most desirous and had Opportunity, met at my House, and there one of them repeated the Sermon, and afterwards they proposed what Doubts any of them had about the Sermon, or any other Case of Conscience, and I resolved their Doubts; and, last of all, I caused sometimes one, and sometimes another of them to Pray (to exercise them); and sometimes I prayed with them myself: which (besides singing a Psalm) was all they did. And once a Week, also, some of the younger sort who were not fit to pray in so great an Assembly met among a few more privately, where they spent three hours in Prayer together. Every *Saturday* Night they met at some of their Houses to repeat the Sermon of the last Lord's Day, and to pray and prepare themselves for the following Day. Once in a few Weeks we had a Day of Humiliation on one Occasion or other. Every Religious Woman that was safely delivered—instead of the old Feastings and Gossipings—if they were able, did keep a Day of Thanksgiving with some of their Neighbors with them, praising God, and singing Psalms, and soberly Feasting together. Two Days every Week my Assistant and my self took 14 Families between us for private Catechising and Conference (he going through the Parish, and the Town coming to me) (Pt. I. 135, p. 83).[10]

Although it is a history, then, it is sometimes difficult to understand the order of happenings or the temporal relationships between one set of happenings and another. So often Baxter is caught between different modes of procedure; and purpose and method, or two different kinds of method, interfere with one another.

The same kind of problem is involved in his conscious effort to write an objective history. He has repeatedly expressed this intention, contrasting his own effort with the slandering and lying reports of others, to which this book is intended to be an antidote. In the course of his longest explanation of this purpose, he points out that false histories have become so common that no sensible person can trust any historian, except through personal knowledge of his integrity, or through evidence given in the work itself of honesty, impartiality, and charity. Then he describes one important way in which he himself has tried to give evidence of his good faith:

I have purposely omitted almost all the Descriptions of any Persons that ever opposed me, or that ever I or my Brethren suffered by, because I know that the appearance of *Interest* and *partiality* might give a fair excuse to the Readers incredulity: (Although indeed the true Description of Persons is much of the very Life of History, and especially of the History of the Age which I have lived in; yet to avoid the suspicion of Partiality I have left it out) (Pt. I. 40, p. 136).

The idea of writing one's life and times is an uneasy concept to begin with: it implies that the two are separate, yet somehow united. This is not to be simply biography, yet neither can it be objective history. Unlike a "scientific" historian, the author is here to remind us that he himself lived and suffered in these times, and that we must see them through his eyes. But that is just what Baxter is trying to prevent us from doing. Wherever he suspects that his eye might be taken for something other than that of a camera, he says he will omit material, even at the risk of destroying the very work which he thinks demands this omission. For his view is that the "true description of persons" is the life of history, and such description to us would seem the least capable of objective handling, and the least essential to objective history.

Baxter thought that he could safely describe Cromwell, because Cromwell let him alone. It did not occur to him that his own doctrinal and political beliefs could be considered subjective, and that they inevitably colored his very negative view of a man who was kinder to him than any other monarch under whom he lived. For the sake of a modern concept of objectivity that he could not entirely uphold, he wrested apart his own experience, and created a work that in yet another way is torn between different goals, different ideals, different times. One is constantly reminded that more than most of the other writers here discussed Baxter spans the century, and that he lived the crucial years of his life in the very midst of wars that finally divided the medieval from the modern world.

The extent to which he did achieve objectivity is very impressive. It is what made him such an object of slander: neither side could feel comfortable with him, because he always spoke the truth as he saw it, and he was practically unique in believing that truth was not the exclusive property of any one human agency. Here he blames the tactics of both Puritans and prelates:

I laboured continually to repress their Censoriousness, and the boldness and bitterness of their Language against the Bishops, and to reduce them to greater Patience and Charity. But I found that their Sufferings from the Bishops were the great Impediment of my Success, and that he that will blow the Coals must not wonder if some Sparks do fly in his face; and that to persecute Men, and then call them to Charity, is like whipping Children to make them give over Crying. The stronger sort of Christians can bear Mulcts and Imprisonments and Reproaches for obeying God and Conscience, without abating their Charity or their Weakness to their Persecutors; but to expect this from all the weak and injudicious, the young and passionate, is against all Reason and Experience: I saw that he that will be loved, must love; and he that rather chooseth to be more *feared* then *loved,* must expect to be hated, or loved but diminutively: And he that will have *Children,* must be a *Father:* and he that will be a Tyrant must be contented with Slaves (Pt. I. 19, p. 14).

This passage is typical of his belief that language, and beyond that human nature, are largely responsible for disagreements thought to be wholly doctrinal. He is applying Bacon's theory of the idols to the problems that are most important to him. But he also finds himself again dividing up goals and methods, results and principles, in concluding that the king has the better cause, the Parliament the better men; or that Cromwell seemed likely to bring about Utopia, but as a usurper, by means that could not be approved.

"Overdoing," he observes, "is the ordinary way of *Undoing"* (Pt. I. 40, p. 27). In his imprisonment under Charles II, when it was suggested to him that now he might move farther from the Church of England party, he responded that he hoped prison would not turn him into an extremist, as he knew it had done with some. There were perils on both sides, and on both sides there were men who truly believed in their cause. Force would inevitably open the division wider. Only loving dialogue could heal the world. That is the keynote of the passage just cited, and of Baxter's best exercise of objectivity.

I began this section with a characterization of the *Reliquiae* as a monumental work, and I would like to end it in the same way, with the suggestion that in all its various kinds of disarray, it is an epic work, by a man whose vision was both microscopic and macrocosmic, passionate and objective. Its purposes, as he explains them, were to praise God, to prevent anyone else from publishing a less accurate account of his life, to counter slander, and to teach young Christians by his mistakes (Pt. I. 213, p. 136). The method he proposes is to relate things as they were, to speak as an objective critic, not as a justifier of either party (Pt. I. 49, p. 30).

The literal truth, uncolored by emotional rhetoric, then becomes of primary importance, and helps to explain the inclusion of so much minute detail, including the extensive use of documents, many of which may be "of no living interest." When Baxter speaks of the poverty of his Kidderminster parishioners, he explains how poor they were by listing several of the highest of their incomes (Pt. I. 137, p. 94). When he mentions the proliferation of sects, he names and describes the sects, their leaders, and their beliefs. When he talks about his illnesses, he goes into graphic detail about symptoms, progress, and cure.

Baxter's Everyman editor, Dr. Lloyd Thomas, cuts extensively when Baxter repeats himself, when he lists, when he gives lengthy reportorial detail, and when he includes documents. That excision cuts Baxter down to less than his life-size, and reduces the work to manageable autobiography. It destroys the real shape of the work, which can, I think, be termed a Puritan epic of a completely different kind than that which Milton achieved, and one necessarily much less valuable esthetically. In this respect, Sylvester's apologetic name for the *Reliquiae* is relevant. He calls it a rhapsody (Preface, b2) by which I think he means what the *OED* defines as "a literary work consisting of miscellaneous or disconnected pieces, etc.; a written composition having no fixed form or plan." And certainly it is possible to view it in that light. But the first definition of a rhapsody is "an epic poem, or part of one," and that definition too goes back a hundred years before Baxter's time. It is so characteristic of the work itself that Sylvester's defining word states weakness and implies strength. Baxter makes no effort to overcome his limitations; he simply makes them part of the work. The literal detail, the repetition, the listing, all are archetypal characteristics of epic, though the kinds of detail and listing are not. Baxter catalogues his physical illnesses, his published and unpublished books and manuscripts, and the names and provinces of his detractors. He also makes less personal lists, for example the names of silenced ministers and sects.

F. L. Powicke objects to the description of this work as a "life and times" [11]—and would also perhaps object to its being called epic —on the grounds that Baxter only describes ecclesiastical affairs, and makes little real effort to give a full history of the period. That is certainly true. Baxter in fact doubted the value of any other kind of history. For him learning was only valuable if it could be useful, and whatever was useful contributed to religious growth. To know the history of the church was to enable oneself to identify with it in its progress and sufferings, and to strive more effectively for its welfare. That is what Baxter did, and that is why he reminded Bishop Wilkins of the Church Fathers.

Furthermore, he includes little that is not his personal knowledge. One almost always has the sense of his immediate presence. But his personal knowledge of the church history of his time has epic scope—it includes revolutions that changed the world. His work, like that of all epics, has basically to do with the history and character of a people, with the ways in which modern Englishmen came to be as they are. And the history of this time could not have been so passionately told by anyone other than Baxter. For it is a story of England divided against itself, and Baxter, like England, is self-wounded. It is thus that his life and times become one, and objectivity fuses with passion, in the whole text, as in this necessarily restrained but very moving account of the effects of self-division:

And when I read this Reverend Man's excessive Praises [of me] and his concluding Prayer for the Success of my Labours, I thought with my self, how little doth the good Man understand how ill the beginning and end of his

words accord: He prayeth for my Congregation, and the Blessing of my Labours, when he hath perswaded me to put an end to my Labours, by setting
up those Prelates who will Silence me and many a hundred more! He perswadeth me to that which will separate me from my Flock, and then prayeth
that I may be a Blessing to them. He overvalueth and magnifieth my Service
to the Church, and then perswadeth me to that which will put a Period to my
Service, and to the Service of many hundreds better than my self. But yet his
Cause and Arguments are honest; and I am so far from being against him in
it, that I think I am much more for it than he: for he is for our Restoring of
the King, that our Ministry may be freed from the obloquy of malicious
Enemies; but I am for restoring of the King, that when we are Silenced, and
our Ministry at an end, and some of us lye in Prisons, we may there, and in
that Condition, have Peace of Conscience in the Discharge of our Duty, and
the Exercise of Faith, Patience and Charity in our Sufferings (Pt. II. 71, p.
216).

Matthew Sylvester said of Baxter's style that "when he spake of
weighty Soul-concerns, you might find his very Spirit Drench'd
therein." [12] In Baxter's writing, as in Lilburne's, it is the man who is
the style.

It is useful and appropriate, then, to turn to Baxter's own comments
on style.[13] He was immensely self-conscious about his choice of a
plain, straightforward, and hasty way of speaking, and defends or
apologizes for it in very many of his works, giving a wide variety of
reasons. He is always trying to prevent us from thinking what he
fears we think about it. His self-divided apologies are likely to be either roundabout or regretful self-defense: his commitment to his
style includes recognition of a desire to write in a different way. And
in the character of his style with which he is most concerned—its
"rudeness"—there is a back-door symbolism quite different from
that employed by Anglicans and intentionally non-literary, but
highly significant in its revelation of why this rude style can be so
compelling. This shadowy symbolism gives him another means of
keeping in touch, however remotely, with more than one possibility
at a time.

Baxter is deeply concerned with the inaccuracies of language, and
here his views are very much like those of the Royal Society,[14]
though his emphasis reflects his central concern for peace, and for
scientific accuracy only insofar as that can be instrumental toward
the achievement of peace. He believes that wars are more often
fought over misunderstandings than over real ideological disagree-

ments. Every word is a *signum* that has three relations—to the matter spoken of, to the mind of the speaker, and to the mind of the hearer. To find words fitted to all these uses, responsive to the subject, and signifying the same thing to speaker and hearer, is almost impossible.[15]

The difficulty is increased when men begin to enjoy playing with words for their own sake; thus it is better to call a spade a spade even if that commits one to a plain, inelegant address. Yet plain talking offends some people. Thus by removing the difficulties of communication in one respect, one may increase them in another. Baxter finds the dilemma insoluble, but the general direction of his thinking is that one must be as plain as possible (thus showing due love and respect to the *subject*) without forgetting to love the person whom one is addressing. To be effective, language must be accurate, and it must be accurately heard. Like Donne, Baxter is upset by the conflicting needs of his congregation, but he chooses not to attempt the kind of sophisticated rhetoric that Donne conceives because in his view that sort of rhetoric creates more problems than it solves. His impulse is to work for more personal and more immediate kinds of communication, to work with one family at a time, or one person at a time. That is how he achieved such an impressive, devoted, understanding congregation at Kidderminster, and he often says that personal conversation with anyone who misunderstood or disliked his writings always cleared up the differences between them.

For Baxter, then, there is no question of a reciprocal relationship with a work of art, because he chooses not to focus on the work that much. His great concern for written language is a sign of his distress over its inadequacies; it is always a means only, and if a better could be found, he would take it. Meanwhile, he makes it very clear that a mutual bond is not ideally to be achieved in address to a large number of people, especially unknown people. Both in print and in person, he strives for greater intimacy. His wish to make the style a clear glass window indicates his sense of how much a barrier between people words can become—a painted window, keeping out the light.[16]

He makes an effort toward partial solution by dedicating his various published works to specific congregations, like his Kidderminster parish. But characteristically he acknowledges that other people are going to read them too, and he also includes a more general dedication, addressed, for example, to hypocrites, doubters or true believers. He is not afraid of the Kidderminster audience; he knows them, and is writing for them the things that he believes they need to hear said. But he is afraid of the reaction of the general audience, because he thinks of them as more sophisticated and less time-bound.

He apologizes for his style to that wider auditory by saying that he is talking to ignorant people (it is not clear how he expected his Kidderminsterians to react to that information), and that a more sophisticated audience must bear in mind that immediate purpose and tolerate the simple language and the prolixity. Like Bunyan, he claims the necessity of a plain style as opposed to a playful one, because when souls are at stake it is no time to play. As for the repetitiousness, ignorant people cannot remember something when you tell it to them only once; the message must be repeated many times in many ways. Baxter undercuts this point, too, by adding that on the other hand, ignorant people have such short attention spans that they cannot listen to a long sermon or read a long book. Always, Baxter looks in more than one direction at the same time, and can solve none of his dilemmas. The problem is that men are mortal, and as long as that is true, communication must be inadequate.

Yet there is something disingenuous in Baxter's defenses of himself. If those unknown readers of his works have souls to be saved, then his directness of address is for them as well as the people of Kidderminster, and meanwhile it is rather hard on the Kidderminsterians to have their limitations advertised—and, one would think, unconducive to a good pastoral relationship. But he wants to eat his cake and have it too—to be a good country parson without sacrificing his reputation among the intellectuals. Our attention, then, inevitably is turned toward him, and his direct statements about himself in relation to his writing.

His seemingly most unequivocal apology is made some years after the silencing of the ministers: because he has been parted five years from his books and three from his preaching, his eloquence and learning are in decline. The reader must expect neither quotations nor ornaments.[17] The rudeness of the style then becomes an emblem of the evils of the age, which must bear the blame, and Baxter's emphasis on his rude style is a way of emphasizing the fallen condition of man.

One of his fullest and most characteristic statements of his own feelings about his style occurs in the concluding pages of the first part of the *Reliquiae*, just before his self-analysis. The passage is worth quoting in full, because so much of Baxter's whole philosophy of life is in it:

And concerning almost all my Writings I must confess, that my own Judgment is, that fewer well studied and polished had been better: but the Reader who can safely censure the Books is not fit to censure the Author, unless he had been upon the Place, and acquainted with all the Occasions and Circumstances: Indeed for the *Saints Rest* I had Four Months Vacancy to write it (but in the midst of continual Languishing and Medicine): But for the rest I wrote them in the Crowd of all my other Imployments, which would allow me no great Leisure for Polishing and Exactness, or any Ornament; so that I scarce ever wrote one Sheet twice over, nor stayed to make any blots or Interlinings, but was fain to let it go as it was first conceived: And when my own Desire was rather to stay upon one thing long, than run over many, some sudden Occasions or other extorted almost all my Writings from me: and the Apprehensions of *Present Usefulness* or *Necessity* prevailed against all other Motives. So that the Divines which were at hand with me still put me on and approved of what I did, because they were moved by *present Necessities* as well as I: But those that were far off, and felt not those nearer Motives, did rather wish that I had taken the other way, and published a few elaborate Writings; and I am ready my self to be of their Mind, when I forget the Case that then I stood in, and have lost the Sense of former Motives. The opposing of the Anabaptists, Separatists, Quakers, Antinomians, Seekers, &c., were Works which *then* seemed necessary; and so did the Debates about Church Government and Communion which touched our present Practice; but now all those Reasons are past and gone, I could wish I had rather been doing some work of more durable Usefulness. But even to a foreseeing Man, who knoweth what will be of longest use, it is hard to discern how far that which is *presently* needful may be omitted, for the sake of a greater future Good. There are some other works, wherein my Heart hath more been set than any of those forementioned; in which I have met with great Obstructions. For I must declare that in this as in many other Matters I have found that we are not the Choosers of our own Imployments, no more than of our own Successes (Pt. I. 212, p. 124).

Lack of time is only one small part of the problem. It is true that, quite aside from his authorship, Baxter's days were so crowded that it is difficult to understand when he could have found time to write. But since he did find it, there is no reason, as far as time alone is concerned, why he should not have written fewer books "well studied and polished." The point is, as I have noted earlier, that Baxter always responded with tremendous urgency to the immediate situation. One can observe this simply in the way he handled the correspondence that is now built into the *Reliquiae*. Troubled people writing for advice, scholars asking for elucidation of difficult texts, controversialists merely trying to engage him in argument, all alike ran the risk of receiving a weighty tome, if not by return post, at least by the morning mail. Many of his books began as letters or impromptu notes. Certainly more consideration might have resulted in more deliberate, less personal work. And yet the personalism, the zeal, the immediacy are important to Baxter, and he regrets in later years the weakening of these characteristics in himself.

A larger problem here is the opposition between microscopic and macrocosmic vision, between the man who does engage wholeheartedly in controversy and personal dialogue, and the one who distinguishes between what is important at the moment, and what will be of durable worth. Baxter's position is, as always, that to a person who is not on the scene, it may look as though he is wasting his energies, and perhaps he is. The point is that although a man can transcend his own mortality enough to understand this, he cannot and probably should not try to transcend it in such a way as to remove himself and his concerns from these immediate, moment-to-moment claims upon his time and talents.

Humanity is not to be redeemed in time. His view of progress before the Revolution may have been radical; but in later years it is clearly conservative. Utopia is a chimera; man is imperfect and sinful, and always will be. That does not mean that one should not engage in social action, however. Man is on earth for just that purpose, to be God's instrument, to work for the salvation of the souls of others and his own. Success is limited and transient, and perhaps finally meaningless in any human terms. But the work is there to be done, and man is there to do it. I think that in this respect Baxter would say that for him to strive for literary immortality would have been to endeavor to bypass his mortal condition. God put him on earth to be human, and human he must be. Again, he accepts and uses all his limitations.

At any rate, passive and predestinarian as any Puritan, he says that it is not up to the godly man to choose. When Baxter has had literary ambitions of his own, they have never been realized. Elsewhere, he says that he never decided in advance what he would write, just as he never set his heart on any given course of action. He made himself God's instrument. In this use of a man, and in the public exhibition of a rude style, God may teach the author humility.

For a final elaboration of this point, Baxter's comments on the style of the Bible may be connected with one other passage on his own writing. The style of Scripture, it would seem, is in the eye of the beholder. Seventeenth-century Anglican writers followed late medieval commentators in speaking of its beauty and elegance, and justified their own style by saying that as God comes to us, we must come to him. It would be irreverent to answer him plainly and rudely, or to unfold the text of a sermon in coarse and vulgar language. Puritans, on the other hand, praised the simplicity and clarity of Scripture, and again on that basis justified their own style, as one which neither played games with words nor made darkness out of light.

Baxter typically begins from neither of these viewpoints. He sets up a situation in which he is to defend Scripture against the charge that it was written by unlearned men. This is his response:

The words are but the Dish to serve up the Sense in; God is content that the words should not only have in them a savour of Humanity, but of much Infirmity, so that the Work of convincing the World may be furthered thereby. And I verily think, that this is God's great Design, in permitting these precious Spirits of Divine Truth, to run in the Veins of infirm Language, that so Men may be convinced in all succeeding Ages, that Scripture is no Device of Humane Policy. If the Apostles had been learned and subtil Men, we should sooner have suspected their Finger in the Contrivance. Yea, it is observable, that in such as *Paul*, that had some Humane Learning, yet God would not have them make much use of it, lest the Excellency of the Cross of Christ should seem to lie in the enticing words of Man's Wisdom; and lest the Success of the Gospel should seem to be more from the Ability of the Preacher, than from the Arm of God.[18]

In the preface to the second edition of *The Saints Everlasting Rest,* he says that most of the errors of the first edition are uncorrected here, because the printer thought that a perfect text would be an offense to those who had bought the earlier one. You may ask, he says, why the errors were made in the first place. They were made because I was sick. Why did I not then wait until I was well? I thought I was dying, "and I am so conscious of my own Imperfections, that I know they will appear in all that I do . . . If great *Austin* so frequently and passionately confesseth so much by himself, *Who am I, that I should hope of better?* So much of this Edition." [19]

Both in the defense of Scriptural style and in the passage on the errors in his own prose, the argument is the same. Imperfection is intrinsic to man. And, again, the very imperfections in one's style accrue to the glory of God. For if it is apparent by its errors that the style is but the instrument, or, as he says, "the Dish to serve up the Sense in," then it will also be apparent that the credit for all revelation and all achievement can be only God's. The imperfect style symbolizes man's mortal condition; the effectiveness of the work demonstrates God's redeeming grace. Thus, again, by accepting limitation and saying that the style is only a dish, he endows it with its own poignant symbolism. Even the small vanity inherent in his excessive defence of his style contributes to this effect.

There are obvious difficulties in the way of using these apologetical defenses for style to construct any kind of esthetic theory. It is important to an understanding of Baxter to see how what I have called his back-door symbolism corroborates the whole pattern and bent of his prose. But his arguments are a negation of esthetic value, and if applied literally could be used to give undue credit to any incompetent writing. It is important not to give undue credit even to Baxter. And part of the intention of this chapter has been to show that he denies himself so much that while his *Reliquiae* will endure as long as the English seventeenth century continues to be interesting, it endures less as literature than as the portrait of a wise and good and much tormented man. He presents a true and moving picture of the conflicts of his age because he bears them within himself, and the reason why his style is moving is that, just because of the intensity with which he rejects a conventional style or viewpoint and conscious self-indulgence, "his very Spirit is Drench'd therein."

This paradox becomes clearer when we turn to direct consideration of Baxter's concept of himself. Here again I must begin with a delineation of Baxter's limitations, and then go on to show how uniquely he uses them. His self-consciousness is of quite a different order from any other discussed in this book, and it is, I think, less coherent: he cannot wholly accept any tradition or ideological patterns of coherence. The limitations of seventeenth-century self-consciousness are especially clear in Baxter, too.

He often talks about self-knowledge in a thoroughly homiletic and conventional way, as the understanding of the state of one's soul in its relationship with God. In examples like the following, almost no psychological penetration is perceptible. A man who spends all his time in the tavern instead of at home is wicked and self-indulgent. If he tells you he cannot stop drinking, he is lying to himself and to you. He is perfectly well able to stop, and if anyone convinced him that he would go to hell tomorrow if he took another glass tonight, he would have no difficulty in remaining sober. That is the general method of approach.

Much more interesting and relevant to our purposes is his clear analysis of the Puritan assumption that man ought to consider himself God's instrument. In order to be a good instrument, he must know himself, which is to say that he must try to know God's will for him, and the means to fulfill it. Implicit in this viewpoint is the belief that too much self-consideration can be more dangerous than too little. Man can easily lose himself by seeking himself because in excessive self-regard he forgets about God, with whose help alone he can achieve true self-knowledge. Baxter also points out in repeated analogies that since man is an instrument, self-knowledge is only the entrance into wisdom. People who spend all their time considering the state of their souls "are like Musicians, that will spend all the Day in setting Instruments in Tune; or like a Mower that spends most of his time in whetting. They are all Day preparing their Tools, while they should be working! And putting on their Armour, and preparing their Weapons, when they should be fighting: And enquiring which is the Way, when they should be Travelling . . . More Letters must be learned than [I,] or we shall never learn to read." [20]

We are properly reminded, not only of Donne and others tuning their own instruments, but also of the many Anglican figures involving the concept of the soul as a mechanical thing acted upon by God, figures which to Leo Spitzer seemed intrinsic to metaphysical wit.[21] The Puritan concept is considerably less meditative and not witty at all. It is also much more concerned with the placement of the instrument in time and with its active participation in the world. Thus one aspect of it is the highly mechanical reading of history according to which all happenings demonstrate the providence of God. Baxter tries to break himself of personal will or plan to go here or there: "And I noted the mercy of God in this, that I never went to any place in my Life, among all my Changes, which I had before desired, designed or thought of, (much less sought); but only to those that I never thought of, till the sudden Invitation did surprize me" (Pt. I. 29, p. 20). A standard formula of Puritan biography—"it pleased God" [22]—is everywhere in this history, applied both to per-

sonal and to public events, always in a way that assumes God's providential love to Baxter and to those whom Baxter favors. Thus both
his illnesses and the ill fortunes of his enemies are signs of God's
mercy. His illness detaches him from worldly things and turns him
toward God; but the ill fortunes of his foes are marks of God's dis-
pleasure. The silencing of the ministers, the plague, and the London
fire are all signs of God's judgment on the very people who caused
or allowed the ministers to be silenced.

The combination of this imposed design with Baxter's insistence
upon literal detail can create a highly comic effect, the obviously abstract and inflexible frame being filled with unique particulars. Here
he is listing the wonderful ways in which God has delivered him
from injury by accidents (another "epic" listing):

> Another time, as I sat in my Study, the Weight of my greatest Folio Books
> brake down three or four of the highest Shelves, when I sat close under them,
> and they fell down on every side me, save one upon the Army; whereas the
> Place, the Weight, and greatness of the Books was such, and my Head just
> under them, that it was a Wonder they had not beaten out my Brains, one of
> the Shelves right over my Head having the six Volumes of Dr. *Walton's Ori-
> ental Bible*, and all *Austin's* Works, and the *Bibliotheca Patrum*, and *Mar-
> lorate*, &c. (Pt. I. 133, p. 82).

One may usefully compare the "metaphysical" effort, in a writer like
Donne, to force an abstraction into a confining and very specific figure of speech: the conflict between the two, when the figure is successful, creates that dazzling union of humor, passion, and intensity
that is called metaphysical wit.[23] Here the effort is to graft a rigid
concept of history upon a very literal, detailed rendering of individual experience in order to prove the working of God's providence
upon Richard Baxter. Inevitably, one is bemused by the fact that
Baxter was struck by a book on the army, but not by the Fathers of
the Church. God's Providence is altogether excessive.

Lilburne's automatic affirmation at every turn, of his rights as an
Englishman, is like this. Because every experience must be newly apprehended, and presents an equal challenge to the actor's vision of
life's meaning in relation to him, it is difficult for Lilburne, and for
Baxter insofar as he adheres to this framework, to sift the unimportant from the important. On the one hand, there is a real capacity to
strip away euphemism and a priori assumptions from experience. On
the other hand, just because those assumptions have been stripped

away, it is urgently necessary to establish new ones, or to establish one's credentials in relation to them, and then to reaffirm those credentials at every point.

This anxiety to determine whether one's every experience fits the proper pattern (or, more accurately speaking, this zealous effort to make all experiences fit) is what the Puritans called self-knowledge. Perhaps its most amusing manifestation is horror of melancholy. Melancholy was associated with religious despair and with doubt of salvation, and it was desirable that a saved man, even in the midst of St. Paul's sufferings, should be full of cheer, for that was a sign of God's grace. One of Baxter's greatest tribulations was that the doctors kept diagnosing his physical ills as "hypochondriack melancholia," and he keeps reassuring the reader (and no doubt himself as well) that this physical disease was not real (or psychological) melancholy, that in spite of all his physical pain, he never for a moment suffered from real melancholy. His discomfort was certainly immense when it got out at one point that his doctors had doubted his account of his symptoms: "I became the common Talk of the City, especially the Women; as if I had been a melancholy Humourist, that conceited my Reins were petrified, when it was no such matter, but meer Conceit. And so while I lay Night and Day in Pain, my supposed Melancholy (which, I thank God, all my Life hath been extraordinarily free from) became, for a Year, the Pity, or Derision of the Town" (Pt. III. 311, p. 173).

In these efforts to make himself and life conform to his idea of the proper character and life for God's instrument, Baxter operates in a thoroughly mechanical way. In fact, his own comments on self-knowledge, together with this treatment of himself, suggest that Baxter took all too literally his belief in his role as God's instrument, dulling irreparably his keener powers of self-analysis. But as always, the facts are not that easy. Side by side with these superficial or simplistic views is the much more adequate account of himself in his self-examination at the end of Part I of the *Reliquiae*, as well as certain less conscious but very present undercurrents that create running themes through the whole book, and provide it with much more coherence than does the imposed historical pattern.

Both conscious and subconscious procedures portray Baxter tuning his instrument. Speaking elsewhere on style, he wrote, "Truth loves the Light, and is most Beautiful when most naked . . . ." [24]

His style is almost always unobtrusive, but in his self-analysis it is as clear as glass. The paragraphing and sentence structure are leisurely, graceful, and almost without identifying characteristics. The tone is dispassionate. The whole essay is organized as a contrast of youth with age, to illustrate "what Change God hath made upon my Mind and Heart since those unriper times, and wherein I now differ in Judgment and Disposition from my self" (Pt. I. 213, p. 124). Some of the differences are general in men: the understanding is less quick, but more profound; both his knowledge and knowledge of his ignorance have increased; his veneration for fundamental truths is greater and he is less interested in idle controversy; he is more than ever convinced of the folly of expecting a golden age. His most moving admission is of his doubts about Christianity; he recognizes that these, too, are a condition of the world, and it is this realization above all that makes him look forward to the removal of all doubt in heaven.

One noteworthy mark of this essay is Baxter's concern with words and books. It is by reference to his earlier works, for example, that he traces his progress: ". . . when I peruse the Writings which I wrote in my younger Years, I can find the Footsteps of my unfurnished Mind, and of my Emptyness and Insufficiency" (Pt. I. 213, p. 125). Language, as always, is blamed for many of the problems of men, especially controversy and dissension. Imperfection in language misleads, zeal in language alienates, slander in language deceives. Yet where is a remedy to be found save in language? Baxter's remedy, I think, is that which would also apply to the soul. Let both be treated as God's instruments, cared for as such, and put wholly at His disposal. The great simple calm of Baxter's style in this essay surely reflects an outstanding characteristic of his soul.

Yet again I have to qualify what I have said. An instrument, like a lute or a scythe, has no consciousness of its own. In this sense, a medieval man might be said to be an instrument if he identified himself by his function. But by the mid-seventeenth century, this way of being was no longer possible for an Englishman in the main stream of events, and certainly not for a man so extremely self-aware as Baxter. On the one hand, he does refuse to think of himself as anything more than one of God's ordinary tools. In his self-analysis, he refuses to discuss "soul-experiments" or "heart-occurrences," by which he means specific psychological and spiritual events, especially those relating to conversion. These, he says, are expected; I have shown in my first and second chapters that they are the characteristic matter of Puritan diaries. Baxter thinks it would be "somewhat unsavoury to recite them; seeing God's Dealings are much what the same with all his Servants" (Pt. I. 213, p. 128). But on the other hand, considering faith and knowledge, he believes with Descartes that his strongest certainty is of his own existence, stronger by far than his certainty of God. Thus when he turns his attention to himself, body and soul, as God's instrument, he has to be interested in himself as an instrument by means of which only the maker of the instrument can be known.

For him, this is a daring thought, and one which he does not permit himself to consider at any great length. But it does emphasize the extent to which he must sometimes have felt himself both separated from the world, and a key to any understanding of it. And it helps to explain the peculiarly vivid self-awareness that is integral to his concept of himself as instrument. In this respect, two matters constantly preoccupy him, and become counterpointing themes in the whole work.

Baxter uses two significant figures to represent his role in history: he was a pen, and a cross-bearer. Both indicate what might be expected of a Christian learned in church history. He is able to defend the Church and to suffer with it. The two figures are not mutually exclusive. The themes that attach themselves to these figures are the theme of slander, which causes spiritual suffering, and the theme of physical pain. Being the potent, active, and provocative force that it is in the fallen world, writing inevitably brings about physical suffering by persecution; and cross-bearing refers to both spiritual and physical oppression. Thus, to be a pen is to be a cross-bearer, and to be the object of slander, hard as it is to bear, is part of the Puritan writer's vocation.

The theme of slander is one which I have discussed in relation to Bunyan and Lilburne, characterizing a figure called the Slanderer as standing for the undervoice of conservatism.[25] But the theme is of such great importance in Baxter that it is appropriate to reopen the subject here. It is obvious now that slander is no exclusive characteristic of the Anglican know-nothing, since Baxter is assaulted equally from the Separatist left and the Royalist right, for continuing to associate himself with the church on the one hand, and for refusing to sign its oaths on the other. In Baxter's discussions of slander, many reasons for its existence and its peculiar effectiveness against Puritan writers become clear.

For Baxter, slander is a degenerative misuse of language more culpable than other misuses because so often deliberate. The Puritan is trying to free language of ambiguities, obscurities, and over-refinements of style in order to make himself as clear as possible; and just because he has such need to be clear, he is particularly vulnerable to the malicious abuse of language represented by slander. Anglicans and Royalists stood by codes of belief that had been operative for centuries. The Puritans were endeavoring, to greatly varying degrees, to redefine, revise, or revolutionize these codes, and slander was an effective method to prevent their true beliefs from becoming known, and thus to minimize useful interchange among themselves, or between them and the conformists. New doctrines were particularly dependent on the good repute of the men who espoused them. Baxter, known as a man with a difficult temper, was widely accused of having murdered a tinker who innocently interrupted his studies (Appendices, p. 117, No. VII). It was a peculiarly appropriate and devastating kind of slander to level against a man whose whole purpose in life was to bring about unity and peace through love. Furthermore, when dissident opinions are being expressed by members of a minority, such men are vulnerable to persecution, which can, and did in Baxter's case, take two forms. Ignorant people, inflamed by misleading stories, persecuted him by direct attacks upon his house and his person.[26] And the Royalist government used informers to charge him with crimes leading to fines and imprisonment, giving Baxter no opportunity to acquit himself of the charges. It was often difficult, under ordinary circumstances, for a Puritan to refute slander, since he had much less easy access to the press than did the establishment, and is was possible for his work to be censored or distorted even in press. He was therefore considerably more vulnerable to gossip and intrigue, both printed and oral, than were his opponents.

But what frightens Baxter perhaps most of all is the prospect that slander may be taken for history. Like many Puritans, he has an instinctive belief in history,[27] in its value as a teaching device, in its revelation of divine purpose, and in its character as a design in which each individual has an ordained place. The prevalence of lying histories destroys the possibility of placing any confidence in the only vehicle by which the pattern and meaning of life can be made manifest.

Aside from the public mischief it causes, slander, as I have already implied, can have a devastating personal effect. It seems to me possible that beyond its particular responsiveness to Puritan theories of language and history, its prevalence at this time may have some relationship to the increasing awareness of people as individuals. A person is more vulnerable to slander than he has ever been before. Such attacks, in turn, must have heightened the self-consciousness of the individual, causing him to analyze his character in their light—and yet, since slander really creates not light but murk, bewildering and exhausting him. While the concept of a public "image" is being explored at this time, it is by no means as familiar as it is nowadays, nor could a man like Baxter in any event have achieved the indifference to slander which is almost essential to a man much in public view. Even Lilburne at one point expresses weariness with public life.

Baxter lists these reasons why the Royalists vilify him: overvaluation of his abilities, which they fear; his blameless reputation; overvaluation of his interest with the people; his conference with the king, contradicting the Royalist views of Bishop Morley; his refusal of a bishopric; his being nearer to them in belief and therefore in a better position to undermine them than other nonconformists. His stress upon their overrating him is typical: he consistently resists both praise and blame. It is his function as reconciler, he says, which is attacked, and his centrality. Again and again, he speaks of himself as caught between two extremes: "This Day, while I am writing these Words, my Pockets are full of Letters sent me, on one side importunately charging it on me as my Duty to conform . . . and on the other side vehemently censuring me as guilty of grievous Sin, for declaring my Judgment for so much of Conformity as I have done . . . And how should I answer these contrary Expectations, or escape the Censures of such Expectants." [28] We are reminded of Donne's and Burton's similar queries about their varied audiences, but their contrary music would not have answered Baxter's need.

I have spoken much of the Puritan use of words as weapons. Baxter has used them in this way in his controversial writing, particularly, he says, in his earlier works. Now he sees that such a practice simply antagonizes those who are attacked, and forces them to defend themselves automatically. Keenness of language, especially prophetic language, may be called slander by the opposition, and it may call forth slander in return. Thus it is better not to engage in this kind of disputation at all, but to adopt in controversy a teaching and learning way of intercourse that begins not with controversy but with love. Yet once attacks are hurled against him, it does not occur to him to respond by turning the other cheek. He did not see any other way to encounter slander than by attempting to answer it, and to clear the record. That is one reason why he wrote so much. It is also one reason why he wrote his history of himself, trying to make it as objective as possible, in order to offset the biased accounts of others.

The very frequent mention and description of slanders against him, throughout the three parts of the *Reliquiae*, keep the reader in mind of all that I have said. In this society words have an immediate and primitive kind of importance. After all, Baxter says of himself, with characteristic humility, "I was but a pen in God's hands, and what praise is due to a pen?" [29] But the life of a pen is in words, and slander can deprive those words of their effectiveness.

On the other hand, as a cross-bearer in Paul's tradition, as a peacemaker, and as a Puritan willing to be responsible for his theories of language and history, Baxter sees that to accept slander may be part of his vocation:

Seeing so many in prison, for this Error, to the dishonour of God, and so many more like to be ruin'd by it, and the separating party, by the temptation of suffering, had so far prevailed with the most strict, and zealous Christians, that a great Number were of their mind, and the Non-conformable Ministers, whose Judgment was against this separation, durst not publish their dislike of it, partly because of sharp and bitter Censures of the Separatists, who took them for Apostates or Carnal Temporizers that communicated in publick, and partly for fear of Encouraging Persecution against the Separatists, and partly for fear of losing all opportunity of teaching them (and some that had no hope of any other friends or maintenance, or Auditors thought they might be silent,) On all these accounts, I, that had no gathered Church, nor lived on the Contribution of any such, and was going out of the world in pain and Languor, did think that I was fittest to bear men's Censures, and to take that reproach on my self, which my brethren were less fit to bear, who might live for farther Service. And at the Importunity of the Book-seller, I consented to publish the Reasons of my Communicating in the Parish-Churches, and against Separation (Pt. III. 80, p. 197).

At this point the two themes of spiritual and physical suffering meet one another. Paradoxically, the spiritual suffering is inflicted by men, whereas he believes his physical illnesses to have been sent by

God for his own good, to free him from love of earthly things. From youth up through extreme old age, he was troubled by a succession of complaints as bizarre, numerous, and painful as can ever have afflicted a man neither psychotic nor moribund. In fact, moribund is exactly what he always thought he was. His constant stress upon his pain, throughout the first and third parts of the *Reliquiae*, is the most exotic, the most personal, and in some ways the most disturbing mark of this work.

Literal as always, he includes complete accountings of his ailments, giving two reasons—that they illustrate God's mercies to him, and that others taken ill in similar ways may find useful his many efforts to discover cures, and his occasional questionable successes. His epic cataloguing of his diseases is once placed in immediate juxtaposition with a cataloguing of his writings—the cross-bearer on the one hand, the pen on the other:

It would trouble the *Reader* for me to reckon up the many Diseases, and Dangers for these ten Years past, in, or from which, God hath delivered me; though it be my Duty not to forget to be thankful. Seven Months together I was lame, with a strange Pain in one Foot; Twice delivered from a Bloody Flux; a spurious Cataract in my Eye (with incessant Webs and Net-works before it) hath continued these eight Years, without disabling me one Hour from Reading or Writing: I have had constant Pains and Languors, with incredible Flatulency in Stomach, Bowels, Sides, Back, Legs, Feet, Heart, Breast, but worst of all, either painful Distentions, or usually vertiginous or stupefying Conquests of my Brain, so that I have rarely one Hour's, or quarter of an Hour's ease. Yet, through God's mercy, I was never one Hour Melancholy, and not many Hours in a Week disabled utterly from my Work, save that I lost time in the Morning, for want of being able to rise early: And lately, an Ulcer in my Throat, with a Tumour, of near half a Year's continuance, is healed without any means. In all which I have found such Merciful Disposals of God, such suitable Chastisements for my Sin, such plain Answers of Prayer, as leave me unexcusable if they do me not good. Besides many sudden and acuter Sicknesses, which God hath delivered me from, not here to be numbred; his upholding Mercy under such continued weaknesses, with tolerable, and seldom disabling Pains, hath been unvaluable.

I am next to give some short account of my Writings since 1665 (Pt. III. 133, pp. 60–61).

Stylistically, one can account for both ailments and books in the epic framework I have described, as epic catalogues. Contextually, one can account for their juxtaposed presence as Baxter himself did: they are evidence of God's mercies. It is also an evidence of God's mercy that despite his illness, he was able to write so much. Beyond this, where he discusses some specific ills, he suggests that their description may contribute to the knowledge and practice of medicine. It is an odd combination of the modern inductive case-history with extremely naive (though characteristically seventeenth-century) medical techniques.

With his first early mention of his ills, he claims brevity, saying that "to recite a Catalogue of my Symptoms and Pains, from Head to Feet, would be a tedious interruption to the Reader . . ." (Pt. I. 9, p. 10). He is not tedious, but as we have seen before, his idea of brevity is unique. Several times during the course of the *Reliquiae* he gathers all his accumulated woes into a single listing, just as he periodically presents his latest bibliography. His explanation is that the listing is necessary, primarily as an account of God's providence, and that to dispose of the subject in this way will enable him to avoid it elsewhere. But it is not that simple. The cataloguing is so vivid that it is not easily dismissed from the mind, and there is constant brief mention of his ailments throughout the *Reliquiae*. He tells us that he consulted thirty-six doctors, including the chief medical adviser to Charles II, and the President of the College of Physicians.

So far as the texture of his prose is concerned, it does support his claim that he was never the victim of "real" melancholy. While the details are vivid, they are not adjectival; considering the number of his illnesses, he lists them rather briskly. Nevertheless, they remain in the mind, and the memory is assisted by the brief mentions, which constantly renew upon his prose the pressure of the imminence of death. He spoke, he often reminds us, "as a dying Man to dying Men." (Pt. I. 32, p. 21). We are returned here to the earlier discussion of the sense of time in his prose, and its discontinuity, every moment being valued in itself, with no certainty of chronology.

Often, physical pain is a way of making persecution seem irrelevant. The court trial in Baxter does not become a climax, as it does in Lilburne and others, because he is constantly expecting a climax of another kind:

After many times deliverance from the Sentence of death, on November Twenty, One thousand six hundred eighty four; in the very Enterance of the Seventyeth year of my Age, God was pleased so greatly to increase my painful Diseases, as to pass on me the Sentence of a painful death . . . A little before this while I lay in pain and languishing, the Justices of Sessions, sent

Warrants to apprehend me . . . carried me (scarce able to stand) to their
Sessions . . . But all this is so small a part of my suffering in comparison to
what I bear in my flesh . . . (Pt. III. 83–85, pp. 198–99).

What follows the trial cannot be anticlimactic; on the other hand,
the *Reliquiae* itself is a constant series of anticlimaxes because Baxter's forecasts of his imminent death never proved to be accurate.
The last event recorded took place six years before he died.

Otherwise, the effect of the illness theme upon the reader can be
described in terms of two different kinds of shocking contrast. One
is constantly aware of Baxter's concern with body and books, body
and mind, a concern which represents in part the Puritan impulse to
wrench one from the other. And one is aware too of the way in
which his narrow-minded preoccupation with his own body is
framed by his wise and broad possession of his times. The microcosm-
macrocosm figure is shifted into a new key. In the Anglican writers
it has been a persistent effort to make man and world equivalent, to
enable man to maintain in himself the meaning of an old order; it has
been a dependency on a metaphor. In Baxter the theme is stripped of
metaphor and torn apart. The world is the everyday world of history and politics. Man is an instrument put into the world to be useful, hence very mindful of his own condition as useful instrument.
Physical illness both untunes and tunes him; it weakens his body, but
it makes him mindful of his maker and his end. In Baxter's pain is
evidenced once more the fragmentation of experiences and conditions that Donne and others, as well as Baxter, had tried so hard to
hold together.

And that it is shown here literally in his pain is emblematic. The
word "psychosomatic" would have to occur to any modern reader
considering Baxter's illness, given his descriptions of it as well as the
diagnosis of "hypochondriac melancholy," a very peculiar ailment,
almost impossible to cure, and said to originate sometimes in depres-
sion and idleness.[30] A psychosomatic disease is, of course, physically
real: it simply demonstrates the inseparability of mind and body.
Baxter's self-divisions were both chosen by him and painful to him
because he is a man divided, much more than Donne was, between
different ways of being. His experience of the world is later than
Donne's, and he has endured the rending of party from party, sect
from sect, brother from brother in sustained and bitter wars. Baxter
himself makes no effort to symbolize his suffering, except perhaps in

his description of himself as cross-bearer who must suffer with the church as every Christian ought to do. The idea of the suffering servant is altogether available, but he has too much humility to emphasize it. Surely, though, we are right to read his illness partly in this way, seeing in his incurably torn body the torn body of his world.

I have tried to show in this chapter that for personal, cultural, and ideological reasons Richard Baxter was prevented from creating a successfully literary self-conscious prose. He could accept neither the mannered style of an Anglican like Donne, nor the singlemindedly aggressive style of a Puritan radical like Lilburne. He sees the power of words used either as symbols or as weapons, but cannot commit himself to either technique because he also sees the drawbacks in each. Standing always on middle ground, in style as in belief, he becomes so preoccupied with defending his middleness, and with rejecting extremes, that in the *Reliquiae* one is always conscious of conflict, of opposite tensions, of being in fact at the eye of the hurricane or the center of the storm, where there is no style and yet no lack of style, calm and yet no peace.

Accepting his vocation to immediate, moment-to-moment action, he could not live within the moment as Lilburne could; he tries to write history, and his effort is blurred both by an "Anglican" indifference to time, and by his "modern" tendency to compartmentalize experience. Accepting his vocation to a rude, prolific, and yet inconspicuous way of writing, he constantly turns upon it, worrying about it, and thereby partly defeating his own ends by forcing the reader to pay attention to the style. Thinking of himself as an instrument, he realizes that the instrument must be effective, and becomes so concerned with his vulnerability to slander and ill-health that he turns the reader's attention upon the instrument, the "I" of his prose.

Such contradictions as these have to be more fully conscious to effect a really impressive work. One may take as an illustration the different ways in which Robert Burton and Richard Baxter (mirror images of each other in so many respects) play ambiguous roles in their own books. Burton is both a ridiculous human being and the colossal Democritus who includes, even as he weeps and laughs over, all mankind. Baxter is both the historical robot hit on the head by a book about the army, and a container and reconciler of all the restricted viewpoints, poses, or styles of his time. Both Burton and Baxter have the epic vision that makes their work epic in scope, and both are aware of playing a dual role, of being both wise commentator and limited actor, as Baxter shows when he criticizes while defending his absolute involvement in wholly transient matters. Yet Burton's duality is a technique consciously written into the work as a literary device. Baxter completely accepts the mechanistic view of history that makes him its dupe, even though at other times his vision is so much broader.

This leads to a further point. Partly because Donne and Burton speak of showing themselves forth in their works, the reader is alert to the evidence of the explicit artificiality of their personae. Bunyan and Lilburne create self-images by attempting to live up to the Puritan stereotypes in which they conceived their necessary historical vocations to reside. Baxter, however, has denied himself a literary persona, and at the same time is less committed than Bunyan and Lilburne to one particular world-view that can define his persona for him. Thus, I think, he is more exposed, more "shown forth" in his work in all his human frailty than any of the others, and for the same reason his work is less literary.

The main task of this chapter has been to demonstrate the prose of a self-conscious man wholly committed to neither an Anglican nor a Puritan world-view. Its paradoxical sub-task has been to explain how Baxter and his times can be so beautifully revealed by means of a prose so inadequate. The explanation is that the prose in its very inadequacy reveals the contradictions and paradoxes, the juxtaposed folly and greatness of an age as they existed in one single mortal man who put himself at their mercy and thereby became his age in all its weaknesses and strengths. Because he did put himself so completely at their mercy, he could never have made himself an epic figure in the way that Burton did, or exercised the control over his autobiography that could have made it a literary masterpiece. But one can think of him as Burton's historical counterpart. It is true that both men now have life only by virtue of their prose. But the effect of Baxter's prose seems to be to present history, and him in history, in all his artless and unguarded human frailty. It is hard to think of Baxter in the present tense, or to think of putting quotation marks around his name to suggest a persona, whereas with Burton or Donne one has no such difficulty. Just as Robert Burton as historical figure is almost unknown, having his whole life in his timeless, and thereby vast, Democritus persona, so "Baxter" as a literary figure seems inconsiderable. The *Reliquiae* seems only to show forth Baxter as wholly mortal man, and thereby as a dubious, heroic defender of human brotherhood against his own and his world's long odds.

CHAPTER VI

SIR THOMAS BROWNE:
ART AS
RECREATION

WHEN DR. THOMAS BROWNE RETURNED FROM EUROPE IN DECEMBER, 1633, he was twenty-eight years old. He had studied at Montpellier, Padua, and Leiden; he had lived and travelled in climates far removed physically, intellectually, and spiritually from that of England. He was probably in Padua in 1632 when Galileo published his *Dialogue on the Great World Systems,* a work which instantly captured the attention of all learned Italy, and led to Galileo's trial and sentencing in 1633. Everywhere were opened to him new doctrines and new worlds. With an M.D. from Leiden, he returned to a required four-year apprenticeship for the Oxford medical degree. Between this time and his thirtieth birthday, he wrote his *Religio Medici,* which is, I think, pre-eminently the work of a young man, pleased with himself and the world, full of his adventures, receptive to new ideas and anxious to test them on his friends, and yet understandably reluctant to commit himself to forthright public expression.

The *Religio* has been so well read and studied for so many generations that it is almost impossible to look at it afresh. Within a few days of its first, unauthorized publication, Sir Kenelm Digby had written a twenty-five-page commentary upon it. It went through eight separate editions during Browne's lifetime, and has been consciously imitated at least eighty-three times.[1] It has been admired and criticized in every age, by men of altogether different styles and temperaments, among whom are Dr. Johnson, Coleridge, Hazlitt, Carlyle, Pater, and Melville. Browne was not "revived" in our century, like other seventeenth-century writers: he did not need to be.[2]

To his contemporaries, he was either an impertinent upstart, perhaps even an atheist, or the kind of spiritual pioneer to whom less original minds can respond instantly with a sense of liberation and gratitude. The *Religio* is spiritual autobiography, but, unlike the Puritan model, it is not concerned with conversion or even with the religious life in its narrower sense. Rather, it is a wide-ranging, many-levelled view of a human mind, the first book of this sort to be written in English, and it must have been a revelation to anyone who had not read Montaigne. Digby simply could not understand the point of it:

> What should I say of his making so particular a Narration of personal things, and private thoughts of his owne; the knowledge whereof can not much conduce to any mans betterment? (which I make account is the chief end of his writing this Discourse) As where he speaketh of the soundnesse of his Body or the course of his Diet, of the coolnesse of his Bloud at the Summer Solstice of his age, of his neglect of an *Epitaph:* how long he hath lived, or may live; what *Popes, Emperours, kings, Grand-Seigniors,* he hath been contemporary unto, and the like: Would it not be thought that he hath a special good opinion of himselfe? Surely, if he were to write by retale the particulars of his own Story and Life, it would be a notable *Romance,* since he telleth us in one total Summe, it is a continued Miracle of thirty years. Though he creepeth gently upon us at first, yet he groweth a *Gyant,* an *Atlas* (to use his own expression) at the last.[3]

There have continued to be readers, like Samuel Johnson, who have felt much the same way, even while appreciating Browne considerably more than Digby did.

On the other hand, it is clear that, to many people, Browne's whole style of thought has seemed immensely valuable, creative, and original. Gui Patin, Browne's contemporary and Dean of the Faculty of Medicine at the University of Paris, wrote to a friend of his: "S'il estoit permis aux scavans d'escrire ainsi librement, on nous apprendroit beaucoup de nouveautez: il n'y eut jamais Gazette qui valut cela; la subtilté de l'esprit humain se pourroit descouvrir par cette voye." [4] If a countryman of Montaigne's could react thus, it is not surprising that Browne should have excited wide-ranging enthusiasms both abroad and at home.[5] John Aubrey's comment is succinct and telling: "1642. Religio Medici printed, which first opened my understanding." [6]

So far, the disagreement would rightly seem to be between those who like a self-centered style and can identify with its "I," and those who are repelled or annoyed by it. But Browne's extraordinary and unexpected complexity is also a problem. The reader is led to expect a straightforwardness and lack of guile which are simply not the primary elements in Browne's manner. Of all those considered in this book, his style is the most open and yet the most inscrutable, his thought the most flexible and yet the most mannered, his character the most naive and yet the most sophisticated, his spirit the most optimistic and yet the most melancholy. One never knows where to begin or end in analyzing his work. To greatly varying degrees, all his critics are right. But it is impossible to wait long and patiently enough to discover whether the pattern that changes like a *trompe l'oeil* before one's eyes has changed for the last time, or whether there is still another dimension qualifying all the others.

Partly because Browne allows nothing to interfere with the perfection of his art, his book seems even frivolous at times. Sentence after sentence is a tour de force, so perfectly wrought that, just as at one extreme, in Baxter and Lilburne, life overcomes art, at the other, in Browne, art begins to overcome life. This is a most important reason for the difficulties as well as the joys his readers have found in him. It points up in him as well a tendency to self-indulgence that allows us to be self-indulgent too. He does not make the reader worry about the state of his soul or the common ills of humanity (although he was certainly familiar with those ills) because, in print at least, he takes them less seriously than do those of his contemporaries who are included here. Instead of compelling, he entices, and that is both a defect and a virtue.

In the seventeenth century, the word "recreation," which Browne uses several times in the *Religio*, could mean either "a fresh creation" or "enjoyment." [7] Both meanings are fulfilled in this prose. Recreating his mind in creating his persona, he built into that persona intrinsic ambiguities that give it some of the mystery of the world (of which it is a microcosm) and of God (in whose image Browne is made). The language of game and play is just frequent enough to keep the reader sensitive to the concept of art as recreation, and the prevalence of words like "love," in such a context, emphasizes Browne's enjoyment of this play. Austin Warren has described this book as having a middle style, halfway between the functional low style of the *Pseudodoxia* and the high style of the *Garden of Cyrus*. [8] One might say that in *Vulgar Errors* Browne is most concerned to make a practical contribution to knowledge, that in the *Garden* (appropriately) he is most at play, and in the *Religio* he is halfway between the two. The many-levelledness and the inherent ambiguities of the book certainly reflect the complex age that he and Baxter span. But (I oversimplify immensely to make this valid point) Anglican Browne liberates himself from Baxter's pain by emphasizing style more than meaning and means more than ends, thus floating above the century's ills, as it were, rather than being submerged by them, and creating an art as fragile and spectacular as a prism. The ambiguities and mysteries of it are there to be enjoyed in themselves.

Ambiguity begins with the circumstances of publication, the preface to the reader, and the relationship between Browne and the "I" of his book. Browne did not publish the *Religio* for eight years after it was written, and then only to counteract a corrupt and unauthorized edition printed by Andrew Crooke in 1642. In his preface he claims that the *Religio* was intended as a "memoriall unto me": "This I confesse about seven yeares past, with some others of affinitie thereto, for my private exercise and satisfaction, I had at leisurable houres composed; which being communicated unto one, it became common unto many, and was by transcription successively corrupted untill it arrived in a most depraved copy at the presse" (Pref., p. 9). While his disavowal of previous intent to publish is entirely conventional, it seems very likely under the circumstances that he would never have printed the *Religio* had not Crooke, and Digby's rumored commentary on Crooke's edition, provoked him into it. On the other hand, in the seventeenth century, a manuscript "communicated unto one" could easily achieve fame for its author without ever being printed at all. And Browne's response to the news of that "depraved" and pirated edition was, charmingly, to prepare an authorized version for the pirate Crooke.[9]

Browne, of course, had the opportunity to revise his book for the authorized first edition, though in some haste, and to revise it subsequently.[10] But he preferred to leave it substantially as it had been, a private memorial only insofar as it makes almost no direct acknowledgment of a reader's presence, and insists that it is by no means intended as an "example or rule unto any other" (which certainly undercuts Digby's criticism). No one is likely to devise so complex a persona for himself without at least a hypothetical audience in mind, and rather than taking notice of "sundry particularities and personall expressions therein," the reader is constantly bemused by the extreme wiliness with which Browne creates this public image.[11]

In his apologetic preface, Browne refers for the first time to "things delivered Rhetorically, many expressions therein meerely Tropicall and as they best illustrate my intention," and asks that such expressions not be put to the "rigid test of reason." His most obvious reason for nervousness about his language is that he is writing what has every appearance of being an autobiographical or personal essay, of a much more original and unrestricted kind than had ever before been attempted in English. And yet the "I," who is not identical with Thomas Browne, often describes and expresses himself metaphorically or symbolically. Sir Kenelm Digby, as we have seen, objected simply to the fact of Browne's considering autobiographical material worthy of publication. But he also objected, and critics have continued in subsequent centuries to object, to certain passages which seem too egotistical when read as Browne's assessment of his own importance.

If a poet were to say, as Browne does, that his life is a "miracle of thirty years," his metaphor would be so protected by the formal and familiar conventions of poetry that no one would be likely to charge the author with a lack of humility, to read the metaphor as statement, or even necessarily to associate the metaphor with the life of the author of the poem. Donne, for example, is able to say, "I'll undo the world by dying"; or "what miracles we harmlesse lovers wrought," without receiving more than the usual amount of personal attention. We are prone, however, to believe that "Browne" is Browne, that the metaphors are statement, and that Dr. Browne of Norwich thinks himself a miracle. All these assumptions may be correct, just as the analogous assumptions may be true of the author of the poem. But Browne remains the more vulnerable author, partly because he is writing prose, and partly because his prose is not consistently symbolic, as Donne's is, for example, in the *Devotions*. Add to this the fact of his immense complexity and ambiguity, which would be unusual and difficult even in a poem, and the treacherous character of the *Religio* for any reader becomes apparent.

Wherever one begins in the *Religio*, the persona is dominant, inextricably involved in every aspect of its style. Also everywhere, implied and expressed, are the persona's contradictory characteristics of change and changelessness, which provide a valuable starting-point because they explain and foreshadow so much else. In one respect, "Browne" seems fluid and changeable, as is proper for a man who, as he says, cannot disagree with another's views, since tomorrow they may be his own. Yet at the same time, the prose is the most obviously artificial to be discussed in this book, and the persona is the most static and carefully posed.

Throughout the *Religio*, transformation imagery, as always in Anglican prose, reiterates the theme of man's changeableness. Much of this, of course, is derogatory, but not all of it. There is the familiar imagery of man's moral degeneration as transformation into beast, as well as an analogous image in which the forms of religion become the shapes of man: ". . . there is not any of such a fugitive faith, such an unstable belief, as a Christian; none that do so oft transforme themselves, not into severall shapes of Christianity and of the same Species, but into more unnaturall and contrary formes of Jew and Mahometan" (Pt. I.25). But man's variousness is also a cause of wonder, because it represents the contrary faces of the globe, and makes of him that great and true amphibium, living in divided and distinguished worlds. Taken one step farther, this thought results in his belief that each man is so changeable that he cannot know who he will be or what he may think tomorrow or next year: "I COULD never divide my selfe from any man upon the difference of an opinion, or be angry with his judgment for not agreeing with mee in that, from which perhaps within a few days I should dissent my selfe" (Pt. I.6).

The discontinuousness of Browne's prose is one cause of difficulty in his interpretation. The paragraphs are independent essays, each with its own number, rather like what Bacon's essays would be if numbered and given a common title. In a lesser way, the same can be said of the sentences. Slow-moving, highly polished, and meditative as they are, each can absorb the attention of the reader for some time on its own merits, and without necessary recourse to those that go before and after. And yet without the corrective aid of the context it is easy for the reader to acquire a false conception of Browne, because he does seem to contradict himself both explicitly and implicitly from moment to moment. One can, for example, cite these two passages:

When I take a full view and circle of my selfe, without this reasonable moderator, and equal piece of justice, Death, I doe conceive my selfe the miserablest person extant . . . [It is a symptom of melancholy to be afraid of death, yet sometimes to desire it; this latter I have often discovered in my selfe, and thinke no man ever desired life as I have sometimes death] (Pt. I.38).

Let me not injure the felicity of others, if I say I am as happy as any. [I have that in me that can convert poverty into riches, transforme adversity into prosperity. I am more invulnerable than Achilles. Fortune hath not one place to hit me]. *Ruat coelum, Fiat voluntas tua* salveth all; so that whatsoever happens, it is but what our daily prayers desire. In briefe, I am content, and what should providence adde more? (Pt. II.11).

Stoicism is the underlying motif that reconciles the two passages, but he is saying the same thing from such different points of view that taking the sense of either passage alone, one could come to different conclusions about Browne's character. The point is that happiness and misery are both relative here, but either state can be fully experienced by Browne at a given moment of time.

A more subtle way in which Browne describes man's changefulness has to do with style, as well as viewpoint. Browne's shifts between humility and pride, for example, occur from sentence to sentence, and section to section, and one has to keep in mind the whole book to have even the smallest degree of confidence in one's ability to describe the persona. Consider the sentences in the following section, where Browne moves from a typically relativistic rhetoric, first, to a quite simple but impressive statement of man's unworthiness before God, and then to a very fancy showing forth of himself as cosmic personality. Any one of these sentences, taken by itself, is easy to analyze or diagnose. In context, the task becomes much more complicated:

AGAINE, I am confident and fully perswaded, yet dare not take my oath of my salvation; I am as it were sure, and do beleeve, without all doubt, that there is such a city as *Constantinople*; yet for me to take my oath thereon, were a kinde of perjury, because I hold no infallible warrant from my owne sense, to confirme me in the certainty thereof. And truely, though many pretend an absolute certainty of their salvation, yet when an humble soule shall contemplate her owne unworthinesse, she shall meete with many doubts and suddainely finde how much wee stand in need of the precept of Saint *Paul*, *Worke out your salvation with feare and trembling.* That which is the cause of my election, I hold to be the cause of my salvation, which was the mercy, and beneplacit of God, before I was, or the foundation of the world. *Before Abraham was, I am,* is the saying of Christ; yet is it true in some sense if I say it of my selfe, for I was not onely before my selfe, but *Adam,* that is, in the

Idea of God, and the decree of that Synod held from all Eternity. And in this sense, I say, the world was before the Creation, and at an end before it had a beginning; and thus was I dead before I was alive; though my grave be *England,* my dying place was Paradise, and *Eve* miscarried of mee before she conceiv'd of *Cain* (Pt. I.59).

The relative straightforwardness of the sentence that begins "And truely" both unifies the paragraph and maintains our sympathy with this man who begins by seeming to parade the strength of his faith in the face of doubt, and ends by asserting his pre-existence in eternity. I do not think it matters that the most important element in that central section is a quotation from St. Paul, though it could be argued that this in itself contributes to our momentary but pervasive relief from concentration upon the "I." At any rate, the paragraph is a medley of styles and moods, very clearly reflecting Browne's sense of man's variety. His persona is like quicksilver; there is no containing him.

And yet, seen in another light, he is not like quicksilver at all. Every picture he draws of himself is a fully posed one. Sometimes one attitude is highlighted and sometimes another, but he himself never changes, even though he says he does. The passage in which he claims never to have been married and wishes men could propagate like trees is famous partly because although he wrote it when he was still single, he was married when he published it, and child followed child (to the number of twelve) as unchanged editions ran through the presses. Joan Bennett defends him on the grounds that chaste bachelorhood was essential to the effectiveness of this whole section,[12] and that is just the point. His persona was set in the prose as if in marble; it was not identical with Browne, nor was it something that could change with time.

The sense of time's discontinuity (and hence of man's), so common in the age,[13] is constantly present in Browne's thought and style. But sometimes he is able to see beyond this condition simply by imagining eternity, and the God of eternity, to whom human time is less than a moment:

. . . for to his eternitie which is indivisible, and altogether, the last Trumpe is already sounded, the reprobates in the flame, and the blessed in *Abrahams* bosome. Saint *Peter* spoke modestly, when hee said, a thousand yeares to God are but as one day: for to speake like a Philosopher, those continued instants of time which flow into a thousand yeares, make not to him one moment;

what to us is to come, to his Eternitie is present, his whole duration being but one permanent point without succession, parts, flux, or division (Pt. I.11).

Since all things are present to God, Browne thereby, with all things, achieves contemporaneity with God. Change is superficial, a temporary result of the Fall. And even if one considers human nature alone, apart from God and theology, it is clear that in all its change-fulness mankind is always the same: "To see our selves againe wee neede not looke for *Platoes yeare*, every man is not onely himselfe; there have beene many *Diogenes,* and as many *Tymons,* though but few of that name; men are lived over againe; the world is now as it was in ages past" (Pt. I.6). The names change; the types remain the same.

For Browne, the moment can be like God's eternity gathered into a permanent point. Discontinuity itself makes possible man's sense of immortality. Translated into art, this attitude means that just because the sentences are so discrete, they are free to celebrate each momentary thought or pose, and so to give the moment its own eternity instead of allowing it to be caught up in the rush of time. Hence, the slow-moving, seemingly almost immobile, repetitious and finely-wrought periods that are his unmistakable characteristic.

The persona, then, is a *trompe l'oeil* partly because "Browne" is both changeable and changeless. This basic fact only opens the way to the patterned ambiguities of that temporal timeless "I." One involves a complexity already hinted at: he is full of what would seem to be unwitting illustrations of his own statement that "all is but that we all condemne, selfe-love" (Pt. II.4). These passages suggest that he delights in himself in spite of himself, and in them he seems particularly young and naive:

. . . I would not entertaine a base designe, or an action that should call mee villaine, for the Indies, and for this onely doe I love and honour my owne soule, and have mee thinkes, two armes too few to embrace my selfe (Pt. II.13).

. . . in the midst of all my endeavours there is but one thought that dejects me, that my acquired parts must perish with my selfe, nor can bee Legacyed among my honoured Friends (Pt. II.3).

I THANKE God, amongst those millions of vices I doe inherit and hold from *Adam,* I have escaped one, and that a mortall enemy to charity . . . Pride (Pt. II.8).

157

The last passage is followed by a lengthy enumeration of all the reasons he has for being proud of himself, so many more than can be numbered by men more vulnerable to this sin!

It is possible, I suppose, although I myself find it difficult, to assume a dry irony in these passages, whereby apparent vanity becomes self-deprecation. But even if we should read them as unmitigated egotism, it is still easy to be charmed by the speaker's enthusiasm, in phrases like "two armes too few to embrace my selfe." And even in these apparently easy passages, there are balancing phrases. Consider the fact that Browne says, "for this *onely* doe I love and honour my owne soule," and "amongst *those millions of vices I doe inherit* . . . I have escaped one" (italics mine). Two things are suggested here. More obviously, Browne is being more objective than he first seemed, and we keep enjoying him partly because we have semiconsciously recognized these qualifications to his egotism. In fact, they make him seem something like an objective critic of himself, enjoying what should be enjoyed while he condemns (not very angrily, to be sure) what should be condemned. Or, again, we can read the passages as an "is-should" conflict: sometimes he likes himself more than he thinks he should.

There is no necessity to choose one reading over another, and in some instances it would be dangerous to do so, since such exclusions would diminish the many-faceted persona. Some of Browne's views of himself are simultaneously compatible; others reflect mood changes from moment to moment. With another rereading, a slightly different interpretation emerges. The whole style of Browne's speech is impetuous and exaggerated. Notice, in each passage, that one thing is emphatically singled out, even though the result is a contradiction between sentence one and sentence three: he loves himself for one reason, his lack of villainy; he is dejected by only one thought; he thanks God that he has escaped one sin, pride. His language runs to extremes: "base," "villain," "not for the Indies," "love," "two armes too few to embrace myself," "all my endeavors," "but one thought that dejects me," "perish," "thank God," "millions of vices," "mortal enemy." This characteristic language of the *Religio* explains our sense of Browne's youthful exuberance, as well as our willingness to enjoy his egotism, for he treats himself only with the same kinds of exaggeration that he applies to everything. If he loves himself, he also says that he loves the world and everything in it; once, in fact, he even embraces the devil, for teaching him a lesson.

Certainly one aspect of Browne's enthusiasm, or of his anxiety to present a proper image, is a willingness to condemn as well as praise himself. There is a critical view that in all these passages Browne is locating himself on the scale of being, uncertain whether he is angel or beast.[14] Just as Burton's commentary on man runs the gamut from god-myth to beast-fable, so Browne swings in self-appraisal from enthusiasm to despair. He tells us that he is by nature melancholy and morose, and that he has contemplated suicide. But this negative inclination, which is very real in Browne, is oddly subordinate, most fully realized not in direct statement but in rhetorical devices to be discussed later, which are easily overlooked. The direct statement in itself does not really convince, because in its unqualified form it is very rare. More usual are images in which Browne praises himself even while seeming not to, as when he says he will be content to "bring up the rear in heaven." The possibility of his going to hell is not part of his consciousness, and his exuberance gives even his essay into *contemptus mundi* a positive twist: ". . . I am not so much afraid of death as ashamed thereof; 'tis the very disgrace and ignominy of our natures, that in a moment can so disfigure us that our nearest friends, wives and Children stand afraid and start at us . . . Not that I am ashamed of the Anatomy of my parts, nor can accuse nature for playing the bungler in any part of me, or my own vitious life for contracting any shamefull disease upon me, whereby I might not call my selfe as wholesome a morsell for the wormes as any" (Pt. I.40).

Compared with his essay on his lack of pride, this passage seems fairly sophisticated, and one is quite willing to grant Browne a tongue-in-cheek attitude. Yet, in another light, his defensiveness here can be lined up with that of other passages, and seen as an extreme self-consciousness that automatically interposes itself between Browne and his critics. The proper Stoical attitude toward death, and the proper Christian attitude, is what he begins with: this is how he ought to think. But he cannot let the reader believe that his is an inferior body, even in the grave.

His self-consciousness can best be illustrated in the very first paragraph of the *Religio*, where the tortuous rhetoric endeavors to dispose of all possible objections before Browne has even begun to consider his subject. It is the most eloquent testimony, also, to Browne's awareness of the presence of readers:

FOR my Religion, though there be severall circumstances that might perswade the world I have none at all, as the generall scandall of my profession, the naturall course of my studies, the indifferency of my behaviour, and discourse in matters of Religion, neither violently defending one, nor with the common ardour of contention opposing another; yet in despight hereof I dare, without usurpation, assume the honourable stile of a Christian: not that I meerely owe this title to the Font, my education, or [the] Clime wherein I was borne, as being bred up either to confirme those principles my Parents instilled into my unwary understanding; or by a generall consent proceed in the Religion of my Countrey: But [that] having in my riper yeares, and confirmed judgment, seene and examined all, I finde my selfe obliged by the principles of Grace and the law of mine owne reason, to embrace no other name but this; neither doth herein my zeale so farre make me forget the generall charitie I owe unto humanitie, as rather to hate then pity Turkes, Infidels, and (what is worse) [the] Jewes, rather contenting my selfe to enjoy that happy stile, then maligning those who refuse so glorious a title (Pt. 1.1).

Except that the distinction is now between "seems" and "is," rather than "should" and "is," the same rhetorical pattern that governed the *contemptus mundi* passage is employed here. First, the negative evidence is set forth. Then, with the transition "not that," Browne opens the defense that is supposed to counteract what has gone before, and sustain "Browne" as an attractive figure in the reader's eyes. There is almost a jungle of qualifying words: "thought," "might," "neither-nor," "yet," "I dare," "not that," "but that," "neither doth," "rather." And this is entirely typical of Browne's method of procedure, as we have already seen in the qualifications of his statements of self-love. He constantly hedges his statements with defensive or qualifying comments that force our awareness that, although he almost never acknowledges an audience, and even goes out of his way to avoid using the second person, he is clearly creating himself for public scrutiny: "The severe Schooles shall never laugh me out of the Philosophy of *Hermes*" (Pt. I.12); " 'Tis not a ridiculous devotion, to say a Prayer before a game at Tables" (Pt. I.18); " 'Tis not a melancholy *Utinam* of mine owne, but the desire of better heads, that there were a generall Synod" (Pt. I.24).

Browne says that no man can ever know another, or even himself. Certainly the whole of the *Religio Medici* is testimony to that fact, even though much of the mystification is also recreational, and even though the book is at the same time a serious effort at self-exploration. He provides a more rounded description of a personality than most writers of his age. We know what "Browne" thought and felt about a wide variety of things—sex, art, love, God, race prejudice, foreign foods. And yet he remains unclear. We cannot know where the expressions of self-love cease to be naive and become either sardonic or schematic, and very likely he did not know either. We cannot know how aware he was of the defensiveness of his rhetoric, although it is obvious that he was aware of a good deal of it. Ironically, his statement on the impossibility of self-knowledge comes in Part II of the *Religio*, on charity, which is considerably less swathed in doubt and qualification than Part I, on faith and hope.[15] It is like a warning that, if he seems to be letting down his guard a bit, we must nevertheless not expect too much.

Yet Browne believed, as I have said, that all men in all ages are alike, in their lack of self-knowledge as in other things. Time, eternity, and human nature being what they are, man, even because of his folly and self-ignorance, can share the experience of the race: ". . . the man without a Navell yet lives in me; I feele that originall canker corrode and devoure me, and therefore *Defienda me Dios de mi*, Lord deliver me from my selfe, is a part of my Letany, and the first voyce of my retired imaginations. There is no man alone, because every man is a *Microcosme*, and carries the whole world about him . . ." (Pt. II.10).

Browne's use of the cosmic personality, which he exploits more fully than any other Anglican, is implicit in passages like this one. Where Burton sought to make himself cosmic by omnivorous reading, Browne does it on the one hand by reference to physiology, which was, after all, his business, and on the other by means of the introspection characteristic of his nature. Both references come to the same thing: Browne assimilates all the world into himself. First, the normal processes of nature yield this thought:

All flesh is grasse, is not onely metaphorically but literally true, for all those creatures [which] we behold, are but the hearbs of the field, digested into flesh in them, or more remotely carnified in our selves. Nay further, we are what we all abhorre, *Antropophagi* and Cannibals, devourers not onely of men, but of our selves; and that not in an allegory, but a positive truth; for all this masse of flesh which wee behold, came in at our mouths: this frame wee looke upon, hath beene upon our trenchers; In briefe, we have devoured our selves . . . (Pt. I.37).

This is a graphic equivalent of what Burton does in chewing up and assimilating his quotations. Here Browne uses the pronoun "we," explicitly joining himself with others. Like Donne, he habitually shifts back and forth between "I" and "we," indicating that uneasy sense of unity with, yet detachment from, others that is everywhere in Anglican prose, as well as the fact that the pronouns themselves are not so distinct for them as they are for us. In Browne, the first person singular is much more frequent than the plural, but the "I" is symbolic and can represent the experience of all.

In the following quotation, he argues that by introspection, man or "Browne" can not only come to know all human nature, but all time and space as well:

Men that look upon my outside, perusing onely my condition, and fortunes, do erre in my altitude; for I am above *Atlas* his shoulders, [and though I seeme on earth to stand, on tiptoe in Heaven]. The earth is a point not onely in respect of the heavens above us, but of that heavenly and celestiall part within us: that masse of flesh that circumscribes me, limits not my mind: that surface that tells the heavens it hath an end, cannot perswade me I have any; I take my circle to be above three hundred and sixty; though the number of the Arke do measure my body, it comprehendeth not my minde; whilst I study to finde how I am a Microcosme or little world, I finde my selfe something more than the great. There is surely a peece of Divinity in us, something that was before the Elements, and owes no homage unto the Sun (Pt. II.11).

Here, where he seems to speak only for himself, the whole passage is tempered by the fact that Browne slips back and forth from "I" to "we," making clear that he is claiming these fantastic powers not for himself alone, but for himself as a representative man—or as Man. If *we* can hold the pattern steady in this light, we are brought into it, and made to see with his eyes. This has not been easy for every reader to do, as a procession of critics, beginning with Sir Kenelm Digby, has made clear. But the shifting back and forth of the pronouns is a key to the fact that in the seventeenth century it is still difficult for a man to think of himself as an isolated individual. The cosmic personality is both a way of maintaining his solidarity with other men, and of celebrating his new sense of selfhood.

Browne does distinguish himself from others more than most writers of his time. His use of the "I" is more insistent and more exuberant. Distinguishing himself from others intoxicates him more than it frightens him, and one senses in passages like this the incipient individualism that reaches both its nadir and its zenith in American democratic man: "FOR my conversation, it is like the Sunne's with all men, and with a friendly aspect to good and bad" (Pt. II.10). In the sixteenth century, this was the metaphor of kings, but by Browne's time the common man is beginning to place himself at the center of the world, where the king once stood. Hence, such passages in Browne as particularly annoyed Kenelm Digby, where he becomes the sun to emperors and popes: "If there bee any truth in Astrology, I may outlive a Jubilee: as yet I have not seene one revolution of *Saturne*, nor hath my pulse beate thirty yeares, and yet, excepting one, hath seene the Ashes, and left under ground all the Kings of *Europe*, have been contemporary to three Emperours, foure Grand Signiours, and as many Popes; mee thinkes I have outlived my selfe, and begin to bee weary of the Sunne . . ." (Pt. I.41).

The sun-king metaphor in Shakespeare goes out with Richard II; and although his Prince Hal tries out the image, he subsequently learns to be a king by becoming a man "of all humours that have shown themselves humours since the old days of Goodman Adam" (1 *King Henry IV*. II.iv).[16] The idea was that the king should contain democracy, but the inevitable next step was for other men to find the same powers and range of feelings and meanings within themselves: ". . . and if I hold the true Anatomy of my selfe, I am delineated & naturally framed to such a piece of vertue: for I am of a constitution so generall that it consorts and sympathizeth with all things . . ." (Pt. II.1). Sunlike, such a man owes no homage unto the sun, and Melville's Ahab only carries Browne's figure to its logical conclusion when he says, "I'd strike the sun if it insulted me." [17] On one level, at least, Browne is heading toward the most extreme kind of democratic individualism, and in this respect he expresses a trend that is at the very most only potential in other Anglican writers.

That this trend is in no way incompatible with what I have called the cosmic personality is evident in Browne as well as in the writers toward whom I have pointed him: Whitman is a good example of the same phenomenon. In both writers celebration of self is celebration of humanity. Yet Browne certainly does not praise humanity, as those later writers do, with lists of names and local habitations.

Though he can believe that he existed before Abraham, he makes no reference to contemporary events. Written in 1634 and published in 1642, the *Religio Medici* has civil war for its context, but we only know that because we know its dates. One of its first readers was Edward Sackville, fourth Earl of Dorset, who was at the same time encouraging Charles I to end the war; its first critic, Sir Kenelm Digby, was a prisoner of war, captured by the Parliament Army. Active in the world though they were, these good Royalists saw nothing to criticize in Browne's abstraction from the world.[18]

He does indirectly mention his European travels in the exposition of a theme in which he seems at first more modern than other writers. That is the "no man is an island" theme, that is sounded in different keys by Puritan and Anglican alike. The note of modernity in Browne is his emphasis on tolerance. In religion, for example, he has himself entertained some choice old heresies. Even now, he cannot dissociate himself wholly from other sects, "we being all Christians, and not divided by such detested impieties as might prophane our prayers . . . (Pt. I.3)." Thus holy water, crucifix, genuflexion, even an Ave Maria bell inspire him to devotion. "At a solemne Procession I have wept abundantly, while my consorts, blinde with opposition and prejudice, have fallen into an eccesse of scorne and laughter" (Pt. I.3). And even with religions utterly opposed to Christianity, persecution is not the answer, being "a bad and indirect way to plant Religion" (Pt. I.25).

Since man not only has the capacity to change from moment to moment, but is truly a little world, carrying within himself the wonders he seeks without, nothing can be really foreign to him: "There is all *Africa*, and her prodigies in us; we are that bold and adventurous piece of Nature, which he that studies wisely learnes in a *compendium*, what others labour at in a divided piece and endlesse volume" (Pt. I.15). No air or diet, tongue or race is strange to Browne: "I finde not in my selfe those common antipathies that I can discover in others . . . my conscience would give me the lie if I should say I absolutely detest or hate any essence but the Devill . . ." (Pt. II.1).

So far, so good. It sounds Whitmanesque. But Browne goes on to say that *if* he "contemnes" anything, it is the multitude. And while this statement is fairly well submerged in the expansiveness of his declaration of human sympathy, it stands for a whole cluster of rhetorical devices that expose this position at the same time that they again emphasize Browne's sense of his unique individuality. Browne sees himself in different lights. He teaches himself to know himself as a cosmic personality, as an ordinary man, and as a man pridefully distinct from others. For a man of his age, he expresses unusual tolerance of other ways of life, but his modern self-analysis is at least partly based in his traditionally conservative hatred of the crowd.

I have already noted Browne's reluctance to speak to the reader directly. More curiously, he seems reluctant to admit the individual existence of anyone except himself. He refers to others by synecdoche, naming them either by a particular part of the anatomy—usually the head—or by abstract states of mind. Thus, in the first instance, "ruder heads," "common heads," "a set of heads," "a multitude of heads," "wiser heads," "many melancholy heads . . . heads ordained only to manifest the incredible effects of melancholy." The effect of this technique is obvious. What one sees when looking at a crowd is heads.[19] Thus Browne deprives people of individuality and human wholeness, and even a laudatory adjective so used can become an insult, as with "wiser heads."

Alternatively, he speaks of "wiser judgements," "ingenuous intentions," "grosser apprehensions," "insolent zeales," "vulgar and common constitutions," always in contexts that reduce people to the abstract feelings they may entertain: "And indeed wiser discretions that have the thred of reason to conduct them, offend without a pardon; whereas ruder heads may stumble without dishonour" (Pt. I.55); "THE vulgarity of those judgements that wrap the Church of God in *Strabo's* cloake and restraine it unto Europe, seeme to me as bad Geographers as *Alexander*, who thought hee had conquer'd all the world when hee [had] not subdued the halfe of any part thereof" (Pt. I.56). Although this reductive technique allows for more variety from person to person, it does not allow for personality, but only for mechanical "humour characters."

Both these devices obviously lend themselves to the formation of larger derisive patterns:

There are questionless both in Greek, Roman, and African Churches, solemnities, and ceremonies, whereof the wiser zeales doe make a Christian use, and stand condemned by us; not as evill in themselves, but as allurements and baits of superstition to those vulgar heads that looke asquint on the face of truth, and those unstable judgements that cannot consist in the narrow point and centre of vertue without a reele or stagger to the circumference (Pt. I.3).

The constellation of words like "allurements," "baits," "asquint," "reel" and "stagger," together with these reductive epithets, describes subhuman creatures (or heads) that are easily caught, have faulty vision, and cannot easily stand upright.

Here, as always, there is a built-in qualification. Browne does not always use such language with equal disparagement. "Wiser zeales" here is not condemnatory. And sometimes he turns these techniques upon himself. One may conceive this whole grouping to be part of a pattern that I have already noted, of locating man on the scale of being. When Browne thinks of himself as "that mass of flesh that circumscribes me," then he becomes a "head"; when he thinks of himself as a mind unlimited by that flesh, then he is "a peece of Divinity." Again, the significance of his techniques depends upon the fact of the *trompe l'oeil* pattern of his prose, and can be read differently from moment to moment. But he calls himself a "head" extremely rarely, while consistently so designating others.

Furthermore, Browne separates himself, by advantageous contrast, from other people. In particular, he is more tolerant than they are, more humble, better able to encounter ritual differences and theological problems, and more capable of exercising his faith: "I CONFESSE I have perused them all, and can discover nothing that may startle a discreet beliefe: yet are there heads carried off with the wind and breath of such motives" (Pt. I.21); "AS for those wingy mysteries . . . which have unhindg'd the braines of better heads, they never stretched the *Pia Mater* of mine" (Pt. I.9). His tendency to exaggerate is illustrated again here. Even in his defects, he likes to be unique: ". . . my selfe could shew a catalogue of doubts, never yet imagined nor questioned [by any], as I know . . ." (Pt. I.21). Yet even at his most self-centered, Browne does not seem vain. There is something almost solipsistic about his reduction of other people to abstractions and heads. It is a way of not having to bother about them, and that is why his rare naming of a particular person or group in order to criticize always disconcerts the reader—as for example, his scornful mention of Jews. As heads and abstractions, people can be ignored, or used as foils, rather than railed against or scorned. They are almost never the subject of his discourse. His readers are able to keep liking him, and even thinking of him as really tolerant and modest, largely because it is easier for them to belong to his cosmic personality, for which he claims these attributes, than to the vulgar crowd. Browne is too self-absorbed for vanity, if that is possible, especially since his cosmic sense of self, and his self-absorption, include his wonder at the variety and mystery of God's world. And before God he is wholly and unequivocally humble and adoring.

There is, he says, a "common peece of divinity within us" that makes all men one. When Browne hears the bell toll, he does remember this, although it is impossible for him to put aside his strong sense of his uniqueness. Two passages will show, in varying degrees, the way in which the two concepts combine:

> I never heare the Toll of a passing Bell, though in my mirth, [and at a Tavern], without my prayers and best wishes for the departing spirit; I cannot goe to cure the body of my Patient, but I forget my profession, and call unto God for his soule; I cannot see one say his Prayers, but instead of imitating him, I fall into a supplication for him, who peradventure is no more to mee than a common nature: and if God hath vouchsafed an eare to my supplications, there are surely many happy that never saw me, and enjoy the blessings of mine unknown devotions (Pt. II.6).

The common nature is mentioned, it is true, but only in such a way as to emphasize Browne's charity in being impelled to pray for a man who "is no more to mee than a common nature." Meanwhile the stress is all on the "I" and "my," and his wonderful assurance that his prayers fall like dew on their fortunate recipients.

In the following passage, the awareness of a common nature is strengthened: ". . . I cannot behold a Begger without relieving his necessities with my purse, or his soule with my prayers; these scenicall and accidentall differences betweene us cannot make mee forget that common and untoucht part of us both; there is under these *Centoes* and miserable outsides, these mutilate and semi-bodies, a soule of the same alloy with our owne, whose Genealogy is God as well as ours, and in as faire a way unto salvation, as our selves" (Pt. II.13). I shall have more to say shortly of other aspects of Browne's rhetoric, which always makes us attend to him even when the emphasis seems to be least personal. And although the statement of underlying unity is clearer here, and the first person plural much in evidence, there is still heavy emphasis on the "I" and the "my," and upon Browne's virtue. The sentence immediately following is a criticism of "statists that labour to contrive a Common-wealth without poverty": even here where he is most concerned with common humanity, he is busy drawing lines between himself and other men, both the statists and the poor.

Thus, while Browne's sense of unity with other men may be as explicitly enunciated as Donne's and Burton's, it is highly qualified by his equally keen sense of his difference from others, and, although he takes no personal credit for this, his superiority to them. And while his cosmic personality is really dependent on his belief in the similarity of men through the ages, together with his doctrinal attitude toward time, the relative extravagance and self-centeredness with which he expresses this personality does place considerable stress on Browne's own importance. At least part of the difficulty is created by his shifting back and forth between symbolic and literal modes of expression, a practice that is essential to his particular kind of autobiography. But there is also an extreme and pervasive ambiguity in the whole work, as I have already pointed out, which forbids any unequivocal critical statement. Browne's is a self-centered persona. But it is not a vain one. His self-praise is praise of man and God. That is clear in his whole essay, as is best illustrated by such terse traditional statements as, "God, who knowes me truly, knowes that I am nothing" (Pt. II.4), or, "Thy will bee done, though in my owne undoing" (Pt. II.14).

That aspect of Browne's book which exposes most clearly of all the difficulty of obtaining an accurate reading of his prose involves a kind of rhetoric of doubt, which is not always apparent to the casual reader, or to a reader not particularly concerned with the style. One of the greatest problems in analyzing the *Religio* is to explain its combination of a generally positive, even, at times, optimistic attitude toward life, with an overwhelming number of seemingly negative rhetorical devices. One could be led to believe that Leo Spitzer's method breaks down here, that the style is at odds with the content, so that while the naive reader happily responds to Browne's enthusiastic portrayal of himself, the more sophisticated one must consider a melancholy that is in the syntax but is perceptible only to the specialist.

Part of the problem is Browne's own deviousness, a phenomenon with many causes, not the least of which is his enjoyment of riddles and complexities for their own sake. When he turns from the long riddling "faith" part of his book to the brief closing section on charity, much, though by no means all, of the caginess evaporates. Concentrating on the doubtful riddling of Part I, the student of style may find just enough of what he expects in Part II to miss its reduction in quantity, while the ordinary reader will have his last and most enduring impression of the book in those relatively positive last paragraphs. More traditionally, the problem can be partially solved simply by a closer look at all the rhetoric: certain less showy but more constant rhetorical devices overbalance the negative ones, while negative devices in context often turn out to be a variety of positive emphasis. Some of the negativism is real, however; its presence and its unobtrusiveness must to some extent be taken seriously, and its purpose and effects explained.

For this part of this chapter, I am particularly indebted to Austin Warren's and F. L. Huntley's enumerations [20] of many of these negative techniques, and I only hope to add to their findings, setting their conclusions in the context of my own argument. A very useful point of departure is a passage in Huntington Brown's book, *Prose Styles: Five Primary Types*. Here Browne's type is identified as prophetic, having its origin in the Bible and in Stoic essayists. Mr. Brown distinguishes between those earlier writers and their seventeenth-century descendants:

Bacon's remark that there is not so much blood in the modern "discoursing wits" as there was in the ancients suggests the broad reflection that any ancient thinker was in a position to lay down the law more confidently about large philosophical issues than any has been in the modern age, when quantitative science and the wide dissemination of the printed word have required him to come to terms with an ever more forbidding system of established fact and therefore with an ever more sharply critical court of public opinion. In the new age there were to be fewer daredevils than formerly who, like Bacon, were ready to venture upon the wholesale invention of serious aphorisms on any and all subjects. The race of Montaigne, Burton and Browne, later revived in Charles Lamb and his following, was cannier. The primary motive in these writers is still oracular and often revolutionary, but the style is discreet, cagey, devious, often jocular. They hurl no old-fashioned challenge at us, to make us think that our fate depends on our assent to their doctrine.[21]

Mr. Brown's essay thus suggests at least a very good partial explanation of the ambiguous mingling of negative rhetoric with a generally positive tone. The ancient exuberance of the prophet is here combined with seventeenth-century self-consciousness and doubt.

Mr. Brown has made the aphorism a mark of the prophetic style and one interesting test of his conclusions is to look at what happens to the aphorism in Browne's prose. It is, of course, markedly present in its usual aggressive form: "God made all things for himself, and it is impossible hee should make them for any other end than his owne glory" (Pt. I.35); "WE tearme sleepe a death, and yet it is waking that kils us, and destroyes those spirits which are the house of life" (Pt. II.12). There is no analytical problem here. The statement is brief, discontinuous from its context, offensive rather than defensive, paradoxical in the second instance, and unsupported by logic. All these characteristics belong to the old prophetic style as Mr. Brown defines it, and they remain central in Browne's prose, except that, as Mr. Brown also demonstrates, his sentences tend to be looser, more verbose, and more mannered than in the classical essay.

The tone of these sustaining sentences is upheld by Browne's characteristically positive and extravagant vocabulary. I have noted earlier that he speaks in extremes; his language is all of love and hate, embracing and battling. And other critics have observed his exuberant Renaissance doubling of words and phrases, often for specific rhetorical purposes, but always, too, for sheer love of language. In this generally positive context all his "skeptical" or "negative" techniques must be seen.

These techniques function on several different levels, not all of which are in Browne's control. It is useful to begin with an explanation of his own which handily confirms Huntington Brown's diagnosis. This is a paragraph taken from the *Christian Morals*, a posthumously published work of Browne's old age, which seems to be a collection of aphorisms built up over the course of many years, and intended to guide his own behavior:

LET well-weighted Considerations, not stiff and peremptory Assumptions, guide thy discourses, Pen and Actions. To begin or continue our works like Trismegistus of old, *Verum, certe verum, atque verissimum est* would sound arrogantly unto present Ears in this strict enquiring Age, wherein, for the most part, *Probably*, and *Perhaps*, will hardly serve to mollify the Spirit of captious Contradictors. If Cardan saith that a Parrot is a beautiful Bird, Scaliger will set his Wits o'work to prove it a deformed Animal. The Compage of all Physical Truths is not so closely jointed, but opposition may find intrusion, nor always so closely maintained, as not to suffer attrition. Many Positions seem quodlibetically constituted, and like a Delphian Blade will cut on both sides. Some Truths seem almost Falshoods, and some Falshoods almost Truths; wherein Falshood and Truth seem almost aequilibriously stated, and but a few grains of distinction to bear down the ballance.[22]

Browne is obviously thinking not only of the "court of public opinion," but also of the nature of truth itself, which seems to him just as
ambiguous as his prose seems to us. His "probably" and "perhaps,"
as well as the essentially ambiguous rhetoric, are intended both to
guard him against that critical public and to express reality as he
knew it. This is not necessarily skepticism; it is simply a matter of
self-expression.

It is possible to read Browne's rhetoric as evidence of what Austin
Warren termed a speculative mind,[23] one that makes very frequent
use of terms like "I think" or "I perceive," not because Browne is
preoccupied with the uncertainty of knowledge based on his own
perceptions alone, but because he loves to exercise his powers of
thought and perception. And indeed he tells us that this is so. But he
also tells us, and thereby confirms another strand of meaning for his
style, that he is so much aware of the uncertainty of human knowledge that he sometimes thinks it worthless for men to bother their
heads with studying at all. Here the techniques do suggest extreme
skepticism. Yet it frequently happens that these techniques are used,
not as negatives, but merely as a means congenial to him of elaborat-
ing or emphasizing an aphorism or a theory: that is to say, negative
words are used positively. Simultaneously speculative, skeptical, and
dogmatic, Browne further complicates his prose by use of these same
"negative" techniques in the way that Huntington Brown characterizes as cagey and devious. Thus he absolves himself from responsibility for his own utterances, and protects himself from any public
reaction.

With all these things going on at once, it is inevitable, and at least
to some extent intended, that the prose should often seem at war
with itself, so that, for example, vocabulary, or even content, quar-
rels with syntax. This phenomenon may be defined by any of
Browne's own comments on the contradictory character of human
nature: "Let mee be nothing if within the compasse of my selfe, I
doe not find the battell of *Lepanto*, passion against reason, reason
against faith, faith against the Devill, and my conscience against all.
There is another man within mee that's angry with mee, rebukes,
commands, and dastards mee" (Pt. II.7). The happy man is attacked
by the man who insists upon subverting the syntax of Browne's
prose into a rhetoric of doubt. Or (another interpretation) the man
who thinks he ought to express doubt and skepticism is opposed by

the man who is irrepressibly optimistic. As the aphorism quoted earlier has it, "Many Positions seem quodlibetically constituted, and like a Delphian Blade will cut on both sides."

This is much to keep in mind at one time, although the task is made easier by the fact that some of these viewpoints have been put forward by previous critics. But as I proceed I shall refer back to these generalizations, and the detailed commentary that now follows should support my conclusion about the immense complexity of this prose. First of all, then, is a technique of hedging about the aphorism with all sorts of qualifiers and disclaimers that make it not a proclamation, but the subject of a lesson. When it is an introductory sentence, the aphorism is, in fact, often used as a noun clause, the subject or object of a sentence which criticizes or limits it, as in the following examples: "THAT Miracles are ceased, I can neither prove, nor absolutely deny" (Pt. I.27); "TO doe no injury, nor take none, was a principle, which to my former yeares, and impatient affections, seemed to containe enough of morality" (Pt. II.7). The aggressive, oracular statement, "Miracles are ceased," would ordinarily in the prophetic style be allowed to stand alone, unsupported by arguments and unqualified by doubts. The piling up of such aphorisms creates an ebullient, confident style that is likely to cause such strong reactions, either admiring or hostile, as Browne's prose has actually inspired in many readers. Combined here with his own critiques, it still retains that virility, but the surrounding material qualifies and softens it.

The commentary on the axiom is not always negative; it may simply contain directions to the reader how to regard the announcement, or expressions of Browne's faith in it, as here: "Beware of Philosophy, is a precept not to be received in too large a sense" (Pt. I.12); "Lord deliver me from my selfe, is a part of my Letany, and the first voyce of my retired imaginations" (Pt. II.10). The contrast is immense between this and such famous openings of Bacon's essays as "Revenge is a kind of wild justice." But for a reflective man, no true prophet, but rather one who is examining the nature of his faith, it makes sense to analyze an aphorism that is given, instead of merely foisting aphorisms on others. The method could typify either a speculative or a skeptical mind considering commonplaces of the medieval scheme of things and the more "prophetic" aphorisms of revolt. But by the ostensible examination of what is presented as *already* a precept, Browne also achieves freedom from responsibility for it. Whether he criticizes or accepts it, the reader is made to feel that it existed before Browne encountered it, and whether he agrees or disagrees with it, he does not have to *be* it, so to speak. The device suggests quotation, it is highly literary, and makes Browne's style appear to be, though it is really not, at the opposite extreme from the oracular.

Browne's dislike of controversy is typical of the self-conscious Anglican. He claims to dislike it partly because he cannot know whether his own ideas will change in a day or two, partly because human knowledge is so necessarily imperfect that controversy is a waste of time, and partly because he has no genius in disputes and considers them a possible danger to faith. Again, there is an apparent reluctance to take responsibility, a desire to be free to speculate and play with ideas that are not threatening to him, or can be handled in an unthreatening way. Illustrative of this attitude are a number of techniques which allow easy retreat from any and all positions, simply on the grounds that perception is faulty, and human knowledge uncertain.

Almost inevitably he qualifies his sentences with phrases like "seems to me," "I perceive," "I think." These sentences do not at first glance suggest any sort of uncertainty. Quite the contrary, they imply a willingness to take responsibility for his own ideas. The word "believe," in particular, frequently used, endows sentences introduced by any of these words with the authority of the Catholic Creed. Many times they are intended as an explicit assertion of faith in the face of impossibility, as here: "I [do] believe there was already a tree whose fruit our unhappy parents tasted, though in the same Chapter, where God forbids it, 'tis positively said, the plants of the field were not yet grown . . ." (Pt. I.10). Yet one is inevitably also alerted to the limited and precarious nature of human knowledge and belief—not because our twentieth-century relativism stands between us and the text, but because Browne himself makes it emphatically clear. The other side of his enthusiastic belief in the impossible is his recognition of the faultiness of a vision that makes truth seem untrue. Browne points out in particular the effect of humour or changing mood upon man's views: "I am not yet so cynical" [which implies he may soon be so]; "in my calmer judgement"; "It is my temper to affect." Many of his speculations include admission of his inability to reach conclusions: "It is a riddle to me"; "I cannot tell how to say that"; "I know not what to make of," and so forth.

Yet this "rhetoric of uncertainty" sometimes has a primary purpose that is not at all uncertain. Most obviously, it can simply signal his love of paradox, as here: "THERE are wonders in true affection; it is a body of *Aenigmaes*, mysteries and riddles, wherein two so become one, as they both become two . . ." (Pt. II.6). But he also uses this language as a way of asserting his absolute certainty about something, in the sense in which one person will say to another, "I can't understand why you think so," meaning, "*Your* idea just doesn't make sense, compared to mine." And beginning thus, Browne may proceed to any kind of dogmatic statement:

IT is a riddle to me, how this [very] story of Oracles hath not worm'd out of the world that doubtfull conceit of Spirits and Witches; how so many learned heads should so farre forget their Metaphysicks, and destroy the Ladder and scale of creatures, as to question the existence of Spirits: for my [owne] part, I have ever beleeved, and doe now know, that there are Witches; they that doubt of these, doe not onely deny them, but Spirits; and are obliquely and upon consequence a sort, not of Infidels, but Atheists (Pt. I.30).

Such phrases are most often employed in these ways; when Browne really introduces his own doubt thus, the subject is one whose resolution he himself considers unimportant. Typically, his rhetoric can operate simultaneously on more than one level, possibly without his being aware of all that it is doing. Even if the "it is a riddle to me" formula expressed either an enjoyable paradox or a dogmatic opposition to others' views every time it was used, it would still suggest, merely by its repeated appearance, the skepticism which Browne does consciously espouse.

Browne is fond of pointing out that all learned disciplines are fallible: "If there bee any truth in Astrology, I may outlive a Jubilee" (Pt. I.41); "yet if (as Divinity affirmes) there shall be no gray hayres in Heaven" (Pt. I.42); "I perceive the wisest heads prove at last, almost all Scepticks, and stand like *Janus* in the field of knowledge" (Pt. II.8). In fact, Browne says, he sometimes thinks study is a waste of time, because life is short, man's mind is incompetent, and all things will be made known in heaven anyway. "If" clauses abound in the *Religio*, as another means both of leaving himself an out, and of expressing human fallibility. Yet it will be observed that here too the tonal ambiguity of his aphoristic sentences occurs. The main clauses of the first two sentences (except for the additional qualification of the word "may") have the positive force as well as the exaggeration and surprise of aphorism, while the "if" clauses, as well as the ascription of the statements to established disciplines, relieve Browne of any responsibility for his utterances.

Browne thinks that error comes not just from the weakness of man's apprehension, but also from the inadequacy of language. Even when language is accurate, man's understanding can easily misread: "It is impossible that, either in the discourse of man, or in the infallible voyce of God, to the weaknesse of our apprehension, there should not appear irregularities, contradictions, and antinomies" (Pt. I.21). But often men are the victims of misuse of language: "THE bad construction and perverse comment on these paire of second causes, or visible hands of God, have perverted the devotion of many unto Atheisme; who forgetting the honest advisoes of faith, have listened unto the conspiracie of Passion and Reason" (Pt. I.19). Browne was very much aware of the power of words, as this passage makes clear. The mischievous possibilities of their misuse may be another reason why he himself handled them at once so impressively and so gingerly. Indeed, with his constant qualification of utterance, he might have had in mind Sidney's classic argument that the poet lies not, because he affirms nothing. So many of his statements, reconsidered, seem to him misleading, and he circles back to avoid possible misunderstanding: "not that I did absolutely conceive a mortality of the soul"; "though not in an implicite but a humble faith"; "which I did never positively maintain or practice." His awareness of the inadequacies of language is expressed, too, in his habitual calling attention to or apologizing for the terms of his discourse: "I hope I shall not injure Truth to say"; "I am now content to understand a Mystery without a rigid definition"; "surely the Heathens knew better how to joyne and read these mystical letters than wee Christians"; "which if I call the ubiquitary, and omnipotent essence of God, I hope I shall not offend Divinity." His skepticism about knowledge receives its most extreme statement in the following passage, which is also very revealing rhetorically: "AGAINE, I am confident and fully perswaded, yet dare not take my oath of my salvation; I am as it were sure, and do beleeve, without all doubt, that there is such a city as *Constantinople*; yet for me to take my oath thereon, were a kinde of perjury, because I hold no infallible warrant from my owne sense, to confirm me in the certainty thereof" (Pt. I.59). Yet here, at its most extreme, the skepticism perhaps ought instead to be read as the most unshakable kind of faith, since he is as sure of his salvation as he is of the existence of the city of Constantinople.

The farthest reach of this way of thinking, which is still an entirely typical and pervasive technique of Browne's speech, is a rhetoric of negativism that can be applied to a wholly positive end. Browne is immensely fond of negative syntactical constructions. Phrases like the following pepper the sections of the *Religio:* "I could not choose but say"; "I cannot but commend"; "it is not unremarkable"; "I would not omit"; "are not without their incommodities"; "I cannot but wonder." The negativism is sometimes so involved that it becomes difficult for the reader to decide what Browne means to affirm:

I think my conscience will not give me the lie, if I say, there are not many extant that in a noble way feare the face of death lesse than my selfe . . . (Pt. I.26).

. . . I would not perish upon a Ceremony, Politick point or indifferency: nor is my beleefe of that untractable temper, as now to bow at their obstacles, or connive at matters wherein there are not manifest impieties . . . (Pt. I.26).

. . . we cannot deny, if wee shall not question those Writers whose testimonies wee doe not controvert . . . there is not one Miracle greater than another . . . I will not say God cannot, but hee will not performe many things, which wee plainely affirme he cannot: this I am sure is the mannerliest proposition, wherein notwithstanding I hold no Paradox (Pt. I.27).

Even when he believes something to be true, he is likely to phrase his sentence as though it were not, leaving the reader with the sense that Browne has certainly said something positive, and yet that somehow he has not fully committed himself to his own saying.

And again here, the very negative can be a clearly positive kind of expression. One of Browne's favorite ways of emphasizing the strength of his feeling or belief on any subject is to say that he cannot help it; he cannot do otherwise: "I could never heare the *Ave Maria* Bell without an elevation" (Pt. I.3); "I COULD never divide my selfe from any man upon the difference of an opinion" (Pt. I.6); "were it [Scripture] of man, I could not choose but say, it is one of the most singular, and superlative Pieces that hath been extant since the Creation" (Pt. I.23). All of these passages have a strongly positive meaning, and Browne's seeming intention is to say that he has an irresistible compulsion to do right, even when (and here the strong emphasis may be a kind of bravado) the right course is also the unpopular one. In context, these forceful utterances never strike the reader as negative. On the contrary, they contribute to the sense of impetuosity and youthful exuberance created by Browne's vocabulary. It is only, as we have seen with other techniques, when they recur again and again, that they begin to take on some importance exclusive of context, and to figure in the whole cluster of negative devices that I have been outlining.

The combination of prophetic aphorism with skepticism, of engagement with irresponsibility, of optimism with despair, is always balanced in favor of the positive side with Browne. His reservations and qualifications, his statements of humility and doubt, only make him seem more human and thus more attractive to the many readers who find him congenial. Such readers, like Coleridge,[24] identify with him and admire his insights and his style. His famous prose rhythms increase the reader's ability to respond: one assents to the content if only to maintain the music unbroken. Browne, meanwhile, is constantly working on the reader to take his meanings in particular ways, to see through his eyes. Sentences are frequently accompanied by instructions how to read them, sometimes, it is true, in the limiting or qualifying sense already observed. Sometimes he suggests speaking in the language of a particular discipline: "Let us speake naturally, and like Philosophers" (Pt. I.48); "Let us speake like Politicians" (Pt. II.1). Or we are given instructions as to the scope or level of the speech: "to speak more narrowly"; "to speak properly"; "to speak strictly"; "in a relative way"; "though not in capitall letters, yet in stenography"; "NOW besides this literall and positive kinde of death, there are others whereof Divines make mention, and those I thinke, not meerely Metaphoricall" (Pt. I.45). Austin Warren has also pointed out Browne's enormous concern with the terms of discourse.[25] The sensitivity about language which Baxter usually confines to his prefaces is part of the texture of Browne's prose.

And yet the prose is not nervous. That is the extraordinary thing, although by this time it should begin to seem almost natural that techniques which would clearly contribute to tension and nervousness in Donne, for example, do not do so in Browne. In every case either there are counteracting techniques, or the technique itself is used in such a way as to render its impression ambiguous. Often the counteraction is provided by the leisurely pace and the high polish of Browne's prose.

Donne can hardly write a sentence without charging it with his febrile intensity; he doubles back on himself, interrupts himself, cuts up the syntax, and creates a stuttering effect by repetition of words in mid-thought. When he does use the aphoristic Senecan curt period, he keeps it relatively short and stark (except for the characteristic repetitions), but his more usual structure is a longer sentence which enables him to expend his excitement without reference to a limited syntactical form. Browne, on the other hand, enjoys a loosened type of curt period, in which he can rise to an "O altitudo" through a gradual enlargement of his original idea. This period allows him considerable freedom to expand his thought leisurely, while retaining enough of a framework for a very obviously studied placement of words within a relatively small space:

THUS there are two bookes from whence I collect my Divinity; besides that written one of God, another of his servant Nature, that universall and publik Manuscript, that lies expans'd unto the eyes of all; those that never saw him in the one, have discovered him in the other: This was the Scripture and Theology of the Heathens; the naturall motion of the Sun made them more admire him, than its supernaturall station did the Children of Israel; the ordinary effects of nature wrought more admiration in them, than in the other all his miracles; surely the Heathens knew better how to joyne and reade these mysticall letters, than wee Christians, who cast a more carelesse eye on these common Hieroglyphicks, and disdain to suck Divinity from the flowers of nature (Pt. I.16).

Here the balancings and reversals, the doublets and the very showy alliteration, support and point up the slow pace achieved by the leisurely, repetitious consideration of the idea. As he proceeds the language unfolds and becomes more decorative: the longest unbroken thought is the last section. There is a moral in the sentence, yet it would be difficult to feel scolded or apprehensive for being "Christians, who cast a more carelesse eye on these common Hieroglyphics." Showy alliteration given no specific meaning in a sentence does, more obviously than any other device, partake of the character of play.

And so I return once more to the concept of art as recreation. At the beginning of this chapter, I pointed out that in the seventeenth century, the word can mean both re-creation and enjoyment. In this sense, Browne's creation of his persona is a re-creation of the great world. His book also shows him recreating himself, in the sense of enjoyment, in two principal ways—by playing with the tenets and apparent contradictions of his faith, and by regarding and enjoying the world, and himself in the world, as the art of God. Since these terms involve and overlap one another (art is play), there is no need to discuss them separately.

The concept of art as game applies to Browne partly because he always accepts the limitations upon his liberty that game requires. In the language of John Huizinga's *Homo Ludens*, Browne is one who obeys the rules, as opposed to the spoilsport who breaks up the game [26] (as Puritans do) when it does not appeal to him: "In Philosophy where truth seemes double-faced, there is no man more paradoxicall than my self; but in Divinity I love to keepe the road, and though not in an implicite, yet an humble faith, follow the great wheele of the Church, by which I move, not reserving any proper poles or motion from the epicycle of my owne braine; by this meanes I leave no gap for Heresies, Schismes, or Errors . . ." (Pt. I.6). Even when he does have doubts, he speaks of them in terms of game—a far cry from the Puritan assertion that it is no time to play when the soul is in peril: "Thus the Devill playd at Chesse with mee, and yeelding a pawne, thought to gaine a Queen of me, taking advantage of my honest endeavours; and whilst I labour'd to raise the structure of my reason, hee striv'd to undermine the edifice of my faith" (Pt. I.19).

Both his refusal to speculate on dangerous ground, and his enjoyment of paradoxes when they provide both safety and liberation, reinforce his typically Anglican consideration of the world, seen in no matter what light, as an artificial construction. As always, there are alternate readings. Seen as bad, the world is the devil's mockshow and a stage of fools. Seen as good, it is the emblematic art of God. As devil's mockshow, it simply exemplifies what one ought to expect of fallen man, and requires no reforming zeal. Neither the laughter of Democritus nor the lamentation of Heraclitus is congenial to Browne:

It is as compleate a piece of madnesse to miscall and rave against the times, as thinke to recall men to reason by a fit of passion: *Democritus* that thought to laugh the times into goodnesse, seemes to mee as deeply Hypochondriack, as *Heraclitus* that bewailed them; it moves not my spleene to behold the multitude in their proper humours, that is, in their fits of folly and madnesse, as well understanding that Wisedome is not prophan'd unto the World, and 'tis the priviledge of a few to be vertuous (Pt. II.4).

Man is responsible to change the world neither by act nor by word, because its limitations are given.

Seen as good, however, the world does provide man with a function, for something unobserved is, as it were, nonexistent (this is also, by the way, an internal argument for at least a semi-public intention for the *Religio*). Man was made to admire God, in Himself and in all His works, both macrocosm and microcosm. Hence, of course, a justification for Browne's willingness to express self-love. And here also is a justification for Browne's extensive use of words involving game and play, for whether the world is the devil's mockshow or God's art it is a subject for recreation.

The most encompassing tone of his admiration of the world is wonder at its mysteries. Since man is God's re-creation of himself, God and man cannot really become chess opponents. Man and his life are art-in-process: hence, the deliciousness of Browne's wonder. Man senses but can never really apprehend the continual creator of his days:

. . . there is therfore some other hand that twines the thread of life than that of nature; wee are not onely ignorant in Antipathies and occult qualities, our ends are as obscure as our beginnings, the line of our dayes is drawne by night, and the various effects therein by a pencill that is invisible; wherein though wee confesse our ignorance, I am sure we do not erre, if wee say, it is the hand of God (Pt. I.43).

It is understandable that man, as part of the creation, can never see the whole, even though in another sense, as microcosm, he *comprehends* it. "Frivolous" but obviously fascinating problems which he mentions without exploring include the question of how the pigeon got back to its mate, where Lazarus' soul was when he was dead, and whose would be Adam's rib at the resurrection. Others worthy of fuller contemplation, are these:

How all the kinds of Creatures, not only in their owne bulks, but with a competency of food & sustenance, might be preserved in one Arke, and within the extent of three hundred cubits, to a reason that rightly examines it, will appear very forcible. There is another secret, not contained in the Scripture, which is more hard to comprehend, & put the honest Father to the refuge of a Miracle; and that is, not onely how the distinct pieces of the world, and divided Ilands should bee first planted by men, but inhabited by

Tygers, Panthers and Beares. How *America* abounded with beasts of prey, and noxious Animals, yet contained not in it that necessary creature, a Horse. By what passage those, not onely Birds, but dangerous and unwelcome Beasts came over . . . These are no points of Faith, and therefore may admit a free dispute (Pt. I.22).

AS for those wingy mysteries in Divinity and ayery subtilties in Religion, which have unhindg'd the braines of better heads, they never stretched the *Pia Mater* of mine; me thinkes there be not impossibilities enough in Religion for an active faith; the deepest mysteries ours containes, have not only been illustrated, but maintained by syllogisme, and the rule of reason: I love to lose my selfe in a mystery, to pursue my reason to an *o altitudo.* 'Tis my solitary recreation to pose my apprehension with those involved aenigma's and riddles of the Trinity, with Incarnation and Resurrection . . . I desire to exercise my faith in the difficultest points . . . (Pt. I.9).

For this purpose, Browne is glad that he did not live in the time of Christ: ". . . then had my faith beene thrust upon me, nor should I enjoy that greater blessing pronounced to all that believe & saw not" (Pt. I.9).

Always, Browne pulls the sting from pain. Two specific illustrations of the means by which he does this suggest, for the last time here, the ambiguousness of his persona. In both, a painful fact is reckoned with. In the first, one has to some extent the impression that he is merely paying lip-service to that fact, that his heart is not really affected by it: "NOW for my life, it is a miracle of thirty yeares, which to relate, were not a History, but a peece of Poetry, and would sound to common eares like a fable; for the world, I count it not an Inne, but an Hospitall, and a place, not to live, but to die in. The world that I regard is my selfe, it is the Microcosme of mine owne frame, that I cast mine eye on; for the other, I use it but like my Globe, and turne it round sometimes for my recreation" (Pt. II.11). The idea of the world as a hospital and a place to die in is in accord with the Stoic philosophy that Browne tries to espouse. But it is muted here, just as all the negatives are muted in the prose. There is here as elsewhere an element of posturing and a suggestion that he has had to remind himself to produce that posture. The figure is so surrounded by words of enthusiasm and play that there is no tragic force in it at all.

On the other hand, Stoicism certainly does not require a tragic attitude, and the negative words and phrases are much too deeply imbedded in Browne's rhetoric to permit the conclusion that this is merely a pose. It is true, as I have shown, that he consciously adopted his qualifications and uncertainties—but they permeated his prose and have to be taken seriously as part of it. Pain is both acknowledged and vanquished.

In this illustration his emphasis falls largely upon the wonder of life. Wonder is even more apparent in my second illustration, where a theological tenet which Browne finds extremely melancholy is presented in such a way as to stimulate and charm the imagination:

THERE is no salvation to those that beleeve not in Christ, that is, say some, since his Nativity, and as Divinity affirmeth, before also; which makes me much apprehend the end of those honest Worthies and Philosophers which died before his Incarnation. It is hard to place those soules in Hell whose worthy lives doe teach us vertue on earth; methinks amongst those many subdivisions of hell, there might have bin one Limbo left for these: What a strange vision will it be to see their poeticall fictions converted into verities, & their imaginary & fancied Furies, into reall Devils? how strange to them will sound the History of *Adam*, when they shall suffer for him they never heard of? when they [that] derive their Genealogy from the Gods, shall know they are the unhappy issue of sinfull man? (Pt. I.54).

He keeps so busy—and keeps us so busy—with the idea of the ancients' discovery that fiction is truth, that there is hardly time left to conceive God unjust, or human fate wretched.

More than most, Browne's prose is entirely responsive to seventeenth-century doubts and tensions. And more than most he makes a game of doubt, and allows himself much play of fancy in his style. I have spoken of his enthusiasm as a sign of youth, but he himself sometimes talks like an old man, and there are signs of a kindred exuberance and irresponsibility in the late Shakespeare and Milton. One never knows where to stop with Browne, but a reading of his prose most attractive to our time might be this. He has seen that the world is not an inn but a hospital, and *therefore* he will make his affirmation. Such a claim can be made much more confidently on behalf of Milton and Shakespeare, because with them the late art is clearly born of a lifetime of tragic insight and artistic discipline. With Browne, one often has the sense that the tragic insight is at best willed and at worst a cliché. Yet his point is, I think, the same as theirs.

Cautious, self-conscious, often claiming melancholy, scarcely willing to make a positive statement about anything, he still says he can compose whole comedies in his dreams—this in a context in which he has been comparing dream and life. Whatever kind of tragedy or comedy the world may be (stage of fools, devil's mockshow, hospital, dream, globe, or fable), it is not remediable. Therefore, let art be play for the sake of God and man, and by the act of re-creation subdue life's pain.

CHAPTER VII

JOHN MILTON:
THE PROSE STYLE OF GOD'S
ENGLISH POET

DURING THE 1630'S, OF MANY YOUNG MEN WHO COMPLETED THEIR education with a continental sojourn, two were Thomas Browne and John Milton. Only three years separated them in age. Within a few years of his return to England, each wrote his first published prose, although neither intended to make a career out of writing prose. Browne's book is a meditative consideration of a personality, formed in travel and study, that can now describe itself at leisure, purposely detached from the immediate and topical world. Milton's early political tracts were written only because of the pressure of that immediate world, which they reflect and embody. Between Browne's *Religio Medici* and Milton's antiprelatical tracts lies the entire difference between the Puritan and Anglican modes of self-consciousness, for Milton was wholly Puritan even in the rich profusion of his greatest art.

It is a fact that Milton rarely uses the first person except as a convenience, and that the tracts in which personal digressions appear are for the most part focused upon some topic, like church government, which he treats passionately but without self-reference. Yet if asked to name one seventeenth-century writer noted for his self-consciousness or his egotism, almost anyone acquainted with the period would think first of Milton or of Donne. Despite Milton's sparing use of the "I," one is always aware of him because of his personal and passionate commitment to every cause he espouses, and because of the character and intensity of his autobiographical statements, which are summarized in his belief that the true poet must himself be a poem. Just as so many of his fellow Puritans added up the evidence to convince themselves that they were saved, Milton repeatedly presents the evidence of his worthiness to be heard, to represent his cause, and, eventually, to be a great poet.

To honor him with even minimal adequacy is to recognize and take seriously the fact that he intends our awareness of him as a man primarily in order to prove to us that, because as man he is true poem, we can take his writing seriously. He points us wholly back from art to life, as all Puritan writers do, but he does it only briefly, only to intensify the art. Unlike other Puritan writers, that is to say, he allows us to examine his autobiography in order to impress upon us his literary qualifications. But these qualifications are for him the signs of grace, which, like other Puritans, he believes to be God-given, and therefore not a matter for vanity.

As one might expect, Milton's prose works are extensive, ranging widely in seriousness, length, style, and subject. The earliest, tentatively dated 1624, is a schoolboy "Theme on Early Rising"; the latest, in order of publication, is *A Brief History of Moscovia*, published in 1682, eight years after his death.[1] Despite the range of topics covered in fifty years of authorship, however, the central preoccupation is liberty, and the central reason for writing is to help men achieve liberty. He believed that reformation was needed in three encompassing fields of human activity: religion, domestic affairs (including education), and politics are the chief subjects of the thirty-nine prose works. For the most part, these subjects are treated without self-reference, and do not concern us here.

But one set of prose pieces well suited to my purposes is a series of five antiprelatical tracts dated between May 1640 and April 1642. Written in English, which is by no means automatic for Milton, they contain explicitly autobiographical passages, and one can find in them a development of self-consciousness or self-confidence that culminates in the last two of the series. Here, apparent opposites join and shift roles, and yet simultaneously remain opposed. Among these, for example, are action and contemplation, time and eternity, dissonance and consonance, prose and poetry. Milton's "I" is typically Puritan, being preconceived and rigid, controversial and time-bound, active and literal, relatively humorless, devoted to nationalism and progress. But because he thinks about poetry rather than salvation in regard to his own calling, when he supplies us with autobiographical details they evoke, not exactly a different world and certainly not an Anglican one, but rather an England perfected, where contemplation and poetry and harmony are intrinsic to life.

If Milton had not been England's greatest poet, we would probably not read the antiprelatical tracts at all, since they are so deeply committed to the future accomplishment of his genius that without its historical existence they would seem at best the products of an over-reaching mind. Because they do assume his poetry of the future and run parallel in theme to some of the poetry already written ("Lycidas" in particular), and because much of the prose is itself poetical, I shall necessarily make frequent reference to the relationships between the poetry and prose insofar as they are relevant to Milton's self-portrayal. It will be most convenient, after providing some necessary biographical information, to begin by following the order of the tracts, giving progressively more attention to them as they become more significant for my purposes, as Milton finds it desirable to speak more and more fully of himself. The analysis of the last tract, in which Milton's presence is most pervasive, will summarize and elaborate the tendencies observed en route.

Milton's early self-portrayal could not help but be complex, partly, no doubt, because of the complex influence of his father. This Puritan businessman and skilled musician, who paid for his son's aristocratic education with money earned from moneylending, brought up his son to enter the church, and bred principles into him that made it impossible for him to swear the necessary oaths. At the age of thirty, the poet had never worked for a living. He was loath to break off studies designed to ripen him into an immortality of poetic fame. The cause which he chose—or which chose him—was, if anything, hostile to the arts, to leisure, to the kind of classical education he had been given. Yet he did break off his studies to descend into a "troubl'd sea of noises and hoars disputes." [2] He emerged only after the Restoration of Charles II, blind and disgraced at fifty-two, the great work still unwritten, so far as anyone could tell. He had apparently put all of himself into a temporal undertaking. It was as he embarked upon that undertaking, which consumed so many years of his life, that he wrote his most autobiographical English prose.

As every reader of Milton knows, because Milton himself explains it, when he returned to England from his European tour, he had no intention of involving himself actively in politics. He had shortened his tour by depriving himself of a visit to Sicily and Greece, because he thought he should not be idly amusing himself at such a time,[3] but he was unprepared to make any more positive contribution to the cause. Filled with grief over the death of his closest friend, Charles Diodati, and unable now to speak to him of his ambitions, he described in a Latin lament for his friend the literary plans and hopes for himself with which he had come home. As a first step he took rooms in London, and shortly thereafter "a pretty Garden-House" [4] in a quiet neighborhood, where he set about continuing his life of studious calm. Apparently against his will, he found himself called —as Donne had always longed to be called, as Donne's heroes Paul and Augustine had been called—to do God's work in the world, which for Milton meant writing controversial prose in defense, not just of the Revolution, but of revolutionary thought and action at home, in the church, and in the state.

In his Latin *Second Defence of the English People*,[5] Milton thus describes his reason for entering into political agitation in 1641. What follows is a translation, which is important to remember because the style must not be expected to be Miltonic:

Meanwhile, as Parliament acted with vigor, the haughtiness of the bishops began to deflate. As soon as freedom of speech (at the very least) became possible, all mouths were opened against them. Some complained of the personal defects of the bishops, others of the defectiveness of the episcopal rank itself. It was wrong, they said, that their church alone should differ from all other reformed churches. It was proper for the church to be guided by the example of the brethren, but first of all by the word of God. Now, thoroughly aroused to these concerns, I perceived that men were following the true path to liberty and that from these beginnings, these first steps, they were making the most direct progress towards the liberation of all human life from slavery—provided that the discipline arising from religion should overflow into the morals and institutions of the state. Since, moreover, I had so practiced myself from youth that I was above all things unable to disregard the laws of God and man, and since I had asked myself whether I should be of any future use if I now failed my country (or rather the church and so many of my brothers who were exposing themselves to danger for the sake of the Gospel) I decided, although at that time occupied with certain other matters, to devote to this conflict all my talents and all my active powers (*PW*, IV:1, 621-22).

Elsewhere, he speaks of the stories he would hear within himself all his life after, if he did not heed his country's call. He thought that he stood at a crucial, decisive moment in human history, that God was again calling the English to be his people, and that both God and England required him.

In the antiprelatical tracts, he sets forth the arguments for separation between church and state, for a church discipline that permits freedom of choice, and for freedom to make individual encounter with God. His vision of the future is formative, and, as other critics have noticed,[6] directly connected with his sense of his own vocation and his reason for choosing to write tracts instead of poems at this time. One is constantly aware both of his sense of vocation and of his self-consciousness about being a late developer. Asked by others or by himself why he was not achieving more, he said that his time was not yet. But his concern over that fact is illustrated in his consistent predating of his work and his long-lasting emphasis on his youth. One means by which he explained why his time was not yet was identification of his own destiny with that of England. In that ideal future, which he believed would be almost the same as, and a certain prologue to, the Second Coming, it would be possible to write poetry celebrating events that in 1641 had not yet occurred, which in fact were never to occur in such a way as to make possible the realization of Milton's dream. Because of its subject matter and because of its context, this poetry would itself be unimaginably beautiful; it could not be written until the world should become worthy of it.

Thus the antiprelatical tracts are in one highly important respect a means by which Milton hoped to make his dearest vocation possible. And the dependency of his vocation upon the course of history reminds us again of the unique inextricability of his poetic gift from his Puritan mind. Foxe's *Book of Martyrs* had made clear to all Puritans the analogy between the calling of the individual and that of the nation, as it had shown that the English were God's uniquely chosen people just as the Jews had been.[7] Typically Milton believed that since God was now preparing "some new and great period in his Church, . . . what does he then but reveal Himself to his servants, and as his manner is, first to his Englishmen; I say as his manner is, first to us." [8] For most Puritans, I believe, the analogy between personal and national destiny must have increased their sense of obligation to themselves and God, since they were called to be saved in and as part of providential history: God's pattern required them now. Any longings for immortality were concentrated upon their hopes for salvation. For Milton the matter was considerably more complex. He believed himself called to be a poet, yet as a Puritan he was required first to accept a temporal historical vocation in order to get to the point in history where he could exercise that more timeless and personally gratifying craft. And he could not choose or foresee when that point in history might come; for that too he must await God's pleasure.

The phrase "egotistical sublime," [9] which has sometimes been applied to Milton, can be a way of describing the sense of self which comes to be expressed under such conditions as these. Critics who have regarded Milton merely as a self-absorbed egotist, or have been repelled by the intensity of his self-concern, would perhaps be less offended if it were possible for them to read him with a fuller awareness of the complex pressures under which he operated, and the moral fervor with which he was imbued. His self-concern, like that of Lilburne, is partly a national concern. It is true that from his youth he had been contemplating for himself "an immortality of fame," [10] last infirmity of noble minds though that might be. But as a literary figure he is typically Puritan in his inability to separate his destiny from that of the English people, and from the beginning he deals with this fact in a manner that could be considered the opposite of egotistical.

His first antiprelatical tract, which probably appeared in May 1641, is called *Of Reformation Touching Church-Discipline in England: And the Causes that hitherto have hindred it*. It is written in two books addressed to a friend, but the tone is throughout public and oratorical, and there is no question that his intention was to reach as many people as possible. The apparently private address may be token modesty about his first tract. This first essay against prelacy is concerned in the first book to refute the arguments from antiquity, in the second, the arguments from politics. The tone is fiery, and the epithets are colorful. Yet, Milton says, defending his zeal, he speaks not out of malice or desire for vain-glory, but for the vindication of truth.

The tract ends with a prayer in which he envisions the coming kingdom, and the poet's place in it. Here, where he first describes his anticipated role, he assigns himself a bardic anonymity:

Then amidst the *Hymns*, and *Halleluiahs* of *Saints* some one may perhaps bee heard offering at high *strains* in new and lofty *Measures* to sing and celebrate thy *divine Mercies*, and *marvelous Judgements* in this Land throughout all Ages; whereby this great and Warlike Nation instructed and inur'd to the fervent and continuall practice of *Truth* and *Righteousnesse*, and casting farre from her the *rags* of her old *vices* may presse on hard to that *high* and *happy* emulation to be found the *soberest, wisest,* and *most Christian People* at that day when thou the Eternall and shortly-expected King shalt open the Clouds to judge the severall Kingdomes of the World, and distributing *Nationall Honours* and *Rewards* to Religious and just *Common-wealths,* shalt put an end to all Earthly *Tyrannies,* proclaiming thy universal and milde *Monarchy* through Heaven and Earth (*Of Reformation, PW,* I, 616).

It was much in this way that in "Lycidas" Milton had referred to himself as an uncouth swain singing to oaks and rills. The third-person pose is partly convention, partly unsureness. He is not yet ready to promise that John Milton will be that idealized poet-priest: hence, he says that "someone may perhaps bee heard." But his mention of himself in the third person is at least in part an acceptance of his complex appointed role in God's design, and it looks forward to his self-representation in *Paradise Lost,* where Puritan instrument and inspired poet are one.[11]

Already, in fact, he is clearly playing more than one role, even as instrument. He is both prophet and thing prophesied, both artist and art. Hence the high tone of the prayer clashes against the savage invective of so much of the essay, as the prophet foresees the time when God's enemies will be cast down, and the poet, freed alike from hoarse disputes and from set forms of prayer, can pour out his unpremeditated verse. Some of the unevenness of tone in Milton's antiprelatical tracts is brought about just by this need to portray simultaneously several different times and states of being. Puritanically, he is dependent on history; yet the fervency both of his prophecy and of his poetic gift allows him to conceive in time the timelessness of sacred verse. To support his reading of the present, he invokes both past and future.

Milton's second tract is called *Of Prelatical Episcopacy, and Whether it may be deduc'd from the Apostolical times by vertue of those Testimonies which are alledg'd to that purpose in some late Treatises.* Printed in the summer of 1641, it is a brief and telling piece of propaganda, rich as *Of Reformation* in redolent epithets, but since it contains no autobiographical material, it needs no further attention here. The third tract, of July 1641, is *Animadversions Upon the Remonstrants Defence Against Smectymnuus.* It is a contribution to the cause of the five Puritans calling themselves Smectymnuus, after their own joined initials, who had attacked and been attacked by the Anglican bishop and controversialist Joseph Hall. In answering Hall's *Defence of the Humble Remonstrance*, Milton chooses the form of a dialogue between the Remonstrant and the Answerer. The Remonstrant is made to quote or paraphrase Hall's arguments for episcopacy, section by section, while the Answerer mocks, attacks, or refutes.

The whole dialogue is stamped with Milton's personality, especially in the imagery, where, for example, the theme of blindness and sight is important. But the casting of his argument into dialogue removes it just about as far as possible from apparent relevance to the subject of this book. Two passages in this sixty-six-page tract, however, require brief consideration, in their respective contexts: these are a defense in the preface of the abusive style of argument, and, in Section 4 of the dialogue, an impassioned apocalyptic outburst that becomes a prayer.

One of several arguments in the preface in favor of the abusive style is that it is utterly sincere: the speaker is moved by sheer love of man and truth, as is proved by the fact that no worldly success can come of what he does: "They that seeke to discover and oppose their [the prelates'] false trade of deceiving, do it not without a sad and unwilling anger, not without many hazards, but without all private and personall spleene, and without any thought of earthly reward, when as this very course they take stopps their hopes of ascending above a lowly and unenviable pitch in this life" (*Animadversions*, *PW*, I, 663). The speaker here is a man who is in the process of committing himself, his eyes, and twenty years of his life to a "lowly and unenviable pitch" that is represented by the ordinary style of the tracts. It is a commitment to polemical prose, rather than to poetry. Yet, as before, he takes a brief moment out of time to practice a strain of higher mood, which is concluded thus:

When thou hast settl'd peace in the Church, and righteous judgement in the Kingdome, then shall all thy Saints address their voyces of joy, and triumph to thee, standing on the shoare of that red Sea into which our enemies had almost driven us. And he that now for haste snatches up a plain ungarnish't present as a thanke-offering to thee, which could not bee deferr'd in regard of thy so many late deliverances wrought for us one upon another, may then perhaps take up a Harp, and sing thee an elaborate Song to Generations. In that day it shall no more bee said as in scorne, this or that was never held so till this present Age, when men have better learnt that the times and seasons passe along under thy feet, to goe and come at thy bidding, and as thou didst dignifie our fathers dayes with many revelations above all the foregoing ages, since thou tookst the flesh; so thou canst vouchsafe to us (though unworthy) as large a portion of thy spirit as thou pleasest; for who shall prejudice thy all-governing will? seeing the power of thy grace is not past away with the primitive times, as fond and faithless men imagine, but thy Kingdome is now at hand, and thou standing at the dore. Come forth out of thy Royall Chambers, O Prince of all the Kings of the earth, put on the visible roabes of thy imperiall Majesty, take up that unlimited Scepter which thy Almighty Father hath bequeath'd thee; for now the voice of thy Bride calls thee, and all creatures sigh to bee renew'd (*Animadversions, PW*, I, 706–7).

This is a forward projection into that time when his "lowly" efforts will after all enable the poet to achieve his high destiny. The concept of stopped hopes meant something, of course, but it was also a rhetorical device. Believing here, as he clearly does, in progress, Milton could not have condemned himself in his own mind to permanent obscurity.

The fact of time again plays a large part, then, focusing the opposition between prelates and Puritans, and explaining the necessity for a visionary prose. It is possible to observe a pattern of improvement in the welfare of God's Englishmen: ". . . thou didst dignifie our fathers dayes with many revelations above all the foregoing ages, since thou tookst the flesh." And time moves forward toward a desired end that is now at hand.[12] In that fulfillment of God's plan, a Song to Generations is an encomium of history as embodied in the men who have known God's mercies and done His will, and thereby helped to bring about His Kingdom. By invoking the future, Milton is enabled to go a step beyond the Puritan repudiation of artfulness as incompatible with the serious business of soul-saving. Now, for haste, there is no time for tuning of instruments, and even thank-offerings must be ungarnished; but then an elaborate Song to Generations, whose mood is here illustrated, may be composed and sung.

It may be said that Milton, like other Puritans, has begun to define or realize himself in opposition to his enemies. "Standing on the shoare of that red Sea into which our enemies had almost driven us," the Saints will raise their voices of joy and triumph, and the poet will take up his harp. But Milton still speaks of himself impersonally and briefly, and the emphasis at any rate is not upon himself, but upon the transformation of England and the coming of Christ. To some extent, his own lack of status still subdues him, as will become clear in the next two tracts, but the impersonality does not then disappear. That is intrinsic to Milton's consideration of himself as God's instru-

ment, a man with a vocation. It is that above all which links the Lilburnian radical with less fiery Puritans like Bunyan and Baxter.

The Reason of Church-Government (March 1642) is Milton's
first signed tract, and the first in which he speaks at length of himself, in a "digression" which is the heart of the piece.[13] The main
concern of this tract on vocation is to show that church discipline is
meaningless compared to the "self-honoring" that should inspire virtuous behavior. Such self-honoring is then illustrated in the digression in several ways. Milton says that his way in the church has been
blocked by the necessity of oath-taking: the prelatical system thus
prevented his self-honoring in the first instance. His desire to write
poetry has been blocked by the necessity to write pamphlets, which
is also the fault of the prelates. On the other hand, God has called
him to write these pamphlets, and though he does it with his left
hand, he necessarily honors self and God through free obedience.
And finally he covenants with the English people to write great poetry when the New Jerusalem shall have been achieved.

When he thinks of himself in his true mission, he thinks poetically.
William Haller speaks of his "style that was hardly prose and not
quite English," [14] and that description fits the digression in *Church-
Government*. The style of Book I is sober and restrained, very much
more polite than that of the *Animadversions*. But at the opening of
Book II it is raised to that cadenced, lofty periodicity which is the
unmistakable mark of Miltonic poetry and prose. The following passage is particularly relevant:

For although a Poet soaring in the high region of his fancies with his garland
and singing robes about him might without apology speak more of himself
then I mean to do, yet for me sitting here below in the cool element of prose,
a mortall thing among many readers of no Empyreall conceit, to venture and
divulge unusual things of my selfe, I shall petition to the gentler sort, it may
not be envy to me. I must say therefore that after I had from my first yeeres
by the ceaselesse diligence and care of my father, whom God recompence,
bin exercis'd to the tongues, and some sciences, as my age would suffer, by
sundry masters and teachers both at home and at the schools, it was found
that whether ought was impos'd me by them that had the overlooking, or
betak'n to of mine own choise in English, or other tongue, prosing or versing,
but chiefly this latter, the stile by certain vital signes it had, was likely to live
(*Church-Government*, *PW*, I, 808–9).

The passage is remarkable for the grandeur of its style, the intensity
of the self-consciousness, and the clarity of the Puritan ethic, which

is profoundly responsible for both the grandeur and the intensity. Milton recognizes that by writing about himself in prose, he is doing something unusual, something that would not be reprehensible if he were writing poetry instead. To speak of prose in this way, as a "cool element," is to assume that it is ordinarily restricted to that "lowly and unenviable pitch" which brings fame to no one.

Milton has already repeated his explanations for the inadequacy of his prose. He is writing out of his "own season," in his green years; there is no time "to pencil it over with all the curious touches of art" and even if there were it would be folly to commit art to "the careless and interrupted listening of these tumultuous times" (*Church-Government, PW*, I, 807). Yet not only must he do this; he will also write about himself in this naked language which affords the author none of the anonymity of poetry. Conventionally masked, "with his garland and singing robes about him," he "might without apology speak more of himself."

It is important to recognize that Milton here indicates his complete understanding of one of the main premises of this book—the fact that first-person narration offers the writer none of the automatic protection of poetry. This is especially true when the author is evidently writing nonfiction, but in any event the idea of a fictitious first person was much less familiar in Milton's time than it is now.

It is typical of Milton to combine such frank insight with some sleight-of-hand. In his very recognition of the difference between poetry and prose, he wrests such poetry from the prose as to protect himself as he writes. He is sitting below in the cool element of prose, but the cool element is the surrounding oration, from which the digression soars with hot intensity. Partly the effect is created by the bewildering Latinate intricacy of the syntax (one reason why Mr. Haller called this prose "not quite English"), which moves according to Milton's musical whims.[15] Partly it is created by a greatly stepped-up and highly poetic supply of imagery replacing the homely pugnacious flyting figures of Book I. Partly it is created by the personal narrative that replaces the impersonal, topical, reasoned discussion of the nature of church government. And whenever the subject is Milton, it is also poetry.

And yet there is a sense in which this section is quite as objective—if Milton is ever objective—as the rest of the work. In the Puritanical intensity of his sense of vocation, he avoids the first person in order to suggest that he has been called, that he is the bearer of the talent, the instrument with which God may write if Milton will move in free obedience. That self-honoring which is conformity between God's will and man's expresses itself in passive constructions, in avoidance of personal pronouns ("the" being substituted for "my"), in ascription of motive forces to agencies other than himself. The intricate perversity of his characteristic syntax may partly be explained by his concern to avoid the first person, which very often leads him to make apparently arbitrary choices of such Latinate constructions as infinitives and ethical datives: ". . . for me sitting here below in the cool element of prose, a mortall thing among many readers of no Empyreall conceit, to venture and divulge unusual things of my selfe, I shall petition to the gentler sort, it may not be envy to me." Other phrases by means of which this particular passage is rendered impersonal are these: "I had . . . bin exercis'd to the tongues . . . as my age would suffer, by sundry masters and teachers"; "it was found that whether ought was impos'd me by them . . . or betak'n to of mine own choise . . . the stile . . . was likely to live" (*Church-Government*, *PW*, I, 808–9).

Certainly one reason for the intricacy of the syntax is that Milton was trained in Latin rather than English grammar. But although in this respect his education was typical in the age, no one else's language came out sounding like his. The way in which his Latin influenced him is unique. Here he begins with impersonal reference to himself, and then gradually drops out subject and verb as he considers the kinds of literature that he may write in the future:

Time servs not now, and perhaps I might seem too profuse to give any certain account of what the mind at home in the spacious circuits of her musing hath liberty to propose to her self, though of highest hope and hardest attempting, whether that Epick form . . . or whether those Dramatick constitutions . . . Or if occasion shall lead to imitat those magnifick Odes and Hymns . . . whatsoever in religion is holy and sublime, in vertu amiable, or grave, whatsoever hath passion or admiration in all the changes of that which is call'd fortune from without, or the wily suttleties and refluxes of mans thought from within, all these things with a solid and treatable smoothnesse to paint out and describe. Teaching over the whole book of sanctity and vertu through all the instances of example with such delight to those especially of soft and delicious temper who will not so much as look upon Truth herselfe, unlesse they see her elegantly drest, that whereas the paths of honesty and good life appear now rugged and difficult, though they be indeed easy and pleasant, they would then appear to all men both easy and pleasant though they were rugged and difficult indeed (*Church-Government*, *PW*, I, 812–18).

Obviously Milton's whole intention in the passage is to describe his hopes for himself. Yet the syntax absorbs and transforms the egocentricity. The "I" is practically silenced, and Milton seems to be carried along by the verbal instructions, or assumed into them, so that he becomes an instrument, a "doer" rather than an asserter, and the subject is less himself than the deeds that he is called upon to perform.

He imagines that the voice of his conscience is addressing him:

. . . this I foresee, that should the Church be brought under heavy oppression, . . . or should she by blessing from above . . . change this her distracted estate into better daies without the least furtherance or contribution of those few talents which God at that present had lent me, I foresee what stories I should heare within my selfe, all my life after, of discourage and reproach. Timorous and ingratefull, the Church of God is now again at the foot of her insulting enemies: and thou bewailest, what matters it for thee or thy bewailing? when time was, thou couldst not find a syllable of all that thou hadst read, or studied, to utter in her behalfe (*Church-Government*, *PW*, I, 804).

Again, Milton's vocation and the inner conflicts which he has had to face are obviously the subject. By making his conscience lecture him on his duty, however, he suggests that he is a called man, learning to listen to the voice, and obey it, rather than following his own desires.

I might note here briefly that in the extremely autobiographical early poem, "Lycidas," Milton uses the first person singular exactly twice. The avoidance of it is certainly less patent, because he does not avoid "me," "my," or "we," but there are analogous impersonal constructions by means of which he makes himself the object rather than the subject: "Bitter constraint, and sad occasion dear, Compels me to disturb your season due"; "Begin then, Sisters of the sacred well,/That from beneath the seat of *Jove* doth spring,/Begin, and somewhat loudly sweep the string." The harsh imagery of the early lines of "Lycidas" implies what he makes clear both in poetry and prose, that he has been called to speak before his time.

Despite the impartial devices, the first person is stifled in neither poetry nor prose. The passage on page 193, with which I began this discussion, is adequate testimony. The combination, in such passages as this, of the present, eagerly assertive first person with the persistent, almost awkward avoidance of it is a way of imitating that conformity between God's will and man's that for Milton was so central a theme. One would ordinarily expect both intensity and tension to come from the collision of personal with impersonal, active with passive. Instead, the joining of the two techniques becomes an illustration of free obedience, as personal will (the first person) and impersonal need (passive voice, etc.) combine. We have seen that Milton's muting of the "I" in passages wholly taken up with himself makes his desires seem to rest on those of God. And often where the "I" does make itself aggressively felt, an overarching periodic sentence prevents the collision of personal with impersonal simply by encompassing both in a larger order. Harmony coexists with the intensity generated by the apparently conflicting forms. The historical tasks of the periodic sentence have been to unite people, to preserve order, and to reflect beauty.[16] These tasks are here fulfilled. Milton's healing music is illustrative of his pervasive effort "to repair the ruins of our first parents." [17] On the one hand, he will expose with all the harsh language at his command the ruins which others have endeavored to patch up or to conceal. On the other hand, he illustrates from his own center the proper means and shape of renewal. The best teacher of others, he says, is the best knower of himself. Teaching others the means of achieving discipline in vocation, he demonstrates these means—outer direction joined with inner purpose—in this digression.

The Reason of Church-Government is an answer to a tract entitled Certain Briefe Treatises, Written by Diverse Learned Men, Concerning the Ancient and Moderne Government of the Church. Of the eight men whose polemics were here included, six were dead, among them Bishop Lancelot Andrewes (PW, I, 738), for whom Milton shows at least a grudging respect. The pamphlet is certainly neither aimed at these men nor addressed to them. Their work is never mentioned by name, and only briefly opposed. The tone of the pamphlet as a whole is comparatively restrained, a fact which emphasizes the ardor of the digression. Further contrast between the "body" and the "heart" of the work is pointed up by Milton's specific designations of different kinds of readers. The body of the work is intended for "the intelligent and equal auditor" ("equal" meaning "judicious") whom he hopes he can convince by means of the digression that his youth should not be held against him. On the other hand, he wishes that in this autobiographical section he might be heard only by "the elegant and learned reader," who perhaps will understand Milton's hopes for himself. For the one reader, Milton employs the language of prose polemics; for the other, the language of poetic prophecy. Yet surely both are included when, in the digression, he makes his covenant with "any knowing reader" to fulfill his promise to write great literature when the time comes. The elaboration of that covenant takes up the greater part of this digression, and is a discussion of the various kinds of literature that might successfully honor God, England, and John Milton. They are epic, tragedy, and hymn, and are sometimes taken to be a knowing prophecy of his future production of long epic, short epic, and drama. His emphasis is primarily on the usefulness to England of these forms, and then briefly on the fact that he would rather not be second-best among the Latin writers. At any rate, as always, he fits himself into history as an English poet who will celebrate English deeds.

The word "covenant" in Milton's time could not but imply a mutual promise, an agreement among the members of a community, since it was commonly used in that sense in revolutionary government and church. Milton may in this way be bargaining with his readers to suggest even more forcefully that his poetry can only be written under certain conditions which they must all, including himself, fulfill. The reader must be available before the work can be written.

It is difficult to emphasize sufficiently the artfulness of this move. The Anglican writer often ignores his audience, and endeavors to make his work appear spontaneous. The Puritan is writing only because he knows he has an audience, but claims the press of history and/or the solemnity of the occasion as a reason to forego artistic sophistication. Milton somehow manages to have everything both ways. He provides an audience for both present and future. And while claiming to write with his left hand only, he covenants in exquisite prose-poetry with his right. This device, which we have seen him playing with already, is a marvelously novel kind of *praeteriteo,* promising poetic excellence in the future in language that offers a sample of it now. The whole is absolutely bound in time, as well as being free of it. Past, present, and future are essential references. Yet the *praeteriteo* bypasses time as well as other things, and as in his poem "On the Morning of Christs Nativity," Milton arrives at the Second Coming while the revolution is still kicking in its cradle. In both cases he goes on to explain what must be done before that second coming can be realized.

Throughout his early writing, Milton shows great sensitivity to the fact of passing time, in his laments that he keeps growing older without producing great work, in his complaints that he has been forced to write before his due season, and in his apparently defensive remarks in the tracts that his arguments ought not to be attacked on account of his youth. Even in *Paradise Lost*, in relation to the search for an epic theme, he speaks of himself as "long choosing and beginning late." And just as one of the main reasons for his beginning late was that he had to fight the battle of free speech, in such issues as whether or not the Book of Common Prayer should be prescribed, so again in *Paradise Lost* he speaks of his "unpremeditated verse," brought to him, as he believed that prayer should be, by direct inspiration, not by mediated rules. Yet, despite the apparent temporal uncertainty of his life, and despite his own insistence upon liberation, there is a remarkable consistency from the very beginning in the portrait of himself which he constructs and in the plans for himself which are eventually fulfilled. Like other Puritans, Milton seems to have said to himself, "This is what I want to be, and I shall be it." He was to be a great poet. First, he must himself be a poem.

The issue is complicated, however, because while the aim of other Puritans is to be saved, Milton's aim at this time is to be the kind of poet who can only exercise his gift after the world has been in effect saved. Throughout the early prose, therefore, he adopts a dual role. As angry Christian, using all weapons available to him to bring down prelacy, he acts wholly in time, at the mercy of moment-to-moment events and requirements. As poet creating himself as poem, he thinks in the timeless context of the New Jerusalem. I said at the outset that, like the other paired opposites in Milton, time and eternity meet. In fact, the Christian warrior and the poet-to-be become conditions of one another, neither intelligible without the other's presence. Thus the timeless idea exists in time, and the angry Christian is made timeless by his idea.

Milton's *Animadversions Upon the Remonstrants Defence Against Smectymnuus* was answered, either by Bishop Hall or by an unidentified champion writing for him, in *A Modest Confutation of A Slanderous and Scurrilous Libell, Entituled, Animadversions upon the Remonstrants Defence Against Smectymnuus*. The fact that the titles keep getting longer is part of the warfare, as each engulfs the one that preceded it. Milton's reply to the *Modest Confutation* at least acknowledges that this practice, unrestrained, cannot go on indefinitely: *An Apology Against a Pamphlet Called a Modest Confutation of the Animadversions upon the Remonstrant against Smectymnuus*.

The *Modest Confutation* returns Milton's attack in kind. Like him, the author uses quotations out of context, and makes aspersions against his opponent's character. At the same time, he claims to have been unable to find out anything about Milton, and says that his remarks are based on Milton's own writing, that, for example, Milton's use of scurrilous language reflects the poet's own character, as does his awareness of the existence of harlots, players, and slop buckets. Certainly Milton had invited this kind of assault, and its force might have been mitigated for him by the fact that he was pilloried only briefly, and as an anonymous figure by an anonymous critic. Yet his outraged response in the *Apology* is predictable. He was triply vulnerable, as sensitive human being, as representative of his cause, and as poet-to-be. His *Apology* is in many respects a harsh and disconnected document, in tone very different from the measured stateliness of *Church-Government*. But it deserves close attention as the culminating tract in the series, written by a now-practiced polemicist, whose developing style is sharpened under the pressure of the Confuter's personal attack.

Over and over again, in Milton's art, one sees suggested the humanist belief that both action and contemplation are essential to the good life. It is a belief that had lost ground since the time of Sir Thomas More and the early humanists, who had thought to be counselors to kings.[18] The division of the two has been posited in this book as one sort of demarcation between Anglican and Puritan writing, and Milton's tracts have implied his belief that only through action and warfare can he arrive at a place where contemplation and poetry can again become possible. Yet, as I have shown, it is not simply a temporal progression, since even in the midst of action Milton demonstrates the contemplative mode. And certainly he does not envisage either heaven or the ideal state as a place where all action ceases. Rather, it is to be a place of harmonious and timeless movement, as described in the final section of "Lycidas":

> There entertain him all the Saints above,
> In solemn troops, and sweet Societies
> That sing, and singing in their glory move,
> And wipe the tears for ever from his eyes.

The very first sentence of the *Apology* demonstrates the larger amount of control and assurance that Milton has now achieved, and will suggest some ways in which to encounter the theme of action and contemplation in this tract. Milton is now committed to his role in this controversy, and he can come immediately and in his own person to grips with the reader and the subject. He is so present that it would be almost impossible to mistake this sentence for one by any English writer other than Milton, and one might even dare to say this about the sentence's first two words alone: "If, Readers, to that same great difficulty of well doing what we certainly know, were not added in most men as great a carelessenes of knowing what they, and others ought to do, we had bin long ere this, no doubt but all of us much farther on our way to some degree of peace and happinesse in this kingdome" (*Apology, PW*, I, 868). There is now no pretence that the tract is written to a single friend, but rather an immediate and peremptory recognition of the presence of readers who are informed of the controversy which the *Apology* sustains. The tract begins *in medias res* with one of Milton's periodic sentences, which is characteristically and awkwardly interrupted, after one word, to embrace the reader, who is never after this released for very long. In content, the sentence takes an immediate and unequivocal ethical stand, expressing impatience that England is not yet perfect, and using the characteristic Puritan figure of a journey. Thus are introduced the themes both of action and contemplation, and of time and eternity. The theme of action and contemplation is also contained in the coupling of doing with knowing.

At the same time, this call for action is expressed in a characteristically Miltonic use of words that slow the thought. They do not repeat, decorate, or cause tension. In a sense, these are unnecessary words: "that *same* great difficulty"; "what we *certainly* know"; "*no doubt but all of us*"; "*some degree of.*" It would be difficult to argue, with the possible exception of the last phrase, that any of the italicized words are essential to the sentence. They are not even a satirical way of mocking the nation's lack of progress. They are simply there to yoke contemplation with action, a sense of calm with the figure of a journey. They add weight, dignity, and sonority to the sentence, and make it more spacious. They announce and illustrate an important theme.

Suggested in these paired opposites of action and contemplation, as they have been in all Milton's prose, are journey and journey's end, revolution and Utopia, tracts and poems, noise and stillness, dissonance and consonance. Throughout the tract, these categories divide and mingle. Rough as the *Apology* is, much of it, like the first sentence, will bear analysis as poetic prose, whereas in *Church-Government* very little besides the digression could be so considered. As soon as anything becomes poetic, it does transcend the chaos of the everyday world, and indicates an ability on the part of the author to transcend or transform it—to have his mind on consonance as well as party politics, and to hold action and contemplation in some kind of fusion where all is simultaneously ill and well.

As the two are separable and often separate, they have their own values and valuations. For the rhetoric of action (in which I here include dissonance and violence), these are harder to discover. Much of the language of both the *Animadversions* and the *Apology* ill befits our concept of literary decorum—or, in fact, of decorum of any kind. And yet Milton uses the word "decorum" with much assurance, as denoting a way of writing which he himself employs, but is regrettably unfamiliar to his opponents. In fact, as Thomas Kranidas has shown in his book *The Fierce Equation*,[19] the idea of decorum was one on which Puritans and Anglicans parted company. We have seen this before in Lilburne. But in Milton it is much more impressive because his writing is much more aggressively "indecorous" than Lilburne's ever was, because he writes with great sophistication and complete consciousness of what he is doing and why. Perhaps he did not want to descend into a troubled sea of noises and hoarse disputes, but he knew very well how to swim in that sea.[20]

The *Apology* differs from earlier tracts, among other things, in that it contains a great deal of literary criticism called forth in part by the attacks of Milton's opponent upon his manner of address. Thus, Milton spends much of his time explaining why he is writing this kind of prose, and what he thinks it is for. His explanation is useful at the outset because it defines for us the kinds of readers for whom he hopes. Again, he suggests two different kinds—the Confuter, and the bystander. He is unsure of the possibility of instructing the Confuter or his party. It may be that Milton can "chase him into some good knowledge, and others, I trust, shall not mis-spend their leisure. For this my aime is, if I am forc't to be unpleasing to him whose fault it is, I shall not forget at the same time to be usefull in some thing to the stander by" (*Apology, PW,* I, 878–79). Elsewhere, less optimistically, he says that only the meek can be taught: others must be discovered and laid open.

The tract, then, will present the savagery of a chase primarily for the edification of the bystander. It is the bystander, in fact, who is forced to take an active interest because he is the person addressed, and it is for him that Milton is concerned to establish his good name. If Milton's target is the Confuter, then the pamphlet is hurled at him in an offensively impersonal way, as if he were an object unworthy of direct communication and incapable of rational discourse. In fact, Milton characteristically deals thus with his enemies, except in the set dialogue of the *Animadversions,* appealing directly only to those whom he believes to be in some way sympathetic already.

The appeal to the reader in the second word of the first sentence forecasts the constant address to him throughout the tract, in contrast to an almost total absence of such a device in previous pamphlets. On almost every page, the reader is summoned at least once, most frequently in close relation to a mention of the author: "let me have pardon, Readers"; "I shall show ye, Readers"; "I conceave, Readers"; "I, Readers"; "to me Readers"; "heare me out now Readers"; and so forth. These insistent phrases put Milton's statements about himself on quite a different ground from that on which we learn about Browne or Burton. Once attacked, he comes out into the open, and he does not confide: he asserts. The reader is allowed to be about as much a bystander as the wedding guest is for the ancient mariner. For the first time, Milton has felt his character assailed, and he is fighting back with an undisguised intensity of appeal.

It is true, however, that he neither courts nor characterizes (at any length) the reader: he only clutches him. He aims, in this indirect but vehement way, at the Confuter, and in polemical warfare he is the first of these writers to give as good as he gets and usually better. Lilburne must surely have admired his skill. The *Apology,* although considerably more restrained than the *Animadversions,* calls his adversary, among other things, "this cursing Shimei," "this Seagull," "dough-kneaded thing," "hip-shot Grammarian," "this cloister'd lubber," "lozell Bachellour of Art," "young queasiness." There are some desultory references to the bishops' smelly feet and socks (or buskins)—a leftover pun on prelates as actors, which Milton thought extremely witty. Still to come, in later tracts, are his really scurrilous attacks on the sexual character and relationships of Salmasius and of Alexander More, where the grossness of his slandering astounds the modern reader.

The language is more easily understandable if one thinks of the pamphlet as a missile, remembering that it is aimed at the Confuter as if he were a standing target. Add to that what we have seen in other Puritans, a feeling that Milton absolutely shares, that words are weapons, or, as he says in *Areopagitica,* "as vigorously productive, as those fabulous Dragons teeth; and being sown up and down, may chance to spring up armed men" (*PW,* II, 492). Remember, too, as this quotation suggests, the magical element in language as primitive warfare—for in this Milton is at least as primitive as Lilburne—which makes namecalling a deadly weapon and character assassination just what the phrase asserts. Milton has joined battle with "Hall," and at stake is the welfare of his own name, which is one with his person in the public eye: "I shall be put unwillingly to molest the publick view with the vindication of a private name; as if it were worth the while that the people should care whether such a one were thus, or thus. Yet those I intreat who have found the leasure to reade that name, however of small repute, unworthily defam'd, would be so good and patient as to heare the same person not unneedfully defended" (*Apology, PW,* I, 870). The battle imagery in Milton's prose has often been remarked upon.[21] It is frequent here, being most often used to strengthen the impression that words are weapons. Milton speaks of his enemy "aiming his slanderous bolts," or "weak arguments headed with sharp taunts," and thus explains his own refusal to support his arguments with references to antiquity: ". . . neglecting the maine bulk of all that specious antiquity, which might stunne children, but not men, I chose rather to observe some kind of military advantages to await him at his forragings, at his watrings, and when ever he felt himselfe secure to solace his veine in derision of his more serious opponents" (*Apology, PW,* I, 872). The tone created by the battle imagery is strongly supported by the fact that Milton's verbs and adjectives, and his images generally, tend to suggest violent action: "ere the brick-bats fly"; "pluming and footing this Sea-gull, so open he lies to strokes"; "that tyranny which the whole Kingdome cry'd out against as stung with Adders, and Scorpions"; "he held the scourgers garments."

Language like this, of course, is common among the tract-writers, and is significant in Milton mainly for its unusual density and violence. More distinctive of Milton is a prevalence of extreme value judgments, also violently expressed. The impression of Milton as stiff-necked zealot may well be strengthened by the eagerness with which he applies all kinds of moralistic epithets: "deceaving glass of other mens opinion"; "rancour of an evil tongue"; "so light as the palm of a bishop"; "to deprave that just government which pride and ambition have shouldered out of the church"; "young divines writhing and unboning their clergy limmes to all the antick and dishonest gestures of Trinculo's, Buffons, and bawds"; "ungentle and swinish breast"; "like a slye depraver"; and so on. His willingness to judge the motives of others, although it is partly a rhetorical device, is also a reminder of the simplicity of his world-view at this age. Even if he had been able to abide Donne's rhetoric, he could not have appreciated the complex psychology of the "I" in the *Devotions Upon Emergent Occasions*.

In larger terms, the whole thrust and organization of Milton's prose is aggressive. The main function of the tracts is as temporal weapon. His awareness in them is double, as I have shown in the contrast between the digression and the main oration in *Church-Government*. It would have been possible, and probably far more literary, for him to end with a vision of the ideal future that could be achieved by the submission of enemies and the cooperation of all sympathetic spirits. But in these tracts, that is not his procedure. They are headed with threats, not promises, and the digressions that hold the vision of the future are set well back from the concluding fusillades.

The *Apology* follows in general the order of topics given in the *Modest Confutation*. Opening with an explanatory prologue in which he defends his right to engage in controversy and in self-defense, Milton then makes some preliminary aspersions against the *Confutation* and goes on to a rather extensive refutation of the Confuter's attack upon his character. His reason for discussing himself first is that without faith in his character his readers will not take his other arguments seriously. But, using this as a prologue, he has had to open with his most personal, positive, and, for the modern reader, his most interesting remarks. He then takes up his opponent's arguments in their original sequence. Two-thirds of the way through, in the eighth section, he makes a digression for the sake of praising Parliament—saying about Parliament what he believes the Confuter should have said—and by this means he achieves an expanse of positive and lofty prose in approximately the same place where the "digression" was inserted in *Church-Government*. There follows a transition, reminiscent of those in "Lycidas," which stands for the whole of section nine:

Thus farre I have digrest, Readers, from my former subject; but into such a path, as I doubt not ye will agree with me, to be much fairer and more delightful then the rode way I was in. And how to break off suddenly into those jarring notes, which this Confuter hath set me, I must be wary, unlesse I can provide against offending the eare, as some Musicians are wont skilfully to fall out of one key into another without breach of harmony. By good luck therefore his ninth Section is spent in mournfull elegy, certaine passionat soliloquies, and two whole pages of intergatories that praise the Remonstrant even to the sonetting of *his fresh cheeks, quick eyes, round tongue, agil hand, and nimble invention* (*Apology, PW*, I, 928).

The final sections are then allowed to build to a climactic tirade against the bishops, which in its passionate metaphors is again reminiscent of the language of "Lycidas." I quote from the midst of a long descriptive period, which shows exactly the note upon which Milton intended to conclude. All the earlier sections exist in large part to earn him the right to use his heavy artillery here:

Who let hundreds of parishes famish in one *Diocesse*, while they the Prelats are mute, and yet injoy that wealth that would furnish all those darke places with able supply, and yet they eat, and yet they live at the rate of Earles, and yet hoard up. They who chase away all the faithfull Shepheards of the flocke, and bring in a dearth of spirituall food, robbing thereby the Church of her dearest treasure, and sending heards of souls starvling to Hell, while they feast and riot upon the labours of hireling Curats, consuming and purloyning even that which by their foundation is allow'd and left to the poore, and to reparations of the Church. These are they who have bound the land with the sinne of Sacrilege, from which mortall ingagement wee shall never be free, till wee have totally remov'd with one labour as one individuall thing Prelaty and Sacrilege. And herein will the King be a true defender of the Faith, not by paring or lessning, but by distributing in due proportion the maintenance of the Church, that all parts of the Land may equally partake the plentifull and diligent preaching of the faith, the scandall of Ceremonies thrown out, that delude and circumvent the faith. And the usurpation of Prelats laid levell, who are in words the Fathers, but in their deeds the oppugners of the faith (*Apology, PW,* I, 952).

The language reaches such a height of intensity because it is more sustained than earlier passages, and because Milton now excludes the low abusive epithets that have been his previous weaponry. Preceded as it is both by his own personal account of himself as one church-outed by the prelates and by his arguments against the bishops, this furious rhetoric is both impersonal and subjective, and his argument is both topical and universal.

These are the primary techniques of Milton's rhetoric of warfare. He can blame them upon "those jarring notes, which this Confuter hath set me," but the Confuter himself has taken exception to the style of the *Animadversions,* and Milton spends a great deal of time in the *Apology* defending his harsh method. He claims justification because he did not (in the *Animadversions*) adopt it on his own behalf; because scorn must be thrown upon a scorner, who cannot be gently taught; because he has a precedent in Scripture language; and because there is force of teaching sometimes in laughter. In a most interesting and eloquent passage, he develops two further arguments, whose juxtaposition is significant. Christ was Lord of all kinds of expression; these were divided up among the teachers of His Church in such a way that any man should be able to find a teacher whose rhetoric would be meaningful and helpful to him, since all men are different and none should be forced to "dissolve that groundwork of nature which God created in him, the sanguine to empty out all his sociable livelinesse, the cholerick to expell quite the unsinning predominance of his anger; but that each radicall humour and passion wrought upon and corrected as it ought, might be made the proper mould and foundation of every mans peculiar guifts, and vertues" (*Apology, PW,* I, 900). Here I think Milton is speaking at least as much for himself as for his hearers. We have seen his predilection for violence and extremity of language, the uncompromising fierceness of his idealism. The preceding passage is followed without a break by a hot, poetic defense of zeal, to which his own commitment is obvious:

. . . in times of opposition when either against new heresies arising, or old corruptions to be reform'd this coole unpassionate mildnesse of positive wisdome is not anough to damp and astonish the proud resistance of carnall, and false Doctors, then (that I may have leave to soare a while as the Poets use) then Zeale whose substance is ethereal, arming in compleat diamond ascends his fiery Chariot drawn with two blazing Meteors figur'd like beasts . . . with these the invincible warrior Zeale shaking loosely the slack reins drives over the heads of Scarlet Prelats, and such as are insolent to maintaine traditions, brusing their stiffe necks under his flaming wheels. Thus did the true Prophets of old combat with the false; thus Christ himselfe the fountaine of meeknesse found acrimony anough to be still galling and vexing the Prelaticall Pharisees (*Apology, PW,* I, 900–1).

To an ardent spirit, he says, "this tart rhetorick" comes much more easily and naturally than a dull style, which for now he chooses to make the alternative. It is evident that he no longer thinks of himself as having to write with his left hand.

Or, at least, it is evident that he can describe in literary fashion his left-handed activities. Once he has broken into poetic metaphor to describe Zeal, and added that the true prophets of old *thus* combatted with the false, it perhaps does not much matter whether he means that the prophets spoke poetically, or that their speaking can be poetically described. Certainly, having summoned the prophets in this way, he must have thought of the poetic power of their words. And they are to justify his practice, which is well illustrated in the long passage already given from the conclusion of the *Apology.* Here the parallel clauses, the repetitions, and the interweaving alliterations make the prose beautiful as well as angry.

The poetic quality even in the anger can make a bridge for us between the two parts of this analysis of *The Apology,* the prose as action and the prose as contemplation. The first part of the discussion concerned some ways in which the prose strikes outward at a target; the second will be more concerned with Milton's consideration of himself. In such self-consideration, he does tend to become more poetic than elsewhere, because he here contemplates the vocation to poetry that he hopes to follow. If in violence he uses a prose hot in anger, in contemplation he contrives to be wholly present and yet detached, coolly passionate.

In explaining the necessity for his self-defense, Milton speaks of "these present times wherein most men now scarce permitted the liberty to think over their owne concernments have remov'd the seat of their thoughts more outward to the expectation of publick events" (*Apology, PW*, I, 870). As so often he grasps the principle behind the practice, here he offers a reason for the public, objective character of Puritan prose. These men do not have time for introspection. But when one's own concernments are separated from the seat of one's thoughts, then various kinds of results are possible. The concernments can be abandoned; they can be attended to in one's spare time; they can be united with the seat of thoughts. Milton suggests all these responses, but his inclination, even when not wholly conscious, is toward the last solution, and toward making his inmost thoughts merely the inner illumination of his outward gaze. Thus, in defending the attack upon his so-called licentious behavior, he says this: "With me it fares now, as with him whose outward garment hath bin injur'd and ill bedighted; for having no other shift, what helpe but to turn the inside outwards, especially if the lining be of the same, or, as it is sometimes, much better. So if my name and outward demeanor be not evident anough to defend me, I must make tryall, if the discovery of my inmost thoughts can" (*Apology, PW*, I, 888–89).

One of the Confuter's least fortunate remarks was the admission that he (the Confuter) probably had as much atheism and corruption latent in him as any man. To Milton, with his anxiety that inside and outside should match, that the poet should be a true poem, this was a horrifying thought. It is responsible for the very many figures of sickness and health in his prose.[22] There cannot be outer health and inner corruption, outer decorum and inner uncertainty, outer order and inner confusion. That is one reason why Milton cannot accept set devotions, traditional order, preservation of any of the forms of the past; all these are efforts to suppress growth from within an age or an individual, and they cause illness that is the more horrible because unacknowledged.

Thus Milton joins the great seventeenth-century controversy over the meaning of the phrase, "the beauty of holiness." For the Anglicans, this beauty was to be achieved in traditional order, which constituted the only stay against confusion. Milton, like the early fathers of the church who loved rhetoric and yet opposed its worldly degradation, took refuge in the Augustinian argument[23] that real eloquence comes from within. While he admits that he is not "utterly untrain'd in those rules which best Rhetoricians have giv'n," he insists that true eloquence is nothing but love of truth, and provides this optimistic account of the reward of virtue:

And that whose mind so ever is fully possest with a fervent desire to know good things, and with the dearest charity to infuse the knowledge of them into others, when such a man would speak, his words (by what I can expresse) like so many nimble and airy servitors trip about him at command, and in well order'd files, as he would wish, fall aptly into their own places (*Apology, PW*, I, 949).

Just as good style is a sign of grace, so bad style characterizes the unregenerate. Bishops being bad men, it is impossible that Bishop Hall should be able to write well, but in case any doubt should remain in the reader's mind, Milton proves Hall's infamy by dissecting his style, which he finds immodest, self-aggrandizing, full of three-inch sentences as if written to measure, and inadequate in grammar. Adherence to traditional order, then, is a means to corruption, not to purity. It results in sentences which are measurable but meaningless, and which eventually break down both in decorum and in syntax, because they have no informing integrity or coherence. It is against this kind of language that his rhetoric is pitched. The illness that he sees festering below the measured speech of others is healthily opposed by his splenetic but not hypocritical prose.

So inside and outside, for him, are one in violence of attack. But, much more importantly, they must be one in his own style and character, for such unity is to justify him. The signs in Milton's prose that proved it likely to live were for him the signs of grace. Inner and outer meet again in his claim that to defend England he must know how to defend himself: "he who will do justly to all men, must begin from knowing how, if it so happen, to be not unjust to himself" (*Apology, PW*, I, 883). And England's cause may be blackened by his ill-fame:

But when I discern'd his intent was not so much to smite at me, as through me to render odious the truth which I had written, and to staine with ignominy that Evangelick doctrine which opposes the tradition of Prelaty, I conceav'd my selfe to be now not as mine own person, but as a member incorporate into that truth whereof I was perswaded, and whereof I had declar'd openly to be a partaker (*PW*, I, 871).

Milton stands for all Englishmen. Significantly, the *Second Defence of the English People*, in which he imagines himself speaking to all

listening Europe, has for its author "John Milton, Englishman."
Here, in the *Apology*, defending what the Confuter calls the "big-
mouth'd" prayer of his *Animadversions*, he says that it ought to be
big-mouthed, since it was "fram'd as the voice of three Kingdomes"
(*PW*, I, 930). His intention from the beginning was to give England
a voice worthy of her greatness, and to do that he must be a
worthy Englishman, that God might speak through him for England.

So far only the amount of meditation and planning which went
into the framing of this position distinguishes him from God's other
Puritan Englishmen, men like Lilburne and Baxter. To some extent,
the same can be said of the means by which he hoped to become
worthy of being God's Englishman. But here he puts extreme and
distinctive emphasis upon a single ideal, that of chastity. The Confuter had claimed that Milton frequented plays and harlots, wore
serge and used obscene language, lived in a "suburb sink." To oppose
this description, Milton documents the growth of his belief in chastity from his early years. For him it did not simply mean abstinence
from sex, since he says immediately that a chaste man may be married. Chastity in fact is just the kind of integrity that unites inner
and outer man, and it preoccupies him, in increasingly sophisticated
form, from *Comus* to *Samson Agonistes*. In *Comus*, chastity prevents
the virgin from being attacked by lions or seduced by Comus; in
"Lycidas," it assures the poet of fame in heaven. In the *Apology*, it
provides him with a defense against the Confuter, and it is so closely
related to virtue, vocation, and beauty that all these are nearly indistinguishable. For Milton, all meet in the autobiographical writings of
the lovers, Dante and Petrarch, who combined chaste and virtuous
living with love of beautiful women who inspired the exercise of
their vocations.

I am certainly not ready to argue the direct relationship between
all these concepts in Milton that he would have claimed. But in all
his writing, even in the prose, side-by-side with the scurrilous abuse
he hurls at his adversaries, there is a purity and beauty of style which
can be read as Milton's literary expression of his ideal. Let me cite as
beauty the extreme mellifluousness of his language, which, as we
have already seen, is particularly marked in passages where he speaks
of his vocation; and as vocation his characteristic personal-impersonal
syntax.

He would not accept an imposed consonance. His earliest comment on prose reflects his appreciation both of its freedom and of its poetic possibilities. In a Latin letter to his teacher Thomas Young, written about 1627 (*PW*, I, 311), he says that although he had previously sent Young a poem, he wanted to write him something in prose as well, with an unfettered pen. His gratitude to Young could not be expressed in the cramped style of poetry, straitened by fixed feet and syllables, but must be given the free language of prose, if possible with Asiatic exuberance. Most of Milton's early poetry is written in Latin, with the exception of short and strictly rhymed English pieces. In the blank verse of *Comus* and the varying verse of "Lycidas," he begins to break the mold. He then returns to Latin for his very beautiful "Epitaphium Damonis," the lament for his friend Charles Diodati, in which he promises to write an English epic. Here, also significantly, he publicly takes his leave both of Latin and of the pastoral style. From now on, although of course he returns to Latin when he needs it, he will be committed to the expression of English matter in English words and forms. It is at this point that he is hurled into polemical battle. The immediacy, the coarseness, and the temporality of the experience were surely what he needed at this time, and were probably more congenial to him than he had expected. Also unexpectedly, his experience in writing English prose taught him so much about how to use the language freely that his obvious choice when he returned to poetry was a blank verse that had much of the unfetteredness of prose.

The opening sentences of the *Apology* will serve to demonstrate the harmony that comes from within. Spontaneously or not, Milton is beginning to write a prose that utilizes the music of blank verse, no sentences cut to order, but consonances freely created:

If, Readers, to that same great difficulty of well doing what we certainly know, were not added in most men as great a carelessenes of knowing what they, and others ought to do, we had bin long ere this, no doubt but all of us much farther on our way to some degree of peace and happinesse in the kingdome. But since our sinfull neglect of practising that which we know to be undoubtedly true and good, hath brought forth among us, through Gods just anger so great a difficulty now to know that which otherwise might be soone learnt, and hath divided us by a controversie of great importance indeed, but of no hard solution, which is the more our punishment, I resolv'd (of what small moment soever I might be thought) to stand on that side where I saw both the plain autority of Scripture leading, and the reason of justice and equity perswading, with this opinion which esteemes it more unlike a Christian to be a cold neuter in the cause of the Church, then the law of Solon made it punishable after a sedition in the State. And because I observe that feare and dull disposition, lukewarmenesse & sloth are not seldomer wont to cloak themselves under the affected name of moderation, then true and lively zeale is customably dispareg'd with the terme of indiscretion, bitternesse, and choler, I could not to my thinking honor a good cause more from the heart, then by defending it earnestly, as oft as I could judge it to behoove me, notwithstanding any false name that could be invented to wrong, or undervalue an honest meaning. Wherein although I have not doubted to single forth more than once, such of them as were thought the chiefe and most nominated opposers on the other side, whom no man else undertooke: if I have done well either to be confident of the truth, whose force is best seene against the ablest resistance, or to be jealous and tender of the hurt that might be done among the weaker by the intrapping autority of great names titl'd to false opinions, or that it be lawfull to attribute somewhat to guifts of Gods imparting, which I boast not, but thankfully acknowledge, and feare also lest at my certaine account they be reckon'd to me many rather then few, or if lastly it be but justice not to defraud of due esteeme the wearisome labours and studious watchings, wherein I have spent and tir'd out almost a whole youth, I shall not distrust to be acquitted of presumption (*Apology, PW*, I, 868–69).

The periodic style, the balanced clauses and harmoniously matched phrases ("wearisome labours and studious watchings") are familiar. Less immediately obvious unless the paragraph is read aloud is the density of consonance as I have marked it through the middle sentences. Sound-matching of this sort is seldom to be found even in poetry. Here it begins to be felt as soon as the prose becomes personal and increases up to the point where the long parallel clauses can take over and bring the period to fulfillment. Such passages remind us, even when Milton is not specifically laboring the point, that he dedicated his life to beauty. And they also help to show that the twenty years of controversy were not wasted years. In the midst of battle he was practising his true vocation.

Vocation is of course intended to be exhibited everywhere in the style of his prose. But it shows up most significantly for us in a way which he could not very well have called attention to, even if he had been aware of it. That is the impersonal personalism of his syntax, which has already been demonstrated at length. In the *Apology*, having been personally attacked and presumably having some little reputation at least, he is freer than previously with the first person. And his personal rhetoric is somewhat more obviously devious. In the following passage he combines a personal reference with an "impersonal" generalization that applies alike to himself and any other hopeful youth—although at thirty-four he could, if he chose, consider himself middle aged:

... if lastly it be but justice not to defraud of due esteeme the wearisome labours and studious watchings, wherein I have spent and tir'd out almost a whole youth, I shall not distrust to be acquitted of presumption. Knowing that if heretofore all ages have receav'd with favour and good acceptance the earliest industry of him that hath beene hopefull, it were but hard measure now, if the freedome of any timely spirit should be opprest meerely by the big and blunted fame of his elder adversary; and that his sufficiency must be now sentenc't, not by pondering the reason he shewes, but by calculating the yeares he brings (*Apology, PW*, I, 869).

The Confuter called Milton a "grim, lowring, bitter fool," but never a youth. This is Milton's own preoccupation—on the one hand, worrying that he has not matured fast enough; and on the other, predating himself in order to assuage his fears and to create sympathy for himself with his audience. The "elder adversary" with his "big and blunted fame" is made a kind of Goliath to Milton's David.

The impersonality into which he swings with a typical participial phrase is itself being used as a device to acquit Milton of any charge of immodesty. But the blending of personal with impersonal in his prose still retains its earlier intention and effect. In the following passage, impersonalism is much more closely connected with his pursuit of his vocation, and it seems accordingly less devious and more spontaneous. Here he is describing his course of life in order to refute the slanderer's charge that he spent his mornings in some unknown low pursuit:

Those morning haunts are where they should be, at home, not sleeping, or concocting the surfets of an irregular feast, but up, and stirring, in winter often ere the sound of any bell awake men to labour, or to devotion; in Summer as oft with the Bird that first rouses, or not much tardier, to reade good Authors, or cause them to be read, till the attention bee weary, or memory have his full fraught (*Apology, PW*, I, 885).

The passage continues as it has begun, using the third instead of the first person and "the" instead of "my," and spreading out clauses by means of participles and infinitives that avoid a subject and predicate.

Rejection of antiquity, of tradition, and, often, of book-learning in general put the Puritan writer on his own, and his vulnerability to slander increased his solitariness. The benefits that he rejected with one hand he retrieved with the other in adopting the myth of history from Foxe's *Book of Martyrs*, and the belief in his role in history as God's instrument. These beliefs, I think, are clearly reflected in the impersonalism of Milton's prose, in passages like those already cited. Wherever one looks in the autobiographical part of the *Apology*, there are phrases that support this reading: "when I was confirm'd in this opinion"; "These reasonings . . . kept me still above those low descents"; "this my minde gave me." Yet, obviously, too, Milton sees God as working through him: Milton's mind, his feet, his reasonings taught him the way. That is chastity—or vocation—Milton's way of showing himself in touch with what the modern theologian calls the ground of our being.

One final way in which he uses the language embraces the others. As I have related consonance to beauty, and syntax to vocation, this last technique, or effect, may be connected with the all-inclusive virtue of chastity. Critics have claimed that Milton wrote English as though it were a foreign language, or a dead language.[24] That tendency, it can be assumed, came of the fact that for purposes of writing and debating he knew Latin better than he knew English, and his English sentences are submitted to Latin syntax. The results are mixed. Sometimes, it is true, his syntax becomes so involved that it is difficult for a modern reader to follow it at all. Sometimes it acquires an unexpected significance, as with the impersonal personalism. And there is a more resonant benefit.

If a dead language is simply one which is no longer spoken, that was not the case with Latin in Milton's time. If it is one which is no longer a national language, and whose vocabulary and syntax are to some extent fixed, then the language—again, like the Latin of his time—acquires by its "deadness" an unexpected life, which is more eternal than temporal, more universal than local, more impersonal than personal. This style, the labored and classical manner of a scholar-artist, has already been extensively illustrated:

Although certainly their actions are worthy not thus to be spoken of by the way, yet if hereafter it befall me to attempt something more answerable to their great merits, I perceave how hopelesse it will be to reach the height of their prayses at the accomplishment of that expectation that weights upon their noble deeds, the unfinishing whereof already surpasses what others before them have left enacted with their utmost performance through many ages (*Apology*, *PW*, I, 922).

Such a style is not quite suitable for tract-writing, the very nature of which demands a popular, ephemeral, immediate, localized style. Tract-writing in fact demands the nationalistic ad-hominem zeal that Milton was very well able to employ. It does not demand this larger, more unwieldy resonance of big words and intricate periods, full of forecasts out of time. It is no wonder that Milton was not the most effective of pamphleteers. But his many-levelled Miltonic music is immensely interesting as the creation of a mind both Puritanical and literary, and especially as the autobiography of this great poet.

One final point which has been implicit in my whole discussion is the extent to which Milton's autobiography is literary. From first to last he speaks of himself as a poet, at first briefly, as someone who may sing the praises of the new order. In *Church-Government*, much of the personal section is devoted to a consideration of the different genres in which Milton would like to excel. In the *Apology* the autobiographical section is a review of Milton's literary education intended to explain both the growth of his moral character and the development of his literary ability:

Next, (for heare me out now Readers) that I may tell ye whether my younger feet wander'd; I betook me among those lofty Fables and Romances, which recount in solemne canto's the deeds of knighthood founded by our victorious Kings; & from hence had in renowne over all Christendome. There I read it in the oath of every Knight, that he should defend to the expence of his best blood, or of his life, if it so befell him, the honour and chastity of Virgin or Matron. From whence even then I learnt what a noble vertue chastity sure must be . . . (*Apology*, *PW*, I, 890–91).

When the literary character of his autobiography is combined with the extensive literary criticism and apologetics, it becomes evident that the tracts, particularly the last two, could be discussed as documents of literary criticism rather than polemics. But for Milton, as we have seen, the two activities are not altogether distinct.

There are of course many reasons why this highly literary prose, created by and creating an "I" whose whole life is based on literature, could never be mistaken for the literary Anglican style. This "I" has devoted himself to a worldly goal, and his tracts are his weaponry. His autobiography, literary though it is, is delivered straightforwardly, though defensively, and involves considerable temporal and factual detail. Most importantly, it is the same kind of spiritual autobiography that other Puritans wrote, except that it is translated into literary terms. He documents the ways in which it was recognized that he had a gift for poetry, just as others documented the incidents that brought them to be receptive of God's grace. His discussions of himself are always a combination of lamentation with rejoicing. In the early prose, he knows he has the gift, but complains of his unripeness; in the poetry, he worries that he has come to write too late. The same kind of nervous assertiveness is observable in other Puritans: This is who I am—but will I make it? In Milton, as in others, the certainty overrides the doubts.

And it does that, finally, because of his acceptance of himself as God's instrument. However we read him, as polemicist, autobiographer, prophet, or literary critic, that is clear. He may lament, like Jeremy (whose words he cites), that God has made him a prophet in an ill time, but he accepts his role. The tracts sometimes seem disconnected because he sees himself called in so many different ways, and they succeed to the extent to which he himself succeeded in making his several vocations into one, in seeing that present rage must prepare for future song, or in seeing how nevertheless to manage raging and song and criticism all at once.

The remarkable thing is that he never loses faith that if he keeps his covenant with God, God will keep it with him. He seems naive in the *Apology*, when he says that when a good man would speak, his words "like so many nimble and airy servitors trip about him at command" (*PW*, I, 949). But that belief is exactly analogous to the usual Puritan reading of Providence, and Milton never gives it up. In the *Apology*, speaking of Parliament, he hopes that in future it may "befall me to attempt something more answerable to their great merits," and that hope, of course, could not be realized. But he did achieve an "answerable style," and he believed that this was because he continued to put himself at God's disposal:

> If answerable style I can obtain
> Of my Celestial Patroness, who deigns
> Her nightly visitation unimplor'd,
> And dictates to me slumb'ring, or inspires
> Easy my unpremeditated Verse . . .

> higher Argument
> Remains, sufficient of itself to raise
> That name, unless an age too late, or cold
> Climate, or Years damp my intended wing
> Deprest, and much they may, if all be mine,
> Not Hers who brings it nightly to my Ear.
>
> (*Paradise Lost*, IX, 20–24, 42–47)

Here is the same impersonal rhetoric that we have traced through all the antiprelatical tracts.[25] And I find myself at this point wanting to take Milton seriously. How else, indeed, could a disgraced, blind, fifty-two-year-old public servant hope to write England's greatest poem? Let us at least say, using the proper language of sober Puritanism, that one can read in the antiprelatical tracts, in bits of the other prose, and finally in *Paradise Lost* and *Samson Agonistes*, the autobiography of a Puritan saint.

CHAPTER VIII

THOMAS TRAHERNE:
THE FOUNTAIN
OF LOVE

PROBABLY THE MOST FAMOUS THING ABOUT THOMAS TRAHERNE IN OUR time is that he was completely unknown before our time, and in being discovered has created two of the literary sensations of the age, first, at the turn of the century, and now again, in the present decade. His story is a classic illustration of the public-private dilemma of the seventeenth-century Anglican. He wrote his meditations in notebooks: they may not be first drafts, but they contain plentiful evidence of the pains of creation—blots, scratches, revisions, excisions, renumberings, and even the remains of cut-out pages. Only one copy of each of the two sets of his meditations is known to exist, and they contain no author's name; hence, the great difficulty with which his work was identified. Although there is reason to suppose that Traherne had an audience in mind, we have no positive proof for whom the notebooks were written. Since they have now fallen into our hands, we may suppose, if we can rise to the occasion, that this seventeenth-century inhabitant of eternity wrote them as much for us as he did for anyone.

The two works most relevant to this study are the *Centuries of Meditations*, first published by Bertram Dobell in 1908, and the newly discovered "Select Meditations," now being edited by Mr. James M. Osborn. While I shall need to refer to the "Select Meditations," [1] my subject is the *Centuries of Meditations* because they are more available at present, because the two books are very much alike,[2] and because the *Centuries*, probably written later, may be considered slightly more typical of Traherne's mature thought and style.

Youngest of the eight writers considered in this book, Traherne was born in 1637, six years after Donne's death, and three years before Burton's. He was not old enough to act as rector of his parish until 1661, a year after the restoration of Charles II, Royalism, and the Church of England. Until then, he was in school, being formed or circumscribed by Puritan teachers, who apparently found him an acceptable pupil, since he was allowed to take a B.A., and in 1657 was granted the incumbency of his parish. Yet one clue to the date of composition of the "Select Meditations" is his profound relief and joy at the re-establishment of the Church of England, and his horror of those who opposed it.[3] He belongs with the earlier Anglican writers, stylistically, in his whole emotional outlook, and in most of his basic beliefs.

He is more of a philosopher than the earlier Anglicans, and more autobiographical, and might very well have been so even if he had not grown up in the age of Descartes, whose *Discourse on Method* was published in the year of Traherne's birth. Certainly he could never have accepted the Cartesian severance of body from soul. But from the beginning he does seem to have shared Descartes' need to build his world-view for himself, from within, and from personal experience, observation, and reflection. At its most facile and its most profound, his mind is originally philosophical, his conclusions self-tried.[4]

His view of good and evil, and his very Anglican assumption that what happiness we have must be absolutely based and founded amidst the evils of the world, are derived from his own childhood, his Edenic infancy, and the replacement of that with the worldly outlook and milieu of the adults he knew: in a clearly autobiographical context, he says that "it is not our Parents Loyns, so much as our Parents lives, that Enthrals and Blinds us" (III.8). In teaching him to value material over spiritual things, he says, they destroyed the sense of wonder and richness with which he was born and gave him instead feelings of deprivation, want, and alienation.

But he was not troubled only by their materialism. Although he himself understands this less clearly, growing up made him aware of certain facts about the world which were incompatible with Eden. All these facts had to do with separations between things and between people. He saw that time and space are real and discontinuous, that they separate moment from moment, place from place, and man from man. He believed in the theory of continued creation, that God did not once make the universe once and for all, but that He continues to sustain and create it with His love from moment to moment. Not only that, but man, made in the image of God, must do the same thing: he too from moment to moment must keep the frame of things entire.

Thus, instead of beginning with wholeness, Traherne begins with disunities and disharmonies which man, in God, can hope to transcend. Man has the remembrance of Eden in his own childhood, and a natural bent toward doing right. In Eden, there is no time or space; there are no artificial separations among things. The actual existence of such separations, however, makes it necessary for him, as a Christian, to try to recover the lost Eden. Out of the very separations and disharmonies of the world, Traherne will achieve felicity:

This World was far better then Paradice had men Eys to see its Glory, and their Advantages. for the very Miseries and sins and offences that are in it, are the Materials of His Joy and Triumph and Glory. So that He is to learn a Diviner Art that wil now be Happy: and that is like a Royal Chymist to reign among Poysons to turn Scorpions into fishes, Weeds into flowers Bruises into Ornaments, Poysons into Cordials. And he that cannot this Art, of Extracting Good out of evil, is to be accounted Nothing. Hertofore, to Enjoy Beauties, and be Gratefull for Benefits was all the Art that was required to Felicity, but now a Man must like a GOD, bring Light out of Darkness, and Order out of Confusion. Which we are taught to do by His Wisdom, that Ruleth in the midst of Storms and Tempests (IV.21).

The physical and spiritual separation of man from God, writer from reader, man from man, moment from moment, meaning from meaning, and even clause from clause, is accepted and then transcended, as Traherne builds upon these separations the harmonies of his style.

In the attempt to understand the texture of this intentionally unitive prose, it is helpful to begin where I believe Traherne begins in thought, with concepts of self and self-love, and the idea that self is only attained in communion with others. Here I shall be less concerned with the *Centuries* directly than with the backgrounds of experience and thought that prepared Traherne to write them. This discussion will lead to his portrayal, in the *Centuries*, of persons in communication and communion with one another, and to analysis of stylistic habits related to this portrayal.

Traherne writes of himself, "He thought that to be a Philosopher a Christian and a Divine, was to be one of the most Illustrious Creatures in the World; and that no man was a Man in Act, but only in

Capacity, that was not one of these; or rather all. for either of these Three include the other two" (IV.3). Traherne formulated for himself a philosophy based upon the concept of self-love, a risky endeavor in the 1660's. Thomas Hobbes' *Leviathan* had been published in 1651, and all the world, it seemed, believed that Hobbes was Machiavelli's own brother,[5] and that self-love, as the world misrepresented its place in his thought, was atheist talk. Traherne therefore took great pains to explain his own very different use of the word.[6]

Since Traherne makes such close analogies between man and God, and since the question of self-love in God is primary for him, it will be best to begin with his treatment of it. God is said to do everything for his own glory. Nevertheless, self-love in God cannot be selfish because true glory "is to lov another for his own sake, and to prefer his Welfare and to seek His Happiness": "Which God doth becaus it is true Glory. So that he seeks the Happiness of Angels and Men as his Last End, and in that his Glory: to wit His Tru Glory. fals and vain Glory is inconsistent with His Nature but True Glory is the very Essence of his Being. Which is Lov unto His Beloved, Lov unto Himself, Lov unto His Creatures" (IV.64). Man in his best state can also operate thus, his self-love fulfilling itself more surely the more he identifies his own welfare with that of God, who always desires the best for man. Self-love, then, is mutual love, a way of blurring boundaries between selves, which, as we shall see again and again, is always what Traherne intends.

In discussing his own development, Traherne considers self-love in a more conventional way, with the first emphasis upon the individual. Dishonorable when it is self-ended, self-love must be satisfied in itself before it can coincide with love of others. In the following passage, he speaks of himself in the third person: "That Pool must first be filled, that shall be made to overflow. He was ten yeers studying before he could satisfy his Self Lov. And now finds nothing more easy then to lov others better than oneself" (IV.55). The image of overflowing, so variously and recurrently used in Traherne's prose, is another means to the blurring of boundaries: one self flows over into another and is thus enlarged and fulfilled. Self-love *becomes* love of others.

One might say that the philosophy which Traherne is here striving to articulate is central to the Judaeo-Christian ethic that commands us to love our neighbor as ourselves. Between self-love and love of others, in most men's experience, there is a great gulf fixed. The difficulties of bridging that gulf are nowhere more clearly described than in what is for my purposes the most interesting passage in the Osborn manuscript, where Traherne complains that his use of the first person is misunderstood. This manuscript was almost certainly written during his years as parish priest in the little village of Credenhill in Herefordshire. He was a young man in his twenties, just out of school, and obviously troubled at times by various criticisms made by his parishioners. What he wanted was to be always talking of God, but his way of doing that was to use the first person, showing himself overflowing with his own sense of God's love:

... profound Inspection, Reservation & Silence, are my Desires. O that I could attain them: Too much openness & proneness to Speak are my Diseas. Too easy & complying a Nature. Speaking too much and too Long in the Best Things. Mans nature is Nauseating & weary. Redundance is Apprehended, even in those things of which there can be never enough ... The vices of men have made those things vices, that are the perfections of Heaven ... Here I am censured for speaking in the Singular number, & saying I ... Felicity is a Bird of paradice so strang, that it is Impossible to flie among men without loseing some feathers were She not Immortal. There it shall be our Glory and the joy of all to Acknowledge, I. I am the Lords, and He is mine. Everyone shall speak in the first person, & it shall be Gods Glory that He is the joy of all. Can the freind of God, & the Heir of all things in Heaven & Earth, forbear to say, I.[7]

The whole course of both the "Select Meditations" and the *Centuries* makes clear that his need to use the first person is no vain egotism on Traherne's part. For him, as we shall see, the "I" fulfills itself in becoming one with God, one with other souls, thereby becoming infinite. In Traherne we have the most explicit representation of the cosmic personality that is afforded by seventeenth-century literature. Startling enough on paper, this mode of speaking must have been difficult indeed for his parishioners to appreciate if he tried to practice it face to face.

And in all probability he did. The sympathetic editor of his *Serious and Pathetical Contemplation of the Mercies of God* says that the author spent most of his time at home thinking and writing about religious matters, "and was so full of them when abroad, that those that would converse with him, were forced to endure some discourse upon these subjects, whether they had any sense of Religion, or not." [8] Again, the proper way to describe his state is to say that he overflowed. Louis Martz rightly sees Traherne's repetitiousness as a technique for reminding and exploring,[9] and as such we find it in much meditative writing of the period. But it is also a manifestation of this characteristic of Traherne, as he himself describes it in the passage cited: "Redundance is Apprehended, even in those things of which there can be never enough." According to the Cambridge Platonist Peter Sterry, who uses much of the same imagery that Traherne does, "the same Word in Hebrew signifies the *Eye*, and a *Fountain*." [10] A simple Trahernian play on the word "eye" as "I," and the Hebrew connection, illuminates in Traherne the central image of the fountain-"I." To ask him to limit his enthusiasm would have been to ask a fountain to flow less copiously.

But at least by the time he came to write his *Centuries*, he had learned much that he did not know at Credenhill. He learned, partly by practice in the "Select Meditations," to commit his exuberance to paper, to vary and control it at least as artfully as the fountain is controlled, and to make his use of the first person as inviting as the fountain's self-expression: "I will open my Mouth in Parables: I will utter Things that have been Kept Secret from the foundation of the World. Things Strange yet Common; Incredible, yet Known; Most High, yet Plain; infinitely Profitable, but not Esteemed. Is it not a Great Thing, that you should be Heir of the World?" (1.3). The "I" of the *Centuries* in fact seems to combine most of these paradoxes. While on the one hand Traherne can speak with immense symbolic grandeur and dignity, making his "I" acceptable because remote from ordinary limited personality, on the other hand he speaks always to an ordinary "you" with whom he wishes to share himself. Moreover, he makes it absolutely clear that without reference to a "you," the "I" would be nothing. Self-love is one with love of others.

This fact in itself, however, does not solve the problem of communication. Certainly Traherne at Credenhill tried to communicate with his people, by speaking as "I" to "you." And although he believed from the beginning that the ideal state is universal harmony, one soul in communion with all, his actual dealings with people apparently produced the opposite effect. Not only were they offended by his mode of communication; he was unable to find in most men any moral sustenance at all: "O my God pitty my weaknes & remember that men were ordained pillers to sustaine me, wings to carry me; lights to illuminat, and freinds to Aid me who now are Enemies Deceitfull lights And floods goeing down to a final end that is Destructive against which I must swim." [11] No reader of the "Select Meditations" could ever conceive of calling this author a "poet of felicity." "O my God," he says, in an early passage on contemporary perversity, "I could be Quickly weary Quickly weary both of Repenting and interceeding." [12] Of course he is also much affected by the immediate background of the civil wars: "Thy Holy Citties are a wildernesse, Zion is a wilderness Jerusalem a Desolation Our Holy and our Beautifull house where our fathers praised Thee is burnt up with fire and all our pleasant Things are layd waste." [13]

Increased distance from the wars has something to do with the difference in tone between the "Select Meditations" and the *Centuries*. More important, though no doubt in some way related, is the increased privacy of his thought. The many references to contemporary England nearly disappear, as do any references to a parish. In his own life, he has gone from the parish at Credenhill to a chaplaincy in a private family. While he acted in some capacity as curate at Teddington when the Bridgman family were in residence at their home there, and while he was immensely loyal to Sir Orlando Bridgman in his fall from royal favor, the very fact of his having the chaplaincy must have made him less vulnerable to parish problems and other external woes.

No doubt, too, he had learned from experience to make himself less vulnerable. Near the beginning of the *Centuries*, he asserts that "I will not by the Nois of Bloody Wars, and the Dethroning of Kings, advance you to Glory"; "I . . . will lead you into Paths Plain and Familiar. Where all Envy, Rapine, Bloodshed, Complaint, and Malice shall be far removed" (1.4). While in "Select Meditations" he speaks of the problems of communication in life, in the *Centuries* he confines himself to illustrating ideal communication in literature. In all these ways, then, the Puritan-educated divine has discovered felicity by committing himself to a more typically Anglican means of self-expression. He still believes that the way to achieve felicity is to bring good out of evil, but evil, in some respects at least, has now become academic. No less real in his thought and style, it is personally less troublesome, just because he can, so to speak, control it more adequately in literature.

The explicit conclusion that he arrives at about communication is identical with that which governs his whole outlook on life. Good friends, like good people, are rare. With one or two or three kindred souls, a pattern of felicity may be worked out, and expressed on paper in universal terms. "And as in many Mirrors we are so many other selvs, so are we Spiritualy Multiplied when we meet our selvs more Sweetly, and liv again in other Persons" (II.70).

The design of the *Centuries of Meditations* is wholly informed by the importance of communion, as is made apparent by the many ways in which the personae of the book—its "I"'s and "he"'s and "Thou"'s—appear and meet and intermingle. Of first importance to an understanding of the book's structure is the relationship between Traherne's view of the aim of God's creation of the world, and his own aim in writing the *Centuries*. According to Traherne, a part of God's creation—man's mind—was originally left blank in order that it might learn to reflect the whole creation. Such reflection—the idea of the world in man's thought—is the aim of creation, and more important than the world itself. And it is as much man's business to continue from moment to moment to approve and sustain that idea as it was God's business originally to create the world. The proper order of the world, then, involves reciprocity and harmony between God and man, man upholding in love what God made in love. Only because of the discontinuity of time and the separation between man and God brought about by sin does this constantly renewed act become difficult or, perhaps, even conscious. By this means the separation between man and God is overcome, man's ruin repaired, and his mind restored to the brilliance and wealth of Eden.

An empty book, says Traherne, is like a child's blank mind, in which anything may be written. Traherne gave to a friend (probably his wealthy patroness, Mrs. Susanna Hopton) [14] the partially-filled notebook in which he had written his centuries. In an accompanying inscription, he suggests that she may want to add to what he has done: "That she may write my Makers prais therin/And make her self therby a Cherubin." [15] By filling the blank pages of the book, imaginatively or in fact, with praise of Traherne's creator, the reader, then or now, can be re-created (made a "Cherubin"); completing Traherne's book, he (or she) proves Traherne's gift, like that of the Creation, to be a mark of the wisest love; and thus, as man approves the Creation, the reader approves the author of this work.

The reciprocal harmony of God and man is imitated by the coopera-tive treatment of Traherne's book. Thus, in the very making of the book, the reader and writer are united, and this achievement leads to sanctification.

While Susanna Hopton may have been the occasion and recipient of the book, Traherne certainly did not think of her as its only reader. Bertram Dobell believed that he started writing it to one per-son, but then decided it was equally suitable for any Anglican.[16] Such language as the following does not suggest the artist addressing his patron: "But Lov can never be reconciled to an Unlovely Ob-ject, and you are infinitly unlovly by Despising GOD, and His Lov so long. Yea one Act only of Despite done to the smallest Creature made you infinitly deformed. What shall becom of you therfore since GOD cannot be reconciled to an Ugly Object? Verily you are in Danger of Perishing Eternaly" (II.30). This is pulpit language, or the language at best of a stern father confessor to one insufficiently penitent. Furthermore, the "you" is addressed in masculine terms, which may be generic, but cannot properly apply to one woman; the "you" is called a "Son of GTD" (I.60), and an "Immortal King," and told, "That you are a Man should fill you with Joys" (II.24). Al-though his language is usually intimate, suggesting that he is on terms of familiarity with the persons addressed, this generalized "you" im-plies a group audience.[17]

This is evident from the way in which he defines the characters of his prose. The universal communion of soul with soul is imitated by the creation of a multitude of personae. Distinctions among all of them are signalled by the use of first, second, and third person pro-nouns. These personae, including the "you" of the reader, are all in a sense aspects of Traherne, the varied selves he sees as he looks upon his own human disunity, and as he sees in himself all mankind. Again, his gaze is inward and literary. The "characters" of his prose invite us to become them partly because they are made up of himself and have no names. Among other things, this technique relieves the "I" of some of its intensity, and goes far toward absolving Traherne of any charge of egotism.

The theme of separation and unity is intrinsic in the creation of these characters. Whether they are the selves of Traherne in differ-ent moods or the selves of different men, the separations among them are indicated as a first step toward the healing of divisions.

Even in indicating the separations, Traherne manages to imply re-union. "I," "you," "thou," and "he" (the latter three both with and without capitals) are, of course, elementary dividing lines between persons; but they are also very immediate and very connective. While peopling his dramatic prose with a number of apparently different characters, Traherne's personae display both separation and unity; they define themselves individually only in the process of (two of his favorite words) communication and communion, the stuff of his ideal and infinite world.

His "I" is capable of a wide range of moods, from that of the limited, finite "I" who makes the blots and the corrections that still testify to the fallible humanity of the author, to that of the "I" who speaks in parables and "will utter Things that have been Kept Secret from the foundation of the World" (1.3). Traherne explains this paradox: "Infinit Worth shut up in the Limits of a Material Being, is the only way to a Real Infinity" (III.20). The soul is an "Infinit Sphere in a Centre" (II.80)—limitlessness bounded.

Traherne's "I" achieves infinity through the graciousness of God, and through his relationships with other centers of consciousness: "To be as GODs, we are Prompted to Desire by the Instinct of Nature. And that we shall be by Loving all as He doth" (II.52). The "you" to whom the book is addressed, as we have already seen, is first to be involved in this love. While the "you" is reminded of his "base and sneaking spirit" (like the "I," he is still part of the fallen world), he is also offered opportunity for redemption in terms scarcely capable of being resisted: "This will Enlarge your Soul and make you to Dwell in all Kingdoms and Ages . . . It will make you a Possessor Greater then the World. Men do mightily wrong themselvs: when they refuse to be present in all Ages: and Neglect to see the Beauty of all Kingdoms" (1.85).

The blend of wonder and certainty suggests intimacy both with his subject and with the person to whom he speaks: "Is not this a Strange Life to which I call you?" (1.45). For here he clearly enjoys and sympathizes with the reader's naiveté. His tone of voice absolutely distinguishes him from a writer like Sir Thomas Browne, who is considerably more interested in himself than Traherne is, more intimate with himself than with his reader, less gentle, more interested in erecting monuments to the wonder that is man than in teaching man how to enter into the wonder of God. The point of view that

Traherne assumes puts him as close as can be to the reader. He reads his mind in saying, "Is not this a Strange Life to which I call you?" He reads it, in a passage like the following, where the point of view puts him inside the reader's skin: "That all the World is yours, your very Senses and the Inclinations of your Mind declare . . . The Powers of your Soul confirm it . . . Neither can any thing but Ignorance Destroy your Joys. for if you know your self, or God, or the World, you must of Necessity Enjoy it" (1.16). If there were a trace of arrogance or dogmatism in Traherne's tone, he might only anger the reader, but there is none, except in those very rare bursts of pulpit language. The "you" is an intimate, whether literally or metaphorically—whether this means Susanna Hopton or any fellow child of God. With this "you," the "I" has no need to pose, and with him he can work out the themes of his philosophy. Another person is necessary to create with him a model of creative love, but one feels that Traherne includes himself as a "you," at least part of the time.

Besides the "you," there are also two "thou"s, who are frequently addressed, and who are distinguished both from the "you" and from the "I." The easiest to identify is Christ, to whom Traherne often turns in prayer or meditation. But he also, like Augustine and others, apostrophizes his own soul, always as "thou." This "thou," like the "you," is advised, consoled, and instructed, often in the intimate language that we have already seen turned outward to another: "But what Life wouldst Thou lead? And by what Laws wouldst Thou thy self be guided? For none are so Miserable as the Lawless and Disobedient . . . Wilt Thou not liv unto Him? Thou must of Necessity liv unto som Thing" (1.71).

The number of possible roles and poses inherent in "I" and "thou" is obviously greater than that in more defined characters. And the roles here are constantly shifting. The "I" alone has a dazzling range of significance, and Traherne is always at his best when he speaks in the first person, which at its best is, for him, a center of consciousness that fuses together all consciousness and the world's meaning. When he speaks to himself, addressing the "thou" of his soul, the "I" is muted; the speaker assumes the role of a catechist, a Socratic adviser whose aim is to make the "thou" experience truth. Dialogue with the "Thou" of Christ or God approaches a familiar meditational type—the soul's colloquy with God. Speaking to the "you" that is the reader, Traherne varies his own role from catechist to fellow lover of God.

The extent and complexity of the role-shifting are greatly increased by Traherne's ability to empathize with others, and by his intention to trace his spiritual growth through the different centuries. In this respect, the third and the fourth are particularly interesting, since they introduce personae not previously encountered. In the largely autobiographical third century, after recounting his childhood and growth, Traherne describes his discovery and immediate appreciation of the Psalms of David. In fact, his discovery of David is truly the discovery of a second self, and many paragraphs (one is tempted to call them stanzas) of the third century are literal transcriptions of parts of the Psalms, with Traherne appearing only occasionally to make a comment. He has here split himself into a prophetic and a pedestrian personality, allowing David's voice to carry all the joy and exaltation which his own "I" had formerly sounded. Two passages must be cited here, to typify Traherne's identification with the Psalmist. In the first, as he has elsewhere done with the "you," he describes how it feels to be David:

He openeth the Nature of Gods Kingdom, and so vigorously and vehemently Exciteth all Creatures to Praise Him, and all Men to do it with all kind of Musical Instruments by all Expressions, in all Nations for all Things as if 10000 vents were not sufficient to eas his fulness, as if all the World were but one Celestial Temple in which He was Delighted, as if all Nations were present before him and he saw God face to face in this Earthly Tabernacle, as if his Soul like an infinit Ocean were full of joys, and all these but Springs and Chanels overflowing. So Purely so Joyfully so Powerfully he walked with God, all Creatures, as they brought a Confluence of Joys unto him, being Pypes to eas him (III.94).

His Soul recovered its Pristine Liberty and saw thorow the Mud Walls of flesh and Blood. Being alive, he was in the Spirit all his Days (III.95).

The theme of communion is here very richly expressed. David, God's child, communicating through the Psalms, thereby reaches communion with God. Thus, part of the reason for the constant quotation of the Psalms is that they represent what Traherne is counseling the reader, and himself, to do. Traherne sees David as one whose soul overflowed with joys. To "eas his fulness," he urged all the creatures of the world to praise God, and thereby to become the instruments of David's praise. By making the world into music, he saw God face to face on earth. David's praise of God merges into God's face, as communication becomes communion. Thus his soul recovers its liberty, achieving the infinity of God. By understanding David so well, Traherne joins his soul with David's, and so shares in the whole process of liberation.

The following passage is a brief illustration of the way in which Traherne gives David the prophetic role, and assumes for himself the interpreter's voice. Typically, this paragraph begins, without explanation, with David's words, but for the sake of the example, I have chosen a meditation in which Traherne-as-interpreter speaks more often than is usual, and this is the whole paragraph, a comparatively short one:

There is a River the streams wherof shall make Glad the City of God; the holy Place of the Tabernacle of the most High. He praiseth the Means of Grace, which in the Midst of this World are Great Consolations. and in all Distresses refresh our Souls. Com behold the Works of the Lord, what Desolations he hath made in the Earth. He exhorteth us to Contemplat Gods Works, which ar so perfect, that when His Secret and just Judgments are seen, the very destruction of Nations, and laying waste of Cities, shall be sweet and Delightfull (III.78).

The first and third sentences are David's (the clause beginning "and in all Distresses" is really part of the second sentence); the second and fourth are Traherne's. While the absence of parentheses does mean that Traherne is concerned to merge his personality with the Psalmist's, rather than to separate it, he here foreshadows a separation-in-unity of his own personality, which is to occur in the fourth century. There he adds a "he" to his range of selves, opening the century as follows: "Having spoken so much concerning his Enterance and Progress in Felicity, I will in this Centurie speak of the Principles with which your friend endued Himself to enjoy it!" Traherne is now both "I" and "your friend." The persons employed in the fourth century indicate a final and not entirely successful effort to describe the final stages of Traherne's spiritual progress.

In the third century, Traherne's identification with David, whom he still continues to speak of as "he," eases the transition to a separation of himself into a "he" and an "I" who play the same roles that "David" and "Traherne" do. The "he," or "your Friend" of the fourth century is a rarified being who has achieved felicity at least partly through the Psalms, and who now through the mediation of the "I" sends down principles to the reader, somewhat as God did through Moses to the children of the Hebrews. Thus he is much further from the reader than he was before, when, acting as guide and friend, he was able to communicate more directly with the "you." Still called a friend (though often capitalized), he now seems to have passed into a stage almost beyond mortal reach.

In discussing the meditational pattern of the *Centuries*, Louis Martz describes this stage as a "process of intellection": ". . . the whole effort of this final stage is to carry the mind as far as reason can be carried—moving ever closer to ultimate Truth by a process of refinement through abstraction." [18] Even considering the device apart from the scheme, we may say that Traherne clearly found it useful to be able to speak about himself with apparent objectivity, when formulating principles based upon his own life. He can thus say things about himself which might otherwise seem vain. Still, there is an ambivalence at times that reveals his own uncertainty, as here where he makes and unmakes claims for his personal righteousness:

I speak not His Practices but His Principles. I should too much Prais your friend did I speak his Practices, but it is no shame for any man to declare his Principles, tho they are the most Glorious in the world. Rather they are to be Shamed that have no Glorious Principles: or that are ashamed of them. This he desired me to tell you becaus of Modesty. But with all, that indeed his Practices are so short of these Glorious Principles, that to relate them would be to his Shame; and that therfore you would never look upon him but as clothed in the Righteousness of Jesus Christ. Nevertheless I hav heard him often say, That he never allowd himself in Swerving from any of these. And that he repented deeply of evry Miscarriage: and moreover firmly resolved as much as was possible never to erre or wander from them again (IV.30).

This "He," at his best and most consistent, is a godlike giver of principles, a being almost beyond human personality. Yet in places like this, he is so clearly limited by personality that the device is weakened by unconscious humor. It is a relief to Traherne, I think, to switch back to his "I," as he does eventually in this century, and to a freer union of his divergent characteristics in a less self-conscious paean of joy and praise, beginning, "O Adorable and Eternal GOD! hast thou made me a free Agent!" (IV.43). While the Lawgiver must be considered intrinsic to the whole work, or to Traherne's concept of being, he fits somewhat uneasily into the flexible system of relationships shared by the other personae.

The "communion" essential to all these personae is achieved mainly by three means. Though they cannot ever be quite separated from one another, they are the primary subjects of the first three centuries: the Cross of Christ; love; and the self, or Traherne. Largely because of the interconnectedness of all Traherne's themes (another communion), it is not always possible to confine a theme or discussion of it to the century of its central location. The more all-encompassing a theme, the more radiant its effects throughout the whole book.

The Cross is the most limited of the three topics, and direct consideration of it is confined to the first century. Here the contemplation of Christ's agony is subordinated to the use of the Cross as ligature and center of the world. That is to say, the Cross is made the symbol of communion, and thereby negates time and space:

If Lov be the Weight of the Soul, and its Object the Centre. All Eys and Hearts may convert and turn unto this Object: cleave unto this Centre . . . (1.59).

. . . our Saviors Cross is the Throne of Delights. That Centre of Eternity, That Tree of Life in the midst of the Paradice of GOD! (1.55).

When I am lifted up saith the Son of man I will draw all Men unto me. As fishes are Drawn out of the Water, as Jeremie was Drawn out of the Dungeon, as S. Peters Sheet was Drawn up into heaven; so shall we be Drawn by that Sight from Ignorance and Sin and Earthly vanities, idle sports Companions Feasts and Pleasures, to the Joyfull Contemplation of that Eternal Object. But by what Cords? The Cords of a Man, and the Cords of Lov (1.56).

Contemplating the Cross, Traherne can see "all Kingdoms," "all Types and Ceremonies," "the most Distant Things in Eternity united" (1.59), "All Nations concentering, and Angels praising." In the light of the Cross, he sees "how to possess all the Things in Heaven and Earth" (1.60).

As the Cross is an infinitely illuminating center, so it teaches communion with other centers. Traherne uses the word "center" to apply to anything that can be said to have a core (as, for example, the earth), but he prefers it to mean something which can organize and shed light on what lies around it. Thus every human soul is a center of the world for the person whose soul it is; yet, for all these souls, the establishment of the Cross of Christ as another center, or pole, is essential:

O Jesu . . . I Admire to see thy Crosse in evry Understanding, thy Passion in evry Memory, thy Crown of Thorns in evry Ey, and thy Bleeding, Naked Wounded Body in evry Soul . . . Thou wholy Communicatest thy self to evry Soul in all Kingdoms, and art wholy seen in every saint and wholy fed upon by evry Christian. It is my Priviledge that I can enter with Thee into evry Soul, and in evry Living Temple of thy Manhood and thy Godhead, behold again, and Enjoy thy Glory (1.86).

The Cross is distinctly a vitalizing force, not the instrument of penitence that it had often been in earlier meditational writing. Introduced as it is by emphasis upon the wonders of God's creation, and then described as the unifying center of that creation, it inevitably possesses this positive power. But Traherne makes no effort to sentimentalize it: the bleeding body of Christ is where the power comes from. That blood is the wine of Communion.

Two supporting motifs are the many words having to do with feeding, and the frequent, familiar echoes of the Communion service itself. The words describing feeding acknowledge the bleeding body as the feast: "Where the Carcase is thither will the Eagles be Gathered together" (1.56); "the Hungry are Drawn with the Desire of a Feast" (1.57). But the figure is more often spiritual, and a reminder of the symbolic meaning of Communion. Christ is "wholy fed upon by evry Christian" (1.86); He will "enable us to digest the Nourishment of our Souls" (1.87); Traherne prays that Christ will "fill me with the Spirit of GOD; that I may overflow with Praises and Thanksgivings" (1.95). The feeding figures lead to figures of overflowing because Communion is creative and reciprocal. Once filled with grace, the communicant can return praises to God, and communicate heavenly truths to others.

In considering Traherne's use of the words of the Communion service itself, it will be helpful to have before us the lines from the Book of Common Prayer that he always has in mind. They occur in the most intense part of the service, directly following the Prayer of Consecration and preceding the communication of the bread and wine to the congregation:

Graunt us therefore gracious Lord, so to eate the flesh of thy deare Sonne Jesus Christ, and to drinke the blood, that our sinful bodies may be made cleane by his body, and our soules washed through his most precious blood, and that we may evermore dwell in him, and he in us, Amen.

And here we offer and present unto thee, O Lord, our selves, our soules and bodies . . . humbly beseeching thee, that all wee which be partakers of this holy Communion may be fulfilled with thy grace and heavenly benediction. And although we be unworthy, through our manifold sinne, to offer unto thee any sacrifice: yet we beseech thee to accept this . . . through Jesus Christ our Lorde . . . .[19]

The prayer that "we may evermore dwell in him, and he in us" is so central in Traherne's thought that evidence of its presence hardly needs to be given. That is the theme of reciprocity which informs everything he says. Certainly it must have been highly important to him that this idea is explicit at the heart of the Communion service. The surrounding language, too, is often embedded in Traherne's centuries, sometimes as fully as in the following passages. Here, at a loss for words, he turns to the liturgy for help:

But Thou O Savior art here upon the Cross suffering for my Sins. What shall I render unto Thee for so Great a Mercy! All Thanksgiving is too Weak. And all Expression too feeble. I giv Thee my self my Soul and Body I offer unto Thee. It is unworthy of Thee, but Thou lovest me. Wash me with thy Blood from all my Sins: And fill me with Thy Holy Spirit that I may be like unto Thee. So shall I Prais Thy Name Acceptably for ever more. Amen.

And now, O Lord, Heaven and Earth are infinitly more valuable then they were before. being all bought with thy Precious Blood (1.75–76).

It is relevant that in the Communion service, the minister is said to communicate the bread and wine to the people. Communication leads to or becomes communion in the most sacred service of the Church, as Traherne must have realized every time he performed that ritual. And communion with God for Traherne was so real as to allow him to be like God: "For then we Pleas God when we are most like Him . . . when our Thoughts are like his" (1.13). "Do you extend your Will like Him, and you shall be Great as He is, and concernd and Happy in all these . . . And when you do so, you are the Universal Heir of God and All Things. GOD is yours and the Whole World. You are His, and you are all; Or in all, and with all" (1.53). The blood of Christ flows in all Christian veins.

In the second century, Traherne turns from emphasis upon the Cross as a way of binding, of healing separation, to emphasis upon love. While the love of God is still strongly stressed, the love of men for one another also becomes an important theme. The meditations on love begin with consideration of God's love for man, and of God's loving preparation of a redeemer to die for man. Love defines God: ". . . by Being Lov GOD receiveth, and is the End of all"

(II.46). He then moves to consideration of the value of love to men. Here, through many variations and extensions of the theme, he says that by loving the soul attains itself, becoming perfect and infinite like God. When every soul communicates infinite love to every other soul, each man is the only end of creation, being infinitely loved by all. Infinitely loved, he can be infinitely loving, and so help to sustain each other man in his lordship of the world. Infinitely loving, each man can also share the joys of all other men, and thereby infinitely increase his own capacities again:

How Happy we are that we may liv in all, as well as one; and how All sufficient Lov is, we may see by this: The more we liv in all the more we live in one (II.61).

Lov having this Wonder in it also, that among innumerable Millions, it maketh evry one the sole and single End of all Things . . . indeed it maketh evry one more then the End of all Things: and infinitly more then the Sole Supreme and Soveraign of all. for it maketh Him so first in Himself: and then in all. For while All Things in Heaven and Earth fall out after my Desire, I am the End and Soveraign of all: which conspiring always to Crown my Friends with Glory and Happiness: And Pleasing all in the same maner whom I lov as my self: I am in evry one of them the End of all things again: being as much concerned in their Happiness as my own (II.55).

The images of feeding and of flowing into one another maintain a unity with the first century. So do figures expressing binding together—ligatures, cords, bonds, and sinews. It seems to me, too, that this century is more repetitious than the others. The reciprocity of love, "I in them and they in me," and so forth, demands this repetitiveness, just as it demands the reflective symbolism of fountains and mirrors:

For as the Sun Beams Illuminat the Air and All Objects, yet are them selvs also Illuminated by them, so fareth it with the Powers of your Soul. The Rays of the Sun carry Light in them as they Pass through the Air, but go on in vain till they meet an Object: and there they are Expresst. They Illuminat a Mirror, and are Illuminated by it. For a looking glass without them would be in the Dark, and they without the Glass unperceived (II.78).

It is apparent here that repetition is no mechanical exercise, but a way of increasing and even creating meaning. Mutual reflection is mutual creation and enlargement. And when the world is the property of each man, man's love becomes valuable, something that God might desire:

Clothe your self with Light as with a Garment, when you com before Him:
Put on the Greatness of Heaven and Earth, Adorn your self with the Ex-
cellencies of GOD Himself. When you prepare yourself to Speak to Him, be
all the KNOWLEDG and Light you are able, as Great as Clear and as Perfect as is Possible. So at length shall you appear before GOD in Sion: and as
GOD convers with GOD for evermore (II.86).

While the personal nature of Traherne's philosophy has been everywhere apparent, he makes himself explicitly the subject of his discourse only in the third century, after he has given full attention to
the Cross and to love, as ways of bringing about unity. Now it is
clear that the self can only serve as center within a context created
by God's love, without which it is nothing. That is one way in
which he now protects his "I" from attack. Moreover, he has from
the beginning prepared us for a symbolic reading of his own history,
since what he has to say is that his life has been a history of the race,
and the first meditations of the first and second centuries are concerned with creation. Thus the "little stranger" of the third century
is but a little Adam, bearing anew the testimony to the perfection
of the world as seen aright. Between his Adamic experience in the
opening paragraphs of the book and his identification with David in
the latter part of the third century, his view that the self is only attained in loving connection with others becomes clear. Traherne has
confirmed in the design of the book his belief that the self is only attained in connection with others. The "overflowing" of the autobiographical section into other parts of the book makes those other
parts in many ways more interesting than it is.

Two other formative elements may help us better to understand
the nature of his persona. One is his ready identification with others,
his ability to merge himself with, lose himself in his subject. He slips
almost accidentally, it would seem, into harmony with Adam or
David; sometimes his sympathy with another man or with God
seems precipitated by a fumbling for the right pronoun, and the variety and quantity of pronouns in constant use in his prose make such
fumbling easy. In the following passage, for example, the pronoun
"me" occurs where one would expect "Him," for God: "Here upon
Earth souls lov what GOD hates, and hate what GOD loves. Did
they keep their Ey Open always upon what He lovs, and see His
Lov to them, and to all, they could not chuse but lov as He does
. . . but they are like the Ey, Mirrors with Lids, and the Lid of Ig-

norance or Inconsideration interposing, they are often times Ec-clypsed . . . they may lov me, or forbear" (iv.86). Thus casually he makes a transition, which to some extent seems not a transition but a merging of himself with God. The identifications, at all times, spring from extreme sympathy with his subject rather than from preoccupation with himself.

This merging of one self, as one word, with another, the striving toward unity in separation, has an important parallel in Traherne's treatment of time, which is dominated by his belief in the doctrine of continued creation, common in the age.[20] According to this doc-trine, Creation is not an event of the past, over and done with, but something which God reaffirms at each moment in preserving the world. Existence is a mercy renewed instant by instant, for which man in turn gives thanks by "upholding" the world in love:

As among Divines it is said, That evry Moments Preservation is a New Cre-ation: and therfore Blessings continued must not be Despised, but be more and more esteemed: becaus evry Moments Preservation is another Obliga-tion: even so in the Continual Series of Thoughts wherby we continue to up-hold the Frame of Heaven and Earth in the Soul towards God, evry Thought is another World to the Diety as Acceptable as the first (II.91).

The possibly frightening implications of a view of continuance that requires such constant attention from God are overcome by the plea-sures available to man in imitating that attention, an activity which Traherne consistently links with creation itself.

The 65th, 66th, and 67th paragraphs of the first century are per-haps his fullest description of the experience of moving back in time to the moment of the original Creation. In the 65th, he begins, "Had I been alive in Adams steed, how should I have Admired the Glory of the world!" and then proceeds to outline an Adamic vision of un-touched creation in psalmic language. Just as, for him, perception, or affirmation, is creation, so the idea of the world in man's mind is more important than the world itself. Thus not only can Traherne intuitively identify with Adam, but, because of his exaltation of per-ception, he can himself renew the world in his mind; and so the world "was Glorious while new: and is as new as it was Glorious." In the 65th meditation he lauds the creation of the world, in the 66th the creation of the body, and in the 67th, the creation of the soul. Unable to conceive of a state of total non-being, Traherne assumes that essence precedes existence, that the soul can long for being before it exists. This kind of imagination makes it easy for him to return himself in thought to that pre-existential state: "Suppose O my Soul there were no Creature made at all, And that GOD making Thee alone offered to make Thee what Thou wouldst." Choosing to be himself and no other, Traherne, at the moment of this constantly and freely remade choice, allows himself to be re-created, and experiences the original joy of creation: "O my Soul, He hath made His Image. Sing O ye Angels, and Laud His Name ye Cherubims: Let all the Kingdoms of the Earth be Glad, and let all the Hosts of Heaven rejoyce. for He hath made His Image, the Likeness of himself, his own Similitude." More soberly, then, he records the Fall: "Being to lead this Life within I was Placed in Paradice without with som Advantages which the Angels hav not. And being Designed to Immortality and an Endless Life, was to Abide with GOD from everlasting to everlasting in all His Ways. But I was Deceived by my Appetite, and fell into Sin . . . I offended in an Apple against Him that gave me the whole World . . ." (1.75).

In these meditational passages, we are confronted again with Traherne's flexibility, his readiness to identify himself not only with another person, but also with an event or an emotion. And as his own personality is enlarged through identification and communion with other persons, so his intense concentration upon a given moment or a succession of moments allows him to transcend the limitations of the idea of continued creation, and to find in the gift of an instant the constant wonder of eternity.

He also tells us that contemplation of eternity itself makes the soul immortal, for the soul's glory is "that it can see before and after his Existence into Endless Spaces":

When my Soul is in Eden with our first Parents, I my self am there in a Blessed Maner. When I walk with Enoch, and see his Translation, I am Transported with Him. The present Age is too little to contain it. I can visit Noah in His Ark, and swim upon the Waters of the Deluge. I can see Moses with his Rod . . . I can Enter into Aarons Tabernacle . . . I can visit Solomon in his Glory . . . No Creature but one like unto the Holy Angels can see into all Ages (1.55).

One can look both to the Middle Ages and to the seventeenth century for an explanation of this sort of passage in Traherne. The whole style of his address here is of course reminiscent of the traditional meditations, which often asked the meditator to put himself into a Biblical or imagined scene. But it has also been pointed out that Traherne's intoxication with the idea of infinity is a product of the spatial discoveries and speculations of his own time.[21] He himself suggests both kinds of influence in the following passage:

When I heard of any New Kingdom beyond the seas, the Light and Glory of it pleased me immediately, enterd into me, it rose up within me and I was Enlarged Wonderfully. I entered into it, I saw its Commodities, Rarities, Springs, Meadows Riches, Inhabitants, and became Possessor of that New Room, as if it had been prepared for me, so much was I Magnified and Delighted in it. When the Bible was read my Spirit was present in other Ages. I saw the Light and Splendor of them . . . This shewd me the Liveliness of interior presence, and that all Ages were for most Glorious Ends, Accessible to my Understanding, yea with it, yea within it. for without changing Place in my self I could behold and Enjoy all those. Any thing when it was proposed, tho it was 10000 Ages agoe, being always before me (III.24).

For Traherne, words like "borders," "limits," "coasts," and "gulfs" are negative. Words like "endless," "infinite," "illimited," "eternal," and "everlasting" are ubiquitous and highly positive. Though he lives in a world of boundaries and discontinuities, he also lives in a world in the process of opening into what would seem to be infinite space. But that external influence is for the most part subsumed inwardly into a celebration of the soul's infinity in God.

Two other words constantly repeated in Traherne's prose are "create" and "conceive." He is always making up little exercises in creation, for example, to convince the reader that this is, as he says, the best of all possible worlds: Why has not God a material body? Why is there a sun? Why not two suns? and so on. If I could be re-created, what would I choose to be? All exercises culminate in man's re-creation of the world in his mind. Out of limited time and space, his imagination teaches him to conceive infinity. Just as he enters all ages in a moment, he can open a fragment of space into the whole universe. Note the successive openings of these paragraphs:

You never Enjoy the World aright, till you see how a Sand Exhibiteth the Wisdom and Power of God . . . (1.27).

Your Enjoyment of the World is never right, till evry Morning you awake in Heaven . . . (1.28).

You never Enjoy the World aright, till the Sea itself floweth in your Veins, till you are Clothed with the Heavens, and Crowned with the Stars . . . (1.29).

Till your Spirit filleth the whole World, and the Stars are your Jewels, till you are as Familiar with the Ways of God in all Ages as with your Walk and Table . . . (1.30).

It is true that he is using the second person here, but he is only asking others to practice what he himself has felt; that is amply documented. "Infinit Worth shut up in the Limits of a Material Being, is the only way to a Real Infinity" (III.20).

Sometimes Traherne checks his joy just short of suggesting that his estate is happier than God's. In a way, then, his use of the cosmic personality is far bolder than that of any other writer discussed here. Burton established his cosmic scope through use of the records made by other minds; Browne and Burton both suggest that they can do it because "men are liv'd over again," and there is nothing new under the sun. In Traherne, on the contrary, everything is constantly both new and eternal; and his sense of self is less bookish than Burton's, less precious than Browne's. The discovery of a new country makes him feel enlarged; so does reading (and identifying with) David; so does communion with God. While both Browne and Burton suggest means of achieving victory over time and make free use of all ages, neither man ever sets his sights on the throne of God, or looks out at the world (as Traherne can) from the throne of God and through God's eyes.[22] Playing characteristically upon the words "I" and "eye," he prays, "O Let me so long Eye Thee, till I be turned into Thee, and look upon me till Thou art formed in me, that I may be a Mirror of thy Brightness, an Habitation of thy Lov and a Temple of thy Glory. That all thy Saints might live in me, and I in them" (1.87).

And yet there is a total modesty and credibility in his performance. We have seen it in his use of traditional instruments—the Cross and the Communion service; in his recognition that the self can only be itself in relation to others; in his assumption that anyone else can and should achieve what he achieves. His unity with God is, just as he tells us, a way of praising the God who made a creature that could return His love. When he overflows, he becomes infinite, but God filled him with the love with which he flows.

Most certainly the impression of modesty, sincerity, and openness that Traherne gives us is much advanced by the absolute coherence of his style on every level. He has very little to say on the subject of

style, and that little is commonplace enough. In a poem which someone has entitled "The Author to the Critical Peruser," introducing
the volume of his poems, he praises "naked Truth," simplicity of
style. The words of the poem are reminiscent of those in a similar
poem by Herbert, which Traherne must have had in mind in writing
these lines:

> No curling Metaphors that gild the Sence,
> Nor Pictures here, nor painted Eloquence;
> No florid Streams of Superficial Gems,
> But real Crowne and Thrones and Diadems! [23]

With both Herbert and Traherne, the concept of "naked truth" requires some interpretation: certainly, they are not interested in the
kind of style that Baxter approved. But they do reject false ornament, contrived for its own sake, as well as the kind of Donnean obscurity that requires the reader to work very hard in order to interpret syntax or symbol. Because their styles are less immediately de-
manding than Donne's, it is easy to overlook the fact that once the
obvious meaning has been understood, there is further delight to be
had in the artful underlining of idea, or in confirming levels of
meaning achieved through thoroughly functional and unobtrusive
techniques. In Traherne, the style follows the theme of healing, clarifying, uniting.

For the modern reader, the one probable intrusion occurs when
the immediacy of Traherne's fresh perceptions, his insistence upon
the moment-to-moment invention or discovery of the world, sometimes gives his prose a hyperbolical pitch. A few of the paragraphs
are overabundant in baroque emotional devices—capitals, exclamations, hyperboles, excessive repetition, especially of certain key
words, emotionally charged language and scenes—like that of the
bleeding Christ upon the Cross:

LORD JESUS what Lov shall I render unto Thee, for thy Lov unto me!
Thy eternal Lov! Oh what fervor, what Ardor, what Humiliation, what Reverence, what Joy, what Adoration, what Zeal, what Thanksgiving! Thou that
art Perfect in Beauty, Thou that art the King of Eternal Glory, Thou that
reignest in the Highest Heavens camest down from Heaven to Die for me!
And shall not I live unto Thee? Oh my joy! O my Sovereign Friend! Oh my
life, and my All! I beseech thee let those Trickling Drops of Blood that run
down Thy flesh drop upon me. O let Thy Lov enflame me (1.62).

Traherne himself says, speaking of life in God: "All Hyperbolies are
but little Pigmies, and Diminutiv Expressions, in Comparison of the

Truth" (II.52). But such zeal of expression is rare beyond the first century. And here as everywhere the constant shifts in tone are helpful, as is the fact that the units are short. A moment can represent eternity, but, paradoxically, is not to be long sustained in human time, and if we momentarily lag in sympathy, at least we are never out of sympathy for long.

This occasional extravagance is the one respect in which Traherne's style is "noticeable," in the way of highly contrived styles. And even here, of course, it would have been less noticeable to Renaissance churchmen familiar with the old meditative traditions, in which the language is so often ardent. More frequently his style is a more unobtrusive and yet more complex reflection of theme.

We have seen that two of Traherne's major themes are communion, which overcomes spatial and temporal differences among people and things; and the sustenance of meaning, of reality, from moment to moment in time. In both of these themes there is a common style; things separate are made to approve, affirm, become one another, but the merging can only be because the separation already is. The urgency of this united theme is wholly and uniquely revealed everywhere in his style, from its most obvious to its most apparently casual details—from imagery and wordplay to the rhythm and punctuation of his sentences.

It is not difficult to find in Traherne puns and wordplays like those used in most Anglican prose, different, perhaps, only in their lack of flashiness and obvious erudition. Sometimes they are real play, a revelling in language for its own sake: "Were there no Needs, Wants would be Wanting themselvs: And Supplies Superfluous" (1.41); "And by how much the more Vile I hav been, let my lov be so much O Lord the more Violent Henceforth" (1.78). More often than we can know, his style is enriched by blurred puns which leave us vaguely uncertain as to whether or not the play is intentional: "*It is the Height of Gods Perfection that hideth His Bounty*" (1.38); "Thou wholy Communicatest thy self to evry Soul" (1.86). The obvious paradox of the second passage is that an infinite being somehow "wholly" communicates itself to finite, unwhole, unwholesome beings, thereby enabling them to achieve wholeness and infinity. Considering the eccentricity of Traherne's spelling and the permissiveness of seventeenth-century spelling in general, no one could be sure that he also meant to connect "whole" with "holy," or to set up vibrations that would suggest all the possible connections among "holy," "wholly," "solely," "whole," and "soul." Yet the interplay and merging of these concepts is as central to his philosophy as half-hidden punning combinations of these words are to his prose. And wordplay itself, the merging of different concepts, imitates his over-all intent to unify.

The more intensely a passage expresses Traherne's concern for unification, the more likely we are to find certain repeated and thematic wordplays, often doubling back and forth in derivation between Latin and English. *Admire* suggests *mirror*, and both suggest *wonder*, a very Trahernian emotion. *Reflection* (the image in the mirror) suggests *reflection* (thought), because *souls* are both *soles* (suns and centers) and *mirrors* (reflectors and admirers). The reflecting back and forth between languages increases the sense of reciprocity which is so integral to Traherne's efforts toward unity:

... as a Mirror returneth the very self-same Beams it receiveth from the Sun, so the Soul returneth those Beams of Lov that shine upon it from God. For as a Looking Glass is nothing in Comparison of the World, yet containeth all the World in it, and seems a real fountain of those Beams which flow from it so the Soul is Nothing in respect of God, yet all Eternity is contained in it, and it is the real fountain of that Lov that proceedeth from it. They are the Sun Beams which the Glass returneth: yet they flow from the Glass and from the Sun within it. The Mirror is the Well-Spring of them, becaus they Shine from the Sun within the Mirror, Which is as deep within the Glass as it is high within the Heavens. And this sheweth the Exceeding Richness and preciousness of Lov, It is the Lov of God shining upon, and Dwelling in the Soul. for the Beams that Shine upon it reflect upon others and shine from it (IV.84).

The figures of the overflowing well and fountain are already familiar, as is the reciprocity between the mirror and the sun. Man (the mirror) is dark without God's sun. Yet God's sun, by Christian wizardry, turns out to be nothing without man. *Sun* translates to *Son*, also to *Sol*, and thence to *soul* and *sole*. God is invisible without his mirror. The soul of man is the sole end of the shining of God's sun. In *soul* and *sol*, God and man, end and means become one.

This now familiar design—the interpenetration of meaning—is repeated in other ways, down to the smallest aspect of Traherne's style. Each brief unit, or meditation, is given its own number and its own separate space. But seldom is it self-contained. Rather, there is a constant interflow of meaning from unit to unit, so that, for example, four successive members of the fourth century begin as follows:

O Adam, we hav given Thee neither a certain seat, nor a Private face . . . (IV.76).

(From the previous unit we have learned that this is Traherne quoting Pico quoting God to Adam.)

O Infinit Liberality of God the Father! . . . (IV.77)   (still Pico)

This Picus Mirandula spake in an Oration . . . (IV.78).

neither is it to be believed, that God filled all the World with Creatures before he thought of man . . . (IV.79).

When the sense is continuous Traherne does not always even bother to capitalize.

Traherne sometimes links his paragraphs musically. From Meditation 25 through Meditation 39 of the first century, there is an intermittent refrain of "You never enjoy the world aright," which links together many of the paragraphs and sentences in a psalmic and at times regular music. This combination of separation with unity is repeated in Traherne's unique sentence punctuation. He uses periods in an apparently arbitrary way, so that often two pieces of a sentence are rent apart at places where we might punctuate more lightly, or not at all. For example:

It [the idea of the world in the mind of man] is better to you, becaus by it you receiv the World, and it is the Tribut you pay. It more immediatly Beautifies and Perfects your Nature. How Deformed would you be should all the World stand about you and you be Idle? Were you able to Creat other Worlds, GOD had rather you should think on this. for thereby you are united to Him. The Sun in your Ey, is as much to you as the Sun in the Heavens. for by this, the other is Enjoyed. It would shine on all Rivers Trees and Beasts, in vain to you, could you not think upon it. The Sun in your understanding illuminates your Soul, the Sun in the Heavens inlightens the Hemisphere. The World within you is an offering returned. Which is infinitly more Acceptable to GOD Almighty, since it came from him, that it might return unto Him. Wherein the Mysterie is Great (II.90).

Traherne's sentences are almost always comparatively short and structurally simple. They are meditational in the sense that they can be considered separately and slowly, for themselves, without requiring the reader to hurry onward for the sake of completing the syntax. And they are often meditational, too, in a density of meaning that demands a careful reading. His idiosyncratic use of periods also emphasizes the short units, often only parts of sentences. The periods break the sentence up more definitely than lighter punctuation could do, and require us to consider separately clauses which are important in themselves, and which otherwise might become too subordinate to a (grammatically) main clause.

At the same time, while we have the advantage of experiencing these sentences separately, we are also forced to remember that they are parts of a whole which they all mirror and illuminate. If Traherne uses more periods than we would, he also uses fewer capitals. And there are often rhythmic as well as grammatical and substantial connections among the separated clauses. Sometimes we can summarize these connections as creating a psalmic effect:

> Were you able to Creat other Worlds, GOD had rather you should think
> on this.
> for therby you are united to Him.
> The Sun in your Ey, is as much to you as the Sun in the Heavens.
> for by this, the other is Enjoyed.

With his fondness for David it is not surprising that Traherne's prose should fall into this kind of rhythm, or that it should include all sorts of other rhythmic effects that help to bind it together. Some of them seem to do no more than that. For sheer alliterative play, for instance, Traherne even outdoes Sir Thomas Browne: "We being then Kings over the Whole World, when we restore the Pieces to their Proper Places, being Perfectly Pleased with the whole Composure" (1.23); "the Slayer of the Serpent is seen with our Souls" (1.57); "He lives most like an Angel that lives upon least Himself" (IV.29). But the music of the last passage rightly suggests that the chief purpose of his alliteration is to create another kind of bond between words and sentences, another kind of chord.

This technique overlaps slightly with a group of devices that make up a reflective or reflexive syntax, in which one sentence or word mirrors another: "GOD is LOV, and my Soul is Lovely! God is Loving, and His Image Amiable" (1.67). Reflecting back and forth, the words imitate the mutual kindling of affection that is being described. The following passage exemplifies a chain reflection, sentences like successive mirrors:

The Misery of your fall ariseth Naturaly from the Greatness of your Sin. For to Sin against infinit Lov is to make one self infinitly Deformed: To be infinitly Deformed, is to be infinitly Odious in His Eys, whose Lov of Beauty is the Hatred of Deformity. To be infinitly Odious in His Eys who once loved us with infinit Lov: to hav sind against all Obligations, and to hav faln from infinit Glory and Blessedness is infinit Misery . . . (II.4).

Traherne also uses mirror images, inverted sentences: "They command you to lov all Angels and Men, They command all Angels and men to lov you" (I.20); "Thou hast made me the End of all Things, and all the End of me. I in all, and all in Me" (I.69). This last is really the point: "He giveth all the World to one, He giveth it to evry one, He giveth it to evry one in giving it to all, and Giveth it wholly to me in giving it to evry one for evry ones sake . . . This is the Effect of Making Images" (I.74). That is to say, image-making, or reflecting oneself in the mirror of others, infinitely increases the felicity of all. The theme of all the prose is that ideal unity whose vision informs the style: "And what shall we think of Christ Himself? Shall not all our Lov be where his is? Shall it not wholly follow and Attend Him? Yet shall it not forsake other Objects. but lov them all in Him, and Him in them, and them the more becaus of Him, and Him the more becaus of them. for by Him it is redeemed to them" (IV.68).

Here is illustrated "the Continual Series of Thoughts wherby we continue to uphold the Frame of Heaven and Earth in the Soul toward God," in which "evry Thought is another World to the Deity as Acceptable as the first" (II.91). Each man, as a separate soul, is precious to God, yet nothing lives or loves which is not active (II.22, 48). The activity of a loving soul is a constant flow of communication, a communion with others achieved as moment flows into moment, clause into clause, image into image, achieved as writer and reader, from separate centuries in time, merge in these centuries in this book.

CHAPTER IX

CONCLUSION

A FINAL BRIEF SUMMARY OF THE VARIATIONS PLAYED BY EIGHT MEN upon two styles of self-expression should help to emphasize the likenesses and differences within and between the two categories, demonstrating, I hope, the extent to which they are both definitive and flexible. This union of precision with variety is possible because the basic characteristics, for the most part, describe shared sensibilities; the variety is achieved through varied emphases and differing techniques. Each different way of expressing the paradigm may be considered one kind of variation upon it: Traherne's "I" thus seems completely different from Burton's, although both are excellent examples of the Anglican cosmic personality. Any given writer can also vary the pattern by really departing from it in one or more characteristics. Such departures occur more often among the Puritans (who differ more among themselves than the Anglicans do), and some at least will be illustrated in the course of this summary. The conceivable range of expression is in fact far wider than that which actually occurred: few other seventeenth-century men could have been included in this study because few were both desirous and capable of expressing successfully so much self-awareness.

The recognizable paradigm for each Puritan "I" is active, timebound, and as simple and visible as possible. This Puritan believes it proper to speak about himself literally, concretely, and spontaneously, using his writing in the service of life. While he chooses not to play, he is anxious to present himself as never melancholy, for melancholy would detract from his certain identity as God's Englishman and God's instrument. By describing his own place and effect in history, he also wishes actively to involve some specific readers or kinds of readers in what he considers important in life.

Bunyan's interpreter "I" tells the story of the younger Bunyan chronologically, making the reader aware of the stages of his conversion. He refuses to play (by which he means, to adopt a "higher" style); and by his use of passive constructions he acknowledges God's work upon him. Although he himself is not yet finished with the journey of life, he can use the story of his youth for the edification of his congregation, to help them while he is in prison. He tells that story with apparent simplicity and directness, selecting, of course, from among the relevant episodes, but seeming to report without embroidery the crucial events of his life. Although he writes from prison, one constantly senses him in the midst of activity, seldom at home, often surrounded by people who have real historical connections with him, physically acted upon by them, by the Bible, or by God. He calls himself the "chief of sinners," as well as the father of his flock. While he can use his past sins in order to be a better father, he is less determinedly cheerful and more introspective than the paradigm, and less insistent upon his own stability.

The reader of Lilburne has, to some extent, to make a variation on the paradigm by putting together the autobiography himself, by collecting the tracts; and the tracts, like Foxe's *Book of Martyrs*, embrace letters, petitions, court records, and other documents. Dated and placed, they help to create history and are embedded in it. Their purpose is to make Lilburne visible, safe, popular, and powerful; their method is to seem to be as true to life, as accurate in describing him as words can be, mingling personal with public material, making inner and outer man match. Inevitably topical, they nevertheless mythologize life. The Leveller leader (varying the pattern again, to the extent that he becomes symbolic) is revealed as the "only Oracle of Truth," "free-born John Lilburne," God's Englishman fighting for the rights of all. Consistently cheerful in the face of persecution, he also sometimes risks absurdity in his serious insistence upon his rights, however trivial. He purposely evokes a kind of "grim laughter" (Milton's phrase) in lampooning authority and false decorum, and in employing Martin Marprelate's new brand of *decorum personae*. For him, spontaneity of utterance is a temporal necessity, as well as an article of faith (putting himself at God's disposal), and a measure of inspiration. Active in themselves as drama, his tracts, in their use of vituperative language, are also intended to function as weapons. For him their success would be the defeat and humiliation of his enemies and the conversion to the cause of the common man, who was to proofread the tracts, sign the petitions, obey the commands, and follow Lilburne.

Milton varies the paradigm by being both Puritan and poet. Having, for the time being, chosen action over contemplation, having recognized the necessity of moving through an uncertain amount of chronological time in order to arrive at the time and place in which worthy poetry can be written, he still manages to some extent to get the best of both worlds, just because he can conceive and describe in time the timelessness of his poetry of the future. Like all the others, like Lilburne in particular, he is anxious to provide the details of his life in order to prove that his inner and outer self are one and the same. He needs to give such proof, however, not only to support his cause, and not at all to attest to his conversion, but to validate his claim for the future, to be God's English poet. He regards his gift, like conversion, as a sign of grace which enables him to write extemporaneously both tracts and poetry. He thinks of himself as God's instrument, signifying this role by use of the third person and the passive voice. His tracts are inevitably many-faceted: with the understanding reader, he covenants in memorable prose-poetry, promising poetic abundance when the new order is fulfilled; for the uncommitted bystander, he provides harsh propaganda; for the enemy, vituperative attacks. The juxtaposition of harshness with delight, of topical propaganda with the less timebound depiction of self, is uniquely exciting.

If Milton varies the paradigm by being both Puritan and poet, Baxter nearly turns it inside out by refusing to choose sides or construct a visible style. Although the plain and hasty extemporaneity of his style troubles him when he thinks of what he might have done with more time, and of what some readers must think of him, for others he knows that the plainness is necessary, and, given his sense that immediate issues must be immediately answered, the extemporaneity is as necessary for him as for Lilburne. Despite his espousal of some conservative values, eventually including the belief that human nature does not change, he still believes in striving for the temporal healing of human disunities in a united church. While his viewpoint transcends time, he chooses to commit himself to time in his daily life, and in an autobiography that becomes increasingly fragmentary and diary-like in its later stages. He varies the chronological pattern by trying to compartmentalize experience, to separate different spheres of activity, different aspects of life from one another. His writing is often extremely topical, his conclusions supported, like Lilburne's, by massive records; but since he is telling the story of his life and times, the effect is less that of a saint's life, than of an epic rendering of church history, which for him was the important history of the time. He tries to be as objective as possible, to tell the story as it happened, although sometimes he has to omit important material because he fears his prejudices may betray him, and although, in his sometimes mechanically providential view of history, he occasionally verges on the absurd. As God's instrument, he sees himself as a pen in God's hands: God's grace will make effective the unplanned work. And he sees himself as a cross-bearer, suffering with and in and for his divided church and world. His writing is for the record: the expected readers are the future generations, who will judge those who wrote the records given in the book, and made the history that the book describes.

All four of these writers intend their work to be of some specific use in the world—as a model for conversion, as incentive to revolutionary action, or as a record of truth for future generations. All four are wearied by slanders against them, and say that they feel impelled to speak about themselves in order to clear their names and causes. All have been isolated, and made more fully aware of themselves and their beliefs, by persecution and by other conditions which made it difficult or impossible for them to do what they wanted or thought themselves called to do. All are highly conscious of having been called to help save their country and the souls of their countrymen, and cannot easily laugh at themselves. Of the four of them, only Bunyan is extensively introspective, because he wants to explain the nature of his conversion. All four, at the time of writing, indicate that they know very well who they are, and would like any readers unfamiliar with them to know it too. None of them is thinking of what he does in terms of art, but primarily in terms of practicality—what it will accomplish. Certain artistic devices are of course essential to that accomplishment. Between perfection of the life and of the work, however, all four writers, at this time, are more concerned with perfection of the life, believing that what goodness the work can have will reflect the goodness of the man as instrument of a good God.

The paradigm for the Anglican "I" is meditative, antihistorical, complex, ambiguous, and obscure. Turning life into art, the Anglican constructs a symbolic cosmic personality that delights in stylistic complications, and even in playful and recreative devices. This persona is introspective, melancholy, sophisticated, and self-amused. Readers are at least implicitly invited to share in the literary life of the book.

Donne meditates in convalescence, recovering his ability to write as if it were synonymous with life itself. While he passes through a series of stages or "stations" in the course of his recovery, chronology is muted by the nature of the disease (the relapsing sickness) and by the cyclic character of his *Devotions*. Not only does he present to us three different faces or moods in the cyclic movement, but he also uses himself symbolically, in despair, in hope, and in faith, turning the bed, the physicians, and the symptoms of his disease into emblems of his spiritual condition. Yet the microcosm-macrocosm imagery, and the shifts from "I" to "we" at once indicate that the "I" stands for all men, and his illness for the spiritual states of mankind. His very closeness to death seems to encourage his puns and plays on language, and he cites in justification his literary God. As the Latin poem of the table of contents makes the story of his experience an *explication de texte*, so Donne becomes subject, author, and critic of his work. One has the sense everywhere of mirrors within mirrors, the historical Donne distant and obscure, despite the immediacy, the eternal present of his discourse.

Burton puts between himself and the reader the useful persona of Democritus Jr., who appears and disappears as Burton pleases. His book grows from one edition to another, not chronologically, but by topic. Its many quotations, fables, myths, and proverbs widen its scope to include all mankind, and to achieve the cosmic personality. Like Puritan works, the book has a practical use, as medicine—but melancholy is a permanent disease of mankind, and the medicine succeeds only if the reader can enter into the book-world, sharing the cosmic persona, enjoying the myths, dealing with the multiple-choice sentences, listening to Burton's gossip, and playing the roles to which he is assigned. Appearances come and go, changing like the flowing river of Burton's style, but laughable, tragic mankind remains always the same. Burton jokes to keep himself and his readers cheerful (telling jokes to make us laugh, rather than, like Donne, making puns that dazzle), but his jokes explain at least some of the reasons for melancholy: they have to do with appearance and reality, the ambiguity of life, the uncertainty of character. Donne's three-faced "I" is almost infinitely varied in the numerous changeable characters who play their roles on Burton's stage of man.

Browne seems to vary the paradigm by appearing to be franker than the others—after all, what is more reasonable than for a doctor to want to defend his religious views? Yet as soon as he starts to speak, he wraps himself in clouds of obfuscation, the style at odds with the content, the content contradicting itself from line to line. He becomes clearer when his subject changes, and the speculations of faith give way to the certainties of love, but the obscurity does not wholly evaporate. The artificiality of the persona is extremely obvious—forced upon our attention in the gleaming sentences polished to dazzling with all the most noticeable devices of rhetoric. The persona becomes cosmic in its rejection of time—the "I" is eternal in the mind of God; in its espousal of the microcosm-macrocosm figure as literally true; in its postulation of a common spark of divinity in man, and of his sameness through the ages. Man as creation comprehends without seeing all; without understanding all, he recreates himself. Browne's exuberant language, his acceptance of rules, his game metaphors, and his enjoyment of "safe" paradoxes, all support the serious playfulness of his endeavor.

Traherne is better described as overflowing than as meditating. His figure is the fountain; his ideal is communion. History and geography for him are means to extend himself—as soon as he learns of a new discovery or another person past or present, that place or person becomes part of him. Self-love is mutual love, and mutual love leads to the infinity of every human soul. In him, too, there is continual creation, continual renewal of life; everything is as it was at the dawn of time, and yet present, and yet infinite. He is neither obscure nor ambiguous on the face of it; he seems far fresher and more natural than the other Anglicans; yet the ease with which he identifies with others gives his persona the fluidity of quicksilver. The reader is invited to add to the manuscript, do the proposed exercises in creation, and share in the bond of mutuality that raises finite to infinite. The mutuality of life is matched by the mutuality of his language, in its half-hidden puns, its interweaving and reflexive syntax, and its distinctive punctuation.

If any common theme is predominant among the Anglican writers, perhaps it is the changeful changelessness of life. For each of them, all changes, yet all remains the same, and that sameness helps to explain the development of the cosmic personality. However, the persona, which shifts back and forth between "I" and "we," is a book-personality; and literary techniques are more consistently and abundantly used than in the Puritan works. Unlike the Puritan writers, too, these, in achieving the cosmic self, try out different roles, seeing the human condition from different viewpoints. Transformation, discontinuity, and appearance and reality are an important part of their consciousness, as shown in many such particular techniques as Browne's aphoristic sentence structure, Burton's jokes, Donne's paradoxes, and Traherne's fluid personae. Whether or not these books are intended to have any practical application, in all of them life has been submitted to art; and the books, in themselves, as literature, invite the reader to meditate, participate, admire.

Some characteristics are shared by Anglican and Puritan writers, but are developed through different kinds of techniques. Of such interesting cross-comparisons, I shall give only three examples here. Both Anglicans and Puritans wish to demonstrate their commitment to other men, to explain their involvement in mankind. The Puritans describe this involvement as an historical and national process. Thus, on the one hand, they emphasize real and metaphorical relations between generations, as Bunyan speaks of his congregation as his children, and Milton calls the Marian exiles "our fathers in the faith we hold." On the other hand, they consistently think of themselves as Englishmen fulfilling their parts in English history, and keeping faith with their countrymen, as when Lilburne insists that his rights are those of all men, or when Milton covenants with his readers to write great poetry when England is ready for it. This identification with other Englishmen is as close as the Puritan comes to a personality that is larger than life.

The Anglicans, thinking of all men past and present as the same, identify themselves with the whole human community. This identification first brings Donne out of the misery of the opening sections of his *Devotions*, causes Burton to laugh and weep for humanity, gives Browne as much tolerance as was probably possible for a man of his time and situation, and leads Traherne to conceive of the infinity of every soul in communion among men. Involved in mankind, each also is man as he achieves the cosmic personality. Yet there is a theoretical and literary air to this feat which is lacking in the Puritan's immediate "topical" encounter with other people.

Both Anglican and Puritan writers, in varying degrees, cultivate the appearance of spontaneity. Donne's characteristic immediacy suggests the apparently real spontaneity of his hastily produced *Devotions* (although the style seems anything but hasty); Burton, at first saying he had no time to revise, sustained his affected dishevelment through edition after edition of the *Anatomy*. Such "spontaneity" is associated with the desired freedom of the Senecan style to meditate as it chooses without obligation to a preordained grammatical pattern. It also has particular explanations in the case of individual writers: Donne wants to create a sense of immediacy; Burton wants to protect himself against criticism, and have fun with his readers. For the Puritan, spontaneity may be intended to indicate direct inspiration and the submission of personal attainment to God's goodness. All these Puritans wished to avoid any suggestion of artificiality or playfulness, and some needed to be quick with their pens to answer immediate needs. Anglican spontaneity often yields unexpected complexities to explication; Puritan spontaneity often leaves questions in our minds, for the answers to which we must apply to history.

In their extreme self-consciousness, these eight writers contributed to the development of a self-conscious language, and of man's capacity for self-analysis and self-expression, in life and in art. Their works are interesting to study for the sake of the personae, and for the sake of the relationships between the personae, the works, and the expected audiences. It is particularly interesting to observe the development of self-consciousness at this time, in the seventeenth century, when no writer has either the desire or the terminology to represent himself as uniquely individual, but wishes only to find a significant meaning for his sense of self in terms of his own traditions.

Perhaps this book may suggest a partial answer to the frequently asked and seldom answered question of why so little fiction was written in the seventeenth century. If, as the Anglicans charged, the Puritans were the rivals of the players, fiction might have been the rival of these nonfiction dramas of seventeenth-century selfhood. At any rate, these works did develop techniques that fiction needed.

Just as the chronological Puritan "I" passes over into fiction almost immediately through Bunyan and Defoe, and as the playful Anglican "I" reappears in symbolic fiction (in early fiction, most notably in Sterne), so the omniscient first-person author may be a development toward which the seventeenth-century cosmic personality was a necessary step. And in our own self-conscious age, whether motivated by psychological or literary curiosity, we can still learn something about selfhood from these explorers of man.

REFERENCE
MATTER

BIBLIOGRAPHICAL
APPENDIX

Cited in this section are books relevant to general background; biographical and critical studies of individual authors; and some of the texts analyzed in this book. Ordinary notes are of course given elsewhere, as usual. It was thought that the following material, which sometimes involves lengthy consideration of scholarly issues and problem texts, might more conveniently be presented here.

GENERAL BACKGROUND

For a brief survey of autobiographical material, see Margaret Bottrall, *Every Man a Phoenix: Studies in Seventeenth-Century Autobiography* (London, 1958), chapters I and II. On the medieval "I," see also Leo Spitzer, "Notes on the Poetic and the Empirical 'I' in Medieval Authors," *Traditio*, IV (1946), 414–22; and Ernst Robert Curtius, "Mention of the Author's Name in Medieval Literature," in *European Literature and the Latin Middle Ages*, trans. Willard Trask (New York, 1953), pp. 515–18. For discussion of Renaissance books on how to know oneself, see Paul A. Jorgenson, *Lear's Self-Discovery* (Berkeley and Los Angeles, 1967). For an excellent brief survey of the modern concept of self, with full bibliographies from philosophy and psychology, see Seymour Pollack, "The Self Concept in the Acute Psychotic Reaction," *Acute Psychotic Reaction*, ed. Werner Mendel and Leon Epstein, *Psychiatric Research Reports*, XVI (May 1963), 49–67.

Some studies concerned with related though not identical issues are the following: A. J. Krailsheimer, *Studies in Self-Interest from Descartes to La-Bruyère* (Oxford, 1962); Henri Peyre, *Literature and Sincerity* (New Haven, 1963); R. D. Altick, *Lives and Letters: A History of Literary Biography in England and America* (New York, 1965); Roy Pascal, *Design and Truth in Autobiography* (London, 1960); G. A. Starr, *Defoe and Spiritual Autobiography* (Princeton, 1965). For a useful defense of the unity between author and "persona" in the literature of the past, see Irvin Ephrenpreis, "Personae," in *Restoration and Eighteenth-Century Literature: Essays in Honor of Alan Dugald McKillop*, ed. Carroll Camden, published for William Marsh Rice University by The University of Chicago Press (Chicago, 1963).

Self-conscious writers whom the seventeenth-century men most consciously chose as models were, as might have been expected, St. Augustine and St. Paul, and it is interesting to notice the different ways in which these precedents are used. Where Bunyan and Lilburne, for example, are more concerned with passages describing Paul's persecution and physical suffering, Donne cites (from I Cor. 9:27) Paul's preaching of himself and his fears that when he had preached to others he himself might be a castaway. Different choices help to define different types of self-consciousness, Puritan versus Anglican.

Certainly it is also relevant to consider studies of prose style that delineate the shift from a public and oratorical to a private and meditational prose, although the present study is concerned less with that shift than with the existence in the seventeenth century of both public and private kinds of self-conscious prose. Both the existence of choices among styles, and the revival of the meditational Senecan mode of discourse accompany and encourage individual styles and personal prose. The definitive scholarship is Morris Croll's and his essays are now conveniently available in one volume, edited by J. Max Patrick and others as *Style, Rhetoric, and Rhythm: Essays by Morris W. Croll* (Princeton, 1966).

JOHN DONNE

There is at present no authoritative biography of Donne. Edmund Gosse in his *Life and Letters of John Donne*, 2 vols. (London, 1899) dealt carelessly with his evidence, and so much new material has been discovered since then that, although it is still necessary to refer to Gosse, it is always wise to check his testimony when possible. R. C. Bald's unfinished biography, on which he had labored some twenty years when he died, was willed, together with all relevant documents, to Professor Wesley Milgate of the National University in Canberra, Australia, who has agreed to complete the book and see it through the press. It is certain to be of immense importance in Donne studies. Meanwhile, Edward LeComte's *Grace to a Witty Sinner* (New York, 1965) is the most interesting and up-to-date of the existing biographies, although flawed badly by lack of proper documentation. Izaak Walton should not be ignored: untrustworthy, he is also irreplaceable. There is much material in articles by R. C. Bald, I. A. Shapiro, and others, and in the introductions to George Potter and Evelyn Simpson's ten-volume edition of *The Sermons of John Donne* (Berkeley, 1953–62). R. C. Bald's *Donne and the Drurys* (Cambridge, 1959) is a thorough treatment of a limited subject.

JOHN BUNYAN

The best biography of Bunyan is Henri Talon's *John Bunyan: The Man and His Works*, English translation (London, 1951). A study which unfortunately was unavailable to me until this book was in final draft is U. Milo Kaufmann's

The Pilgrim's Progress and Traditions in Puritan Meditation (New Haven, 1966). It contains much that is relevant to consideration of the Puritan "I."

JOHN LILBURNE

For the details of Lilburne's life, his own writings are almost sufficient. The biographies are Pauline Gregg, *Free-born John: A Biography of John Lilburne* (London, 1961), and M. A. Gibb, *John Lilburne the Leveller* (London, 1947). Miss Gregg's book includes a complete bibliography of Lilburne's tracts.

ROBERT BURTON

After this chapter was completed, I read Rosalie Colie's chapter on Burton in her *Paradoxia Epidemica* (Princeton, 1966), "Burton's *Anatomy of Melancholy* and the Structure of Paradox"; it is by far the best short study of Burton that I have seen. Also by Miss Colie is "Some Notes on Burton's Erasmus," in *Renaissance Quarterly*, XX (Autumn 1967), 335–41. Ellen Louise Hurt's unpublished Ph.D. thesis, "The Prose Style of Robert Burton: The Fruits of Knowledge" (University of Oregon, 1964), notices some of the same characteristics of Burton's style with which I am concerned, although her whole approach is quite different from mine. Jean Robert Simon's *Robert Burton (1577–1640) et L'Anatomie de la Mélancolie* (Paris, 1964) is a major contribution to Burton studies. It includes previously unknown biographical material, considerable analysis of the content of the *Anatomy*, and several useful chapters on language and style; these are cited in the notes, when relevant to material considered here. Both M. Simon and Miss Hurt are interested in a systematic laying out of the elements of Burton's style, as contrasted to my intensive analysis of the dynamic effect of Burton's "I" upon his work.

There is no adequate modern edition of *The Anatomy of Melancholy*, and it would therefore be very difficult at present to make a definitive full-scale analysis of Burton's prose style. This present study, for example, makes no effort to consider Burton's stylistic revisions from edition to edition, or details like spelling and punctuation, which have been standardized in every modern edition.

The section on religious melancholy has been properly edited by Dennis Donovan as a Ph.D. dissertation, "Robert Burton's *The Anatomy of Melancholy:* 'Religious Melancholy' A Critical Edition" (University of Illinois, 1965). Although this work is partial and as yet exists only in manuscript and on film, I have used it where I could because it is superior to the other possibilities. Elsewhere, I have used the text edited by Holbrook Jackson for Everyman's Library, 3 vols. (London, 1932). This text is based on the sixth edition of the *Anatomy* (the last prepared by Burton for the press, and therefore the fullest) collated with the fifth. I have collated Jackson's text with a film of the Huntington Library copy of Burton's sixth edition, and in the one passage I have cited where Jackson's text is actually misleading, I have given the punctuation of the original version. Elsewhere, his modernizations have no real bearing on any of my conclusions. I have consistently omitted Jackson's translations of Burton's Latin, however, since this one very easily-made change brings us much closer to the original text.

RICHARD BAXTER

The best biography of Richard Baxter is Geoffrey F. Nuttall, *Richard Baxter* (London, 1965). Most of the biographical facts, and the best picture of the man, are to be found in the *Reliquiae Baxterianae*, ed. Matthew Sylvester, 1696. J. M. Lloyd Thomas's introduction to his abridged *Autobiography of Richard Baxter being The Reliquiae Baxterianae (1696)* (London, Everyman, 1931), is the best commentary on Baxter that I have seen.

My decision to use the 1696 edition of the *Reliquiae* needs some explanation. The book was written over a much longer period of time than Baxter ordinarily devoted to any manuscript; it was therefore subject to more than the usual number of interruptions; and it was left at his death, in imperfect form, to his friend Matthew Sylvester, who edited it and published it five years later, in 1696.

In his preface, Sylvester insists that reverence for Baxter's own words necessitated absolute fidelity to the manuscript. At the same time, though, he admits to numerous typographical errors resulting from his inability to see the manuscript through the press; some pages lost through his own careless-ness; and a very few corrections of the manuscript. J. M. Lloyd Thomas, editor of the modern Everyman abridgement, points out also that some pas-sages have been changed or omitted. He harshly terms the folio "a confused and shapeless hulk, and in a great measure a dossier of documents, many of them of no living interest" (*Autobiography*, p. xxx).

Lloyd Thomas's introduction to his edition shows him to be an extremely sensitive interpreter of Baxter. But his intention in his text is to "satisfy the immediate needs of the general reader." In making his selections, he says, "I have looked upon myself as the curator of a strictly limited museum who may be led to choose, for the sake of the representative character of the whole collection, some specimens wrought in baser metal or with poorer craftsman-ship than others intrinsically more valuable" (*Autobiography*, pp. xxxv and xxxii). Such a selection certainly has its worth, but it cannot be used as the basis for a style study, nor, I think, can it really teach us to know Richard Baxter. For his *Reliquiae* is not a museum, but a portrait of a man and his age. To allow ourselves to be content with some representative samples is to lessen very much our chances of understanding why the whole work might *look* like a museum, even though it is not one.

For lack of a better, then, we must rely on Sylvester's edition. Dr. Lloyd Thomas was certainly right to complain about it. From the point of view of any modern editor, it is completely inadequate. A collation of the text with the whole manuscript is not possible, since (in eerie imitation of the character of its author) the manuscript somehow came to be divided, and part of it is completely missing. The remaining sections are divided between the British Museum and Dr. Williams's Library in London, which specializes in Baxterianae. This remaining material can, I think, be considered typical of the whole, especially since we have the greater part of the second section, which is the most problematical. Collation of text with manuscript does reveal a great many variations, of which I have recorded typical examples below. None of these variations, however, affects the kind of style study which can be achieved upon the *Reliquiae*, since Sylvester's alterations, omissions, and additions are never extensive enough to affect either the texture or the structure of the work, and I have argued in Chapter V that there are no significant "minor" techniques in this style.

I cannot agree that the work is meaninglessly shapeless, or that Sylvester's editing significantly changed the form that Baxter gave it. So far as can be determined, Sylvester never tampered with the structure of the book. Not only did Baxter express himself thus and in this order to begin with, but he even reread at least parts of the manuscript, making occasional revisions and marginal notes. If it is true, as he says of all his writing, that he "scarce ever wrote one Sheet twice over, nor stayed to make any blots or Interlinings, but was fain to let it go as it was first conceived" (Pt. I. 212, p. 124), then the *Reliquiae* must have been exceptionally carefully done. There is nothing to suggest that without Sylvester the work would have been substantially different, even if Baxter had been able to see it through the press himself.

And that, incidentally, is something that he was rarely able to do. Again and again, he complains of the printing problems that always beset Puritan writers. Many times a book could not be legitimately printed, and had to be done hastily and surreptitiously, or not at all (Baxter claims never to have given countenance to such publication, but it did befall some of his writing). He speaks of some of his books being pirated, and badly printed. Available printers were likely to be unskilled or temperamental. And restrictions on Baxter's own person sometimes made it impossible for him to travel to London, where, in later years, his printers were established. If nothing else interfered, sometimes it was his own work that kept him from careful proofreading. It was quite in the spirit of his publishing history that he left his manuscripts to a man who was himself too busy to proofread. Thus, the smaller inaccuracies of language of which Sylvester and his publisher were guilty tend to preserve rather than to obscure Baxter, and make much less difference to our reading than they could with another author.

It may also be useful at this point to make some comments on the manuscript, since it is not easily available. The best approach to the Baxter manuscripts is a pamphlet entitled *The Baxter Treatises*, compiled in 1959 by the Rev. Roger Thomas, present librarian of Dr. Williams's Library. This pamphlet lists twenty-two volumes of manuscript material. Parts of the *Reliquiae Baxterianae* and the supporting documents which Baxter intended to incorporate (and which Sylvester did incorporate) into the text are scattered through a number of these volumes. Volume 22 in this catalogue is a photostat of part of Egerton No. 2570 in the British Museum, which contains the manuscript materials separated from Dr. Williams's Library. This part of the manuscript includes from the *Reliquiae*, about 74 pages of Part I, and 48 pages of Part III. The volumes in Dr. Williams's Library have about 130 pages of Part II, a number of documents from Part III, and the additions for the years 1675 and following.

Collation of manuscript and text reveals numerous differences between the two, but none that affect the structure or tone of the work. Most of the changes are minor, and some are undoubtedly printers' errors. The following is a representative list, with illustrations provided where the type of change seems significant:

a) less responsible italicizing in text. Baxter italicizes for emphasis; the text often italicizes two words, where Baxter has underlined only one.

b) translation of Latin phrases

c) abbreviations written out

d) spelling in general regularized and modernized

e) additions for clarity or caution:

MS: "In the Diocesane Party I utterly disliked 1. Their Extirpation of the true Discipline of Christ . . ."

Text: ". . . true Discipline of Christ as we conceive, by *consequence* though not intentionally . . ." (Pt. II. 12, p. 141)

f) changes in individual words, accidental or clarifying

g) slight stylistic revisions

h) updating:

MS: "There was no Name to this Paper, but long time after I learnt that it was Mr. *Peter Gunning's* now Doctor and publick professor of D. in Cambridge."

Text: ". . . Mr. *Peter Gunning's*, afterwards Bishop of Ely . . ." (Pt. II. 33, p. 150)

i) extensive excision or revision. This is rare. Its purpose is generally tact. For example, the text omits mention of a paper supposed to have been written by a Catholic, attempting to excuse Charles II's love life (Pt. II. 83, p. 218).

j) revision of text according to marginal notes:

Discussing a controversy with a Catholic, he explains, in the manuscript, why he has not yet published a refutation of the Catholic's latest argument. Later, in the margin, he writes, "Since then I have published a full rejoinder to which I can procure no answer." The text omits the explanation, and simply adds the later information to his account of the controversy, thus: "And when he came no more to me, nor gave me any Answer, I printed all together; which made him think it necessary at last to write a Confutation: whereto I have since published a full Rejoinder to which I can procure no Answer" (Pt. II. 83, p. 219).

BIBLIOGRAPHICAL APPENDIX

SIR THOMAS BROWNE

The best life of Browne, which is also an excellent critical work, is Frank Livingstone Huntley's *Sir Thomas Browne: A Biographical and Critical Study* (Ann Arbor, 1962). In considering Browne's persona, I have found useful N. J. Endicott, "Some Aspects of Self-Revelation and Self-Portraiture in *Religio Medici*," *Essays in English Literature from the Renaissance to the Victorian Age*, ed. Millar MacLure and F. W. Watt (Toronto, 1964), pp. 85–102.

A brilliant, if sometimes eccentric, Ph.D. dissertation, which I saw only after this chapter was completed, is John R. Mulder's "Literary Scepticism: Montaigne and Sir Thomas Browne" (University of Michigan, 1963). To me the most interesting part of the dissertation is the stylistic analysis, which I find so impressive (despite my reservations) that if I had seen it first, I might not have had the courage to write this chapter at all. Mulder's intention in bringing Montaigne together with Browne is not to prove an influence, but to cite parallels. The question of influence is one which will certainly occur to the reader during the course of this chapter. It was raised during Browne's time, and he responded thus: "Many things are casually or favourably super-added unto the best Authors & sometimes conceats & expressions common unto them with others, & that not by imitation butt coincidence, & concurrence of imagination upon harmonie of production . . . In a peece of myne published long agoe the learned Annotator (Commentator) hath parallel'd many passages with other of Mountaignes essayes, whereas to deale clearly, when I penned that peece I had never read 3 leaves of that Author & scarce any more ever since" (Sir Geoffrey Keynes, ed., *The Works of Sir Thomas Browne*, 4 vols., Chicago, 1964, III, 290). Browne is here responding to the 1656 edition of the *Religio Medici*, with annotations by Thomas Keck. Mulder discusses the issue, rightly chooses not to decide whether or not Browne was telling the truth, and explains his own study of the parallels as one which may simply help to define the relevance of skepticism in Renaissance literature.

JOHN MILTON

For autobiographical details, see, as with all the Puritan writers, Milton himself. The definitive biography has long been David Masson's seven-volume *The Life of John Milton* (London, 1859–94). The impending publication of William R. Parker's biography has been announced by Oxford University Press.

THOMAS TRAHERNE

The rediscovery of Traherne began when a number of poems and meditations, at first ascribed to Henry Vaughan, were correctly identified and published by Bertram Dobell—the poems in 1903, and the *Centuries of Medita-*

tions in 1908. If we had nothing else, these would be more than enough to have established Traherne as a major literary figure. In 1963, Holland Brothers of Birmingham advertised in their catalogue, without any especial fanfare, a manuscript whose title page was missing, but which began each following section with this or the equivalent heading: "Select Meditations: The Second Century." The manuscript was described as written "in a very small neat and perfectly legible hand," "ca. 1650, in a contemporary calf bound volume, rubbed and worn," containing verse and prose of high quality. And if this were not enough in itself, Holland Brothers included samples of both prose and verse. The author's name scarcely needed to be included. This manuscript was acquired by James M. Osborn of Yale University, its identity was confirmed by Louis L. Martz, and it is to appear under Mr. Osborn's editorship in a companion to the two-volume Oxford edition of the *Centuries, Poems, and Thanksgivings.*

For a fuller description of these discoveries, see, for the earlier-discovered work, the introduction to H. M. Margoliouth's edition of Thomas Traherne, *Centuries, Poems, and Thanksgivings,* 2 vols. (Oxford, 1958). Or, for even more detail, see Bertram Dobell, ed., *Poems of Thomas Traherne* (London, 1903). For the "Select Meditations," see James M. Osborn, "A New Traherne Manuscript," *Times Literary Supplement,* October 8, 1964, p. 928. The same story in greater detail is given in an unpublished address, "A Meditation Upon Traherne," delivered by Mr. Osborn to the Fellows of the Pierpont Morgan Library on October 7, 1964. A brief description of the manuscript is included in an appendix in Louis Martz's *The Paradise Within: Studies in Vaughan, Traherne, and Milton* (New Haven, 1964), pp. 207–11.

We still know very little about Traherne. Gladys Wade's biography, *Thomas Traherne* (Princeton, 1944), is a mass of speculation based on very little evidence. H. M. Margoliouth includes almost all the known factual material in fifteen pages of his introduction to the *Centuries, Poems, and Thanksgivings.* Carol Marks has taught us a great deal more about his intellectual life than we knew before in a series of articles which culminate in an edition of Traherne's *Christian Ethicks,* ed. Carol Marks and George Guffey (Ithaca, 1967). Her articles are as follows: "Thomas Traherne and Hermes Trismegistus," *Renaissance News,* XIX (Summer 1966), 118–31; "Thomas Traherne's Commonplace Book," *Bibliographical Society of America,* LVIII (1964), 458–65; "Traherne's Church's Year-Book," *Papers of the Bibliographical Society of America,* LX (1966), 31–72; and "Thomas Traherne and the Cambridge Platonists," *PMLA,* LXXXI (December 1966), 521–34. I have also found useful A. L. Clements, "On the Mode and Meaning of Traherne's Mystical Poetry: 'The Preparative,'" *Studies in Philology,* LXI (July 1964), 500–21; and Helen C. White, *The Metaphysical Poets* (New York, 1936).

In an important essay on Traherne's *Centuries,* included in his book, *The Paradise Within,* Louis Martz demonstrates the usefulness of considering the *Centuries* in the light of a synthesis of the principles of Augustinian mysticism, showing convincingly that Bonaventure's *Itinerarium Mentis Deum,* when used with caution, provides a good outline of the *Centuries.* Another

organizational principle is suggested by Victor Rowley, in "Thomas Traherne's *Centuries* and Aristotle's Theory of Change" (Unpublished M.A.
thesis, Ohio State University, 1967), p. 58: "The first century might be seen
as proposing the end or object of happiness in order to enkindle desire; the
second presenting the means, particularly the world and divine love; the
third considering an individual soul committed to perfection; and the fourth
the rules for the quest." Like other Anglican works, the *Centuries* reflect different aspects of themselves to different readers, or even to the same reader.

NOTES

1. *The Essayes of Montaigne,* trans. John Florio, intro. J. I. M. Stewart (New York, 1933), Bk. II, Ch. XVIII, p. 602.
2. However, I do not wish to preclude the possibility that further research might turn up other varieties of self-consciousness. The deist Herbert of Cherbury belongs in neither of these categories, for example; and there ought to be a self-conscious "I" (perhaps Peter Sterry's) among the Cambridge Platonists, although they may have to remain indirectly represented by Traherne.
3. See, for example, the differing views of Christopher Hill, William Haller, Charles and Katherine George, and John F. H. New.
4. See U. Milo Kaufmann, *The Pilgrim's Progress and Traditions in Puritan Meditation* (New Haven, 1966), and Louis Martz, *The Poetry of Meditation* (New Haven, 1954).
5. I am considering this literary, ideological view of time here as literary characteristic, and do not intend to suggest that in his writing or out of it the Anglican is unaware that chronological time governs the daily lives of men. In *Religio Medici,* in fact, Browne makes obvious the artificial and self-conscious nature of this view of time by turning to it whenever he wants particularly to assume his cosmic personality.
6. See Susan Snyder, "The Left Hand of God: Despair in Medieval and Renaissance Tradition," *Studies in the Renaissance,* XII (1965), 18–59.
7. *Complete Prose Works of John Milton,* ed. Don M. Wolfe and others, 4 vols. to date (New Haven, 1953–   ), I, 663.
8. Hence, the Puritan accusation that the Anglican preaches the wisdom of words rather than the Word of Wisdom. The source of the phrase is St. Paul's, "For Christ sent me not to baptize, but to preach the gospel: not with wisdom of words, lest the cross of Christ should be made of none effect" (I Cor. 1:17). Christian rhetoricians from Augustine on cited this verse, and in Donne's time it became almost a battle cry in the attack of the Puritans on Anglican preaching. On this use of the phrase, see William Haller, *The Rise of Puritanism* (New York, 1938). See also my *Contrary Music: The Prose Style of John Donne* (Madison, 1963), Ch. V, for fuller analysis of Anglican use of words.

9. See *Contrary Music*, Ch. V.

10. The three styles or faces of the *Devotions* are described in *Contrary Music*, Ch. VII.

11. Milton, *Prose Works*, II, 492.

12. The word "instrument" is Puritan jargon. A striking and certainly influential example of this way of thinking is to be found in Cromwell's letters to Parliament, reporting on military successes. Repeatedly he says he wants to report the battles fully enough to do justice to God's goodness, but not to describe the feats of individual men, who merely acted as God's instruments. *The Writings and Speeches of Oliver Cromwell*, ed. Wilbur Cortez Abbot, 3 vols. (Cambridge, Mass., 1937-45).

13. See Donald R. Howard, "Chaucer the Man," *PMLA*, LXXX (September 1965), 337-43.

14. Here, as so often, I find Bernini's St. Theresa an apt analogy. The saint is in ecstasy; and she is beheld by heavenly hosts and secular chapelgoers, as well as by art lovers. Donne's *Devotions* must have been written while he was still at death's door, and were already in press before he was well enough to leave his bedroom. Thus, still in the grip of the illness or ecstasy with which the *Devotions* are concerned, he was able to say of them, "my friends importuned me to print them, I importune my friends to receive them printed." See R. C. Bald, "Dr. Donne and the Booksellers," *Studies in Bibliography: Papers of the Bibliographical Society of the University of Virginia*, XVIII (1965), 79-80.

15. For meditative style as a type of seventeenth-century prose, see, in particular, the following essays by Morris Croll: "Attic Prose: Lipsius, Montaigne, and Bacon," and "Attic Prose in the Seventeenth Century," in *Style, Rhetoric, and Rhythm: Essays by Morris W. Croll*, ed. J. Max Patrick and others (Princeton, 1966).

16. Among the many works discussing Puritan autobiography, the best, I think, remains Haller's *Rise of Puritanism*. Useful bibliographical material is contained in William York Tindall, *John Bunyan, Mechanick Preacher* (New York, 1934); G. A. Starr, *Defoe and Spiritual Autobiography* (Princeton, 1965); Margaret Bottrall, *Every Man a Phoenix: Studies in Seventeenth-Century Autobiography* (London, 1958). For a how-to-do-it book on Puritan autobiography, see John Beadle, *The Journal or diary of a thankful Christian* (London, 1656). Beadle's work is especially interesting because he not only gives directions how to write autobiography; he also defends its unique value as a genre.

CHAPTER II. DONNE AND BUNYAN: THE STYLES
OF TWO FAITHS

1. I. A. Shapiro, "Walton and the Occasion of Donne's *Devotions*," *Review of English Studies*, N.S., IX (1958), 18-22.

2. Edward LeComte, *Grace to a Witty Sinner* (New York, 1965), p. 190.

3. See Mrs. Bunyan's testimony in "A Relation of the Imprisonment of Mr. John Bunyan," in John Bunyan, *Grace Abounding to the Chief of Sinners,* ed. Roger Sharrock (Oxford, 1962), pp. 127–28.

4. Henri Talon, *John Bunyan: The Man and His Works,* English translation (London, 1951), p. 74.

5. It has been remarked that Bunyan's conversion experience falls into a standard Puritan pattern. William York Tindall asserts that "the details of Bunyan's conversion could be supplied by a diligent anthologist from the autobiographies of other preachers" (*John Bunyan, Mechanick Preacher,* New York, 1934, pp. 33–34). While Tindall's book has been much attacked, and this observation is surely exaggerated, Bunyan did want his conversion to conform to the rules. He had to have certain experiences in order to achieve approval among his co-religionists; the harder the conversion, the greater the assurance of God's favor. Donne in his own time was thought too fancy, a preacher of the wisdom of words rather than the Word of wisdom (an attack levelled at all the "witty" preachers), and in subsequent generations has been thought too melodramatic as well, too mindful of the effects he might be achieving, exploiting his own illness in order to create an interesting pose. (See, for example, on Donne's sermon "I," William R. Mueller, *John Donne: Preacher,* Princeton, 1962, pp. 248–50.) If Bunyan was too imitative, Donne was too mannered: in both cases, such criticism really implies, there is a lack of spontaneity, a striving for effect at the expense of truth to experience.

6. For discussion of how-to books on the art of self-knowledge, see Paul A. Jorgenson, *Lear's Self-Discovery* (Berkeley and Los Angeles, 1967).

7. Isaiah 38.

8. See *Peake's Commentary on the Bible,* ed. Matthew Black (London, 1962), p. 515.

9. R. C. Bald, "Dr. Donne and the Booksellers," *Studies in Bibliography: Papers of the Bibliographical Society of the University of Virginia,* XVIII (1965), 79–80. Quoted by permission of the publisher.

10. Izaak Walton, *The Lives of John Donne, Sir Henry Wotton, Richard Hooker, George Herbert, and Robert Sanderson* (London, World's Classics, 1956), p. 78.

11. *Ibid.,* p. 74, citing in full a letter from Donne.

12. See Sharrock, p. xxxvi. Sharrock does point out that the Great Fire destroyed a number of copies, and adds that early editions of Bunyan are generally extremely rare; they were all read to pieces.

13. On this, see J. Paul Hunter, *The Reluctant Pilgrim: Defoe's Emblematic Method and Quest for Form in Robinson Crusoe* (Baltimore, 1966). Mr. Hunter calls the Puritan method emblematic, but I believe that his distinction between Puritan and Anglican technique is somewhat analogous to mine.

14. Substantiation of this is everywhere apparent in the literature. For modern commentators on the Puritan pilgrim, see William Haller, *The Rise*

of Puritanism (New York, 1938), and Hunter, *The Reluctant Pilgrim;* for Puritan pilgrim and Anglican microcosm, see Michael Walzer, *The Revolution of the Saints: A Study in the Origins of Radical Politics* (Cambridge, Mass., 1965).

15. Bunyan does not always use this device for this purpose. The "as I thought" can be simply a distancing device, for separating the Bunyan who thought this way from interpreter-Bunyan. But in any event the distancing involves a detachment that allows for the possibility of errors on the part of Bunyan-in-process.

16. There was, from the thirteenth century, civil relief for defamation in local courts, and later in ecclesiastical courts, but slander was not a criminal offense until 1609, when the first criminal case was tried. See William F. Walsh, *Outlines of the History of English and American Law* (New York, 1926), pp. 399–400. See also W. S. Holdsworth, *A History of English Law*, 7 vols., VI (Boston, 1927). Holdsworth points out that the relaxation of censorship under Parliamentary government made much more important the establishment and development of libel laws (p. 377).

    Sir Francis Bacon speaks at length of the evils of scurrility, commenting as follows on the relative efficacy of Puritan and Anglican name-calling: "Nevertheless, I note, there is not an indifferent hand carried towards these pamphlets as they deserve; for the one sort flieth in the dark, and the other is uttered openly . . ." (*The Works of Francis Bacon, Lord Chancellor of England,* ed. Basil Montague, 3 vols., Philadelphia, 1884, II, 413). Walsh, *Outlines of the History of English and American Law,* points out that, according to precedent in Roman law linking defamation of character with breach of peace, truth of the libel was no defense for the speaker/writer, since his remarks in any case could be said to create a breach of the peace (p. 400). An anti-establishment "libeller" would of course be in every way more vulnerable to such a charge than a member of the party in power.

17. In his sermons, Donne repeatedly comments on the fact that "that language in which God hath spoken in his written word, the Hebrew, [has] the least consideration of Time of any other language" (*The Sermons of John Donne,* ed. George R. Potter and Evelyn Simpson, 10 vols., Berkeley, 1953–61, IX, 335–36). See also *Sermons,* VIII, 76–77, and 144–45.

18. Directly influenced by St. Augustine, this passage reminds us of Augustine's influence upon Donne's consideration of time. See St. Augustine's *Confessions,* Book XI.

19. For a full analysis of the rhetorical evidence for this conclusion, see my *Contrary Music: The Prose Style of John Donne* (Madison, 1963), Ch. VII.

20.   . . . Spirante *columba*
             Suppositâ pedibus, revocantur ad ima *vapores* . . .

    In this case, he is clearer about the treatment in the poem than he is in the meditation, although the added clarity does not inspire greater confidence in seventeenth-century medicine.

21. *Contrary Music*, Ch. VII.

22. For total contrast with Donne in this particular detail, see *The Journal of George Fox*, rev. John L. Nickalls (Cambridge, 1952). Fox hears voices commanding him to do things whose purpose he does not even understand —for example, to walk barefoot in the snow to the town at hand (whose name he does not know) and cry through the streets "Woe to the bloody city of Litchfield." After obeying, he devises an explanation having to do with ancient persecution of Christians in Litchfield. The founder of the Quakers, he represents an extreme openness to visions and voices (direct communication with God), compared to which Bunyan's experiences seem almost ordinary.

23. See my *Contrary Music*, Ch. V.

24. On the literary mysteries and delights of the Bible as seen by Renaissance commentators, see Israel Barroway, "The Bible as Poetry in the English Renaissance," *Journal of English and Germanic Philology*, XXXIII (1933), 447–80.

25. For sources in Puritan homily of many of Bunyan's techniques, see Haller, *The Rise of Puritanism*, and Kathrine Koller, "The Puritan Preacher's Contribution to Fiction," *Huntington Library Quarterly*, XI (August 1948), 321–40.

CHAPTER III. JOHN LILBURNE
THE EYE OF A POLITICAL RADICAL

1. J. Milton French, *The Life Records of John Milton*, 5 vols. (New Brunswick, 1949–58), V, 144. As Mr. French says, the portrait was reproduced in the *Burlington Magazine for Connoisseurs*, LXXXIV (1944), facing p. 151, "as a picture of John Lilburne or possibly of John Milton." He himself thought it "sufficiently different from the other known pictures of the poet to be difficult to accept as genuinely of Milton." Elizabeth Meyer, Secretary of the Department of Paintings of the Museum, says that the Museum accepts it as a painting of Milton. But it is apparent from the discussion in the *Burlington Magazine* that the Museum was interested primarily in identifying the painter, rather than the subject. The painting is now on extended loan to Fairleigh Dickinson University in Rutherford, New Jersey.

2. On Lilburne's fine eyes, however, I have only hearsay evidence. In *The Great Rebellion, The King's Peace: 1637–1641* (London, 1955), p. 206, C. V. Wedgwood speaks of his "neat unimpressive features, distinguished by fine eyes," but her usual careful documentation is missing. Lilburne was accidentally run through the eye with a pike while walking in Moorfields in 1645, but he also mentions being afflicted with blindness some years earlier. See Pauline Gregg, *Free-born John: A Biography of John Lilburne* (London, 1961), p. 116. Milton speaks of his own eyes in 1654, when he was wholly blind, as clear, bright, and unclouded. See

Second Defence of the English People (1654), in *Complete Prose Works of John Milton,* ed. Don M. Wolfe and others, 4 vols. to date (New Haven, 1953–), IV:1, 583.

3. William Haller, *The Rise of Puritanism* (New York, 1938), p. 287.
4. John Lilburne, *Innocency and Truth Justified* (n.p., 1645), p. 8.
5. Milton, *Prose Works,* I, 821.
6. G. P. Gooch, *English Democratic Ideas in the Seventeenth Century,* 2nd ed. (Cambridge, England, 1954), p. 124; Don M. Wolfe, *Milton in the Puritan Revolution* (New York, 1941), p. 261. See also Gregg, *Free-born John,* and M. A. Gibb, *John Lilburne the Leveller, passim.*
7. Samuel R. Gardiner, *History of the Great Civil War, 1642–1649,* New Impression, 4 vols. (London, 1911), III, 245, quoting "Letter of Intelligence," April 26 [1647], Clarendon MSS, II, 502: "The whole army it seemed—to use the words of a report which had just been made from Saffron Walden—was 'one Lilburne throughout, and more likely to give than to receive laws.' "
8. William Prynne, *Lyar Confounded,* "To the Impartial Reader," quoted in William Haller, *Liberty and Reformation in the Puritan Revolution* (New York, Columbia paperback, 1963), p. 263.
9. *The Just Defence of John Lilburne* (1653), in William Haller and Godfrey Davies, eds., *The Leveller Tracts 1647–1653* (New York, 1944), p. 455.
10. *Ibid.,* p. 453.
11. See, for example, Joseph Frank's excellent book, *The Levellers* (Cambridge, Mass., 1955), p. 256. Note in contrast the only really affirmative critical view, that of William Haller, who compares Lilburne's prose favorably to Bunyan's, in *The Rise of Puritanism* (New York, 1938), pp. 283–84.
12. See Erich Auerbach, "Figura," in *Scenes from the Drama of European Literature,* trans. Ralph Manheim (New York, Meridian Books, 1959), and *Mimesis: The Representation of Reality in Western Literature,* trans. Willard R. Trask (Princeton, 1953), pp. 73–76, 156–62, 194–202, and *passim.* As I understand it, the figural interpretation requires the linking of two figures, the later of whom (or which) explains or fulfills the first, as so much of the Old Testament was said to typify and be explained by the New. The second figure may be the same one as the first (as Dante's Beatrice in her two different existences), or a different one (as Adam and Christ). In this way, Milton, I think, looks forward to his transformation into ideal poet in the ideal state. Lilburne can be called figural only in the much looser sense in which the age in which he lived was thought to be a fulfillment of prophecy, or Biblical type, and in his utter dependence on real life for his existence as symbol.
13. On this difference between the Levellers and other Puritan sects, see Haller and Davies, eds., *The Leveller Tracts,* p. 40.
14. *The Picture of the Councel of State* (1649), in Haller and Davies, eds., *Leveller Tracts,* p. 212; *The Oppressed Mans Oppressions declared* (n.p.,

1648), p. 26; *As You Were* (Vianon, 1652), p. 32; *Legall Fundamentall Liberties* (London, 1649), pp. 19–20.

15. The person addressed in this letter is not identified, but the tone and content, unique in Lilburne's repertoire, are such as to make it seem highly probable that his wife-to-be was the recipient. See *Letter to a Friend* (1638), appended to *Innocency and Truth Justified*.

16. These are included in *The Resurrection of John Lilburne*, 2nd ed. (London, 1656).

17. Lilburne, *Londons Liberty in Chains discovered* (London, 1646), pp. 26–27.

18. *An Alarum to the House of Lords*, published anonymously (n.p., 1646), p. 9.

19. *Resurrection of John Lilburne*, pp. 2–3.

20. *A Worke of the Beast* (London, 1638), p. 30.

21. *Innocency and Truth Justified*, p. 11; pp. 24–25; pp. 26–27.

22. For more studied "artless art" and for the traditions of the plain style, see Wesley Trimpi, *Ben Jonson's Poems: A Study of the Plain Style* (Stanford, 1962).

23. See, for example, Gregg, *Free-born John*, pp. 325 and 356–58.

24. *Truths Victory over Tyrants and Tyranny*, quoted in Gregg, *Free-born John*, p. 295.

25. *The Marprelate Tracts*, ed. William Pierce (London, 1911), p. 17. For discussion of the importance of Martin's announcement, see John S. Coolidge, "Martin Marprelate, Marvell, and *Decorum Personae* as a Satirical Theme," *PMLA*, LXXIV (December 1959), pp. 526–32.

26. *An Impeachment of High Treason against Oliver Cromwell* (London, 1649), p. 24.

27. Thomas Kranidas, *The Fierce Equation* (The Hague, 1965), pp. 50–104.

28. *As You Were*, pp. 15–16.

29. Quaker practices are comparable—addressing all men as "thee," refusing to remove hats, the levelling "steeple-house" language. And Lilburne was eventually to become a Quaker (see last pages of this chapter). See *The Journal of George Fox*, rev. John L. Nickalls (Cambridge, 1952).

30. *Triall of Lieut. Collonell John Lilburne* (Southwark, 1649), p. 120.

31. *The Oppressed Mans Oppressions declared*, p. 9.

32. A.L. Morton, "The Place of Lilburne, Overton, and Walwyn in the Tradition of English Prose," *Zeitschrift für Anglistik und Amerikanistik*, VI (1958), p. 8.

33. *Letter to a Friend*, p. 19. See also *Londons Liberty in Chains discovered*, p. 58; *Come Out of Her My People* (n.p., 1639), p. 6.

34. *Come Out of Her My People*, p. 6.

35. *As You Were*, p. 33.

36. *As You Were*, p. 5.

37. *Mercurius Pragmaticus*, January 18–25, 1648, quoted in Gregg, *Free-born John*, p. 236.

38. It is estimated that the normal impression of a pamphlet was 1500 copies,

though in the case of very popular tracts it could go as high as 10,000. It is further estimated that each copy had ten readers. A normal pamphlet then could be expected to have 15,000 readers, and it was very much worth Lilburne's while to be prolific. See Frank, *The Levellers*, pp. 94–95.

39. For what Lilburne learned—and a good deal more—see J. G. A. Pocock, *The Ancient Constitution and the Feudal Law; A Study of English Historical Thought in the Seventeenth Century* (Cambridge, England, 1957).

40. *The Lawes Funerall* (n.p., 1648), p. 8.

41. *The Clarke Papers*. Selections from the Papers of William Clark, Secretary to the Council of the Army, 1647–1649, 4 vols. (Westminster, 1891–1901), ed. C. H. Firth, for the Camden Society, I, 22–23. This aim is listed in a paper called "Advertisements for the Managing of the Councells of the Army," which includes several other suggested types of propaganda.

42. Gregg, *Free-born John*, p. 229.

43. *Londons Liberty in Chains discovered*, p. 35.

44. *Come Out of Her My People*, p. 34.

45. *Oppressed Mans Oppressions declared*, p. 15.

46. *Come Out of Her My People*, p. 34.

47. *"To the Honourable the Judges of the King's Bench*. The Humble Petition of Lieut. Col. *Iohn Lilburne* Prisoner in the Tower of *London*," appended to *The Prisoners Plea for a Habeas Corpus* (n.p., 1648), B1.

48. *Come Out of Her My People*, pp. 26–27.

49. Milton, *Prose Works*, I, 663.

50. For comments on both Renaissance specialization and primitive concepts of language, see Marshall McLuhan, *The Gutenberg Galaxy* (Toronto, 1962). For primitive language as weapon, see also Robert C. Elliott, *The Power of Satire: Magic, Ritual, Art* (Princeton, 1960).

51. On the importance of Foxe in the age, see William Haller, *The Elect Nation: The Meaning and Relevance of Foxe's Book of Martyrs* (New York, 1963).

52. See Leslie Hotson, *The Commonwealth and Restoration Stage* (Cambridge, Mass., 1928). Ch. I, "Players and Parliament," makes very clear that the "equation between stage players and 'state mountebanks' " was commonplace. The following is a quotation from Hotson, with interpolations from a contemporary pamphlet quoted on the same page: "The proceedings of the Commons are a series of amusing mistakes [*Comedy of Errors*]; the army men, on the other hand, are grimly determined to bring the King to trial" ["their first show should be a King and no King, personated to the life, but wholy Tragicall"], p. 29.

53. Haller, *Rise of Puritanism*, p. 254.

54. *Ibid.*, p. 258.

55. *Impeachment of High Treason against Oliver Cromwell*, p. 2.

56. *Triall of Lieut. Collonell John Lilburne*, pp. 44, 47.

57. *Ibid.*, p. 119.

58. *Lawes Funerall*, p. 3.

59. *Triall of Lieut. Collonell John Lilburne*, p. 120.
60. *Ibid.*, p. 141.
61. *Worke of the Beast*, p. 11.
62. *Ibid.*, p. 20.
63. *Ibid.*, pp. 20 and 23.
64. On this point, see Haller, *Rise of Puritanism*, pp. 283–84.
65. *Worke of the Beast*, p. 30.
66. *Worke of the Beast, Come Out of Her My People.*
67. For example, *Legall Fundamentall Liberties*, "Printed in the grand yeer of hypocriticall and abominable dissimulation. 1649."
68. *Legall Fundamentall Liberties*, pp. 22 and 24–25.
69. If Lilburne's imprisonment kept him from telling the printer to make this addition (which is possible, but not inevitable, given his resources), then we may be able to blame the declaration's irrelevance on the printer. The inclusion of odd documents, however, is entirely in Lilburne's spirit, and it is also true that he did not like to leave pages blank.
70. *Oppressed Mans Oppressions declared*, p. 13.
71. For figures on pamphlet circulation, see note 38.
72. *Londons Liberty in Chains discovered*, p. 72.
73. *Ibid.*, p. 57.
74. The places where one must criticize the tracts as literature are the places where they are too lacking in design, too full of the clutteredness of life, or where Lilburne expects us to know things that in the twentieth century we cannot be expected to know. These defects have been amply described by Joseph Frank, whose negative assessment of Lilburne's prose is accurate enough from his point of view. There is nothing to be gained, at any rate, from pushing very hard in the other direction. Lilburne's is a very limited, very minor sort of art, made remarkable only because he is remarkable, because he is the "I" of his prose, and because he forces us to encounter him in it. The best short critique of his prose is, I think, Morton's in "The Place of Lilburne, Overton, and Walwyn in the Tradition of English Prose." Morton very sensitively describes both its shortcomings and its strengths.
75. *Resurrection of John Lilburne*, pp. 5 and 14.

CHAPTER IV. ROBERT BURTON:
THE ANATOMY OF DEMOCRITUS, JR.

1. I speak here of the sixth edition, the last which Burton prepared for the press, and the one which is ordinarily cited. The first edition, in quarto and smaller by more than half, is a much less impressive affair. See Bibliographical Appendix for a discussion of Burton texts.
2. "Known to few, unknown to fewer, here lies Democritus Junior, to whom Melancholy gave life and death." The epitaph is cited by Douglas

Bush in *English Literature in the Earlier Seventeenth Century*, 2nd ed. (Oxford, 1962), p. 295, n. 1.

3. *Ibid.*

4. Jean Simon, *Robert Burton (1577–1640) et L'Anatomie de la Mélancolie* (Paris, 1964), p. 26. See also William R. Mueller, *The Anatomy of Robert Burton's England* (Berkeley, 1952), and Laurence Babb, *Sanity in Bedlam* (East Lansing, 1959).

5. See Marshall McLuhan, *The Gutenberg Galaxy* (Toronto, 1962), and Walter J. Ong, "Oral Residue in Tudor Prose Style," *PMLA*, LXXX (June 1965), 145–54.

6. See, for example, Ben Jonson's admiring description of Selden as one who, without leaving home, has learned to know all times and places. "An Epistle to Master John Selden," in *The Complete Poetry of Ben Jonson*, ed. William B. Hunter, Jr. (New York, Anchor Books, 1963).

7. John Donne, writing to Sir Henry Goodere, in *Letters to Severall Persons of Honour*, ed. Charles Edmund Merrill, Jr. (New York, 1910).

8. Entry for May 31, 1669, *The Diary of Samuel Pepys*, transcribed by the Rev. Mynors Bright, ed. with additions by Henry B. Wheatley, 2 vols. (New York, 1946), II, 1086.

9. Bergen Evans, in consultation with George J. Mohr, M.D., *The Psychiatry of Robert Burton* (New York, 1944), Ch. I, "The Man," pp. 1–24. He presents a very little supplementary evidence. Jean Simon also attempts this, in his chapter, "La Personnalité de Burton," in *Robert Burton et L'Anatomie de la Mélancolie*.

10. See Rosalie Colie, *Paradoxia Epidemica: The Renaissance Tradition of Paradox* (Princeton, 1966), Ch. XIV.

11. For very similar comments by a writer whom Burton could have had in mind, see the following passages in Thomas Nashe, who quotes a phrase from Martial that Burton uses here "(*quicquid in baccam venit*)" and praises the "extemporall" style throughout his works: "Pierce Penilesse His Supplication to the Divell," in Ronald B. McKerrow, ed., *The Works of Thomas Nashe*, 5 vols. (Oxford, 1958), I, 195.17; and 199.4.

12. Burton did undertake considerable stylistic revision in the course of bringing out these editions. Donovan gives the best account of it in his introduction to "Robert Burton's *The Anatomy of Melancholy*: 'Religious Melancholy' A Critical Edition" (Unpublished Ph.D. dissertation, Urbana, 1965). A fuller but more limited study is Robert G. Hallwachs, "Additions and Revisions in the Second Edition of Burton's *Anatomy of Melancholy*: A Study of Burton's Chief Interests and of His Style as Shown in His Revisions" (Unpublished Ph.D. dissertation, Princeton University, 1942). The revisions which they discuss are for the most part (aside from the extensive additions, of course) minor alterations intended to polish phrases, improve sentence structure, and clarify ideas. They prove that Burton was concerned with his style, but they do not really affect the over-all air of dishevelment, which is of course intentional.

13. Here one ought to be aware of Montaigne, who is obviously Burton's

model. See *The Essayes of Montaigne,* trans. John Florio, intro. J. I. M. Stewart (New York, 1933), Bk. III, Ch. IX, p. 871: "May it please the gentle reader, to suffer this one part of Essay to run on, and this third straine or addition of the rest of my pictures peeces. I adde, but I correct not: First, because he who hath hypothekised or engaged his labour to the world, I finde apparence, that he hath no longer right in the same: let him, if he bee able, speake better els where, and not corrupt the worke he hath already made sale off; Of such people, a man should buy nothing, but after they are dead: let them throughly thinke on it, before they produce the same. Who hastens them? My book is alwaies one: except that according as the Printer goes about to renew it, that the buyers depart not altogether empty-handed; I give my selfe law to adde thereto (as it is but uncoherent checky, or ill joined in-laide worke) some supernumerall embleme. They are but over-waights, which disgrace not the first forme, but give some particular price unto every one of the succeeding, by an ambitious pety subtility. Whence notwithstanding, it may easily happen, that some transposition of chronology is thereto commixt: my reports taking place according to their opportunity, and not ever according to their age. Secondly, forsomuch as in regard of my selfe, I feare to loose by the exchange: My understanding doth not alwaies goe forward, it sometimes goes also backeward: I in a manner distrust mine owne fantasies as much, though second or third, as I doe when they are the first, or present, as past. *We many times correct our selves as foolishly, as we taxe others unadvisedly.* I am growne aged by a number of yeares since my first publications, which were in a thousand five hundred and foure score. But I doubt whether I be encreased one inch in wisdome. My selfe now, and my selfe anon, are indeede two; but when better, in good sooth I cannot tell. *It were a goodly thing to bee old, if wee did onely march towards amendment.* It is the motion of a drunkard, stumbling, reeling, giddie-brain'd, formeles, or of reedes, which the ayre dooth casually wave to and fro, which way it bloweth."

14. Dom Jean Leclerq, *The Love of Learning and the Desire for God,* trans. Catherine Misrahi (New York, 1961), pp. 89–90. This is quoted by McLuhan, *Gutenberg Galaxy,* pp. 89–90. Bernard of Clairvaux's homilies on the Song of Songs had provided the Middle Ages with both the figure of indigestion arising from overintellectualism and the figure of spiritual assimilation of Christian truth as physical digestion: *Sermones in Cantica,* in *Patrologia Latina,* ed. J. P. Migne, CLXXXIII (Paris, 1854), Sermon XXVI, ii, and Sermon XXXVII, iv. For further comments, see my *Contrary Music: The Prose Style of John Donne* (Madison, 1963), pp. 85-86.

15. For a helpful chapter on Burton's sources, use of his sources, and methods of translation, see Simon, *Robert Burton et L'Anatomie de la Mélancolie.*

16. The sources for these quotations are the Book of Common Prayer (1 and 2), Catullus (3), and Vergil's *Aeneid* (4 and 5).

17. See, for example, Hardin Craig, *The Enchanted Glass* (New York, 1936), p. 244.

18. The "fictionalizing" of what would normally be scientific data is carried on in all sorts of ways. For example, because many of the phrases listed on p. 85 of this chapter are emotionally loaded, their use makes the giving of data equivalent to an insistence on the veracity of tales. In this respect, too, note his treatment of hypothesis as fiction in Pt. II.2.3: Tycho and other scientists have hypotheses; hypotheses "be but inventions, as most of them acknowledge"; hence, "Tycho hath feigned I know not how many subdivisions of epicycles in epicycles . . . ."

19. Burton justifies himself at some length in the preface to the section on love-melancholy: an old discreet man is fittest to discourse of love; love is a species of melancholy; many worthy men have provided precedents; it will provide some relief in this harsh treatise, and will both profit and please; I have yielded to numerous requests in this matter.

20. On mating palm trees, see Robert E. Hallowell, "The Mating Palm Trees in DuBartas' 'Seconde Sepmaine,'" *Renaissance News*, XVII (Summer 1964), 89–95.

21. See J. Max Patrick, "Robert Burton's Utopianism," *Philological Quarterly*, XXVII (October 1948), 345–58. While claiming that this Utopia is a "significant social document," Mr. Patrick also points out that Burton is rather vague about the means by which it might be put into effect.

22. Directions for writing sermons are given in numerous manuals, among which are Richard Bernard, *The Faithfull Shepheard* (London, 1607), and Bartholomew Keckermann, *Rhetoricae Ecclesiasticae Sive Artis Formandi et Habendi Conciones Sacras*, 3rd ed. (Hanau, 1606). It is sometimes difficult to remember that Burton was an Anglican divine, but he was, and the *Anatomy* is his homily.

23. George Williamson, *The Senecan Amble* (Chicago, 1951); Morris Croll, *Style, Rhetoric, and Rhythm: Essays by Morris W. Croll*, ed. J. Max Patrick and others (Princeton, 1966).

24. Leonard Goldstein, "Science and Literary Style in Robert Burton's 'Cento out of Divers Writers,'" *Journal of the Rutgers University Library*, XXI (June 1958), 55–68.

25. William Mueller singles out for special mention a satiric, a lyrical, and a scientific style, in his *Anatomy of Robert Burton's England*, pp. 27–30. See also Jean Simon's sensitive analysis of Burton's style in *Robert Burton et L'Anatomie de la Mélancolie*.

26. For discussion of the frontispiece, see William R. Mueller, "Robert Burton's Frontispiece," *PMLA*, LXIV (December 1949), 1074–88; and Ellen Hurt, "The Prose Style of Robert Burton: The Fruits of Knowledge" (Unpublished Ph.D. dissertation, University of Oregon, 1964), pp. 246–48.

27. Jean Simon devotes a chapter to Burton's wit, in his *Robert Burton et L'Anatomie de la Mélancolie*.

28. Because the Everyman punctuation of this passage is misleading, I have corrected the punctuation (making no other changes) by reference to the sixth edition of the *Anatomy*.

29. John Milton, *Of Education* (1644), *Complete Prose Works of John Milton*, ed. Don M. Wolfe and others, 4 vols. to date (New Haven, 1953–   ), II, 366–67. See also Sidney's *Defense of Poesie*, for the fullest exposition of the view that this is the task of literature.

30. Leo Spitzer has called this theme central to metaphysical wit. See Leo Spitzer, "Marvell's 'Nymph Complaining for the Death of Her Fawn': Sources Versus Meaning," *Modern Language Quarterly*, XIX (September 1958), 237–40.

31. As such, the figure is very common in the age. For one of countless illustrations, see John Donne, *The Sermons of John Donne*, 10 vols., ed. George R. Potter and Evelyn Simpson (Berkeley, 1953–61), VI, No. 10, ll.169 ff. I cite this particular example because it is lengthy and acknowledges the debt to Chrysostom. Burton also quotes Chrysostom's transformation passages in the *Anatomy*, Pt. III.4.2.6. I have not yet found in Chrysostom the passages which Donne and Burton quote. I have seen many analogous ones, however. See the several series of homilies in *A Select Library of the Nicene and Post-Nicene Fathers of the Christian Church*, ed. Philip Schaff, 14 vols. (New York, 1907–17), Vols. IX–XIV. Examples of beast-transformation passages are in Volume XIV, pages 20 and 130.

32. Donne, *Sermons*, IV, No. 13, ll.102–12.

33. *The Essayes of Montaigne*, trans. John Florio, Bk. III, Ch. IX, p. 871.

34. Sir Thomas Browne, *Religio Medici*, in *The Works of Sir Thomas Browne*, ed. Geoffrey Keynes, 4 vols. (Chicago, 1964), I, Pt. I, Section 6.

35. E. M. Forster, *Abinger Harvest* (New York, 1936), p. 190. This is quoted by McLuhan, *Gutenberg Galaxy*, p. 203.

CHAPTER V. RICHARD BAXTER: THE EYE OF THE HURRICANE

1. After inventing this figure, as I thought, I discovered that I must have had at the back of my mind a paragraph in J. M. Lloyd Thomas's introduction to his abridged edition, *The Autobiography of Richard Baxter being The Reliquiae Baxterianae, Abridged from the folio (1696)* (London, Everyman, 1931), p. viii: "Throughout his extraordinary career, all the dramatic issues of that turbulent era are seen energetically alive and struggling for mastery. To understand him in the range and subtlety of his rich and powerful mind, were to understand also the political and religious forces that incessantly clashed in fateful conflict all around him. For many of these he was himself the storm-centre. He stood within the tempest on a lonely eminence and looked out into the far future in all directions."

2. Several critics have pointed out this odd qualification to Puritan individualism, associating it often with Calvin, and thus with Presbyterianism in particular, which would account for its particular importance in Bax-

ter. See, for example, Michael Walzer, *The Revolution of the Saints: A Study in the Origins of Radical Politics* (Cambridge, Mass., 1960), Ch. II.

3. Baxter is said to have referred to himself thus on his deathbed. See William Orme, *The Life and Times of the Rev. Richard Baxter with a Critical Examination of His Writings*, 2 vols. (Boston, 1831), I, 353, quoting from Dr. William Bates' funeral sermon on Baxter.

4. Roger L'Estrange, *The Casuist Uncased*, 2nd ed. (London, 1680).

5. Bishop Wilkins is quoted by the editors of *The Practical Works of the Late Reverend and Pious Mr. Richard Baxter, in Four Volumes* (London, 1707), I, iii.

6. Florence Higham, *Faith of Our Fathers* (London, 1939), p. 91. This information is not documented.

7. The relevant clause in Baxter's will reads thus: "All my MSS to the said Mr. Matthew Silvester, but he only to print them with the approval of Mr. Lorrimer, Mr. Doelittle, Mr. Morris, or Mr. Williams." The will is reprinted in *Transactions of the Shropshire Archeological Society*, 4th Series, IX (1923–24), 145.

8. Geoffrey F. Nuttall, *Richard Baxter* (London, 1965), pp. 129–30, and 132–36 (a list of titles). See also Orme, *Life and Times of the Rev. Richard Baxter*, II, 327: "The best method of forming a correct opinion of Baxter's labors from the press, is by comparing them with some of his brethren, who wrote a great deal. The works of Bishop Hall amount to ten volumes octavo; Lightfoot's extend to thirteen; Jeremy Taylor's to fifteen; Dr. Goodwin's would make about twenty; Dr. Owen's extend to twenty-eight; Richard Baxter's, if printed in a uniform edition, could not be comprised in less than sixty volumes, making more than from thirty to forty thousand closely-printed octavo pages!"

9. *Practical Works*, III, vi.

10. See Frederick J. Powicke, *A Life of the Reverend Richard Baxter 1615–1691* (Boston and New York, 1924), pp. 92–94; also p. 52.

11. *Ibid.*, p. 128.

12. The funeral sermon, "Elisha's Cry after Elijah's GOD," p. 14. The sermon takes up the final pages of the 1696 edition of the *Reliquiae.*

13. These comments are to be found in the prefaces to the *Practical Works*, and in the *Reliquiae Baxterianae*. The history of the plain style is relevant to this discussion, for which see Wesley Trimpi, *Ben Jonson's Poems: A Study of the Plain Style* (Stanford, 1962); the footnotes contain extensive references to primary and secondary sources. Among these, see in particular R. F. Jones, "The Moral Sense of Simplicity," in *Studies in Honor of Frederick W. Shipley* (St. Louis, 1942), pp. 265–87.

14. See Thomas Sprat, *History of the Royal Society*, ed. Jackson I. Cope and Harold Whitmore Jones (St. Louis and London, 1959), p. 113.

15. *Practical Works*, III, 882.

16. For a contrast of this viewpoint with that of George Herbert in his poem "The Windows," see my article, "Celebration of Word and World in

Lancelot Andrewes' Style," *Journal of English and Germanic Philology,*
LXIV (April 1965), 255-56.

17. *Practical Works,* II, 964.
18. *Ibid.,* III, 98.
19. *Ibid.,* III, vi.
20. *Ibid.,* II, 792-93.
21. Leo Spitzer, "Marvell's 'Nymph Complaining for the Death of Her
    Fawn': Sources Versus Meaning," *Modern Language Quarterly,* XIX
    (September 1958), 237-40.
22. For a good typical example, see the autobiography of the Baptist merchant
    and minister William Kiffin (1616-1701), *Remarkable Passages in the
    Life of William Kiffin,* written by himself and edited from the original
    manuscript, with notes and additions, by William Orme (London, 1823).
23. See my *Contrary Music: The Prose Style of John Donne* (Madison,
    1963), Ch. III.
24. *Practical Works,* IV, 358.
25. See especially Chapter II, note 16, for more speculation on the causes of
    slander, and for references to the history of law.
26. Morgan, *The Nonconformity of Richard Baxter,* p. 67, mentions, for
    example, a bullet shot into his house in 1665.
27. Baxter's views are fully expressed in the *Reliquiae* and other works. See,
    for example, his biography of his wife, *Richard Baxter and Margaret
    Charlton; A Puritan Love-Story, Being the Breviate of the Life of Mar-
    garet Baxter,* by Richard Baxter, 1681, with introductory essay, notes,
    and appendices, by John T. Wilkinson (London, 1928), pp. 61-65. Here
    he speaks of the reasons for writing biography, connecting biography with
    history. John Beadle's contemporary how-to-do-it book on biography
    makes the same connection, *The Journal or diary of a thankful Christian*
    (London, 1656), Ch. V.
28. *Practical Works,* III, 882.
29. Orme, *Life and Times of the Rev. Richard Baxter,* I, 353, quoting from
    Dr. William Bates' funeral sermon on Baxter; these are said to have been
    among Baxter's last words.
30. R. James, in *A Medicinal Dictionary,* 3 vols. (London, 1743), gives illu-
    minating information on this disease, which was thought to originate in
    the hypochondria, or abdomen. "If we thoroughly consider its Nature, it
    will be found to be a spasmodico-flatulent Disorder of the *Primae Viae,*
    that is, of the Stomach and Intestines, arising from an Inversion or Per-
    version of their peristaltic Motion, and, by the mutual consent of the
    Parts, throwing the whole nervous System into irregular Motions, and
    disturbing the whole Oeconomy of the Functions . . . no Part or Func-
    tion of the Body escapes the Influence of this tedious and long protracted
    Disease, whose Symptoms are so violent and numerous, that it is no easy
    Task either to enumerate or account for them." Much of James's descrip-
    tion does suggest what we would call hypochondriac or psychosomatic

illness: "No disease is more troublesome, either to the Patient or Physician, than hypochondriac Disorders; and it often happens that, thro' the Fault of both, the Cure is either unnecessarily protracted, or totally frustrated; for the Patients are so delighted, not only with a Variety of Medicines, but also of Physicians . . . On the contrary, few physicians are sufficiently acquainted with the true Genius and Nature of this perplexing Disorder; for which Reason they boldly prescribe almost everything contained in the Shops, not without an irreparable Injury to the Patient." James lists among its causes grief and an uneasy mind, especially among the languid and sedentary.

CHAPTER VI. SIR THOMAS BROWNE: ART AS RECREATION

1. See Geoffrey Keynes, *Bibliography of Sir Thomas Browne* (Cambridge, England, 1924), pp. 187–208.

2. The list of his twentieth-century editors is remarkable evidence of his continued widespread popularity. The major editors of the *Religio Medici* include English Geoffrey Keynes (1928), French Jean-Jacques Denonain (1953), and Italian Vittoria Sanna (1958), whose text Keynes found so admirable that he reprinted it in his 1964 edition. As Browne himself claimed, he is truly cosmopolitan (*The Works of Sir Thomas Browne*, ed. Geoffrey Keynes, 4 vols., Chicago, 1964, Vol. I, *Religio Medici*, Pt. II. 1).

3. Sir Kenelm Digby, *Observations Upon Religio Medici*, 3rd ed., corrected and enlarged (London, 1659), pp. 33–34. Bound with fifth edition of *Religio Medici*.

4. *Lettres de Gui Patin*, Nouvelle Edition, ed. Paul Traire (Paris, 1907), I, 430.

5. Apparently he was claimed as a kindred spirit by men whose religions ranged all the way from Roman Catholic to Quaker. See Simon Wilkin, *Sir Thomas Browne's Works*, 4 vols. (London, 1836), I, lxiii.

6. *Aubrey's Brief Lives*, ed. Oliver Lawson Dick (London, 1958), p. xxviii.

7. Rosalie Colie points this out repeatedly in her *Paradoxia Epidemica: The Renaissance Tradition of Paradox* (Princeton, 1966), a work, incidentally, which takes all its chapter epigraphs from the *Religio Medici*.

8. Austin Warren, "The Style of Sir Thomas Browne," *Kenyon Review*, XIII (Autumn 1951), 678.

9. Vittoria Sanna, however, suggests that Browne may have compromised with Crooke rather than be harassed by the Puritan authorities for views expressed in the unauthorized edition. Some toning-down of his opinions does take place, but I think the evidence to support her suggestion is insufficient. See Vittoria Sanna, ed., *Religio Medici, Annali Delle Facoltà*

di Lettere-Filosofia e Magistero Dell'Università di Cagliari, XXVI (Cagliari, 1958), Parte II, p. lviii.

10. On Browne's revisions, see also Jean-Jacques Denonain, ed., *Religio Medici* (Cambridge, England, 1953).

11. To dramatize the artificiality of Browne's style and pose in works like the *Religio Medici*, other critics have usefully contrasted it with the style of his letters. See J. R. Sutherland, *On English Prose* (Toronto, 1957), pp. 29–30; and Austin Warren, "The Style of Sir Thomas Browne," *Kenyon Review*, XIII (Autumn 1951), 677–78.

12. Joan Bennett, *Sir Thomas Browne, a Man of Achievement in Literature* (Cambridge, England, 1962), pp. 7–8.

13. See Georges Poulet, *Studies in Human Time*, trans. Elliott Coleman (New York, Harper Torchbooks, 1959), pp. 14–15.

14. F. L. Huntley, *Sir Thomas Browne: A Biographical and Critical Study* (Ann Arbor, 1962), p. 106.

15. This fact was first called to my attention by John Fleischauer, who discovered that on the basis of its affirmative character he could assign to Part II a passage of the *Religio* taken out of context. John R. Mulder, "Literary Scepticism: Montaigne and Sir Thomas Browne" (unpublished Ph.D. dissertation, Michigan, 1963), makes extensive use of the contrast in his analysis.

16. See my article, "The Renewal of the King's Symbolic Role: From Richard II to Henry V," University of Texas *Studies in Literature and Language*, IV (Winter 1963), 530–38.

17. Herman Melville, *Moby-Dick or, The Whale*, ed. Luther Mansfield and Howard Vincent (New York, 1962), p. 162.

18. See Huntley, *Sir Thomas Browne*, Ch. IX, "Interlude: Browne's First Critic."

19. An interesting example—and one relevant to the Anglican persona—is the frontispiece to Thomas Hobbes' *Leviathan* (1651). Rising out of his countryside, the cosmic king is composed, from waist and wrists up to his neck, of his small subjects. Turned reverently toward him and away from the reader, they are a crowd of heads.

20. See Warren, "The Style of Sir Thomas Browne," and Huntley, *Sir Thomas Browne*, Ch. VIII, "*Religio Medici*: Substance and Form."

21. Huntington Brown, *Prose Styles, Five Primary Types* (Minneapolis, 1966), p. 79.

22. Browne, *Christian Morals* (Pt. II. 3), in *Works*, I, 260–61.

23. Warren, "The Style of Sir Thomas Browne," p. 686.

24. S. T. Coleridge, *Miscellaneous Criticism*, ed. Thomas Middleton Raysor (Cambridge, Mass., 1936), pp. 253 and 257: "I have never read a book in which I felt greater similarity to my own make of mind—active of inquiry, and yet with an appetite to believe—in short an affectionate visionary!" "This book paints certain parts of my moral and intellectual being (the best parts, no doubt), better than any other book I have ever met with;—and the style is throughout delicious."

25. Warren, "The Style of Sir Thomas Browne," p. 684.
26. John Huizinga, *Homo Ludens*, English edition, (London, 1949), Ch. I.

CHAPTER VII. JOHN MILTON: THE PROSE STYLE OF GOD'S ENGLISH POET

1. "Chronology of Milton's Prose Works," *Complete Prose Works of John Milton*, ed. Don M. Wolfe and others, 4 vols. to date (New Haven, 1953–   ), I, xv–xvi.
2. *Reason of Church-Government* (1642), *Prose Works*, I, 821.
3. See Rose Clavering and John T. Shawcross, "Milton's European Itinerary and His Return Home," *Studies in English Literature*, V (Winter 1965), 49–59. There has been considerable critical controversy on this subject because it has been thought that Milton claimed to have given up his tour even though he remained in Europe for more than five months after he received news of the troubles at home. Clavering and Shawcross convincingly argue that he claimed to have and did only *shorten* his stay, considering the completion of the professional part of his tour at least as essential as ever. There is a suggestion that several months after he received the political news, he did curtail his trip for personal reasons upon receiving news from his family.
4. Edward Phillips, *The Life of Mr. John Milton* (1694), in *The Early Lives of Milton*, ed. Helen Darbishire (London, 1932), p. 62.
5. Since this work is written in Latin, it is disqualified for admission to a study of English prose style. However, a study of it would probably not yield any results significant for this study that cannot be obtained through analysis of the English tracts.
6. Arthur Barker, *Milton and the Puritan Dilemma* (Toronto, 1942), pp. 16–18. See also Michael Fixler, *Milton and the Kingdoms of God* (Evanston, 1964), esp. 101 ff.
7. This story is well documented in William Haller's *The Elect Nation: The Meaning and Relevance of Foxe's Book of Martyrs* (New York, 1963). Here again, as with Lilburne, we may usefully employ Erich Auerbach's term "figura," a word which he uses to describe the result of connecting figures from two different parts of history (i.e., Moses and Christ), or from outside of history, or of connecting an historical figure with an ideal version of the same (Dante on Beatrice or Milton on himself as future bard). The historical figure remains very much in the "here and now," while at the same time endowed with some kind of allegorical, or patterning, universal significance. See Erich Auerbach, *Mimesis: The Representation of Reality in Western Literature*, trans. Willard R. Trask (Princeton, 1953), *passim*, and his essay, "Figura," in *Scenes from the Drama of Western Literature*, trans. Ralph Manheim (New York, Meridian Books, 1959).
8. *Areopagitica* (1644), *Prose Works*, II, 553.

9. The phrase is originally that of Keats, in discussing Wordsworth. See Letter from Keats to Richard Woodhouse, October 27, 1818, in Hyder Rollins, ed., *The Letters of John Keats, 1814–1821*, 2 vols. (Cambridge, Mass., 1958), I, 387.

10. Letter to Charles Diodati, 1637, *Prose Works*, I, 327.

11. Auerbach's term "figura" seems entirely appropriate here. See my note 7.

12. The cyclical interpretation of history that Milton had accepted is now abandoned, as new revelations enable history to be finally fulfilled.

13. In length, it is about one-seventh of the whole. It is characteristic of Milton to inject discussion of himself into works which are not intrinsically personal, as we have already seen in brief, and thereby to connect microcosm with macrocosm, his own vocation with that of England. These discussions are compartmentalized in such a way as to seem to some modern readers to be proof of Milton's egotism. We have justly been reminded that as classical oration *The Reason of Church-Government* legitimately uses self-defense as part of the ethical proof (John S. Diekhoff, "The Function of the Prologues in Paradise Lost," *PMLA*, LVII, 1942, 697–704; Merritt Y. Hughes, *Ten Perspectives on Milton*, New Haven, 1965, p. 248). This argument is a healthy defense against those who attack Milton's egotism. But to say with Merritt Hughes that the autobiographical passages would have struck Milton's contemporaries as "a rather casual . . . proof of sincerity" is surely going too far in the other direction. There is nothing casual about Milton, and if his readers thought there was, then they were as mistaken as the "egotist" critics of today. Furthermore, while Milton would not have denied his debts to the classics, he would not have leaned upon them either. Just as he refused to marshal classical support for the whole unsettling decorum of his prose, we do not need to seek classical source or precedent to explain the effects that he wished to create in *Church-Government*, in the *Apology Against a Pamphlet*, and in the *Second Defence of the English People*. His intention is not always the same. *Church-Government* is cool and measured discourse compared to *Apology*, and in epic scope *Second Defence* soars above both.

14. William Haller, *Liberty and Reformation in the Puritan Revolution* (New York, Columbia paperback, 1963), p. 50.

15. The question of Milton's Latinity is not going to be settled here. I should like merely to register my awareness that there are extreme differences of opinion on this subject, to provide some of the relevant bibliography, and to explain why I take the position I do. T. S. Eliot, in his controversial first essay on "Milton" (1936), reprinted in *On Poetry and Poets* (New York, 1957), restated for our time a belief that had been current long before, that "Milton writes English like a dead language" (p. 159). William Haller's gentler and much more admiring phrase, "not quite English," keeps the notion current among Milton's friends. Critics who wish to keep Milton English cite Harris Fletcher, *The Intellectual Development of John Milton*, 2 vols. (Urbana, 1956);

or E. M. W. Tillyard, *The Miltonic Setting, Past and Present* (London, 1949). Tillyard says that "far too much has been made of the supposed Latinization of Milton's style" (p. 122). But he goes on to say that the Latinizing (which does really exist) is part of the epic heightening of his poetry, and is chiefly manifest, in the poetry, in short phrases and suspended verbs. The main peculiarities, he says, are quite un-Latin. Ronald D. Emma, in *Milton's Grammar* (The Hague, 1964) takes samples of prose and poetry to find statistical proof that the grammar is not latinate. I think that his evidence is too limited to be conclusive, and that, in any case, as his reviewer in the *London Times Literary Supplement* (December 31, 1964, p. 1182) points out, regardless of the facts about some grammatical details, the style as a whole continues to give the effect of Latinate periodicity. And even Emma admits that Milton's style is not pure English idiom. In *Prose Works* IV:1, the most recent translators of Milton's Latin speak of the Latinity of his English, pp. 296 (Donald C. Mackenzie) and 545 (Helen North). Donald Mackenzie says, "Milton came as close as anyone could to writing Latin in English." I have tried to show in this chapter that the texture of Milton's prose has many aspects, and to some extent, and from another point of view, this conclusion would support Tillyard's. Milton's use of passives, for example, is based partly in his desire to express impersonality. He does, very often, have such immediate reasons for his choice of construction. But my findings show that the latinity is there and relevant. In view of my very severe limitations as a classicist, I am glad that I can cite the opinions of classical scholars. But it is obvious that the subject remains controversial and needs some undivided attention from scholars extremely well trained both in Latin and in English.

16. I can only support this generalization by reference to the traditions themselves, the texts (like Cicero's *De Oratore* and Quintilian's *Institutio Oratoria*) that describe them, and the critical studies that analyze them. Among these are, especially, *Style, Rhetoric, and Rhythm: Essays by Morris W. Croll*, ed. J. Max Patrick and others (Princeton, 1966); Izora Scott, *Controversies over Cicero* (New York, 1910); Wilbur S. Howell, *Logic and Rhetoric in England, 1500–1700* (Princeton, 1956); Ruth Wallerstein, *Studies in Seventeenth-Century Poetic* (Madison, 1950).

17. *Of Education* (1644), *Prose Works*, II, 366–67.

18. See, for example, Sir Thomas Elyot, *The boke named the governour*, "Proem"; and Sir Thomas More, *Utopia*, Pt. I. The diminishing public role of Renaissance humanism is well described in G. K. Hunter's *John Lyly: The Humanist as Courtier* (Cambridge, Mass., 1962).

19. Thomas Kranidas, *The Fierce Equation: A Study of Milton's Decorum* (The Hague, 1965). Kranidas cites and discusses Milton's most significant uses of the word. For an earlier expression of a relevant decorum, see *The Marprelate Tracts*, ed. William Pierce (London, 1911), p. 17. See also John S. Coolidge, "Martin Marprelate, Marvell, and *Decorum Personae* as a Satirical Theme," *PMLA*, LXXIV (December 1959), 526–32.

20. In an interview published in the *New York Times Book Review* XLIV (June 15, 1966), Pablo Neruda reminds us of a whole literary tradition in which political and topical references, and very specific name-calling, are completely acceptable, as they have seldom been in English. This is the tradition, after all, of Dante, who described in great detail the infernal abodes of many of his own contemporaries. Milton's defense of his practice is based both on Scripture language and on the Puritan preference for religious zeal over lukewarmness, but it is useful too to remember with Neruda that the need to defend his behavior might not even arise in a culture warmer, less temperate, and in some ways more congenial to Milton (witness his love of Italy) than our own.

    However, on this point, see also J. Milton French, "Milton as Satirist," *PMLA*, LI (1936), 414–29. Mr. French reminds us both of the astounding fertility of Milton's genius for epithets (adding up, with no pretense of completeness, an eleven-line list of invectives from *Of Reformation*) and of the off-color jokes in Milton's *Prolusions*. The example of the *Prolusions* is particularly instructive in reminding us of the relative propriety of such language in seventeeth-century England, since Milton surely would not have risked censure in these public academic exercises.

    Michael Walzer suggests another point of reference in *The Revolution of the Saints: A Study in the Origins of Radical Politics* (Cambridge, Mass., 1965), Ch. III, "Two Case Studies in Calvinist Politics: Huguenots and Marian Exiles." Reminding us that in 1649 Milton called Knox, Goodman, Whittingham, and Gilby "our fathers in the faith we hold," he also mentions the flood of invective that these exiles sent toward England in pamphlet form.

21. See James H. Hanford, "Milton and the Art of War," *Studies in Philology*, XVIII (1921), 232–66.

22. On this see Kranidas, *The Fierce Equation,* and Kester Svendsen, *Milton and Science* (Cambridge, Mass., 1956), pp. 186–87, and 191–92.

23. But it is important to remember that Milton does not claim these precedents. For him, it is important that the rhetoric should justify itself.

24. T. S. Eliot, *On Poetry and Poets*, p. 159. See also my note 15, in this chapter.

25. Epic conventions are of course relevant here, but they should not be made wholly to explain Milton's manner.

CHAPTER VIII. THOMAS TRAHERNE:
THE FOUNTAIN OF LOVE

1. I am most grateful to Mr. Osborn for making available to me his xerox copy of the manuscript, as well as the manuscript itself, and for allowing me to cite passages from it in this chapter.

2. See James M. Osborn, "A New Traherne Manuscript," *Times Literary Supplement*, October 8, 1964, p. 928, and Louis Martz, *The Paradise Within: Studies in Vaughan, Traherne, and Milton* (New Haven, 1964), pp. 207–11.

3. Thomas Traherne, "Select Meditations," (Unpublished manuscript), I. 85.

4. Carol Marks, whose publications are cited in my bibliographical appendix, says this repeatedly. So does K. W. Salter, *Thomas Traherne: Mystic and Poet* (London, 1964). And from Miss Marks this conclusion comes with special authority, because it is only through her research that we have begun to realize the extent of Traherne's massive borrowings from other writers. The innocent poet of childhood yields to the scholar; but the scholar in turn yields to a man who proved his hypotheses upon his own heart and brain.

5. For this story, see Samuel I. Mintz, *The Hunting of Leviathan* (Cambridge, 1962).

6. Because Traherne explicitly condemns Hobbes in his *Christian Ethicks*, and of course because Hobbes was such a figure in the age, it is tempting to believe that Traherne had read him. But his references to Hobbes are savage in so uninformed and imprecise a way that finally it is easier to believe that Traherne just did not know what he was talking about, either because he had not read Hobbes, or possibly because he had read him blinded by prejudice.

7. "Select Meditations," III. 65.

8. "To the Reader" in *A Serious and Pathetical Contemplation of the Mercies of God* (1699). This is cited in full in Thomas Traherne, *Centuries, Poems, and Thanksgivings*, ed. H. M. Margoliouth, 2 vols. (Oxford, 1958), I, xxxi–xxxii.

9. Martz, *Paradise Within*, pp. 43–54.

10. Peter Sterry, *The Rise, Race, and Royalty of the Kingdom of God in the Soul of Man* (London, 1683), p. 141. Quoted by Carol Marks in "Thomas Traherne and Cambridge Platonism," *PMLA*, LXXXI (December 1966), 533. I am not proposing an influence. Such an analogy was available even to a man without Hebrew. But whether or not Traherne was aware of the Hebrew connection, the "I" as fountain is his prose.

11. "Select Meditations," III. 2.

12. *Ibid.*, I. 84.

13. *Ibid.*, I. 92.

14. There is no proof that he wrote the *Centuries* for Mrs. Hopton, but they were in her possession. He knew her in his days as rector at Credenhill. When he went with Sir Orlando Bridgman to London, the separation from her may have been painful, for his friends were few and very dear to him ("Select Meditations," II. 38). It is speculated that she gave him the notebook in which he wrote his *Centuries*, and that the hundred-mile separation that he laments in one of them (I. 80), which is the distance between London and Credenhill, is evidence that he wrote his meditations for her. In this event, the book seeks to repair a separation and sustain a familiar world.

15. The use of the word "cherubin" here is more precise than it might seem to be, as Gladys Wade points out, in *Thomas Traherne* (Princeton, 1944), p. 183, quoting Aquinas in what might be taken as a description

of the *Centuries:* " 'Cherubin' comes from a certain excess of knowledge; hence it is interpreted 'fullness of knowledge,' which Dionysius expounds in regard to four things: the perfect vision of God; the full reception of the Divine light; their contemplation in God of the beauty of the Divine Order; and in regard to the fact that possessing this knowledge fully, they pour it forth copiously upon us!"

The shared use of a single notebook does literally occur in the "Select Meditations," which break off suddenly like the *Centuries*, leaving blank pages, some of which were used by Traherne and some of which contain entries in an as yet unidentified hand.

16. Bertram Dobell, ed., *Centuries of Meditations* (London, 1908), pp. xiii–xiv.

17. Miss Wade hypothesized a group around Mrs. Hopton, but Miss Marks points out that evidence for that is nonexistent. See Wade, *Thomas Traherne*, pp. 81–82; Carol Marks, "Traherne's Church's Year-Book," *Papers of the Bibliographical Society of America*, LX (1966), 38–40.

18. Martz, *Paradise Within*, p. 100.

19. The 1645 abolition of the Book of Common Prayer was never effective. The book had, in effect, been martyred, and became more popular thereby, as the Puritans, from their own experience, should have known it would. The prayers that Traherne always has in mind had surely been there years before the Restoration, and I take my quotations from the old Jacobean Prayer Book: The Book of Common Prayer (London, 1603), N2ᵛ and N3ᵛ.

20. See Georges Poulet, *Studies in Human Time*, trans. Elliott Coleman (New York, Harper Torchbooks, 1959), p. 14.

21. Rosalie Colie, *Paradoxia Epidemica: The Renaissance Tradition of Paradox* (Princeton, 1966), pp. 146–49.

22. His own experience should be that of every man: "Nothing is in vain, much less Infinity. Evry Man is alone the Centre and Circumference of it. It is all his own, and so Glorious, that it is the Eternal and Incomprehensible Essence of the Deitie." *Centuries*, v. 3.

23. Margoliouth, ed., *Centuries, Poems, and Thanksgivings*, II, 2. Herbert's "Jordan I" and "Jordan II" both explain his esthetic theories, but "Jordan II" is a little closer in language to Traherne. The first stanza follows:

> When first my lines of heav'nly joyes made mention,
> Such was their lustre, they did so excell,
> That I sought out quaint words, and trim invention;
> My thoughts began to burnish, sprout, and swell,
> Curling with metaphors a plain intention,
> Decking the sense, as if it were to sell.

See *The Works of George Herbert*, ed. F. E. Hutchinson (Oxford, 1941), p. 102.

INDEX

Alleyn, Edward, 15
Andrewes, Lancelot, 4, 197
Anglican "I": characteristics of, 252, 254; revived in symbolic fiction, 256
Anglican writers: described, 3, 5, 7, 9; compared with Puritan writers, 254–55; use of words, 269n8
Aubrey, John, 150
Auerbach, Erich, 57, 274n12, 286n7
Augustine, St., 187, 229, 260, 272n18

Bacon, Sir Francis, 125, 154, 172, 272n16
Bald, R. C., 19, 20, 260
Bastwick, John, 69
Baxter, Richard: reasons for inclusion of, 6–7; centrality of, in religion and politics, 14, 115, 116, 118, 141; time in, 115, 118, 122–24, 144, 146; life of, 116–17; self-dividedness, 115, 118–19, 127–28, 130, 145; self as instrument, 115–16, 132, 135, 137–39, 145, 146, 281n2; as peacemaker, 116, 118; on style, 116, 128–34, 137, 141–42; illness of, 118, 126, 136, 142–46; concern with slander, 124, 140, 142, 146; on language, 125, 128–29, 138; on history, 127, 136; on Biblical style, 133; self-knowledge, 134–35, 137; vocation, 139, 142, 146; characteristics of "I," 250–51
—Practical Works, 121
—Reliquiae Baxterianae: division between content and style in, 118; summary of, 119–20; structure of, 119–24, 262–63; compared with Baxter's other books, 120–21; imitative of Baxter's life, 120–21; length of, 120–21; 1696 edition, 120–21, 262–64; documentation in, 121; illness as theme in, 122, 145–46; theme of slander in, 124, 139–42; objectivity in, 124–26; reasons for writing, 126;

microscopic and microcosmic vision in, 126, 132, 145; epic characteristics of, 126–27, 136, 143, 147; comic effects in, 136; self-analysis, 137–38; melancholy in, 137, 144; self as cross-bearer, 139, 142; self as pen, 139, 142; on words as weapons, 141–42; suffering as theme in, 142–45; rejection of persona, 147; manuscript of, 262–64; publication of, 263; textual variants, 264
—The Saints Everlasting Rest, 121, 133
—compared with: Donne, 115, 116, 129, 135, 141, 145–46, 147; Lilburne, 116, 128, 136, 146, 147, 250–51; Burton, 120, 141, 146–48; Bunyan, 130, 147; Puritan and Anglican writers, 147; Browne, 152, 177; Milton, 193, 211; Traherne, 242
Beadle, John, 270n16
Bennett, Joan, 156
Bergson, Henri, 64
Bernard of Clairvaux, 279n14
Bernini, Giovanni Lorenzo, 270n14
Bible, 22, 42, 45–47, 48, 50–51, 54, 59, 61, 169
Book of Common Prayer, 38, 119, 199, 234–35, 291n19
Boyle, Robert, 117
Bridgman, Sir Orlando, 225
Brown, Huntington, 169–70, 171
Browne, Sir Thomas: life of, 149, 156; melancholy in, 182; responsiveness to seventeenth-century doubt, 182; characteristics of "I," 253; supposed influence of Montaigne, 265; mentioned, 254
—Christian Morals, 170–71
—Garden of Cyrus, 151
—Religio Medici: description of, 6; reputation of, 149–50; distinguished from